What they're s̶a̶
How to Race

MW00397280

"Bravo! Jeff Hollobaugh has produced a masterful, comprehensive, insightful and historic book on *How to Race the Mile*."

—Ryan Lamppa,
Founder, Bring Back the Mile

"The mile is such an interesting race because it's the perfect combination of speed, endurance, tactics, and sometimes pure luck. *How to Race the Mile* expertly captures each of these elements in a conversational tone with some of the world's greatest milers, past and present. This book should be required reading for all mile hopefuls, from high school to the professional ranks. If you want to race (and win) the mile, there's no better place to start."

—Amanda Eccleston
NCAA Division II Champion, Division I All-American

"The combination of Jeff's engaging storytelling and the revealing insights shared by the legends who lived these moments in mile history makes this both a compelling read for the fan as well as an invaluable resource for the savvy athlete and coach."

—David Mitchell
announcer, New Balance Nationals
& Nike Cross Nationals

How to Race the Mile

*Learning Effective Tactics
from Great Runners and Races*

By Jeff Hollobaugh

Mercury-Chronicle™ Books

HOW TO RACE THE MILE: LEARNING EFFECTIVE TACTICS FROM GREAT RUNNERS AND RACES

© 2015 Jeff Hollobaugh

Mercury-Chronicle™ Books

3130 Kensington St, Dexter, MI 48130

ISBN-13: 9781508718215

ISBN-10: 1508718210

Cover Design – Riley Hollobaugh.

Photo by Randy Miyazaki, Track and Field PhotoMagazine.

Dedicated to the best family a guy could have.

Table of Contents

Preface 1

1. Tactics of Old 13

2. Successful Front-Running 21

3. The Pitfalls of Leading 54

4. The Mid-Race Move 68

5. The Long Kick 87

6. The Short Kick 121

7. How to Beat a Kicker 157

8. Running the Rounds 171

9. Racing Indoors 190

10. Racing Behind Rabbits 203

11. Tools in the Toolkit 227

12. The Unexpected 247

13. Advice from the Great Ones 265

Index of Names Dropped 304

Notes 318

Photo Credits 323

Preface

"The days of tactics are fast disappearing."

Legendary New Zealand coach
Arthur Lydiard in 1982[1]

"You train to race… then you have to train for tactics."

Legendary American coach
Ron Warhurst in 2014

As this project grew, both in size and time consumed, it evolved into a different beast than I originally had imagined. Truly, there was no linear way to organize the material. The chapters ended up being organized by racing style: "Leading," "Kicking," etc. However, every single race includes multiple stories. One man's brave attempt to lead may have occurred in the same race as another's wise choice to sit and kick. There are two sides to every coin (or 12 sides to every Olympic final). Plus, I did not always focus on the winner's tactical choices—I may have thought the better lesson came from one of the other competitors.

The chapters include three very different elements:

My commentary, in which I discuss general trends and effectiveness of various tactics.

Race histories, in which I highlight certain races that I believe are excellent teaching tools as to the effectiveness of various tactics. Note that this book is not a history itself, and the races chosen were not to demonstrate historical trends. Nor do they represent any sort of "greatest races ever" list. The selected races have a U.S. bias because one of the key factors for me was whether I could access enough decent material to reflect the tactical choices and the racers' thought processes.

"What They Say" – These are comments from runners and coaches, which hopefully will have the effect of the reader sitting in a room with some terrific athletes and thinkers and hearing them talk about racing. One of the beauties of this is that not all of the voices agree. You very well may hit concepts where you notice that one star athlete says, "X is the only way to go," while another athlete—just as qualified—says, "only idiots do X." The reader/racer has to think and sort these things out. Indeed, the point of the book was to generate more thinking and discussion of tactics in the event.

Another advantage to hearing the athletes' voices directly is that, as a former teacher, I know very well that there are many different learning styles among students and athletes. Two athletes may say essentially the same thing, but one may get the point across better to some of my readers by making a video game comparison, while the other's explanation may work better for another group of readers.

Other things to be aware of while you are reading:

Name dropping – You'll find a lot of that here. I realize it's hard to expect runners born in the late 1990s or 2000s to have a great working knowledge of the racers of the 1960s and 1970s, no matter how famous they might have been at the time. So in the back I have included a detailed index to many of the names that appear in the book.

Splits – I have paid a great deal of attention to including accurate split times for the various historical races that I discuss. One of the primary sources I went to for these was *Track & Field News* and its companion results publication, *Track Newsletter*. No one on earth takes splits more seriously or does a better job of recording them. Both are indispensible publications to the track fan.

Where splits may be inaccurate—or off slightly—are in those cases where I was forced to take them myself from videos of varying quality.

My terms are exact for distances mentioned in splits. If I wrote "quarter," "half," or "three-quarters," then I am referring to a mile race in which splits were taken at the imperial measurements, not at the 400m mark (yes, it's possible, even on a metric track). The same goes for the numerical equivalents (440y, 880y, 1320y). A 440y track is 402.34m, and at 4:00-mile pace, a lap would take about 0.3 seconds longer.

Men vs. women – While I interviewed as many female athletes as I did males, I found it difficult to come up with as many good historical examples of various tactical styles demonstrated by female runners. It is certainly not for lack of merit.

Rather, in the early decades of women's running, many of the important 1500/mile races were not especially close and thus did not yield very instructive tactical lessons. Furthermore, I ran into too many cases where the key figures in a contention have since been identified as users of performance-enhancing drugs. As a youth coach myself, I find it quite awkward to write, "See how brilliantly this doper outsmarted the rest of the field." I recognize that many of the runners I talk about in this book are to be held up as role models, and that indeed played a factor in the decisions I made as to whom to include.

Those Early Races

Every spring, at our local middle school, we put on an event called the "Derby." It's a wonderful gathering, and an obvious boost to recruiting for our running programs. Throughout the school year, every fifth and sixth grader in our school runs the "mile" (really a 1600m) in "Phys. Ed." class. Every boy who runs under seven minutes and every girl under eight qualifies for the Derby. Near the end of the school year, usually on a beautiful day, they line up for a four-lap race on the track with the entire student body watching. Sometimes the band is even there and plays the national anthem. For 10 and 11-year-olds, this is a big deal.

And here's how they race. The boys and girls run separately, but the races look very similar. In fact, from the split times to the final times, there's not really much difference at this age. Usually the boys end up with the faster times, but sometimes it's the girls.

Most of the field starts out in a crazed sprint to get to the front. A few, working on their pessimism skills, drop to the back immediately. By 300m, some of the front-runners are already feeling rigor mortis. When they pass by the starting line (in about 1:15), some are clutching their stomachs. Some eyes are glancing to the crowd, looking for Mom—for anyone—to say, "Oh honey, you don't look well. It's okay if you stop."

By 800m (second lap 1:40), the field has boiled down to two or three contenders, as some of the early leaders have dropped out or resigned themselves to the jog of shame toward the back of the pack. At 1200m, (another 1:40 lap), what has emerged is the leader's unquenchable need to overpower all challengers, so every time one of the pursuers comes close, the leader sprints for 25 meters. Truly, it can be painful to watch.

Finally, on the last lap, little happens as the top runners all plan and rest for their final kick, which will not begin until they hit the straightaway. As soon as they can see the finish tape in front of them, they explode. They need to see it, though. Sprinting before they see it would be an unthinkable foray into the abstract—If they can't see it, how do they know it's really there? After 10 meters of sprinting, the challenger usually gives up, and our hero crosses the line in around six minutes, a moment of glory that stays with the jubilant child forever.

That, ladies and gentleman, is unvarnished mile racing, and it is how neophytes with no experience race four laps. It is quite unlike children playing football and basketball on the playground. In any pick-up ball game, many of the players seem to have an instinctual grasp of the game. I believe that comes from TV exposure, perhaps sitting on the sofa between Dad and a bigger brother, who both comment on the idiotic moves that various players might make. On the playground, these ball players know how to avoid idiot moves.

Not so with the mile, because precious few of our young runners have actually seen televised mile races. And those who are from running families, and they're so used to winning every race from the front that they don't have a clue what to do when actually challenged.

For many of these runners, next comes middle school and high school track. There they learn about even pacing—though for many, that takes years to sink in, and some are resistant to it altogether. They learn never to look over their shoulder in a race. If their coach is an old track buff, he will tell them that's how John Landy lost to Roger Bannister in the biggest mile race ever. The youngsters have never heard of Landy, though Bannister might ring a bell.

They have to learn not to run too wide, another difficult concept for many. But once they figure out the geometry of curves, they resolve to run the shortest distance possible. Another batch of curb huggers is born.

As they encounter more and more talent near their level, they have to learn to run in a pack. That first elbow can be a tough one to deal with. Sometimes the victim runs to Mom, who asks the coach or starter to have the offender disqualified. Or they run to Dad, who asks why they didn't elbow the little jerk back. Or, raised on a steady diet of televised mixed martial arts matches and bad reality television, they haul off and slug their rival, and end up getting disqualified themselves.

Then they have to learn—while they are processing the concept of staying next to the curb—not to get boxed in. They get indignant when they get to the key point in the race, their engines ready to ignite, the finish line in sight, and there is a wall of rivals that will not let them through. I've seen wonderful runners finish in tears—"It's just not fair!" they want to scream.

But in a Darwinian way, it's absolutely fair.

It's tough learning how to race. And as they move up the food chain, so to speak, and run against more runners at their level, it gets even tougher. When there's a big range among the abilities of the runners in a race, the win usually will go to the best runner out there—the one with the highest current level of fitness.

However, when everyone in a four-lap race has a time within a few seconds of one another, the game has changed. Suddenly it's not the "best" runner winning, but the smartest or the luckiest. In fact, the more often runners race competition at their own level, the more they will need to use smart tactics in order to win. Smart tactics come from experience, and the right kind of experience can be hard to come by for runners who spend 80% of their season running against runners who aren't at their level.

Prior to the 1996 Olympic Trials, 1500m favorite Steve Holman told a reporter, "My goal is not to let people who haven't trained as hard as I have in the race. If I do, I become the rabbit. The Trials should reflect who is the fittest. If someone beats me, they have to run pretty fast to do it."[2]

Those are honorable words, but on closer examination, they don't hold up for a winning strategy, unless the speaker has a level of fitness that puts him many levels above his competition. At the top, that rarely happens anymore. How are the Trials going to pick the fittest athlete unless one of them is willing to take the pace out hard and risk his own chance of making the team? In Holman's case, he seemed to leave it up to others to generate a fast pace that would favor his strength. Of course, they didn't—and why would they? The Trials is distinctly not about picking the fittest runner—it's about picking the best possible competitors for the Olympic Games 1500m, which is usually a kicker's race, not a time trial.

For many young runners, competition is all about testing their inner limits, running their own races, and scoring personal records as often as possible. They are told to, in effect, use the other competitors as pacers to help generate those PRs. If that describes your outlook on racing, you might find yourself distressed by some of the viewpoints expressed in this book. Lining up at the start with the sole goal of running personal records is not racing, it is time trialing. This book is unapologetically about racing—trying to beat as many competitors as possible to the finish line.

Much can be said about learning from the successes and mistakes of others. From my own experiences watching 35 years of championship races, to the words and memories of the world's top milers and their coaches, this is the ultimate guidebook for the tactics of racing the mile (and the 1500m & 1600m). Enjoy.

—Jeff Hollobaugh

"When you lined up on the track, it was all on you. It's not like it was a team sport where you had to rely on somebody else to get you the ball or the puck or to be in the right position. You either made the correct decisions or you didn't. For the most part, it's pretty black and white when the race is over... how you could have improved or what you could have done better."

-Kevin Sullivan
Three-time Canadian Olympian

"Right when the gun goes off, that is so fun for me because you've bottled up all this energy and this nervous feeling and everything. I always feel like that's the ultimate form of freedom. When that gun goes off, you have the right and the freedom to just go, and not think about all those nerves anymore. All that just goes away, but everything is still possible, because it's so early in the race."

-Heather Kampf
Nine-time All-American

"There's just no disputing that the strategy in the 1500m is by far more apparent than any other race in track & field. It's just what's so compelling and why I love it so much. From the gun to the finish you really have to be aware. You can't shut off your brain. You have to be aware of it. Maybe that's why I fall asleep in other races, like the 5K. I love the way that you have to think and the way you have to evaluate every other runner the entire time, and you really can't count anybody out, either."

– Cory McGee
Four-time NCAA finalist

Conversion Chart
for 1500-1600-Mile

1500	1600	MILE
3:26.0	3:41.2	3:42.5
3:30.2	3:45.7	3:47.0
3:35.3	3:51.2	3:52.5
3:40.4	3:56.6	3:58.0
3:45.0	4:01.6	4:03.0
3:50.1	4:07.1	4:08.5
3:55.2	4:12.5	4:14.0
4:00.3	4:18.0	4:19.5
4:05.4	4:23.5	4:25.0
4:10.0	4:28.4	4:30.0
4:15.1	4:33.9	4:35.5
4:20.2	4:39.4	4:41.0
4:25.3	4:44.8	4:46.5
4:30.4	4:50.3	4:52.0
4:35.0	4:55.3	4:57.0

Adapted from the *Big Gold Book* from *Track & Field News*.
Used by permission.

Making Sense of the Times

Throughout this book, times are mentioned frequently. It can often be difficult for the newcomer to put them in perspective. Knowing what the world record was at any particular time in history isn't much of a help, since there is so little correlation to what the world's best might do in a rabbited record attempt, versus what they might do in a championship race. While there have been a few world records that have fallen in the 1500m in international championships, they are the exception. Typically, in a tactical race where winning is far more important than the final time, the results are slower, sometimes significantly so.

The table below is organized by decade, and will give the reader an idea of what the fastest runners were clocking in those years (including U.S. high school leaders, where pertinent). It also shows what it took to win an Olympic or World medal, as well as the range of winning times in the national championships in the United States. As you can see, sometimes the range between fastest and slowest winning times can be quite striking.

MEN

What it took in the 1930s

1500	Mile
Leaders: World--3:47.8; US--3:48.8	Leaders: World—4:06.4; US-4:06.7; HS—4:21.2
Fastest Olympic medalist: 3:47.8	Fastest USA Winner: 4:15.0
Slowest Olympic medalist: 3:52.8	Slowest USA Winner:4:15.0
Fastest USA Winner: 3:48.8	Fastest NCAA Winner: 4:08.3
Slowest USA Winner:3:54.2	Slowest NCAA Winner: 4:19.3
Fastest NCAA Winner: 3:53.0	
Slowest NCAA Winner: 3:53.1	

What it took in the 1940s

1500	Mile
Leaders: World--3:43.0; US—3:48.2	Leaders: World—4:01.4; US-4:05.3; HS—4:20.0
Fastest Olympic medalist: 3:49.8	Fastest NCAA Winner: 4:09.6
Slowest Olympic medalist: 3:50.4	Slowest NCAA Winner: 4:19.1
Fastest USA Winner: 3:47.9	
Slowest USA Winner:3:58.4	
Fastest NCAA Winner: 3:54.3	
Slowest NCAA Winner: 3:54.3	

What it took in the 1950s

1500	Mile
Leaders: World--3:36.0; US--3:41.5	Leaders: World--3:54.5; US-3:58.7; HS—4:12.2
Fastest Olympic medalist: 3:41.49	Fastest USA Winner: 3:57.9
Slowest Olympic medalist: 3:45.67	Slowest USA Winner:4:11.5
Fastest USA Winner: 3:47.5	Fastest NCAA Winner: 4:03.5
Slowest USA Winner:3:52.0	Slowest NCAA Winner: 4:13.8
Fastest NCAA Winner: 3:47.3	
Slowest NCAA Winner: 3:50.7	

What it took in the 1960s

1500	Mile
Leaders: World--3:33.1; US--3:33.1; HS--3:39.0	Leaders: World--3:51.1; US-3:51.1; HS—4:02.4
Fastest Olympic medalist: 3:34.91	Fastest USA Winner: 3:51.1
Slowest Olympic medalist: 3:39.6	Slowest USA Winner:4:04.9
Fastest USA Winner: 3:38.1	Fastest NCAA Winner: 3:57.7
Slowest USA Winner:3:43.1	Slowest NCAA Winner: 4:05.3
Fastest NCAA Winner: 3:39.9	Fastest NCAA Indoor Winner: 3:58.6
Slowest NCAA Winner: 3:44.2	Slowest NCAA Indoor Winner: 4:08.0

What it took in the 1970s

1500	Mile
Leaders: World--3:32.03; US--3:34.6; HS--3:43.4	Leaders: World--3:48.95; US-3:51.11; HS—4:02.4
Fastest Olympic medalist: 3:36.33	Fastest NCAA Winner: 3:57.06
Slowest Olympic medalist: 3:39.33	Slowest NCAA Winner: 4:00.06
Fastest USA Winner: 3:36.40	Fastest NCAA Indoor Winner: 3:57.89
Slowest USA Winner:3:42.4	Slowest NCAA Indoor Winner: 4:04.7
Fastest NCAA Winner: 3:37.01	
Slowest NCAA Winner: 3:39.89	

What it took in the 1980s

1500	Mile
Leaders: World--3:29.46; US--3:29.77; HS--3:45.5	Leaders: World--3:46.32; US-3:47.69; HS—4:03.59
Fastest OG/WC medalist: 3:32.52	Fastest NCAA Indoor Winner: 3:58.06
Slowest OG/WC medalist: 3:42.02	Slowest NCAA Indoor Winner: 4:05.3
Fastest USA Winner: 3:34.92	
Slowest USA Winner:3:46.83	
Fastest NCAA Winner: 3:35.30	
Slowest NCAA Winner: 3:45.42	

What it took in the 1990s

1500	Mile
Leaders: World--3:26.00; US—3:31.52; HS--3:43.18 Fastest OG/WC medalist: 3:27.65 Slowest OG/WC medalist: 3:40.69 Fastest USA Winner: 3:36.24 Slowest USA Winner:3:45.85 Fastest NCAA Winner: 3:37.54 Slowest NCAA Winner: 3:47.54	Leaders: World--3:43.13; US-3:49.31; HS—4:02.01 Fastest NCAA Indoor Winner: 3:55.33 Slowest NCAA Indoor Winner: 4:03.54

What it took in the 2000s

1500	Mile
Leaders: World--3:26.12; US—3:29.30; HS—3:38.26 Fastest OG/WC medalist: 3:30.68 Slowest OG/WC medalist: 3:38.02 Fastest USA Winner: 3:34.82 Slowest USA Winner:3:44.00 Fastest NCAA Winner: 3:37.05 Slowest NCAA Winner: 3:44.72	Leaders: World--3:44.95; US-3:46.91; HS—3:53.43 Fastest NCAA Indoor Winner: 3:56.84 Slowest NCAA Indoor Winner: 4:12.75

What it took in 2010-2014

1500	Mile
Leaders: World--3:27.64; US—3:30.90; HS—3:45.74 Fastest OG/WC medalist: 3:34.08 Slowest OG/WC medalist: 3:36.83 Fastest USA Winner: 3:35.75 Slowest USA Winner:3:50.83 Fastest NCAA Winner: 3:39.09 Slowest NCAA Winner: 3:50.25	Leaders: World--3:47.32; US-3:50.53; HS—3:59.71 Fastest NCAA Indoor Winner: 3:54.74 Slowest NCAA Indoor Winner: 4:02.54

WOMEN

What it took in the 1980s

1500	Mile
Leaders: World--3:52.47; US--3:57.12; HS—4:16.6 Fastest OG/WC medalist: 3:53.96 Slowest OG/WC medalist: 4:04.15 Fastest USA Winner: 4:03.70 Slowest USA Winner: 4:14.62 Fastest NCAA Winner: 4:09.85 Slowest NCAA Winner: 4:17.90	Leaders: World—4:15.61; US-4:16.71; HS—4:35.24 Fastest NCAA Indoor Winner: 4:30.63 Slowest NCAA Indoor Winner: 4:44.87

What it took in the 1990s

1500	Mile
Leaders: World--3:50.46; US--3:58.43; HS—4:21.77 Fastest OG/WC medalist: 3:55.30 Slowest OG/WC medalist: 4:04.70 Fastest USA Winner: 4:02.41 Slowest USA Winner:4:13.47 Fastest NCAA Winner: 4:08.25 Slowest NCAA Winner: 4:21.06	Leaders: World—4:12.56; US-4:20.93; HS—4:42.94 Fastest NCAA Indoor Winner: 4:33.04 Slowest NCAA Indoor Winner: 4:39.19

What it took in the 2000s

1500	Mile
Leaders: World--3:55.33; US--3:57.40; HS—4:14.50 Fastest OG/WC medalist: 3:57.90 Slowest OG/WC medalist: 4:05.27 Fastest USA Winner: 4:01.01 Slowest USA Winner:4:10.44 Fastest NCAA Winner: 4:06.19 Slowest NCAA Winner: 4:14.63	Leaders: World—4:17.75; US-4:20.34; HS—4:35.42 Fastest NCAA Indoor Winner: 4:29.72 Slowest NCAA Indoor Winner: 4:42.17

What it took in 2010-2014

1500	Mile
Leaders: World--3:56.54; US--3:57.22; HS—4:04.62 Fastest OG/WC medalist: 4:02.67 Slowest OG/WC medalist: 4:10.74 Fastest USA Winner: 4:03.91 Slowest USA Winner:4:28.62 Fastest NCAA Winner: 4:13.25 Slowest NCAA Winner: 4:18.10	Leaders: World—4:22.66; US-4:22.66; HS—4:39.28 Fastest NCAA Indoor Winner: 4:27.18 Slowest NCAA Indoor Winner: 4:39.76

Chapter 1: Tactics of Old

*"I heard the mile described once—it's long enough
to create suspense and drama, but short enough that
we don't fall asleep watching it."*

— Paul McMullen

S ince the dawn of modern track & field, racing tactics have played a
critical role in the history of the 1500/mile. Medals lost and won,
legends made, winning streaks ended—all the drama of our sport and
its classic event so often comes down to the decisions athletes make in the
heat of battle.

Nowhere was that more true than in the early years of our modern sport at
a little track in London that no longer exists, located not far from Stamford
Bridge, the stadium where the Chelsea Football Club now plays. It was
called Lillie Bridge. Both athletic fields derived their names from actual
bridges that had been in the vicinity, one that has a long history. In 1066 at
the site, King Harald defeated an invading Viking force at the Battle of
Stamford Bridge. Not that it did him much good—he was killed three weeks
later by the invading Normans at the Battle of Hastings.

The First Battle of Lillie Bridge took place on August 31, 1885. The two
greatest professional milers of the era lined up to sort out once and for all
who was the best miler. One of them was the world record holder, William
Cummings, who four years earlier had run 4:16.2 on a 603y track in a
downpour.

Yet it was the challenger, Walter George, who mastered the tactics of the moment and lived on in history.

In the late 1800s, a fierce divide existed between amateur track and professional track. Both featured regular, well-attended events, as well as quality competition. George ruled the amateur world; he was a chemist with a bevy of training notions that would seem ludicrous by today's standards, including running in place and the occasional cigar. Meanwhile, Cummings was getting more attention (as well as money) on the professional side. In 1885, after achieving all he could on the amateur side (there were no Olympic medals to win at that point), George turned pro and challenged Cummings to a mile race.

The big match: Cummings on the left, George on the right.

Their first clash took place that summer and truly was a bizarre affair. It was held at Lillie Bridge, which featured two tracks, one a cinder rectangle a third of a mile long (with sharp corners), the other a quarter-mile bicycle racing track. Cummings won the coin toss and chose the big rectangle. Betting was heavy as the rain came down. George went for the early lead and hit the quarter in 58.6. Neck-and-neck, they slowed to 2:01 at the half. At three-quarters, they hit 3:07½, on pace to destroy the world record. However, back then, records weren't nearly as important as the head-to-head competition on which the 30,000 spectators put money down. With 220y to go, Cummings broke, and started to walk. Once George realized he had the win in the bag, he started to walk as well (clearly, no world record bonuses had been promised).

Cummings' fans screamed at him to start running again, and he did. George took off as well, and hurried to the finish in 4:20.2, some 65 yards ahead of Cummings. The time was only four seconds slower than the world record, which surely would have fallen had the combatants not walked.

The Second Battle of Lillie Bridge took place nearly a year later, on August 23, 1886. It would be one of the last athletics meetings at the site, which lost a bit of its luster the next year when a riot tore it apart. It was demolished in 1888.

Over 20,000 spectators came to watch the rematch between George and Cummings, this time on the quarter-mile bicycle track. Once again, George had a plan, and he was determined to stick with it. He started with a 50-yard sprint to achieve a safe lead, and then he found a slower rhythm. He passed the quarter in 58¼ (back then, times were usually taken in quarter-second increments), and the half in 2:02. He hit three-quarters in 3:07¼, but still Cummings held on. On the turn, Cummings flew past George, in a decisive move perhaps intended to break the chemist's spirit. He gained as many as eight yards against his rival. George, however, held back his kick until 300y to go. He caught Cummings, and then pulled himself two yards ahead. Cummings, this time, collapsed. George made it to the finish in 4:12¾, a new world record by nearly four seconds. So many people swarmed the track that Cummings, on getting to his feet, could not even make it to the line.

George's 4:12¾ remained the world record for a full 29 years until Norman Taber of the United States barely nipped it in a race on Harvard's track.

As a historian, it's hard to say that we saw any new tactical trends develop in the 1500m and mile from the 1930s through the 1970s—leading, following, surging from the middle of the race—it had all been seen before. It can be argued that various runners adopted signature tactics and strategies. Glenn Cunningham had his mid-race burst in the 1930s. Jack Lovelock surprised the world with his 300m sprint in the 1936 Olympics, perhaps pioneering a finish that is fairly standard now. Even in the 1970s, with Filbert Bayi leading championship races and winning, we did not see his peers adopt the same strategy, so it really wasn't much of a trend.

In terms of trends that affected many runners and races, though, the growth in the use of pacing rabbits that came with the sport's professionalization in the 1980s had a huge effect on the event. That not only changed the way most professional invitational races were run, but it also weakened the ability and the confidence of runners to lead their own races.

The second major development—one that indeed was far more gradual as training knowledge became more scientific and worldwide—was the increase in the number of medal-caliber runners. This greater depth has affected virtually every major championship by creating situations where, more and more, any runner can win, depending on how the tactics unfold.

"Because he did not have the finishing speed of some of his rivals, Glenn had to depend on his superior endurance to run them into the ground. Glenn liked to charge into the lead at the halfway point and then try to keep a grueling pace until the end. This half-mile burst became a Cunningham trademark. Opponents dreaded the Kansas Ironman's long surge to the finishing tape."[1]

—Nathan Aaseng
on Glenn Cunningham

Tactics of Old: Race Histories

1936 Olympic Men's 1500m:
Lovelock unveils his big secret

Jack Lovelock wasn't even sure he wanted to run the 1500m at the Berlin Olympics. The slight New Zealander thought he might want to compete in the 5000m instead, and even showed up for the heats of the longer run. Luckily, a team manager told him to not bother. He was meant for the 1500m. After all, he had been saving something for it.

On the track that day, in front of 105,000 spectators, the shy Oxford scholar would face some of the great ones: 1932 Olympic champ Luigi Beccali, American record holder Glenn Cunningham, and world indoor record holder Gene Venzke, who had beaten Cunningham at the Olympic Trials.

For the first lap, Lovelock settled in the middle of the pack as the pace at the front ran torrid, led by Britain's Jerry Cornes, with Beccali on his tail. Cornes led at the 400m in 61.5 (Lovelock 61.7). He followed Cunningham's move to the lead on the backstretch, and as he got to second place, Fritz Schaumberg moved up on his outside and effectively boxed him in. No worries, as Lovelock seemed quite comfortable on the rail, and didn't seem to be bothered even as the tall German squeezed his running lane smaller and smaller. Glenn Cunningham moved to second at 700m and Lovelock found himself in fourth. Cunningham still led at the 800m in 2:05.0 with the Swede Eric Ny a half-stride behind (Lovelock 2:05.6). Beccali ran fourth.

The racing began with 500m to go, and Lovelock showed mastery in moving to the outside smoothly and accelerating alongside Cunningham, while Ny took the lead as the bell rang (3:05.4). Coming off the turn, Lovelock decisively passed Cunningham, and he passed the fading Ny on the 1200m line. He unleashed a sprint that broke open the field quickly—a sophisticated, modern burst that current fans might be surprised at when they see the video. "Jack Lovelock came out of nowhere," Cunningham later wrote in his autobiography.

In his book, *Conquerors of Time*, author Lynn McConnell describes a feint—that when Lovelock began his sprint just before the backstretch, Cunningham looked over at him, ready to respond. Lovelock then eased for a stride, as Cunningham relaxed again. Then Lovelock took off.

Cunningham followed, and Beccali, the "Milan Powerhouse," chased hard, rightfully worried that the race would get away from him. The pursuers could get no closer. Lovelock's choppy, short stride churned away at the cinder track. He looked over his shoulder once, saw no one, and sped across the line, taking more than a few strides to slow down and stop. He certainly looked like he could have maintained that sprint longer, but, as it was, it carried him to the world record, a second faster than Bill Bonthron's 1934 standard.

Lovelock (in black) tucked into the pack for the first lap as Cunningham led.

His final 400m took 57.2, his last 300m only 42.4. Note that Cunningham dipped under the existing world record as well. Said Cunningham, "There's nothing you can say when you lose to a runner like Jack Lovelock. He must be the greatest runner ever."[2]

Lovelock was a great thinker, too. He revealed after the race that he had sandbagged for several years, knowing that he could mount a powerful long finish, but refusing to show it in public. He intentionally saved it for the Olympics. "That's what fooled Cunningham, Luigi Beccali and the others. They thought I could sprint only about the last 70 meters and were not prepared when I started my run."[3]

Lovelock told another reporter, "I could have run another hundred at the same pace. I eased down at the finish feeling perfectly fresh. I felt I had to beat Cunningham, a great runner and a great competitor. After a big lead at 50 yards [to go], I eased up. The main idea is winning, not records."[4]

Results (6 Aug 1936): 1. Jack Lovelock (New Zealand) 3:47.8; 2. Glenn Cunningham (USA) 3:48.4; 3. Luigi Beccalo (Italy) 3:49.2; 4. Archie San Romani (USA) 3:50.0; 5. Phil Edwards (Canada) 3:50.4; 6. Jerry Cornes (Great Britain) 3:51.4; 7. Miklós Szabó (Hungary) 3:53.0; 8. Robert Goix (France) 3:53.8; 9. Gene Venzke (USA) 3:55.0; 10. Fritz Schaumberg (Germany) 3:56.2; 11. Eric Ny (Sweden) 3:57.6; 12. Werner Böttcher (Germany) 4:04.2.

1939 Mile of the Century:
A failure of politeness?

The word "hype" wasn't even used in 1939, but plenty of it was in evidence when mile world record holder Sydney Wooderson of Great Britain traveled across the Atlantic to take on American great Glenn Cunningham.

The men had different styles. Cunningham was known for driving a hard pace, sometimes taking the lead at halfway and burning his way home. Wooderson made his plans clear to reporters on the day of his arrival in New York: "It's possible, don't you know, that none of the chappies will want to set the pace. I shan't. My main purpose in coming to America is to beat Cunningham. Hang the time."[5]

British sportswriters were worried the Americans would gang up on the tiny (5-0) Englishman: "One hopes the Americans will resist any temptation to run as a team. If something out of the ordinary is to be accomplished, there will be little room for mere victory tactics."[6]

However, that may be what happened in the five-man race in front of 30,000 fans. The Americans refused to lead. An impatient Wooderson went to the front, hitting the quarter in 64 and the half in 2:08. Charles Fenske lurked right behind him, with Cunningham running third. Battling a stiff wind, he slowed to 3:14 for the three-quarters. Not until the final turn did the Americans attack. With 200 yards to go, Blaine Rideout of North Texas went by first, bumping Wooderson and "appearing to throw the little Briton off his stride."[7]

According to the Associated Press report: "There is no doubt Rideout's bump was accidental. It was clearly seen from the stands. With Wooderson striding along easily on the inside, the Texan made a sudden effort to crowd through from third place and grasp the lead. He cut it too fine as he attempted to edge past Wooderson and hit him with his left leg. The 123-pound Briton half stumbled out several yards from the inside lane, and never fully recovered his long stride."[8]

Photos showed Wooderson stepped on the rail before the stumble.

Cunningham tried to seize the moment and dash through the sudden opening, but Wooderson recovered quickly enough to block him and force him to take the long way around.

Then the mad rush past Wooderson began. Wisconsin grad Charles Fenske finished fastest, holding off Cunningham for a 4:11 win (57 last lap). Archie San Romani grabbed third, and Rideout stayed ahead of Wooderson for fourth.

Flopperoos!

Wooderson Performance in 'Mile of the Century' Will Rank High in List of Disappointments

By JOE WILLIAMS

NEW YORK—It won't be long now until the historians start work on their annual reviews of the sports season. A lengthy and somewhat morbid chapter on the busts—or to be charitable, the disappointments, of the year will not be out of order.

The American newspapers weren't kind to Wooderson.

Wrote Bob Mamini, "Many officials down at the track thought Wooderson was all through when the accident occurred. They thought Sydney made an error in setting the pace when the wind was kicking up across the field. They thought he should have abandoned all idea of a record right then and dropped back to let the bigger Americans break the force of the breeze."[9]

Rideout apologized to Wooderson immediately after the race, but Wooderson's coach told reporters, "What good does that do now?" The world record holder vowed never to race in the United States again.

Results *(17 June 1939): 1. Charles Fenske (US) 4:11.0; 2. Glenn Cunningham (US) 4:11.6; 3. Archie San Romani (US) 4:11.8; 4. Blaine Rideout (US) ?; 5. Sydney Wooderson   (GB)   4:13.*

Chapter 2: Successful Front-Running

"They have to catch me."

—*Filbert Bayi*

Perhaps it's the purest, most beautiful way to win a race, to lead from start to finish. Nothing demonstrates more strength and dominance. This concept has crept into our lexicon of sports-writing cliches: "wire-to-wire," to have never given the opponent one smidgen of hope that they could possibly win.

It is the tactic that dreams are made of. And it can come true. It just takes an overwhelming level of dominance. Historically, it is untraceable, in the sense that as one of the most basic—and unsophisticated—racing styles, it has been practiced since the very first race, which certainly happened not long after the first human steps. It is also the most widespread at the elementary levels of the sport and can be seen at any middle school track meet. Yet the use of leading at the highest levels of the sport is rare, simply because it is so difficult to manage in an evenly matched competition.

The physical cost of leading. Undoubtedly, there is a physiological cost to leading a race, in the sense that the lead runner will bear the brunt of the wind resistance. In the world of cycling, it has been found that the riders drafting behind the leader are expending approximately 39% less energy. In running, the effects are nowhere near as great, but they are substantial and real. Griffith Pugh's groundbreaking 1971 study showed that at a 4:10 pace for the 1500m in still air, lead runners expend 7.5% of their energy simply in overcoming the air resistance. The runners following can save up to 80% of that energy. At higher speeds, the leader uses even more energy to break the wind. Pugh speculated that the following runner basically saves one second per lap. The math is clear: simply in physiological terms, unless the leader is superior to the rest of the field by at least four seconds over the 1500/mile, running from the lead simply provides an advantage for the follower. As Pugh wrote, "The effect of shielding is, of course, well known to athletes and team managers, but they have regarded it as a subjective effect. The observation that it has a physiological basis may enable them to use it with greater tactical understanding than before."[1]

In a nutshell, that explains why for so many runners, leading is a recipe for losing.

Prefontaine's style? Writing after watching Treniere Moser and Mary Cain kick to the finish in the 1500m at the 2013 Nationals, former Olympic distance runner Vicki Huber Rudawsky wrote an opinion piece citing Steve Prefontaine, criticizing the notion of a kicker's race. She quoted Prefontaine: "Nobody is going to win a 5,000-meter race after running an easy 2 miles. Not with me. If I lose forcing the pace all the way, well, at least I can live with myself."

Wrote Rudawsky, "I certainly have lost my share of races after having taken the lead. In the NCAA Cross Country Championships in 1987, I led for more than a mile before being passed by eight women in the final 200m. People probably best remember me leading the Olympic 3,000m final for just over a lap before being solidly passed by five women and tiredly holding on for sixth place.

"Was I stupid for taking the lead either time? Would I have raced any differently knowing the outcome? No... I didn't always win, but in the end, I could walk away knowing that I ran my own race, not someone else's."[2]

If how you race is more important than the result of the race, go for it. Run the "Prefontaine way." If it builds your self-esteem and makes you feel like a braver, tougher, stronger person—wonderful. But remember the basics. Boil racing down to its original point, whether it is two kids racing along a beach or scientifically trained athletes hammering down the homestretch in the Olympics—the point of racing is to see who wins. And while winning is not everything, the fact is that most of us would trade one of our "brave" losing races for the first place medal.

My own Prefontaine imitation. In fact, when I think back to one of my own races, that point becomes abundantly clear. It was the area championship in the two mile, and I was favored to win since I had the fastest time going in, a 10:00 indoor clocking. That was a couple months

Steve Prefontaine's front-running style created legions of fans.

earlier, so I knew I had more speed in me for this race. It had a lot of personal importance, as my brother had won the title twice and I hadn't yet. I knew I would have competition; one of my rivals had beaten me in a mile earlier in the season, and he had a great kick.

Two other factors doomed me. One, I'd had words with my father the previous year when, in this very race, I kicked past another athlete at the end to avoid the shame of last place (I struggled with anemia my junior year, and clocked only 10:29). Second, I had been reading Tom Jordan's amazing biography of Prefontaine. I had determined, before the race started, that I would run in such a way that I would make both my father and Prefontaine proud of me.

After the first few laps shook out, I found myself in the lead, with my rival running right behind. I started running surges to break him. Occasionally I would craft a small gap, but he always came back. I had trained for surges, so I was confident that I could destroy him. I had trained hard and fast. My rival had a reputation for not training at all. I will swear that at the start of one race, he stepped up to the line reeking of pot. So yeah, I was confident.

Surge, surge, surge—I lost count. By the last lap, my confidence and strength faded. He passed me. I tucked behind him. I knew how to kick. I waited until there was a half-lap left. I moved out, hit the gas... and the tank was empty. Nothing... I had nothing. I stumbled home in 9:56, a PR, but three seconds behind my rival.

Yes, my dad was proud of me. And yes, I could tell myself that I had run the classic Prefontaine race. It was small consolation; I would rather have won.

As the years passed and I watched thousands more races over the years, I looked back on that race with regret. My rival and I were too close in ability for me to try to break away. The evidence of that was that he had previously beaten me in the mile that season. I was probably the "stronger" two-miler, but not by a lot.

What should I have done? Made him lead. No matter how slow the pace, my money says that at the end of the race, I would have destroyed him with my kick. Instead, I dismembered my kick and left it scattered fruitlessly over the previous seven laps.

Bottom line—surges and Prefontaine races are wonderful self-esteem builders—if you're strong enough that you would have won that race anyway. But if your competition is close, all you're doing is serving them up a win.

Because of the obvious challenges involved, there haven't been too many front-running milers over the years. On the women's side of the equation, we have seen far more front-running success, especially in the early years (before 1990, or so). That owes much to the lack of distance running depth in those years. Less talent was crowded at the front of the pack, so it was easier for a world-class female to outrun her pursuers.

Successful Front Running: Race Histories

Our natural starting point is the race that, for the modern era, at least, is the iconic representation of front-running success: wire-to-wire, upset victory, world record. Please, look at the videos of the 1974 Commonwealth Games, and prepare to be amazed. Filbert Bayi was the greatest practitioner of this style ever. The wiry mile/steeplechase specialist came from Tanzania, a country with little distance running history before he emerged, and not much in the decades since his retirement. What he accomplished in his career made him forever the poster boy of successful front-running. He defined the style, and when you hear stadium announcers refer to "brave" front-running, you need to know that no one ever did it more courageously—and consistently—over four laps.

Bayi did not start out as a superstar. He grew up on a farm in Karatu, about a three-hour drive from the Kenyan border. He could see Mount Kilimanjaro from his house. When he was 17, he moved to the capital city, Dar es Salaam. The largest, busiest city in the country, it had a population of over 300,000—a far cry from the four million-plus that live there today. Set upon being a runner, he started training with a group and building on the fitness he got from running to and from school as a child (about eight miles a day). One of his new training games stood out: he would race the city buses in Dar es Salaam, stopping when they stopped, sprinting after them when they took off, a curious form of urban fartlek.

Bayi improved, but was not an overnight sensation. He finished ninth in the 1972 Olympic steeplechase, and then got stuck in the 1500m heats, where his 3:45.4 set a national record. In that heat he complained of being boxed in. He also said that in training he found he did not like running in crowds and getting his feet occasionally tangled with others. He told CNN, "Your life is in danger when somebody spikes you. I thought the only way to avoid spiking was to run from the beginning in front of everybody."[3]

One of his first successful displays of his front-running came at the All-Africa Games in January 1973, where he led the 1500m the entire way, winning in 3:37.18 over 1968 Olympic champ (and 1972 silver winner) Kip Keino. Even more impressively, Bayi had weathered a bout of his chronic malaria in the weeks before the race. He says, "To understand [why I started front-running] you have to go back to the first time I led, 1973 in Lagos, Nigeria. At that time, my competition was Kip Keino. The only way to beat Kip Keino was to run from the front. At that time, Kip Keino, Jim Ryun, and the others, they all would sit and kick when they were running a mile or 1500m. Kip Keino had a lot of speed. I decided the best way to run was to overpower the other runners."

He continued winning against top competition all that summer, often employ-ing the same tactics. At this, Bayi was very effective. In Helsinki in June 1973, against a stellar field, he led through the 400m in 53.6, the 800m in 1:51.6. He held on through 1200m in 2:52.2, and won in the fastest time in the world, 3:34.6. It was the third-fastest time in history to that point. Observers thought he would break Jim Ryun's record of 3:33.1, but Bayi apparently tied up in the last 50m. Behind him, the defeated included Olympic 800m winner Dave Wottle (who kicked from sixth to second in the last straight), Steve Prefontaine, and Kenyans Mike Boit and Ben Jipcho (the day after his steeplechase world record).

Wottle recalls that race: "I ran the 800m against Dieter Fromm and ran 1:45.3. And the next day I had to run against a guy named Filbert Bayi, who I didn't even know about. He went out in about a 1:51 for the first two laps and never came back. Back then, you know, he'd go out that fast, and you'd just sit there and go, 'Well, he's going to come back. He just can't keep that pace up.' He just kept going around. He never came back to us."

"Unless you are in a class of your own"

Peter Rono, the 1988 Olympic champion, says we won't be seeing too many Filbert Bayis in the future, especially in championship races:

"Unless you are in a class of your own. Maybe one out of many will come. But not really—you'll not see a lot of that.... You have a lot of respect for people like [2012 Olympic 800m champ David] Rudisha who take it from the gun and go all the way. You don't see much of that in the middle distances or the long-distances where somebody just decides to take it out on their own from the start. Most championships are tactical and that is why sometimes they are slow."

Just a few days later in a mile race in Stockholm, Bayi again went for the lead, but this time even faster. He hit the 400m in 52.5, the 800m in 1:51.1. Veteran Jipcho ran up to 10m behind, but passed a fading Bayi on the last turn and won in 3:52.17. Bayi held on to clock 3:52.86. Jipcho had never been rattled by Bayi's crazy pace: "That was fine. I can do my best when just behind the leader."[4]

A couple years later, he told a reporter, "I knew his tactics. I knew where to start sprinting, with 300m to go."[5]

Jipcho beat Bayi again that summer at the US vs. Africa meet. Weeks later, in Nairobi, Bayi went out faster still (52.0, followed by a 1:52.0 split). He was run down by Kenyan John Kipkurgat. It might be that Jipcho and

Kipkurgat did Bayi a favor by spreading the word that the Tanzanian was beatable, if only one stayed patient and hunted him down gradually. Yes, Bayi was fearless, but 52.0?—maybe he was foolish as well.

Those races set the stage for the 1974 Commonwealth Games, held in the Down Under summer, that is to say, January and February.

1974 Commonwealth 1500m:
Bayi Shocks

On this day in Christchurch, New Zealand, the 1500m field was loaded. The veteran Ben Jipcho, the world's top-ranked miler with a 3:52.17 best, had just been crowned *Track & Field News* Athlete of the Year for 1973. New Zealander Rod Dixon won the bronze at the 1972 Olympics and had a 1500m best of 3:37.3. Mike Boit, a Kenyan 3:37.4 performer, and Filbert Bayi, the 20-year-old Tanzanian who was the third-fastest of all-time with his 3:34.6, also lined up.

"Everyone was picking John Walker to win the race," Bayi remembers. "No one was picking me. Despite that I had run 3:34 in Europe.... Leading was the best way for me to win the race."

Bayi shocked no one when he went to the lead. He had spent a year building a reputation that served him well here. His opponents, believing that patience was on their side, let him go. At 200m he had a three-meter lead. At 400m (54.9), he led by at least 10m. By 800m (1:52.2), he had nearly a 15m lead. The question became one of who would run him down. Boit led the chase. At 800m, Dixon ran in third, while Jipcho and John Walker started moving up through traffic. Bayi, perhaps a bit nervous, regularly looked over his shoulder.

At 1100m (2:50.8 for Bayi), Dixon, Boit and Walker led the pursuers. On the turn, Boit started falling apart, while Jipcho made his move up from fourth place once he hit the penultimate straightaway. He passed the New Zealanders with 30 seconds left in the race only to have Walker and then Dixon pass him back on the turn. With 100m left, Bayi still had a two-plus meter lead, but Walker, on fire, started closing the gap. Jipcho came back and started battling Dixon for the bronze.

Then, with a mere four seconds left in the race, it happened. Instead of succumbing to Walker's charge like a dying horse, Bayi glanced to his right, sensed Walker's approach, and sprinted again, hitting the line a clear winner. His 0.36 winning margin was truly more impressive than the numbers seem—he had crushed Walker and the field.

Then the shock truly registered. Bayi's 3:32.16 had broken Jim Ryun's nine-year-old world record of 3:33.1. Walker had also dipped under it with his 3:32.52, and Jipcho's lifetime best of 3:33.16 could be considered a statistical tie of the mark. Poor Rod Dixon had run 3:33.89, a time which would have been the second-fastest in history the day before. Here, it didn't give him a medal.

Did Bayi die out there? He slowed, but he still managed a 55.3 final lap with a sprint on the end. Did he succeed because of anyone else's mistakes? Hardly. Walker, Jipcho and Dixon all ran nearly perfect races. Boit probably burned himself out a bit by leading the second pack for so long.

Interestingly, Bayi didn't make much of his little sprint at the end. He told reporters, "I heard shoes behind me, but when I saw they were not so near, I didn't increase my pace. If I had been pressed, the time might have been 3:30."[6]

One would think that a race like this for a 20-year-old would presage much faster things to come, but fate was to deny Bayi those opportunities. Oh, he still had successes: a world record in the mile the following year, a silver in the steeplechase in the 1980 Olympics. But a boycott (related to South Africa's apartheid policies) kept him out of the 1976 Games, and politics and money stymied many of the hoped-for rematches with Walker. To make things worse, he was dogged his entire career by malaria, which would weaken him greatly whenever it recurred. So his first major championship success had to remain his greatest moment.

"To me, to win that race in a world record was exciting."

Could Jipcho have won?

Years later, Jipcho insisted that he could have won the race if it hadn't been for interference. "John Walker and Rod Dixon blocked me all the way. They allowed Bayi to run. I think their coach told them not to worry about Bayi, to worry about Jipcho because I had won the 5000m and the 3000m steeplechase.... When they blocked me, Bayi won."[6]

The video doesn't back Jipcho's memory very well. He was boxed by the Kiwis on the second-to-last turn, but got out with 300m left. He passed them both on the back stretch, but ran out of steam on the turn. They passed him back, and on the homestretch he caught Dixon for bronze. Did he have a chance for gold? Not with his legs that day.

Results *(2 February 1974): 1. Filbert Bayi (Tanzania) 3:32.16; 2. John Walker (New Zealand) 3:32.52; 3. Ben Jipcho (Kenya) 3:33.16; 4. Rod Dixon (New Zealand) 3:33.89; 5. Graham Crouch (Australia) 3:34.22; 6. Mike Boit (Kenya) 3:36.84; 7. Brendan Foster (England) 3:37.64; 8. Suleiman Nyambui (Tanzania) 3:39.62; 9. David Fitzsimmons (Australia) 3:41.30; 10. John Kirkbride (England) 3:41.91; 12. Randal Markey (Australia) 3:44.56.*

1973 Hayward Field Restoration:
Prefontaine takes on Wottle

Surely there are other track fans that fantasize about time travel—not just to pick winning lottery numbers, but to drop in on track meets they wish they had seen. The 1973 Hayward Field Restoration Meet would be one of those. The main event would be a mile race between Steve Prefontaine, nearing the height of his abilities and still burning with the disappointment of his fourth-place finish at the Munich Olympics, and Dave Wottle, the ultimate racer who had left Munich with a gold medal that Pre only dreamed about. Yet this was more than just a race—to Wottle it was an eye-opening experience about what it takes to be a class athlete.

This event was set up to raise funds to rebuild the west grandstands at Oregon's historic track. According to Tom Jordan in his classic book *Pre*, the organizers put it together with just five days notice.

Some of the history of the mile match-up appears to have gotten tangled, as the Oregon track website says, "In a rare appearance as a rabbit, Prefontaine paced '72 Olympic 800m gold medalist Dave Wottle through an attempt at the American record..." In other contemporary accounts, it reads as if this was a pure race between the two legendary runners. Which was it really?

"It was both," clarifies Wottle. "Prefontaine agreed to pace me to a world record in the mile. *And* we were racing." The two had roomed together at the AAU Champs in Bakersfield, California, and had made plans to travel the European circuit together that summer. "He came up to me after he ran the three mile and I ran the half. He said, 'What do you say you come up to Eugene prior to our going to Helsinki? We'll go after the world record.' He said, 'I will bring you through into 2:56 flat,' which back then was pretty unheard of for the mile. We used to go out in 3:00 or 2:59 back then. A 2:56 was fantastic. I said, 'Sure, sounds great.' So I went up there."

The World and American record back then was Jim Ryun's 3:51.1, set six years earlier in Bakersfield. For either runner, it would be a stretch, though one would think an 800m/mile runner with a 1:44.3 world record to his credit would have a better shot than a 13:22.8 guy. Not that it mattered much—sometimes, it's just about taking that shot.

Gary Atchinson led the field through a 58 first lap and stepped off the track at about 650m. Pre then went to the front and hit the half in 1:56.8. "He took off," says Wottle. "You can't have a better rabbit than Prefontaine. He hit 2:56 flat, right on pace. And then every man for himself for the last lap. Pre was a frontrunner anyways. He was basically saying, 'I'm going to pace myself to a world record. I'm going to go out quick and hit the pace and bring it through in a good time and then we'll race for the record.' "

Wottle, who had recently won the NCAA mile title, ran a step behind.

Then Pre appeared to kick with 300m left. He couldn't shake Wottle, who stormed past with about a half-lap to go. The Bowling Green senior won handily in 3:53.3 to 3:54.6. The first eight runners set lifetime bests.

Their post-race quotes tell much of the story. Said Wottle, "I was waiting for the right time to kick. I felt I had him going into the last lap. He tried to break it at the three-quarter mark, but I hadn't even started to breathe hard then. I found out what I had always thought, that I can kick after a 2:56 or 2:57 three-quarters." He also had something left in the tank: "If somebody had come up on my shoulder, I had something left and could have gone faster."

Said Pre: "I'm not making excuses, but the mile is not my race. I don't train for it. I can race with anyone—with a little speed work I can do much better."

"To me it was a very basic strategy," recalls Wottle. "All I had to do was hang with him for three laps and put myself in position to win on the final lap. So that was really my strategy there. I didn't think it through like Liquori with Ryun in 1971 where he just said, 'Hey I'm going to go out and take the kick out of him in the last 600 yards.' I wish there was more to it. I wish I could say that I was [a good tactician].

"A lot of people on the Internet say about that [Olympic] 800: 'What a great tactical race.' It wasn't a great tactical race. I didn't go in thinking I was going to run that race. You don't go into Olympics and give the guys 10 yards and reel them in at the end. That's not really the greatest strategy. Same with the 1500m. It burned me a lot of times."

After the race, Wottle embarked on a victory lap but was surprised when Prefontaine joined him. "I remember Pre came up jogging beside me and held my arm up alongside him. I'm kind of ashamed to say, I was kind of like, 'What are you doing? Why are you holding your arm up next to mine? I just beat you.' And what he was doing was saying, 'You were able to run a 3:53, because I was able to run a 2:56 three-quarters. That race was a shared victory.' I think he was also kind of giving his endorsement to the Eugene crowd that I was okay.

"I can remember just thinking that to me it was one person wins, one person loses, but he had the perspective that I wished I had. He kind of knew that often times, it's not you. It's your competitors and your coach and all the other things. It all mixes together to develop a world-class runner. I wish I had the perspective back then."

Postscript: It's worth noting that Wottle even had some kick *after* the Hayward Field race. He had thrown his trademark golf cap to the infield of Hayward Field, and a kleptomaniac fan grabbed it and ran away. Wottle chased him out of the stadium and into a nearby field, where the young man fell down and Wottle skinned both his legs tripping over him. He got the hat back.

Results (20 June 1973): 1. Dave Wottle (Bowling Green) 3:53.3; 2. Steve Prefontaine (Oregon) 3:54.6; 3. John Hartnett (Villanova-Ireland) 3:54.7; 4. Paul Geis (Oregon TC) 3:58.0; 5. Ken Elmer (Canada) 3:58.5; 6. Jim Johnson (Club Northwest) 3:58.8; 7. Scott Daggett (Oregon) 3:59.8.

1974 USTFF Men's Mile:
Wohlhuter kept them guessing

In conventional terms, if anyone would be figured to have lethal kicking skills, it would be a world record holder in the half mile. However, when Rick Wohlhuter lined up to defend his USTFF title, he had other plans. Facing off against Len Hilton, a 1972 Olympian in the 5000m, Wohlhuter adapted his strategy accordingly. "I knew, from a tactical perspective, his tendency was to hang back a little bit and then have a strong finish," Wohlhuter recalls. "So I thought that I would take advantage of that fact and lead the race and push it through earlier at a faster pace. And then hold on."

Wohlhuter, whose PR was 3:58.8 at the time, hammered from the gun, hitting 57.7 for the quarter. Hilton ran 58.4. Hilton drew closer over the next lap, just 0.2 behind Wohlhuter's 1:58.0 at the half. But the gap started to grow again as they passed the gun 2:58.2-2:58.6. Wohlhuter closed the deal with a 56.9, finishing in a PR 3:55.1, with Hilton 1.6 seconds back. "He congratulated me on that race. 'Great race,' he said, 'I hung back a little too long and you got too far ahead of me.' So I guess from a tactical perspective my strategy was to get out in the lead and don't let up, and just hold on, because I was also looking for a fast time as well."

Wohlhuter adds, "I know some runners had said after the race they were concerned whether I was just going to hold back and outkick them at the end or if I were to get into the lead, I would build up too much of a lead too quickly. I guess there were some concerns about that since I was really an 800m runner as opposed to really being a pure miler."

Results (1 June 1974): 1. Rick Wohlhuter (U Chicago TC) 3:55.1; 2. Len Hilton (Pacific Coast) 3:56.7; 3. Bruce Fischer (U Chicago TC) 3:58.5; 4. Ted Castaneda (Colorado) 3:58.5; 5. Keith Palmer (Kansas St) 3:59.2; 6. Jeff Shemmel (Kansas St) 3:59.4; 7. Paul Craig (Texas-Canada) 3:59.8; 8. Mike Peterson (Colorado) 4:00.8; 9. Jim Crawford (unattached) 4:09.8; 10. Randy Smith (Wichita St) 4:12.6.

1975 International Freedom Games Men's Mile:
Did Bayi Game the Field?

The year before, Filbert Bayi had made his name as the ultimate frontrunner. His wire-to-wire world record at the Commonwealth Games 15 months before staggered the imagination. In the time since, though, others had emerged as worthy contenders. Tony Waldrop had run a 3:53.2 mile at the Penn Relays the year before. Rick Wohlhuter had broken the world half-mile record with his 1:44.1 in Eugene (worth a 1:43.4 for meters, far better than the existing 800m record). He had also clocked a 3:54.4 in Helsinki. Marty Liquori had gotten over his injuries and appeared to be in fine form after running a 3:55.8 early in the indoor season.

Perhaps all the pieces were in place for Bayi to challenge his Tanzanian record of 3:52.6, and even Jim Ryun's world record of 3:51.1, set nearly eight years earlier in California. Before the race, Liquori admitted to *Sports Illustrated's* Ron Reid, "The worst part about it is you're chasing Bayi and on your shoulder, you've got Wohlhuter. To run against them, you've got two different strategies. Which one are you going to use? If you use a strategy that's good against Bayi, you might be playing into Wohlhuter's hands. If you use the right strategy against Wohlhuter, you might be helping Bayi. It's almost like the Olympics. You've got to go out and run your type of race and hope you get to the finish line first."[7]

Eight men lined up at the start, and Bayi stood in lane one, next to Wohlhuter. When the gun sounded, Bayi flew into the lead and steadily extended the margin. By 200m, he had more than five meters on Britain's Walter Wilkinson.

"I run hard at the start because that way I don't have to run in a bunch. They have to catch me," he told reporters afterward.[8] He passed 440y in 56.9. By that point, Eamonn Coghlan had realized that the pace he was refusing to follow wasn't actually insane, but was on target for a record attempt. However, he was already too far behind. He moved up to second and passed the line at 59.0.

By the half mile, Bayi had 15-20 meters on the field. He hit the mark in 1:56.6, his second lap of 59.7 too slow for world record pace, and he looked around to see where the competition was. Coghlan had made up some of the ground—he hit halfway in 1:58.0. Liquori ran a couple strides behind at 1:58.4.

On the third lap, Bayi ran a 58.7, a minor improvement. Still, it was slow enough by international standards that it gave Coghlan hope, and on the backstretch he made a serious charge to narrow the gap. Coming off the turn with 500m to go, Coghlan came up right behind Bayi, with Liquori a step behind. That's when the Irishman tried a cheeky inside pass, even though the Tanzanian hadn't strayed to the outside. Bayi let him get six inches ahead, and then he let loose with a smooth sprint that destroyed Coghlan. "He looked over his shoulder when I came up on him," said Coghlan. "Then he just picked up the pace. He wasn't sprinting or kicking hard, though. He just seemed to be gliding."[9]

He passed three-quarters in 2:55.3 and built a two-stride lead over Coghlan on the turn. With 300m left, Liquori pulled even with Coghlan, who charged again after Bayi. Just when it looked like he might pass him, the

African sprinted away again.

On the last turn, Liquori passed Coghlan and came close to Bayi, who produced a devastating sprint on the homestretch to cap off a 55.7 final lap. He won by eight meters and his 3:51.0 nipped a precious tenth from Ryun's record. Liquori at 3:52.2 had the distinction of running the fastest losing time in history at that point.

Analyzing it today, it is clear that Bayi's 56.9 opener was nothing outlandish, and certainly didn't drain his strength. His next two laps were relatively easy, and allowed him to gather his strength so that he could toy with and crush a solid field of runners. On that last lap, he showed brilliance in the psychological game especially, three times letting the competition get close to him and three times sprinting away almost tauntingly.

The world record was not something that concerned him. During the race, he simply wanted to destroy his competitors. At the time, Bayi told reporters, "When I run from the front, I know what kind of strength I have." He also put himself in the position to completely control the race.

Writer Neil Amdur reported that Bayi had told a friend that the slowdown in the middle was intentional: "I knew that would let them gain on me. I figured that would get their adrenaline going. They would think they could win. I knew it would take something out of them when they tried to pass me and couldn't."[9]

Said Liquori, "When I was racing [Jim] Ryun, I had to take the initiative and lead. Now I'm chasing Bayi like Ryun did me the last 600 yards or so. It's a lot easier to chase someone than be the guy getting chased. The problem with Bayi is he's potentially so much faster than I am."[6]

Reached in Tanzania recently, Bayi addressed whether he purposely slowed with a lap to go to let Coghlan catch him. "At some point, Eamonn Coghlan and the others were going to come after me. I knew how to beat them from running against them indoors. At 1200m, when Coghlan comes to catch me, I knew he would do that. It was simply a matter of running away, of summoning my strength, knowing that they are running behind me. That's the only tactic that I was using."

Results *(17 May 1975): 1. Filbert Bayi (Tanzania) 3:51.0; 2. Marty Liquori (USA) 3:52.2; 3. Eamonn Coghlan (Ireland) 3:53.3; 4. Rick Wohlhuter (USA) 3:53.8; 5. Tony Waldrop (USA) 3:57.7; 6. Reggie McAfee (USA) 3:59.5; 7. Walter Wilkinson (Great Britain) 4:06.2; 8. Sylvanus Barrett (Jamaica) nt.*

1978 CYO National Invitational Men's Mile: Dick Buerkle's gambit

The thing about Dick Buerkle that made his performance here so surprising was that Dick Buerkle wasn't a miler. He had made his name as a

5000m type, and in quite a big way. A 4:28 high school miler when he showed up at Villanova as a walk-on, he slowly bloomed under the tutelage of James "Jumbo" Elliott. By the time he graduated, he had improved to 8:46.2 in the two-mile, and had made NCAA All-American three times. Over the next few years, he specialized in the 5000m, winning nationals in 1974, the same year he defeated Steve Prefontaine in an indoor two-mile. In 1976, he won the Olympic Trials in 13:26.60, with a final mile of 4:11.3. Dick Buerkle was the furthest thing from a nobody. Yet he had specialized so much in the longer distance, that in the mile, where he had run a 3:58.0 as far back as 1973, he was not considered a real threat.

In 1978, Buerkle decided on a change of pace. He spent the cold winter in Buffalo thinking about and training for the mile. He showed up at the Muhammad Ali meet in Long Beach to try a 1500m. The event, rarely contested indoors back then, featured some weak records. Buerkle's coach, Bob Ivory, told him not to leave it to the kick. "He said to spread out my effort over the entire race, rather than just sprinting over the last lap. So I thought I'd give it a shot," recalls Buerkle.

He took it out hard, a pace the newspapers called "blistering"—56.8, 1:56.5, 2:56.8. He couldn't hold it, but his pacemaking allowed winner Wilson Waigwa of Kenya to record the second-fastest time ever, 3:38.6. In second, Paul Cummings scored an American record 3:39.8. Buerkle faded to third in 3:40.0, ahead of Filbert Bayi's 3:41.9.

At the CYO National Invitational in College Park, Maryland, the mile rookie balanced out the pace a little better. Facing the legendary Filbert Bayi—and without a rabbit—Buerkle set out to break the world record of 3:55.0 set by Tony Waldrop in 1974. He went out hard, hitting the quarter in 57.4. He slowed to 1:59.0 at the half. The pace continued to lag. "I didn't think I had a chance when I heard the three-quarters time [2:58.4]."[10]

Just a couple yards ahead of Bayi, Buerkle gave it everything over the remaining laps on the 160-yard board track. He showed speed no one knew he had, blazing a 56.5 for the last quarter. He just barely snagged the record with his 3:54.93. "I only pulled it out because I thought that Bayi was too close."[11]

Buerkle added, "My coach, Bob Ivory, said a few months ago, 'Americans have to go out and run hard every lap. Too many American milers are just kickers.' So I said, why not? I wanted to find out how fast I can run. I guess I did."[10]

Buerkle's mile glory was short-lived. An ankle injury emerged at Millrose two weeks later, and he lost the rest of the season. He produced some solid races in 1979, but retired a year later after making the Olympic team in the 5000m. That was the year the Americans boycotted the Moscow Games. "I waited a long time and trained very hard to compete in Moscow. This was my last shot," said the 32-year old.[12]

Dick Buerkle, here leading Matt Centrowitz in a 5000m race.

Results (13 January 1978): 1. Dick Buerkle (New York AC) 3:54.93; 2. Filbert Bayi (Tanzania) 3:58.4; 3. Paul Cummings (Pacific Coast Club) 4:00.2; 4. Ken Schappert (Florida AA) 4:05.2; 5. James Peterson (Georgetown) 4:13.9.

1983 World Champs Women's 1500m: Mary vs. the Soviets

Mary (Decker) Slaney didn't surprise anyone with her tactics in Helsinki, though she shocked many with her victories. It might be said that one of the major factors why she chose frontrunning was that she had no experience with any other kind of race. She was not equipped to run in a pack, and that perhaps led to her problems the next year at the Los Angeles Olympics.

For what it's worth, in the months leading up to Helsinki, Slaney gave lip service to the idea of running in a pack: "It is hard for me to run behind. I don't do it often, and I feel uncomfortable tucked behind someone else. But I need to learn to, and I think it's just a simple matter of not having done it enough. When I tried it at Pre last year, I had to run by Paula [Fudge's] side. I felt like I was going to run up her heels or something."[13]

The 3000m final came four days before the 1500m and Slaney led from the gun, bringing five survivors with her into the final lap. Once she hit the homestretch, she produced a kick that held off her competitors and gave her the gold.

The weather conditions were a bit more trying for the 1500m final, with temperatures in the low 60s and gusting winds that perhaps slowed her pace. Slaney didn't take the lead immediately, as she ran on the inside after the gun and waited to see what would happen. When no one else made a move she eased into the frontrunner role and sped up. From that point on, Zamira Zaytseva of the Soviet Union ran at her side and just a few inches behind. She had not contested the 3000m, but had watched her teammates succumb to Slaney's kick. She knew she had to position herself optimally.

Slaney hit 64.04 at 400m with Zaytseva in tow. Wendy Sly of Great Britain and Italy's Gabriella Dorio held the next two spots. The key positions stayed frozen over the next two laps, as Decker passed 800m in 2:10.92 and 1200m in 3:16.7.

On the backstretch, Zaytseva pulled even with Slaney, but was unable to get any breathing room. Behind, the Soviet's teammates had challenged for medal positions. Going into the turn, Zaytseva finally edged past Slaney, cut in on her aggressively, and soon had a stride or two on the American. Had Slaney met her match? Once they entered the homestretch, Slaney unleashed her legs and started reeling Zaytseva in. Perhaps the Russian had burned up her resources in getting to the lead, leaving nothing to respond to a challenge. With 10m to go, Slaney passed her. Zaytseva panicked, overstriding. She fell just before the line and rolled across behind the victorious American.

"She cut me off on the turn. She moved in on me and I had to let her go by. Down the stretch I was worried because I couldn't get my momentum back," said Slaney.[14] Later, Slaney told reporters that she was so distressed by Zaytseva's bumping that she "thought about taking a swing at her."[15]

"I think we will have to change our tactics," said Zaytseva.

Many in athletics journalism hailed this as a sea change in international competition, a shift of distance running power from the Soviet Union to the United States. Actually, it was more of a blip on the radar. Disregarding the 1984 Olympics that the Eastern Bloc boycotted, over the next 20 years in World/Olympic competition for women from the 800m to the 10,000m, the Soviet Union/Russia won 30 medals compared to the four captured by the U.S.

Results (14 August 1983): 1. Mary (Decker) Slaney (USA) 4:00.90; 2. Zamira Zaytseva (Soviet Union) 4:01.19; 3. Yekaterina Podkopayeva (Soviet Union) 4:02.25; 4. Ravilya Agletdinova (Soviet Union) 4:02.67; 5. Wendy Sly (Great Britain) 4:04.14; 6. Doina Melinte (Romania) 4:04.42; 7. Gabriella Dorio (Italy) 4:04.73; 8. Brit McRoberts (Canada) 4:05.73; 9. Christina Boxer (Great Britain) 4:06.74; 10. Cornelia Bürki (Switzerland) 4:11.61; 11. Ivana Kleinová (Czechoslovakia) 4:15.12; 12. Maria Radu (Romania) 4:19.03.

2009 NCAA Men's 1500m:
Fernandez Dares the Field

At the NCAAs in Fayetteville, Arkansas, German Fernandez of Oklahoma State faced a host of weighty pressures. A high school superstar now in his first year of college, so far he had lived up to and exceeded potential. As a prep from Riverbank, California, he had produced the most remarkable state meet double ever, clocking 4:00.29 for 1600m to break Ryan Hall's state record, and coming back two hours later to run 8:34.23 for 3200m. Three weeks later he set a national high school record of 8:34.40 for two miles, passing 3000m in a record 7:59.82.

His freshman track campaign for Oklahoma State coach Dave Smith was nothing short of legendary. Indoors he ran miles of 3:56.50 and 3:55.02, the latter a world junior record. Outdoors he ran an American junior record 13:25.46 for 5000m, but laid low in the 1500m, only notching a PR of 3:42.80 prior to Nationals. He would be facing one of the toughest NCAA fields ever, with seven others in the 3:37s or better.

One of those tabbed as a favorite was Oregon frosh Matthew Centrowitz, a noted kicker who had clocked 3:36.92 and won the Pac-10 race as well as the West regional. However, Centrowitz finished last in his heat due to a foot injury.

German Fernandez

In the final, Fernandez wasted no time at all, sprinting to the lead from the start. He wanted to be in control of the race, but he clearly did not intend to burn away his competition with a sizzling pace. He hit the 400m in a sane 60.88, and spread out the field a little with his 59.2 second lap. By the time he passed 1100m, five remained in his tow. His kick already begun, he hit 1200m in 2:57.81, his third lap a 57.7.

Coming off the last turn, three still threatened Fernandez: Stanford's Garrett Heath, New Mexico's Lee Emanuel, and Dorian Ulrey of Arkansas. The result seemed up in the air until Fernandez produced a remarkable sprint with 50m to go, pulling away to win in 3:39.00.

Fernandez said, "I knew I wanted to keep the pressure on and I knew I needed to save for the last 100m. I kept thinking, 'I'm almost there.' I thought I was going to get caught, but I had that extra gear. I always knew I had that extra gear in the last 100m, so I just had to time it perfectly... I kind of didn't want to take the pace, but I had to make this an honest race."

Fernandez presented the perfect example of someone who led just so that no one would interfere with his kick. His last lap took 55.30, his last 800m, 1:53.63, not much faster than Heath's 55.56/1:53.73. The key was that Fernandez gave himself a head start by being in the lead when the kicking began.

Coach Dave Smith said, "He ran a phenomenal race today and showed a lot of confidence in leading from the start. He basically told the field, `Come and get me if you can,' and they couldn't."

Results *(13 June 2009): 1. German Fernandez (Oklahoma St) 3:39.00; 2. Garrett Heath (Stanford) 3:39.51; 3. Lee Emanuel (New Mexico) 3:39.66; 4. Dorian Ulrey (Arkansas) 3:39.93; 5. Matthew Gibney (Villanova) 3:40.58; 6. Liam Boylan-Pett (Georgetown) 3:41.11; 7. Austin Abbott (Washington) 3:41.15; 8. Jeff See (Ohio St) 3:41.18; 9. Craig Miller (Wisconsin) 3:41.31; 10. Michael Coe (California) 3:41.64; 11. Jordan McNamara (Oregon) 3:42.42; 12. David McCarthy (Providence) 3:44.55.*

2013 NCAA Indoor Men's Mile: Lalang Lonely Out There

Sometimes the lead isn't that hard to get. Surely that's how Kenyan Lawi Lalang felt, running at the NCAA Indoors. He had a unique backstory: he had shown up to claim his scholarship at Arizona three years earlier despite having no racing experience whatsoever. His only promise at that point was that his brother, Boaz Lalang, had won the Commonwealth Games a year earlier in the 800m.

Now all eyes were on the 21-year-old, as he started the first final in what would be a difficult one day mile/3000m double. He shot out to the lead with a 28.9 first lap on the 200m banked track in Fayetteville. No one joined him out there—the closest was Wisconsin's Austin Mudd 0.4 back. So Lalang kept going, but he certainly was running at a reasonable pace in a field full of sub-four-minute milers: 29.7, 30.0, 29.9. He hit 800m in 1:58.5, which gave him a nearly 13-meter lead. At 1200m he clocked 2:57.2—a 2.6-second lead over Ryan Hill of NC State and defending champion Chris O'Hare of Tulsa (and Great Britain).

Considering that Lalang paced his breakaway evenly and that it was well within his abilities (he had run 3:54.56 at Millrose a few weeks earlier), he put himself in great position for the final two laps. For one, he was not stressed by his pace. Second, the burden of passing would be on his opposition. And third, and most importantly, he had a significant head start when the sprinting started.

O'Hare folded immediately after three-quarters, but Hill and Mudd both ate into Lalang's lead—Hill doing that penultimate lap a full second faster than the leader. On the last lap, Lalang just fought to stay ahead, his legs stretching to cover real estate as fast as possible. His last 200m took 27.49, his last 400m, 56.27. In contrast, Hill had closed in 26.38 and 54.17. But it was too little, too late. For no good reason, he had let Lalang get too far out in front, and apparently overestimated his own finishing speed.

Hill himself said, "I gave Lawi way too much room. I thought he would come back to me a little more… So I'm kicking myself for that because he

Lalang was surprised to be running alone from the start.

wasn't actually running that fast... I should have just run right up on his shoulder. I think I could have outkicked him possibly."

Said Lalang, "I was surprised nobody went with me early on. I said to myself, 'It doesn't seem I'm running fast, but no one is around.' With two laps it seemed I was going to take it, so I said, 'Let me just go for it.' "

Results *(15 March 2013): 1. Lawi Lalang (Arizona) 3:54.74; 2. Ryan Hill (NC State) 3:55.25; 3. Austin Mudd (Wisconsin) 3:57.93; 4. Tyler Stutzman (Stanford) 3:59.70; 5. John Simons (Minnesota) 3:59.71; 6. Chris Fallon (Ohio St) 4:02.28; 7. Chris O'Hare (Tulsa) 4:02.96; 8. Michael Atchoo (Stanford) 4:04.92; 9. Robby Creese (Penn St) 4:08.82;... dnf—Raul Botezan (Oklahoma St).*

2013 Euro Team Champs Men's 1500m:
Özbilen Goes For It

İlham Tanui Özbilen—if the name doesn't ring a bell, maybe his old name will: William Tanui Biwott. In 2009 he broke the world junior record for the mile with his 3:49.29 at age 19. He was one of Kenya's most promising young talents, but in 2011, he was lured away to begin representing Turkey internationally under a new name. He won the World Indoor silver in 2012 and followed that up with an eighth-place finish at the London Olympics.

Running for his adopted country, Özbilen had a tough fight on his hands at the Euro team meet in Gateshead. Among the 11 other entrants, eight had PRs under 3:38. One loomed particularly dangerous: Carsten Schlangen of Germany. Perhaps had he been born in another generation, international fans would have known Schlangen better. A veteran nine years older than Özbilen, he had a best of 3:33.64 and won Euro silver in 2010. However, he has faced the predicament of many top European racers—a difficulty getting places on the starting line in Diamond League events that are awash with faster African talent.

Özbilen faced the choice of dueling with Schlangen on the last lap of a conventional race or trying something more bold. Schlangen might have been the favorite here, with a 3:35.07 seasonal best that topped Özbilen's. However, one would think Özbilen had the speed to handle a kick—a week later he would run a personal best of 1:44.00 for the 800m. And in the Olympic 1500m, he had the fastest last lap of the field (52.5), though he started too far back for it to do him any good.

At the Euro Team Champs 1500m, Özbilen went for curtain number two and ran bold, blasting out from the gun. France's Simon Denissel followed in second. Schlangen led what became the chase pack, backing off on the pace after Özbilen hit 25.2 for the first 200m. The Turk hit in 53.72 for the 400m, with Denissel in tow. The chase pack was already 15-meters back at that point, with Schlangen running 56.5. At 800m (1:51.08, a 57.36 lap), Özbilen's lead had widened, as Denissel lost his grip and fell 20-meters behind. Schlangen's pack was back another 25m. For the third lap, Özbilen managed a 58.63 (2:49.71) and led by 50m.

Schlangen continued to lead the second race until the final straight, but the last lap he battled hard with Britain's promising Charlie Grice. However, Özbilen had built up an effective safety cushion at the front, and would not be challenged. He ground out his last 300m in a painful 48.86 (last 400m—63.8), winning by 1.19 seconds (about 8-meters) over Grice, with Poland's Marcel Lewandowski edging Schlangen for third.

Said Özbilen, "That was my plan, to lead from the start. A little windy, but the wind was going to everybody. So I knew that if I got a little bit in front, about 10 meters, it would be difficult for them [to narrow the gap]."

Őzbilen at 2012 World Indoor

Results *(22 June 2013): 1. İlham Tanui Őzbilen (Turkey) 3:38.57; 2. Charlie Grice (Great Britain) 3:39.76; 3. Marcin Lewandowski (Poland) 3:39.82; 4. Carsten Schlangen (Germany) 3:39.95; 5. Adel Mechaal (Spain) 3:40.58; 6. Yegor Nikolayev (Russia) 3:41.80; 7. Oleksandr Borysyuk (Ukraine) 3:42.41; 8. Andréas Dimitrákis (Greece) 3:43.23; 9. Simon Denissel (France) 3:43.68; 10. Merihun Crespi (Italy) 3:43.92; 11. Vegard Ølstad (Norway) 3:44.08; 12. Maksim Yuschanka (Belarus) 3:44.32.*

2013 World Champs Women's 1500m:
Simpson shows how to stay in it after leading

Jenny Simpson makes it clear: "leading the race was not planned." Sometimes, though, things happen. "A funny combination of events," as she puts it. An armchair coach—or even this author—might have said only a fool would lead a World Championship final when Abeba Aregawi seemed unbeatable in the months leading in. Simpson, though, is anything but a fool.

She had surprised the world by winning the title in Daegu two years earlier. She followed that with a considerably less happy Olympic year (she didn't make the final in London). So at the end of 2012, she returned to her college coach, Mark Wetmore, who had guided her to a U.S. steeplechase record and a 3:59.90 for Colorado. A hard winter of training put her in amazing shape for her title defense. Her slowest time leading up to Moscow, 4:03.35 at Drake, was faster than anything she ran the previous year. "I knew I'd made a real significant gain in physical ability and in confidence."

Yet the competition loomed much larger than before. Abeba Aregawi, the Ethiopian-born Swede, had finished fifth in London and ran undefeated in the 1500m prior to Moscow. Hellen Obiri had run 3:58.58 to win at the Prefontaine Classic. Faith Kipyegon, just a teenager, had pushed Aregawi to the line in Doha, clocking 3:56.98 to the Swede's world leading 3:56.60. Genzebe Dibaba of Ethiopia had run 3:57.54 at Doha and also seemed like a credible threat.

In planning the race with her coaches, Simpson refused to discuss the final until she had safely made it through the semis. She felt snakebit from the previous season: "I'm a little bit superstitious, and I know I don't want to just have the final in my mind and have it taken away again."

When they did sit down to plan, Simpson remembers, "We talked about the most serious competition—or the most prepared competition—and we talked about how being fast was better than the race being slow for me.

"Then I woke up the morning before my final. And we saw that I had been randomly drawn in lane one for the start of the race. I think that for most distance people, lane one is the worst lane you can possibly get, because you're starting out so fast, the tempo of the race is truly set in the first 200m and 300m, and nobody wants to lead. And yet you are the person that everyone is going be collapsing in on. Lane one is horrible. I definitely was not happy when I saw that."

Then came the delay of the start, as the officials wanted to give Bohdan Bondarenko the stage for a world record attempt in the high jump. "So they held us. They didn't start the race until quite a bit after when they said it was going to begin. People got really nervous and amped up. We had been standing out there for so long and we were way beyond warmed up and ready to go. I think that all that just got me really quickly off the starting line."

When the gun fired, Simpson shot to the lead. Teenager Mary Cain came in from the outside and the two bumped elbows a little before Cain dropped back behind her. Obiri moved to a stalking position a half-stride behind Simpson's shoulder. Likewise, Aregawi put herself just off Obiri's shoulder. Simpson led the crowded pack—running up to four wide—through the 400m in 65.76. Behind her, the places shuffled a bit. Zoe Buckman of Australia edged ahead of Cain on the inside and put herself behind Obiri, as Aregawi kept her options open on the outside. "When I found myself in the lead," says Simpson, "I remember thinking, 'This is a safer place. And I feel like I can handle this, and I don't want to give it up.'

"I thought, 'I need to control this race. I don't necessarily have to go out and be crazy and run it as fast as I can. But if I'm going to be in the lead, I have to keep it, and I need to control the race from here. I think that mentality kept me from making a huge mistake. I remember thinking, 'This isn't too fast, it isn't too slow. This is really comfortable. I know I can run the whole way this way, and so there is no reason to give up the lead,' So I had a lot of conviction. I just felt like if I was in this position, I better own it and I need to run smart and hard the whole way and not give it up until I have to."

After 600m, Dibaba made her move to join the leaders, but in the space of the homestretch she slipped back again as Moroccan Siham Hilali brought herself nearly even with Simpson and Aregawi. At 800m to go, the Swede made a move to edge ahead of Simpson into the lead before the turn. Simpson responded and calmly held her off. "At that point I had so much invested in the race, I already had 700m of leading. I thought, 'I can't give it up and give other people hope,' I had just done a lot of the work." She passed through 800m in 2:13.95, a 68.19 lap. "I wasn't leading the race so that people could take over and sprint past me and it would be a free-for-all at the end."

Around the next turn, Aregawi ran just off Simpson's shoulder, as Dibaba again made a bid to join them at the front. Simpson started to increase the pace with 500m to go. "One of the horrible things about being the leader is that you can't see and you can't sense very much of what is going on behind you. So I didn't want to be caught off guard. I needed to be the first person to start winding it up. If I didn't do that all of a sudden three people would be passing me. And then I would have absolutely no control over what happens over the last 400m. I'd be just like everybody else vying for position."

At the bell, Simpson (3:03.75) still led by half a stride over Aregawi, Yekaterina Sharmina of Russia, and Buckman. Rather than fold under the pressure of their kicks, Simpson again upped the ante at the front. Aregawi edged ahead at 1200m (3:18.97). Simpson's third lap took 65.04. Thirty meters later, when Obiri tried to pass Simpson as well, she responded with another gear change. "I definitely wanted to stay in contact with [Aregawi]. I definitely was still fighting to win the race. But at the same time on the very top of the final curve, when Helen came up on me, I'm bridging the gap between wanting to win and fight for the win, and still protecting the silver medal. There is a very short period of time on the top of the turn where I really had to defend my space."

Coming off the turn, the gains Aregawi made became apparent. She sprinted for gold. Simpson, however, rather than folding after carrying the lead for so long, decisively outstripped Obiri and Kipyegon to grab the silver a stride behind the Swede. Her last lap took 59.24. Afterwards, Aregawi, who

Simpson: "I feel like I can handle this, and I don't want to give it up."

finished in 58.84, said, "Today, the race suited me perfectly."

Simpson looks back on it thoughtfully: "I think in that instant that I was focused on defending my second-place position, Abeba Aregawi got just the ground on me that I wasn't able to make up the last hundred meters. I don't know, looking back, do I think there's anything I could've done to still win it? I don't know. I definitely was running as hard as I could."

As for taking the gamble of leading a championship, Simpson says, "I think sometimes the reason that people get eaten alive when they're leading, is the entire time, they don't want to lead. They don't want it. They have been forced into that position and they're hating every single second of it. I don't know. Maybe it's because I'm kind of a positive person. Or maybe I have a screw loose or something. But I think once I was in the lead it hearkened a little back to my steeplechasing days when I led a lot of races, I said to myself, 'I'm comfortable here, I'm safe here,' It's so much less likely that you will fall when you're in the lead. And I was really happy to have that position. And then I didn't want to give it up."

Results *(15 August 2013): 1. Abeba Aregawi (Sweden) 4:02.67; 2. Jenny Simpson (US) 4:02.99; 3. Hellen Obiri (Kenya) 4:03.86; 4. Hannah England (GB) 4:04.98; 5. Faith Kipyegon (Kenya) 4:05.08; 6. Yekaterina Sharmina (Russia) 4:05.49; 7. Zoe Buckman (Australia) 4:05.77; 8. Genzebe Dibaba (Ethiopia) 4:05.99;*

9. Nancy Langat (Kenya) 4:06.01; 10. Mary Cain (US) 4:07.19; 11. Siham Hilali (Morocco) 4:09.16; 12. Yelena Korobkina (Russia) 4:10.18.

O'Sullivan on Simpson

Sonia O'Sullivan won a World silver in the 1500m herself 18 years previous. Her thoughts on the race:

"Once you make your mind up that that's what you're going to do, and you stick with it, then you are just going to have to go for it. She led from the front. It was controlled, 65-seconds. You can manage that. So really what she was doing was grinding it out. The second lap probably wasn't as fast as it needed to be. What you need to do is get rid of a few people and it becomes a smaller race. The tactics become a bit more obvious, what you need to do. You have fewer people to fight off and less risk of people falling and pushing and shoving when you reduce the numbers. So that didn't really work that well, but she's obviously very strong and able to finish off after leading from the front.

"If you can do that without worrying about people sitting behind you, then it's the way to go. You might as well have clean space and run on the inside of the track, rather than be behind and wondering what to do. It wasn't one of those typically slow championship races. And it wasn't superfast, but it was fast enough to stretch people enough that it was going to feel difficult no matter what with 300m to go. If they had gone really slow for the first few laps, then that last 300m is definitely a lottery and anyone can win. I think when you make it a true-run race where you go for it and you make it a race that not everybody in the field is capable of, then you test people."

2013 Big 10 Men's 1500m:
A great move on a bad day

To say the weather was unseasonable is an understatement. The spectators on that day in Columbus wore hats and coats, and still shivered in the wind as the flags blew taut. Andy Bayer was the defending champion and had placed fourth in the previous year's Olympic Trials, but that did not guarantee him anything. The fifth-year senior had to face Penn State's Robby Creese, who had run a 3:57.11 mile indoors, as well as Ohio State's Chris Fallon, who had run a 3:41.13 two weeks earlier.

Remembers Bayer, "I had been hurt, during cross country and the beginning of indoor, we had done a lot of strength-work coming back but my speed wasn't there. At the Big 10 meet, for the 1500m, we came up with this plan, because typically it will be kind of honest, but never that fast. Coach [Ron] Helmer wanted me to get out like I was trying to run a PR in the

1500m. To surprise people a little bit. It was at Ohio State, and it was like 50 degrees and 25mph winds. And so it wasn't the best race ever to be in the lead. But Coach Helmer was like, 'I think if you can get a jump on them, they'll have to do just as much work to catch up to you.'

Bayer went with the plan. With the wind howling, he jetted the first 200m, building a 5m lead. He continued his dash, "I went out the first quarter in 57 in the wind and had 2-3 seconds on the field. And then I just probably ran 60s from there on. He was right. It was just about perfect."

About halfway through the race, Rob Finnerty made a bold move to try to catch Bayer, but it took too much out of him. He fell back disheartened after Bayer went through 800m in 1:58. Then Robby Crease made a charge at the end, but the gap that Bayer had built was still too much to overcome. "The whole last 500m, [Crease] kept making moves to catch up to me, but the wind was hitting him in second just as much as it was me in first and he never quite could catch me."

Concludes Bayer, "It was actually one of my proudest, I thought, because I was leading from wire to wire. It was kind of exciting."

Analyzing it now, it's clear that the weather played a critical role. Bayer's opponents had to fight serious winds just to stay close to him, let alone catch him. However, don't underestimate the part that Bayer's strength played in this race. He fought the winds the entire distance, alone.

Results (12 May 2013): 1. Andy Bayer (Indiana) 3:44.24; 2. Robby Crease (Penn State) 3:45.39; 3. Chris Fallon (Ohio State) 3:48.37; 4. Rob Finnerty (Wisconsin) 3:48.53; 5. John Simons (Minnesota) 3:49.27; 6. Alex Hatz (Wisconsin) 3:49.50; 7. Adam Behnke (Indiana) 3:50.03; 8. Brannon Kidder (Penn State) 3:51.50; 9. Robby Nierman (Indiana) 3:51.77; 10. Brendon Blacklaws (Michigan) 3:54.54; 11. Liam Markham (Illinois) 3:56.48; 12. Alex Brend (Minnesota) 4:02.12.

2014 USA Indoor Women's 1500m: Kampf says "Why not?"

A perfectly legitimate reason to lead is to open up the chance for a slightly different outcome. At least, that was the case for Heather Kampf, running in the altitude of Albuquerque against big-time kicker Mary Cain. "My coach and I, we were saying, it's been the Mary Cain Show basically all indoor season, and she's pretty predictable. The race seems to be predictable whenever she's in it. Everyone kind of allows her to do whatever she wants to do, and then kick down and win. So we said, there has to be someone out here who's courageous enough to try something else. And that had to be me. We'll try to do something different and see if it works."

Another plus was that the officials had jammed 15 women into the final, creating more than the usual potential for thrills and spills. Kampf avoided all of that by forcefully putting herself into the lead and running the first 400m in 66.7. Behind her, Cain and training partner Treniere Moser bided their time. Kampf slowed a bit for the next couple laps, hitting 800m in 2:16.0. At the end of the next lap, Cain made her move.

Kampf watched a procession of other names go past her: Moser, Morgan Uceny, Katie Mackey, Amanda Winslow. Then she fought back, passing them one-by-one. On the last lap, she got past Winslow and secured third behind Cain and Moser.

Heather Kampf

Says Kampf, "I had been committed for a very long time and had been mentally visualizing myself in the front of that race at USAs. I still think that strategy is what got me to third. It sort of took out the legs of some of those other athletes earlier on in the race when I was pacing it, rather than allowing a 1500m at altitude to be a 1500m at altitude as it usually is. So just because that had been kind of my mantra and my mentality going into the whole year, that I am comfortable in the front. I like to lead, why not do it here?"

Cain won in a very impressive 4:07.05—a time that owed much to the early pace. She closed in 61.05. For Kampf, that third place finish ended up being worth a spot on the U.S. team at the World Indoors, as Cain eventually pulled out of the meet.

Results *(23 February 2014): 1. Mary Cain (Nike) 4:07.05; 2. Treniere Moser (Nike) 4:09.93; 3. Heather Kampf (Asics) 4:13.04; 4. Amanda Winslow (Oiselle) 4:14.38; 5. Katie Mackey (Brooks) 4:16.24; 6. Sarah Brown (New Balance) 4:17.81; 7. Becca Friday (adidas Rogue) 4:18.70; 8. Morgan Uceny (adidas) 4:20.49; 9. Rebecca Tracy (unattached) 4:22.55; 10. Sara Vaughn (Brooks) 4:22.93; 11. Dana Mecke (unattached) 4:23.44; 12. Carmen Graves (Roanoke Valley Elite) 4:26.51; 13. Melissa Agnew (Twin Cities TC) 4:27.32; 14. Amanda Mergeart (unattached) 4:28.32; 15. Brigitte Mania (Connecticut) 4:31.10.*

2014 USA Champs Women's 1500m:
The obvious time to lead

Sometimes, leading makes all the sense in the world. When the athlete is confident and is physically the best in the field, it can be wise to get up front and out of trouble and just run. Jenny Simpson, 2014 version, showed that kind of confidence and strength at the USA Championships.

Not long after the start, Simpson went to the front, running alongside teenager Mary Cain for a while. She hit 400m in 68.76—a modest pace, but still a stride ahead of Katie Mackey and Cain.

By 800m (2:13.73), Mackey still stuck close to Simpson, with Cain and Morgan Uceny holding third ahead of Florida's Cory McGee. A few seconds later came the sort of event that Simpson was wise to avoid. Morgan Uceny, a victim of falls in the 2011 Worlds as well as the 2012 Olympics, tripped again and went down hard. No one else went down, but Simpson herself was victim to a mass pile-up in a Diamond League race in 2013. She surely knows the pitfalls of exposing yourself to that kind of situation.

With a lap to go, Simpson looked confident and controlled. The field had started to string out, though she was still pursued by Mackey and Cain. Simpson's kick started spreading the competition out even more, opening up two meters on Mackey, with Cain another two back. She hit 1200m in 3:17.54, a 63.81 circuit. With 200m left, Cain caught Mackey as Simpson now ran five meters ahead.

Coming off the final turn, Cain appeared to gain ground on Simpson, but the veteran still had plenty in reserve. She powered away and left little suspense to the finish.

Craig Masback, a former miler of note himself, commented in the telecast that Cain's coach, Alberto Salazar, told him that they considered Simpson at another level, and that Cain was running to place second.

Mackey wasn't. She says, "Obviously I respect Jenny. She has proved herself on multiple stages over the last couple years, at nationals and also the world level, winning a gold and winning a silver. So I think there is that respect from most of the American athletes towards Jenny. Actually how I raced was because I respected Jenny so much. I wanted to just go, and I wanted to follow her... My perspective going into it—I remember cross

Jenny Simpson won by running confidently from the front.

country nationals the year that Jenny was favored to win and then she didn't. I remember seeing her, and realizing she was human.

"I think it's important to remember that everyone out there is human and has good days and has bad days. We've all trained very hard and worked very hard, we get up, we put our shoes on, and train. Really what we do is not that dissimilar, and so I have to go into the race with the attitude of, 'Hey, I've worked really hard to be here, just as everybody else. What I'm doing is not that much different than what everybody else is doing. I don't necessarily think that anyone deserves to win more than anybody else'. So you kind of have to respect the athlete's ability, but when it comes into the race you almost have to turn that off and you have to go the other way with it, 'Hey they're human and anything can happen.' I want to race as well as I can today. Anytime you step on the line, the point of the race is to win. That's kind of how I approach it."

Sarah Brown is another who objects to the notion of running for second: "If you limit yourself and think like that, then... Jenny's obviously the class of the field. This is not a hidden fact. Anything can happen on that day, so if I were in position, I would never try to put myself out of it. I think at that point when you step on the line, you just have to put yourself – at this level – you have to put yourself on an equal playing field. You can't dwell on someone else."

Results (29 June 2014): 1. Jenny Simpson (New Balance) 4:04.96; 2. Mary Cain (Nike) 4:06.34; 3. Katie Mackey (Brooks) 4:07.70; 4. Sarah Brown (New Balance) 4:08.57; 5. Gabe Grunewald (Brooks) 4:09.68; 6. Heather Kampf (Asics) 4:10.60; 7. Cory McGee (Florida) 4:12.16; 8. Stephanie Charnigo (NJNYTC) 4:12.66; 9. Stephanie Brown (Arkansas) 4:12.93; 10. Amanda Eccleston (unattached) 4:16.92; 11. Kate Grace (Oiselle) 4:18.97; 12. Morgan Uceny (adidas) 4:24.01.

Successful Front Running: What They Say

Francie Larrieu Smith on whether Filbert Bayi at his peak could win a modern championship 1500m: "I think what would happen in today's world is that everybody would know that Filbert's going to go out fast and so we're all going to hold on the best we can and try to kick. There are athletes that are inherently gifted with speed. There was a period of time that I considered myself one of those people. All you had to do was get me close to the finish line, and I knew I could outkick people. But the problem was being there. You had to train hard enough to be good enough to be there, but once you were there, chances are the person with the best speed is going to win no matter what. I mean, Filbert might have had good speed, but we just didn't know it because of the way he ran and the era in which he ran. He may have been able to kick, we don't know."

Heather Kampf on why she likes running at the front: "One of the big reasons that I like running in front is I like to control the race. I like to keep it honest. I'm not really a fan of traveling all the way to a meet to jog around the track. So I feel that I'm really strong in a multi-faceted kind of way, so that even if I do take out a race and make it an honest pace and everything, I'm still going to have something left in the end and I trust that even if someone takes over that lead, I'll still have something in the end. But also, my back kick is the thing that gets me in a lot of trouble and makes me famous for falling in races because it seems like people get tripped up on that and end up tripping me. And if I run from the front and run a little bit scared, then I just know, 'Stay out of the way - stay out of the way - stay out of the way!' But when I'm in the middle of the pack, it's harder for me to sort of focus on who's in front of me, who's beside me, behind me, all the time, so I don't run super comfortably in the middle of tight packs."

Sarah Brown on the fearless mentality: "In high school, I always had led. Even in national races, I would take the lead going from the gun. And when I first started racing, that was all I knew as a kid, I would just do the same thing. Because in my mind – I didn't come from a running family – the point of a race was to try and win. There is no question I would just go out and lead from the front, and never thought about anything, like if it was windy and tucking in. When I got to college and all of a sudden I was running behind people in packs, it was very different for me. It took a little bit, because I wasn't comfortable in it. I was definitely running a lot more uptight with that kind of scenario…. I think my first two years in college I struggled a little bit – I'm not saying it was based on racing tactics or anything in particular – I think that that kind of changed a lot about me and who I am now. I'm trying to embrace some of those mile race take-the-lead mentalities. I think that a more fearless mentality is actually beneficial. Tactics are important and having a race plan and executing that race plan. But I think sometimes you do just have to be fearless and taking the lead is part of that."

Cory McGee on staying in front: "My senior year in high school, at the Millrose Games, I feel like that's the best strategy I ever had. I finished second the first three years, and then finally my senior year, it was absolutely the best. I went into it with absolute confidence. I was set on my strategy. I knew that I was going to challenge it from the gun and go for it, and I wasn't going to let anybody pass me. That's what I did. Emily Lipari was in the race, and she had beaten me in a lot of championship races before that, and she would usually get me right in the last 50m. So I just made up my mind that I was going to push the pace and that's what I did, and I'm really proud of that race. It's one that I still look back on and get butterflies in my stomach. It's probably one of my happiest moments in high school. It was definitely the race that I always hoped to win. It's my favorite indoor meet. I think that that was a big one for me, and I was really confident in my strategy and confident in the way I went about it."

Renato Canova on trends in racing: "I don't think it's possible, at the moment, to find somebody successfully leading a top race from the start. Filbert Bayi was a clear exception, in a sport without rabbits, when also the mentality of the best athletes was very different (look at Ron Clarke, Kip Keino, Vladimir Kuts, Herbert Elliot and several others).

"Now, the best we can expect, is somebody having the courage to take the lead with 500m or one lap to go, such as Morceli, El Guerrouj, Aouita, Cram did. After El Guerrouj quit running, nobody, in the last 10 years, had this type of courage. In Monaco [2014], for the first time one athlete, Asbel Kiprop, finally tried again this type of race, having in his mind the target of attacking the world record. He didn't succeed, but became the best rabbit ever for Silas Kiplagat."

Kevin Sullivan on what it takes: "I think front running is certainly more difficult nowadays, when you don't necessarily have one guy who is clearly that much better or that much more confident than the rest of the field that they can just go from the front the whole way. [Asbel] Kiprop probably has the ability to do it. But you never really know which Kiprop is going to show up on any given day. But certainly, when he's on, he has the ability to. But there's nobody right now that's really that head-and-shoulders above the rest of the world that I think in a championship race would feel confident enough just to go to the front and lead the whole thing."

Sarah Brown on the right kind of aggression: "If you look back in history—we're talking about some people who hold the records—they weren't sitting and kicking. They were out there leading it. I think that's a brave mentality, and it's showing the right kind of aggression. Jenny Simpson's not afraid to take these Diamond League races and lead them. And I think that speaks volumes of her whole mentality and what she's going after. I think that's part of the reason that she is able to go after the American record because she is fearless in that sense."

Chapter 3: The Pitfalls of Leading

"My main quote with all my kids I coach in high school—I'm always telling them— you lead, you lose."

—*Jeff Atkinson*

T he previous chapter might have gotten some readers excited about the prospects of leading an important race from the gun. In truth, more often than not, the strategy fails for a variety of reasons:

Pace misjudgment: The leading runner sets out on a brutal pace intended to burn off the field. However, because the runner is not in touch with his or her own fitness level, they overreach. The only person who gets destroyed is the early leader. This is a failing we see time and again, usually at the younger levels of the sport.

Underestimating the competition: Even if the early leader has a competent grasp of their own fitness level and runs a pace within their ability, it is unlikely they are as familiar with the fitness level of every other runner in the field. Unless the leader is significantly more fit to begin with, they are just setting up the race so that someone else can outkick them.

Inexplicable nervous reaction: I know more than a few runners that this has happened to, including myself. Something throws them off or screws up their warm-up routine. When they step on the track, they're not really ready to go. It doesn't take long before they find themselves someplace they'd rather not be—in the front or the back.

In my case, it was a 3000m race at a big high school invitational in Ohio many years ago. My family got lost on the way there and arrived late. I went on the track with no warm-up, having missed every section except for the fast one. The kind-hearted official let me in. On the starting line, I realized I was standing amidst a host of state champions from Ohio and surrounding states. I had been to the state finals too, but I had to buy a ticket.

The gun fired, and it was as if I blacked out. When I opened my eyes at 200m, everyone else was behind me. It made no sense, since I didn't have the leg speed to lead a run in my PE class. In my inexperience, I couldn't process the fact that I had no business being there, so I kept going. At 400m, I bettered my PR. Strangely, I felt no pain or anaerobic debt. At 800m, another PR! That's when I convinced myself that I had suddenly been anointed by the gods. I started imagining the headlines! This wasn't a sad accident of pacing, this was the revelation of a new distance running star!

Then, in the space of about 10 seconds, everyone in the race passed me. Absolutely everyone. Someone elbowed me. Someone else muttered, "Idiot." Next thing I knew, I was in dead last. I still felt "good," however, my legs just weren't working as well as everyone else's. Spectators laughed at me. I remember that the three-hour ride home seemed longer than that, and my parents didn't say much.

Once you find yourself in the lead of a race accidentally—and you know it's wrong—you have to fight the natural urge to go with it. It takes quite a bit of poise to run wide and let people pass until you can tuck into the appropriate place in the pack. Obviously, it's best to perform a repositioning move like that *before* you die out there. Once you find yourself back in the right position, your job is to find a rhythm and focus on the rest of the race, in effect wiping clean your mental slate of the early stages. Dwelling on a screw-up will only hurt you later in the race. Move on.

The pitfalls of leading: Race Histories

1970 MLK Freedom Games Men's 1500m: Keino looked back

One of the highlight races of this meet at Pennsylvania's Villanova University, the 1500m featured Olympic champion Kip Keino of Kenya facing off against a host of American challengers including Marty Liquori on

Kip Keino building a huge lead in the MLK Freedom Games against Marty Liquori (far right). Despite the immense gap, he wasn't able to hold it.

his home track. Organizers had paid $8,000 to bring in Keino and a Kenyan 4 x 880 team to lend more flavor to the meet.

Keino took to the lead immediately, cruising through the quarter in 59.6. Liquori wasn't too far off, at 60.7. Then the Kenyan put the squeeze on the field, hammering his next lap in 56.6 for 1:56.2 at halfway. Liquori felt the hurt on that one, and fell back by more than 20 yards.

On the third lap Keino eased again, giving Liquori some hope. They were 2:56.9 and 2:58.1 respectively as they charged into the final 300m. Liquori smelled blood, and went hard after the veteran, finally passing him with 50m to go. Keino almost stopped then, but realized Liquori's teammate Chris Mason was finishing fast. Forced to sprint again, the Kenyan star held on for second.

Said Liquori of his first win in four tries against Keino, "That was his race. He went out fast and dared the rest of us to catch him. I knew I would win when he looked back on the final lap. He knew I had him when I got within five yards in the stretch."[1]

At the finish line, Liquori turned and gestured at Keino—a bit of showboating that was not out of character for the New Jersey native. Perhaps that motivated Keino to tell reporters that he wasn't really trying: "I wanted him to win. It is good for him here."[1]

Results (16 May 1970): 1. Marty Liquori (Villanova) 3:42.6; 2. Kip Keino (Kenya) 3:43.8; 3. Chris Mason (Villanova) 3:44.1; 4. Byron Dyce (Jamaica) 3:44.3; 5. John Lawson (Pacific Coast Club) 3:45.0; 6. Howell Michael (William & Mary) 3:47.8; 7. Dave Wright (Villanova) 3:48.8.

1976 Olympic Trials Men's 1500m: Byers loses his head

In 1976, the U.S. had no supreme mile specialist. Dave Wottle, the 1972 Olympic 800m champ, had always believed himself to be more of a miler, but he had retired. Jim Ryun was also gone, and Marty Liquori had announced his move to the 5000m before losing the season to injury. That left Rick Wohlhuter—the world record holder at the half-mile, and no slouch at the full distance—as the man to beat.

Ohio State junior Tom Byers only made it into the final after an appeal of a foul in the semi and figured he didn't have a chance. Just a 4:18 high school miler three years before, in Columbus he had run 3:37.5 for 1500m as a freshman, grew his hair long, and built a reputation as a rebel. With his long hair flowing, he figured "What the hell," and took his shot. Sometimes, though, the excitement takes over. "I got so excited I lost my head."[2]

Byers raced past 400m in 53.6 and 800m in 1:51.3, stunning the audience and his fellow competitors. The "legitimate contenders" had to work hard to reel him in after he built up a 20m lead. Matt Centrowitz went after Byers aggressively, while Wohlhuter bided his time. "The pace drew the field out and it turned to my advantage," said the 27-year-old Chicago insurance man.

Said Wohlhuter, "I expected Matt to go out slower and come on stronger as the race progressed. I figured I could win, but I knew Matt would be tough… There was a point there I decided I had to get back to Centrowitz. I felt if I lost contact I would possibly be fighting for second or third."[3]

Centrowitz might have had a chance to win, but perhaps he followed Byers' pace too closely. His own splits were 54.7, 1:52.8 and 2:52.3. "I remember looking at the clock on the first time around and I couldn't read it. I'd never seen those numbers before."[3]

Eventually, Mike Durkin, one of Wohlhuter's training partners, got past Byers as well, with 500m left. He caught the leaders before they edged away on the homestretch. Byers faded to last place in 3:55.9. "I couldn't concentrate," said Byers. "I can't believe it… God, it blows my mind."

Said Wohlhuter "He wanted to take it out hard and more or less steal the race, but his plan backfired."[4]

Jenny Simpson on the psychology of the chase pack

"There is this strange thing that can happen in a race that if somebody does something exceptional early in a race or part way through a race. Even though the people next to you are your competitors, you kind of work together to go after that person. At the first sign of weakness at the very front, you can sense this camaraderie between the other people. You really begin working on trying to chip away at that perceived weakness. I have had that experience at other races, as well. It's so much more obvious in a longer race like the 5K or the 10K but it certainly can happen in the 1500m. So when you put yourself out early in a race, I think you run the risk of exactly that happening, instilling in your competition a sense of camaraderie to bring you down. Yes, the chase pack becomes piranhas. And they're coming after you."

Reflecting on the race recently, Wohlhuter explains, "The rest of us runners weren't probably accustomed to that kind of pace, although, being a half-miler, it wasn't bad for me. I'm thinking along the way, 'Gee, I could get a good time out of this. I just have to hang in there.' That pace was so fast that it knocked out some very good runners, and I am sometimes amazed that I got into the top three places which made the team. But I held on, and the other two runners that qualified for the team were strength runners which a race like that might favor."

Results *(27 June 1976): 1. Rick Wohlhuter (U Chicago TC) 3:36.47; 2. Matt Centrowitz (Oregon) 3:36.70; 3. Mike Durkin (U Chicago TC) 3:36.72; 4. Mike Make (unattached) 3:37.05; 5. Mike Slack (U Chicago TC) 3:39.09; 6. Rick Musgrave (Colorado) 3:40.73; 7. Steve Scott (UC Irvine) 3:48.9; 8. Ken Popejoy (U Chicago TC) 3:53.9; 9. Tom Byers (Ohio St) 3:55.9.*

1995 NCAA Men's 1500m:
Hyde tries to run away

In any race situation, there are multiple narratives that could be told. One man's disaster is another man's victory. For William & Mary's Brian Hyde, the story was all about confirming that he was indeed a world-class runner. The Michigan native had popped a world-leading 3:35.84 in May, stunning everyone, including his coach, Walt Drenth. His previous best had been a mere 3:42.5.

With that time, he came to Knoxville wearing the favorite's mantle, even though the field included defending champ Graham Hood and indoor champ Kevin Sullivan. He publicly laid out his plan for the race: "If I think I can run 3:35 from the start, I'll lead. I think I have a better chance off a faster pace if I'm leading. Some guys can change pace faster than me. I think I'm better off from the front."[5]

Sullivan, meanwhile, came to Knoxville expecting a race against Hood, a fellow Canadian. He was somewhat disappointed when the Arkansas star left the track after trying to warm-up for the final, a victim of plantar fasciitis. "I knew that Graham was dinged up going into it, but he looked good in the prelims, I remember. He was certainly one of the big focuses for me. For a couple of reasons. One, obviously, the talent, being a 1:45 800m runner and Olympic finalist in the 1500m, you certainly don't take somebody like that lightly. But also, we raced each other all the time in high school. It was a really big rivalry that then translated over into the collegiate ranks. So yes it did change things emotionally, I think, because whenever Graham and I raced—not that we weren't focused on others in the race—but we were always focused on each other as well."

With no Hood present, Sullivan had to plan how to run a race with Hyde likely leading, and the dangerous kick of Paul McMullen probably factoring on the last lap. Jon Wild took the early lead, before Hyde took over. They hit 400m in 60.1, 800m in 1:58.7. This would be no slow race. Hyde upped the ante with a 57.5 third lap. Sullivan, meanwhile, ran fairly relaxed in second. With 300m to go he sensed a weakness: "I think Brian was just kind of stuck in a pace at that point. And this was one of the times where I think everything just kind of clicked for me, and I floated by Brian and accelerated on the backstretch and Paul [McMullen] was chasing me the whole way, but I had enough of a gap that he wasn't able to close in on that gap at all over the last

Brian Hyde: "I think I'm better off from the front."

300m so it was just really kind of a strong move, a three-stage acceleration from 300m home."

Sullivan closed with a 54.9; his last 800m took 1:52.6. McMullen (55.9 final lap) couldn't match that speed in the stretch.

To make the move, Sullivan had to have a clear path to get to the front. For that he thanked his coach, Ron Warhurst. "Ron's big thing, the one thing he will always tell you, is to not let yourself get stuck on the rail, to always make sure that you're trying to work yourself to the outside, even if it means running extra distance. He'd be like, 'Yeah, you've got to run a little extra distance, but it's better to put yourself in a position to challenge for the win than to be stuck somewhere where you're hoping for a medal.' That was a lot of the focus when we were running in college there. Positioning was always a big thing for Ronnie."

Results *(3 June 1995): 1. Kevin Sullivan (Michigan) 3:37.57; 2. Paul McMullen (Eastern Michigan) 3:38.74; 3. Passmore Furusa (LSU) 3:40.41; 4. Michael Cox*

(Kansas) 3:40.69; 5. Michael Morin (Arkansas) 3:40.80; 6. Ken Nason (Villanova) 3:41.24; 7. Brian Hyde (William & Mary) 3:41.34; 8. Jon Wild (Oklahoma State) 3:41.40; 9. Balázs Tolgyesi (Nebraska) 3:41.52; 10. Scott Anderson (Princeton) 3:42.14; 11. Eric O'Brien (Georgetown) 3:47.97.

1995 World Champs Men's 1500m: McMullen tries leading

In 1995 in Goteborg, Sweden, McMullen put himself into the front of the race at the start. Still a rookie at the international level, the U.S. champ hit the first lap in 57.43 and stayed in front till nearly 800m. Considering the athletes lined up behind him, he had little chance of staying in front. Defending champion Noureddine Morceli had broken the world record a month earlier with his 3:27.73. Hicham El Guerrouj was quickly rising to prominence and had recently run a 2:16.85 for the kilometer. Vénuste Niyongabo had 1:45.13 speed and had clocked 3:30.78 three weeks earlier. And Olympic champion Fermín Cacho had experience and a dangerous kick. McMullen explains why he made the decision to run from the front:

"The prelims and the semifinals in that race were brutal. I got hit really hard coming down the homestretch in the prelims by Abdi Bile. He just extended his arm outright and hit me so hard across the chest it took my breath away. I mean, I ran right through it, but I was just like, 'Holy cow, these guys are so physical. I can't believe it.' Then in the semifinals with 500m to go, Julius Achon, who was known on the circuit as one of the most unpredictable runners, does a 'I-think-I'm-going-to-jump-over-one-lane-all-at-one-time-and-not-even-look-behind-me,' and he trips Reuben Chesang of Kenya, and both of them hit the deck right in front of me. As they rolled, I jumped them like a moving steeplechase barrier but one of their feet kicked up as they're rolling—the bottom of their spike catches on the bottom of my foot. I stumbled badly and one knee hit the track. This is with 500m to go in the World Championships semi-final—usually you're done. Just walk off the track and be reinstated, but that was not in my nature. I've broken many tackles in football and reached the end zone and in my naivety I believed I could still advance. I got back up and regained my stride and locked my vision on the last couple of guys as the bell rang. Julius, on the other hand, came by me like a rocket in a panic to catch back up. No more than 100m later I went right by him and began to close on the straggling casualties of Hicham El Guerrouj's kick. As I approached the final 100m, Vyacheslav Shabunin of Russia glanced back and saw me coming with a head of steam and I dug deep one more time to edge him by five hundredths of a second to earn the last spot in the final.

"Those events created Coach Parks' and my front running strategy in the final, concluding, 'The back is not the place to be in this thing. Just get to the front and whoever passes you, hold your position on the rail until the final kick.' But I did not intend for everybody to just follow me for two laps. I didn't think they would all follow me until 800m to go, but they did. And then, when they did go, they didn't give me much room. It was [Vénuste] Niyongabo from Burundi—he cut me off really bad, to where I had to cut my stride to not trip him and tip toe to miss stepping on the rail. Then I started to gradually slip backwards until the bell rang.

"I got a lot of great pictures from that race, I spent so much time at the front! But the outcome wasn't ideal. I dug deep in the semifinal to get to the final with the last 400m sprint. So that's what stinks. You can't get the lactic acid out of your legs. You just can't. You drink plenty of water and get plenty of sleep, run some strides, get a massage, but you can't be there when you want it. You can try to convince yourself, I feel great, this is going to be awesome, then they all start running like a rocket. And you're like, 'Oh man, I can't keep up with this stuff.' That's how it goes, man. And then you got your mom, 'Why don't you just go out there and beat all those guys? It's just running in circles. You're so fast, just outrun them all.' Oh, no, not quite that easy."

In the end, Morceli crushed the field with his 51.28 last lap, winning in 3:33.73 despite slowing down before the finish and blowing kisses to the crowd. Said the Algerian, "I never know what to expect in a race. The race was a little bit fast, not like what I had expected. I expected it to be a little bit slow."

Results (13 August 1995): 1. Noureddine Morceli (Algeria) 3:33.73; 2. Hicham El Guerrouj (Morocco) 3:35.28; 3. Vénuste Niyongabo (Burundi) 3:35.56; 4. Rachid El Basir (Morocco) 3:35.96; 5. Kevin Sullivan (Canada) 3:36.73; 6. Kader Chékhémani (France) 3:36.90; 7. Mohammed Suleiman (Qatar) 3:36.96; 8. Fermín Cacho (Spain) 3:37.02; 9. Gary Lough (Great Britain) 3:37.59; 10. Paul McMullen (USA) 3:38.23; 11. Niall Bruton (Ireland) 3:39.15; 12. Isaac Viciosa (Spain) 3:41.12.

2004 Olympic Women's 1500m:
Yevdokimova Gets Nothing for Trying

Jenny Simpson wasn't the first woman to try to run away from the field in a major international championship. Disregarding some of the chemically questionable Eastern Bloc runaways we saw in the 1970s and '80s, one race that stands out is Natalya Yevdokimova's in the 2004 Athens Olympics. The Russian, 26 at the time, was the youngest on the Russian team. Both of her teammates, older and more experienced, also made the final. Olga Yegorova was a 32 year-old veteran with a best of 4:01.00. Tatyana Tomashova, 29, had a best of 3:58.52.

Many speculated that with three in the final, the Russians would engage in team tactics. Britain's Kelly Holmes had won the 800m five days earlier and figured to be a strong favorite with her fearsome kick. So, yes, it would make sense for the Russians to take turns hammering the pace to give one of them the chance to outkick a fatigued Holmes. Yet that's not how the race played out.

Yevdokimova, only a 4:04.61 runner the previous year, had improved to 4:01.57 in taking second at the Russian nationals behind Gulnara Galkina, who had run the 5000m in Athens. She finished ahead of Tomoshova and was arguably the best Russian on the starting line in Athens. But it was Yevdokimova who took the pace out hitting 63.59 and 65.05 (2:08.64) for the first two laps. Holmes lagged far back, second-to-last at 400m, and ninth at 800m. Though it was quite fast, the Russian didn't really lose anyone. Yevdokimova ran even, steady splits, and the field stayed with her, packed quite closely at times. So from 800m on, Holmes was never farther back than five or six meters.

Holmes benefited from Yevdokimova's pace.

Positions barely changed through 1200m (3:12.82), except that Holmes had moved up to third. Lidia Chojecka of Poland challenged Yevdokimova on the backstretch but the Russian fought her off. Holmes started sprinting with 200m left, and nearly pulled even with the Russian on the turn. Everyone else was sprinting also, and the traffic forced Holmes wide. She needed about 10 strides on the homestretch to catch Yevdokimova. By then, the feeding frenzy had started. Romania's Maria Cioncan passed her on the inside while teammate Tomoshova passed her on the outside. They would join Holmes on the medals stand.

Yevdokimova would have to console herself with a personal best in fourth place, and the knowledge that she set the pace in a race where seven of the 12 finalists had set PRs, six of them breaking 4:00, the most ever in an Olympics.

Said Holmes, "I was trying to place myself in the right position and put myself where I had to make a move. I wouldn't ordinarily move up as quickly as I did, but the pace was so quick. I had to use all my guts to hold on for dear life. I was running as fast as I could."[6]

Results (28 August 2004): 1. Kelly Holmes (Great Britain) 3:57.90; 2. Tatyana Tomashova (Russia) 3:58.12; 3. Maria Cioncan (Romania) 3:58.39; 4. Natalya Yevdokimova (Russia) 3:59.05; 5. Daniela Yordanova (Bulgaria) 3:59.10; 6. Lidia Chojecka (Poland) 3:59.27; 7. Anna Jakubczak (Poland) 4:00.15; 8. Elvan Abeylegesse (Turkey) 4:00.67; 9. Carmen Douma-Hussar (Canada) 4:02.31; 10. Natalia Rodriguez (Spain) 4:03.01; 11. Olga Yegorova (Russia) 4:05.65; 12. Hasna Benhassi (Morocco) 4:12.90.

2012 NCAA Men's 1500m:
Fernandez leads differently this time

In 2009, German Fernandez won the NCAA title as a freshman, running a solid pace through 800m, and then outkicking the field from the front. It was an act of immense confidence and savvy. Three years later the Oklahoma State runner faced a different situation. He had been plagued by injuries in the years since, and only started running in mid-April after his most recent injury. Perhaps he could muster a kick, but it was unlikely he could burn out the field as he did in 2009.

That explains why Fernandez went to the front early—to keep the pace slow. He hit 400m in 64.5, and brought his competitors through 800m in 2:06.0. Behind him, Andy Bayer of Indiana lurked, along with Lawi Lalang of Arizona.

Says Bayer, "The whole first three-quarters of the race I had stayed right on German's shoulder and he led and my plan the whole time was just to make a move, wait till 150 or 100m to. That was my plan, but I intended to respond to any other move that happened."

Things stayed steady until the 1200m mark, when Erik van Ingen launched the attack. Immediately the race ignited. Miles Batty chased the lead. He said, "400m to go, I expected things to go a little more than they did. Then when it wasn't going with 300m to go, I was like, 'Hey, make a move. We're all probably going to kick the same, might as well be in the front when it all starts and get a head start."

Fernandez faded to the back as did Lalang. Bayer went to the front but had to battle Miles Batty on the turn. Finally Bayer relented and Batty took the inside lane.

Andy Bayer

"On the backstretch, German was still in the lead and I was following him," says Bayer, "but right before 200m to go is when Miles took off, and I went with him and was kind of on the inside. The whole turn he was a half-stride ahead of me, but for a while I was trying to hold him out. I kind of had a famous quote where I told one of the interviewers my final thought with 100m to go was, 'Quit cutting me off, you jackass.' "

Batty said, "It was probably a little iffy as far as what I did, but I was just trying to hold my position all the way to the rail. I'm not going to go out for him either, so I kind of forced him to go around."

It wasn't over, though. Bayer came around the outside for another go at Batty and chased him down the homestretch. "I fought him for a while and decided that I wasn't going to get by on the inside. So I just let him go around me and decided with 150m to go that once we hit the homestretch, I would try and come back around him." Neck-and-neck as they approached the line, the two both dove for the finish. Bayer picked himself off the track the winner by a mere 0.01. Batty produced the faster last lap, 53.50, but Bayer only needed that 53.78 since he was ahead with a lap to go.

Of the dive, Batty, who had dived at the NCAA Indoor finish that year, said, "Indoors was probably more of a conscious decision. Today was more lean-lean-lean until I fell. I was like, 'Whoops!' probably makes me look bad doing that twice in a row at a championship, but I wanted to give it all I had."

Says Bayer, "I thought with 80m to go I was maybe going to run away from him. I got even with him, but then he put up a strong fight. We were together the last 50m and then I felt with the last step and a half I had finally gotten the lead on him, and that's when he dove. I responded, and I rolled across the line thinking that I had won but not being really sure. I had jumped up immediately, and was looking at the board, and then the result came up what seemed like forever later. I was pretty ecstatic, jumping all over the place."

"I don't think I was going to beat him either way," admitted Batty. "I pretty much gave myself the biggest advantage I possibly could by forcing Bayer to go outside. He still got me... You always want to win. The last 100m, all I was thinking was go-go, come on, this is mine. The last second—it sucks."

For Fernandez, the feeling could only have been worse. He said, "The plan was not for me to lead at all. I wanted to be in contention with 500m left... I felt good, I just can't find that gear."

Results (9 June 2012): 1. Andy Bayer (Indiana) 3:43.82; 2. Miles Batty (BYU) 3:43.83; 3. Ryan Hill (North Carolina State) 3:44.24; 4. Michael Hammond (Virginia Tech) 3:44.47; 5. Rob Finnerty (Wisconsin) 3:44.53; 6. Rich Peters (Boston U) 3:44.66; 7. Duncan Phillips (Arkansas) 3:44.77; 8. Erik van Ingen (Binghamton) 3:45.00; 9. Sam McEntee (Villanova) 3:46.41; 10. German Fernandez (Oklahoma

State) 3:46.62; 11. Lawi Lalang (Arizona) 3:46.82; 12. Chris O'Hare (Tulsa) 3:51.64.

The Pitfalls of Leading: What They Say

Dick Buerkle, on whether the days of the front-runner are over: "Nothing's ever over. There have just been patterns. Somebody could come along that could lead and make people hurt. You make the folks behind you hurt enough and they might give up. It's tougher with people relaxing behind you, it makes it tough because they can feed off you. But if you make them hurt, it's a little different."

Peter Snell, on the 1962 Empire Games in Perth, Australia, where temperatures soared over 100-degrees Fahrenheit. Though Snell was coached by Arthur Lydiard, the mercurial coach Percy Cerutty beseeched him to break the meet record in the mile: "I'd summed up the conditions and my own physical being and decided to run a waiting race. I told Perce an easy run would be quite satisfactory. After all, the Empire Games is scarcely the place for foolhardy solo exhibitions of virtuoso performances. Forty-five thousand people and the Duke of Edinburgh might be watching and waiting for fireworks, but my concern was to win, not entertain them at risk of failure."[7]

Snell jogged the first lap in 66-seconds, forcing his opponent to panic and take the lead on the second lap. "He was to pay dearly for this." Snell won comfortably in 4:04.6.

Chapter 4: The Mid-Race Move

"I knew if someone came with me,
they were going to be
hurting just as much as I was."

—*Alan Webb*

For many competitors in a championship race, it makes sense to hang back on the first lap. That gives them the vantage point to size up the field and to watch the front of the race to see what others might be planning to do. Another very obvious reason to wait at least a lap before making a move is the accurate assessment of the runner's own strength. Very few have what it takes to lead a race from the start successfully. It stands to reason that a larger population of runners can handle a kick from 600-1200m out.

For the purposes of this chapter, that is the challenge we are focusing on here, making a decisive move anywhere from 400m to 1000m in a mile race, or 400m to 900m in a 1500m. (Kicks of a shorter duration will be covered in following chapters.)

Who is the ideal candidate for a mid-race move? It's a strategy that favors the strength runner—the higher mileage athlete, perhaps, or the 5000m runner moving down in distance. If you know you can get outkicked in a slow race, it makes perfect sense to go somewhere in the middle. You may be able to burn the kick out of the speed merchants. The risk is obvious: you may have company. You may simply be acting as the rabbit to give everyone else a faster time when they outkick you. However, some athletes are better than others at kicking from a hard initial pace. If that describes you, perhaps then you want to be the one to make that earlier pace hard. In any case, this underlines the importance of knowing your own capabilities, as well as those of the competition.

The Mid-Race Move: Race Histories

When Swedes ruled the world of miling: Gunder Hägg leads rival Arne Andersson in a race in Stockholm's Olympiastadion. Combined, they set 10 world records at 1500m and the mile during the 1940s. In 1947, a former rabbit of theirs, Lennart Strand, tied the 1500m mark. A year earlier, he made his mark in the United States at the national championships.

1946 AAU Men's 1500m:
The Swede puts a twist on the mid-race move

In post-war America, it took years for the sport to regain its strength. The generation's best, healthiest athletes had spent the previous years fighting, and untold numbers of potential greats died in those years. Training for running races seems a little trivial when the free world is fighting for democracy. These were lost years, and while there were a few solid American milers in 1946 such as Gil Dodds, they were not in the same class as the Swedes. The best Swedish runners, Gunder Hägg and Arne Anderson, had spent the war years whittling away at the 1500/mile records. They could afford to—Sweden had been neutral during the war, and they were able to keep training. Even after Hägg and Anderson had been banned on professionalism charges in early 1946, their countrymen still dominated the four-lapper. At the end of 1946, of the top 10 on the world list at 1500m, eight were Swedes.

Strand (right) won silver in the 1948 Olympics
behind teammate Henry Eriksson.

Lennart Strand made his name in the war years as a rabbit for several of the world records set by Hägg and Arne Anderson. In 1946, though, he emerged as the world's best, running list-leading times of 3:48.0 and 4:06.6. He decided to do a six-week racing tour through America that summer. He had amply proven his kicking abilities in his first U.S. race, a 1500m at the Compton Invitational, defeating Johnny Fulton easily in 3:51.6. They had gone through the first 800m in 2:09.5, then Strand shut it down with a 59-second third lap and a 43.1 for the final 300m.

In one of his more interesting results, he traveled to San Antonio, Texas, to compete in the 1500m at the AAU National Championships. With the sun beating down to the tune of 94-degrees (34C), Strand decided not to bother warming up—who knows how it would affect him? Instead, he decided to use the first lap of the race as his warm up, jogging a 65.4 well behind the pack. Once he felt comfortable, he shot to the lead on the second lap, and proceeded to run Americans Les MacMitchell and Tommy Quinn into the ground, winning by over 30 yards in 3:54.5. His last lap was a blazing 56.5.

1984 Olympic Men's 1500m: Scott's big move

Anyone watching the videos of Sebastian Coe's successful defense of his 1500m gold in the Los Angeles Games would agree that Coe could not have lost that race, short of someone throwing an octopus at the track and beaning him. That day, Coe, the world record holder in the 800m and the mile, had the unique ability to run any pace and still kick better than anybody on earth.

Before that day, however, many were thinking that Steve Scott's moment had come. The American record holder won the silver at the inaugural World Champs the year before and had the experience and the speed to run with anyone. *Track & Field News* even tabbed him the favorite. Perhaps the hometown boy had a bit too much pressure on him—and big expectations sometimes inspire big moves.

The 1500m heats started just three days after defending champ Coe won the silver in the 800m. The first round mixed fast and slow. Jose Abascal of Spain won his in 3:37.68. Coe got a lucky rest and cruised to a 3:45.30. The semis the next day sizzled. Abascal ran 3:35.70 to win his, ahead of American Steve Scott (3:35.71) and Coe (3:35.81). The second semi was nearly as fast, with Briton Steve Cram (3:36.30) topping American Jim Spivey (3:36.53). Britain's Steve Ovett, the world record holder, ran fourth in 3:36.55. He had suffered through a last-place finish in the 800m and even spent time in the hospital with respiratory distress—a possible victim of LA's smog.

When the final came around, Coe made a move to the front but was edged by Omar Khalifa and Joseph Chesire. Italian Riccardo Materazzi ran on Coe's right. After 200m, Coe stumbled as Steve Scott came up on inside. Approaching 400m (58.85), Coe moved outside to get on Khalifa's shoulder.

Then, at 500m, Scott made his move. It didn't look like he was planning to break the race open there; it looked more like a panicked response to getting boxed. He had stayed right behind Coe until they neared the 400m. Scott, finding himself trapped, dropped back to let Materazzi pass as well as José Abascal, who was moving up quickly. Once he got free, Scott stormed down the backstretch in a move that looked faster than it was (about 14.8 for that 100m). He led for the next lap but it was at a pace he should have been able to handle (57.8). It may have been that he planned to take the sting out of Britain's kickers.

Coe stayed on him, and with 800m to go, ran in second. Scott led at 800m in 1:56.81. At 900m, Coe was moved back to third by the rush of Jose Abascal, who passed Scott. Coe stayed on him, passing Scott to move into second at the 1000m mark. Then Scott faded as both Cram and Ovett passed him. Abascal hit 2:39.05 with a lap to go. Ovett dropped out just before Abascal hit 1200m in 2:53.2, Coe in second, Cram in third.

With 200m left, Coe responded to Cram's attempt to take the lead and went past Abascal to the fore. He looked back several times on the turn before unleashing a forceful sprint on the straightaway that Cram could not respond to. Coe won in an Olympic record 3:32.53, running a 53.3 last lap and 1:50.0 for his final two. Scott finished a forlorn second-from-last.

Coe later wrote, "I had made the pre-race decision not to allow Steve [Cram] to control the race over the latter stages. It was a decision born of hard experience and a study of his racing. I knew he was always at his best and most comfortable mentally when he was leading the race. With a long, uninterrupted run for home, I didn't want to allow him to draw upon that strength. And I knew it didn't really matter what happened; I just had to stop him under all circumstances from getting ahead of me in the last lap."[3]

Steve Scott's story

The genesis of Steve Scott's race plan came out of the 1983 World Championships, a race that went out in a pitifully slow 64.98. He and his coach Len Miller decided that the Olympics would be a faster race that would give him a better chance at gold.

"We sat down in October and November, and said the Olympic final is not going to be run like that. It's not going to be a slow race, it's not going to be tactical. We're going to get out and go after it. The race is going to be won in 3:32. That's kind of the race plan that we set out. In the beginning, I was kind of for it, and then in time, I lost confidence in that race plan... because I don't lead. I'm not someone who's going to lead from the beginning, or even after the first lap. You won't find me leading until sometime late in the third lap. And so, to take over the lead, it created a lot of anxiety for me. This was even in the months leading up to it. We didn't really practice it. Well, we tried to practice it, but it really didn't work out so well. In the big-time races I didn't practice it. It wasn't a race plan that I had confidence in.

"So when the actual race came, I would have been much better off to just sit

---

and let the race develop as it was going to develop. We really went through the first lap pretty decently. I think we were around 60. There was nothing wrong with that. It's not like the 65 that we went out in at Worlds. So after the first lap, I came up into the lead and I pushed that second lap, pushed it pretty hard, and I'm thinking, okay, I've got to have 10 yards on the field, and I looked behind me, and they were all sitting right on me. I didn't lose anybody. That's a big mistake. You start looking backwards, that's the direction you're going.

"I kept going another lap, and we're coming in with a lap to go and then one went by me, then two, then three, then four, I mean, everybody went by me except Ovett, who dropped out. That was just poor tactical planning. It wasn't something I was really comfortable with. And that was the thing. If I could have changed after the first lap and said, 'I'm not doing it,' I would have been totally relaxed. But taking the lead created so much tension and anxiety. It was building up for months. If I had just sat back, I'm sure it would have been a whole different outcome. I don't think I would have beaten Coe on that day, but I think medaling was a possibility."

Results (11 August 1984): 1. Sebastian Coe (Great Britain) 3:32.53; 2. Steve Cram (Great Britain) 3:33.40; 3. José Abascal (Spain) 3:34.30; 4. Joseph Chesire (Kenya) 3:34.52; 5. Jim Spivey (USA) 3:36.07; 6. Peter Wirz (Swi) 3:36.97; 7. Andrés Vera (Spain) 3:37.02; 8. Omar Khalifa (Sudan) 3:37.11; 9. Tony Rogers (New Zealand) 3:38.98; 10. Steve Scott (USA) 3:39.86; 11. Riccardo Materazzi (Italy) 3:40.74;... dnf—Steve Ovett (Great Britain).

1988 Olympic Games Men's 1500m:
How to come up with a race plan after the first 400m

This Olympic final remains tactically interesting from several different perspectives, but it's especially curious that two very similar mid-race moves resulted in drastically different outcomes for Peter Rono and Jeff Atkinson.

Rono, 21, was raised in a small village near Kapsabet, Kenya. In the epicenter of Rift Valley running excellence, pursuing the sport seemed like an obvious choice. It didn't hurt that he attended the legendary St. Patrick's School in Iten, where he was coached by Brother Colm O'Connell. Just after his 18th birthday, while still in high school, he ran a 3:39.2 to place second in the Kenyan national championships, held at high altitude. That got the attention of Jim Deegan, the coach at Mount St. Mary's University. Already a World Junior silver medalist when he showed up in Maryland, as a freshman he made it to the semis of the World Championships in Rome. Even though Rono had run a PR of 3:35.59 in June, his appearance on the starting line in Seoul frightened no one. He was, after all, the youngest man in the field, and favorites Peter Elliott and Steve Cram tend not to be scared of NCAA Division II champions.

Atkinson, 25, had starred at Stanford but had never won an NCAA title. While he was a ferocious competitor on the track, he also had a reputation as a laid-back surfer type. Many were surprised by his Olympic Trials win, but it had come in a season when he had chopped more than five seconds off his 1500m PR, all the way down to 3:36.10.

Rono and Atkinson were the eighth and eleventh fastest runners in the field, respectively.

In a field packed with veterans, all eyes focused on the big names. The *Track & Field News* formchart picked Saïd Aouita, Steve Cram, and Abdi Bile for the medals. Aouita pulled out after the semis with an injury, and Bile also turned up injured. Peter Rono was not included in the top 10 picks, and only merited mention in the last sentence as a possible finalist.

Kenya had placed three in the finals, and the team coaches were urging the runners to help each other with the pace. Recalls Rono, "Originally Joseph Chesire was supposed to take the lead from the start. But when we were warming up, [the Kenyan] coach came and told the guys there are three people who could win. It could be the British and the Americans or the Kenyans. And he didn't mention names because my coach Jim Deegan was there. Chesire was supposed to rabbit, but he also thought he could win. The only problem was he didn't tell us he wasn't going to rabbit anymore."

Who are they cheering for?

"When we were going into the stadium something very interesting happened that I thought about many years later. I looked around the stadium and I saw the flags. The British had their flags and were yelling, 'Go Peter!' I also looked at the Germans and they had their flags and were yelling, 'Go Peter!' And I looked at the Kenyan guys, and they were saying, 'Go Peter!' And I thought that everybody wanted me to win! I didn't know that there were also Peter Elliott and Jens-Peter Herold. The day actually was the day for the Peters."

–Peter Rono

Ireland's Marcus O'Sullivan took the early lead with Omar Khalifa of Sudan running off his shoulder. The Brits, Steve Cram and Peter Elliott, stayed close in third and fourth. Rono ran in last for the first lap; Atkinson third from last. O'Sullivan clocked 59.65 for his opener.

"When the race started, obviously it was slow, and I'm in the back looking around and seeing Chesire still in the back with us. So after one lap, I decided each one of us was on our own. So I took my own plan. I changed my strategy myself. I realized we had very fast runners like Peter Elliott who had run 1:42 that year. We also had Steve Cram who was obviously a very good kicker. We also had Steve Scott who was very, very good. So I realized the only thing to do was to start leading the race at halfway and start running very, very hard and start burning these guys out."

Rono made his move—from 500m to 700m, he shot into the lead with a 27.4 half-lap. Once he was safely in the front, he eased the pace over the next 100m before he passed through 800m in 2:00.31 and began his long drive to the finish.

Atkinson at that point lagged in second-to-last. He jumped the field on the backstretch, and made it to Rono's shoulder midway through the turn. However, since Rono began his big drive to the finish at the same time, Atkinson's move was significantly more expensive than Rono's original move to the front. Atkinson took 26.7 for that half-lap, and couldn't afford to take a breather like Rono did—the real racing had already begun, and he was already in oxygen debt.

Rono gradually upped the ante after 800m, hitting 100s of 13.7, 13.6, 13.4, 13.3, 13.0, 12.3 and 12.6. He had passed 1200m in 2:56.65 with Atkinson right behind; a few steps later, the American imploded, and the field moved around him like a river around a boulder.

On the final turn, Rono's biggest challengers were the Brits and Jens-Peter Herold. He kept glancing over his shoulder to gauge their progress. On the straightaway, he put on his best sprint and managed to stay ahead of the hunters, after leading for the last 800m of the race in 1:50.8. His last lap had taken 52.83. "We were all going at top speed and they didn't pass me. They wanted to pass me and they didn't pass me."

Atkinson, however, had finished with a 57.7. His mid-race move came at 700m, a half-lap too late to get the jump on anyone.

Said the winner of his improvised plan, "My strategy worked.... Something that not many people realize is that I did not lose any race that year. Including the NCAA [D2] and including the Kenyan trials where I had run a 3:36 at altitude. That is the equivalent of a 3:34, and people didn't see that. But I knew I had the speed, I had the endurance, and I had never lost any race that year."

What many coaches often dismiss as a sign of weakness—looking frequently over the shoulder—may have been key to Rono's success. The secret of winning on a long drive over the best milers in the world is always keeping another gear in reserve. Rono needed to monitor his pursuers closely so he could save his very best gear for when he really needed it. If he spent it too early, he would have lost.

"Physically I knew that the only way to probably win when the race was slow was to run very fast from 900m to go because you don't want to take a very good sprinter all the way to 200m," says Rono. "You don't want to do anything with Peter Elliott or Steve Cram [in the last 200]."

Quipped the disappointed Cram in a 2012 interview, "We let him win—Rono was running off the front and we were all watching each other."[3]

Behind Cram's finish

Three weeks before the Games, Steve Cram attempted a world record for the 1000m. With 150m to go, he pulled a calf muscle. He said, "That upset all of my preparations and confidence and I couldn't do the fine-tuning work needed, and entered the Olympic final with many doubts. Peter [Elliott] will tell you that in the final everyone was waiting for me to do something, and because of my lack of self-belief, I ran a very poor tactical race... When I crossed the finish line I cried and that was something I'd never done before. I was so frustrated that I wanted to go back and do it all over again."

Results (1 October 1988): 1. Peter Rono (Kenya) 3:35.96; 2. Peter Elliott (Great Britain) 3:36.15; 3. Jens-Peter Herold (East Germany) 3:36.21; 4. Steve Cram (Great Britain) 3:36.24; 5. Steve Scott (USA) 3:36.99; 6. Hans Kulker (Netherlands) 3:37.08; 7. Kip Cheruiyot (Kenya) 3:37.94; 8. Marcus O'Sullivan (Ireland) 3:38.39; 9. Mario Silva (Portugal) 3:38.77; 10. Jeff Atkinson (USA) 3:40.80; 11. Joseph Chesire (Kenya) 3:40.82; 12. Omar Khalifa (Sudan) 3:41.07.

Jeff Atkinson on the 1988 Olympic race:
Mistakes and what-ifs

"The Games were the same exact strategy as all my previous races. The only difference is that at the international level, things heat up faster and sooner. In the semi final, I did that move and got a nice position and then I got passed back down the home stretch with 400m to go and got pushed all the way back into eighth or ninth place. That was a mistake and so I had to kick my way up a little harder than I wanted to to make the final. I made it, no problem, but I had to eke a little more juice than I wanted to, and I had to come from farther back.

"So when I got to the final, I said I can't let that happen. Once I achieve a position, I can't let it slip back on the tractor wheel as I call it. And so I was a little overcommitted to that particular plan, which ultimately was my downfall because I needed to be a little more flexible. Like I said, in an international race it really heats up sooner, so had I moved my positioning back 100 or 200 yards, that's what it would take, because that's exactly when Peter Rono moved to the front. Coming up on two laps to go, 900m to 800m to go, and he did it very gently because that's when the race lagged. So he gets up there and I take off down the backstretch to get my position, and *everybody* decides to do that. It happened all 200m earlier than normal, and that forced everybody to run a whole lot faster, and I had to go farther around to get to that spot I liked on the leader's shoulder. The result was that that lap

Jeff Atkinson

was about a 55 which would normally be close to a last lap. You know, last lap speeds can be 51 – 52 – 53. But that lap, the penultimate lap was I think 55. I got to the bell, I was in a nice spot, I held off a couple of people on the turn, but I then was gassed with 300m to go. So it didn't so much as backfire as I wasn't strong enough to make the move in that way. Or had I been smarter or more experienced, I might've recognized it was going to happen a little earlier and I would eke my way up there.

"Rono got there and nobody was running, and he got a nice position and he had to lead some more, but the pace was slow enough, and he was strong enough that that wasn't too detrimental for him. Would it have worked for me? Had I followed him up, I might've been closer. I wouldn't have had to make that big move on the backstretch. I still would've had to put some energy into the backstretch when everybody goes wide, and starts loading up. So would he, and so would I. It would've been another fight there just to hold that position, but might've been less juice overall. Less energy overall."

2004 Olympic Trials Men's 1500m: Webb at his finest

In a career that generated more ink (virtual and otherwise) than possibly any other American miler, Alan Webb always faced the burden of his potential. So often the articles covered not what he had done, but what he still might do. Yet, when one slices and dices his career and throws out the record attempts, looking solely at the competitive races, it's easy to come to the conclusion that nowhere was he better than at the Olympic Trials.

Only 21, Webb ran as the favorite, yet there were others who thought they might challenge him. In the semi, he tried a mid-race breakaway and ended up getting reeled in by Michael Stember. Defending champion Jason Lunn also had designs on the race.

The final took off extremely fast, then slowed. Webb had the lead at 400m in 59.11, but seemed content and relaxed in that position. However, he started putting his opponents in pain with his next circuit of 57.94. Everything indicated that he would continue to gradually apply the pressure. It is a technique that can generally only win if the leader is stronger than everyone in the field to begin with, strong enough to generate a kick to defeat anyone lucky enough to hang on until the end.

Webb, though, always had a flair for the big, dramatic move. As the field came off the turn toward the 800m mark, he produced an acceleration that stunned the field and killed the hopes anyone might have had to beat him. By the end of that straightaway, he led by 25m. He simply continued to pour it on, hitting 1200m in 2:52.58 (a 55.53 circuit). He tired at the end, but his lead couldn't be challenged. He ended up winning by 2.32 over Charlie Gruber.

Stember struggled with a torn shoe and ended up far in the back. He said, "I knew if Alan got a jump, it would be hard to catch him. When he is four seconds better than the rest of the field, it was basically two races and I should have tucked in early and focused on winning the battle for second."

"I'm the defending champion," said Lunn, "but all I could do was run for second today. I didn't expect Alan to open up such a big gap, even though everyone knew he would make a move. I figured it would be after the 400m or as late as 600m to go."

Said Webb, "I knew it was going to take a really decisive move to break away from those guys. I knew if someone came with me, they were going to be hurting just as much as I was."

Results *(18 July 2004): 1. Alan Webb (Nike) 3:36.13; 2. Charlie Gruber (Nike) 3:38.45; 3. Rob Myers (unattached) 3:38.93; 4. Chris Lukezic (unattached) 3:40.05; 5. Jason Lunn (Nike) 3:40.81; 6. Nathan Robison (unattached) 3:40.99; 7. Donald Sage (Stanford) 3:41.26; 8. Said Ahmed (Arkansas) 3:42.77; 9. Chris Estwanick (Nike Farm Team) 3:43.03; 10. Zach Griffin (Nike Farm Team) 3:43.38; 11. Michael Stember (Nike) 3:47.42; 12. Scott McGowan (New Balance) 3:49.50.*

2005 World Champs Men's 1500m: Webb's crazy sprint

Alan Webb, the wunderkind of American miling, came to Helsinki in great shape. His confidence was high in every aspect but his kick, so he planned a daring mid-race move. The race went out with a slow first lap, 60.73. Reyes Estevez of Spain led with Webb off his shoulder. The pace lagged even more on the second lap, and as they neared the 800m, Rashid Ramzi came up on Webb's shoulder, perhaps increasing the pressure on him.

The leaders hit the 800m in 2:03.78.

That's when Webb made The Move. He exploded from the 800m mark into a full-out sprint. TV commentators caught his next 100m in 12.3. While he shook the field up, he didn't lose them. Kipchirchir gradually reeled him in over the next 100m, and Ramzi came along as well.

"He ran like 26-point for the next 200m," said Ron Warhurst, who briefly coached him several years earlier. "He thought he was going to run away from everyone."

On the British TV feed, in response to one of the commentators calling the move "suicidal," mile great Steve Cram said, "I had the word 'crazy' on my lips because I'm not sure that Webb can sustain anything like that. Now all he's done is stretched them out and slowed again.... He stretched them out but they're all still there. Ramzi's still there."

Approaching a lap to go, Webb slowed the pace, while staring at the stadium screen to assess the situation behind him. On the next turn, Ramzi jumped him, leading Ivan Heshko as they passed 1200m in 2:57.52, a 53.79 circuit. On the backstretch, the bottom dropped out for Webb, as he watched the field stream around him. "He started looking like, 'I thought I broke them,'" said Warhurst.

The runners ahead of Webb chased the medals. Ramzi never wavered in first place, though the fast kicks of Adil Kaouch and Rui Silva put some pressure on him. He ran a 54.19 closer to win in 3:37.88, then a few days later captured the 800m gold in 1:44.24. Webb, meanwhile, finished a dispirited ninth in 3:41.04, more than three seconds behind the winner.

He said afterward to reporters, "Nobody wanted to do anything. All those guys are kickers." With more time to think, he later told *Runners World*, "I've gotten more praise for this ninth place finish than I've ever gotten in my life for finishing ninth in a race. People knew I tried. It wasn't for a lack of effort.... It's an extremely difficult task to run a race like that, just because there's uncertainty in those races. You don't know what the pace is going to be, or who's going to be in the races.

"You're always changing tactics, from one round to the next. There are different circumstances; there are different people in the race. You have to be able to think on your feet and change things. If I could do the race over again, would I run it differently? Yeah, but that's not to say that if I didn't know what was going to happen, would I still have chosen that choice? Yeah, I probably would have chosen to do the same thing."[2]

Ironically, Ramzi quipped after he won, "There were no tactics in the race." His last 800m took only 1:49.1, as he reacted to Webb's move and won using a long kick.

Webb had described his strategy as all or nothing—he wanted to go for the win, instead of second or third. In reality, there was no choice there.

There rarely is. A smart kicker's race might have seemed like more of a crapshoot, but it may also have gotten him a medal—of any color. The bold mid-race move? It only served to impress those who don't know how championship 1500m races work—with added cheers from the Prefontaine acolytes who haunt Internet message boards.

In 2005, Alan Webb came to Helsinki's Olympiastadion as anything but the favorite. His best time of the year was a 3:33.16, and the only race he had won since Nationals was a low-level 800m in Ireland. He would be facing off against Rashid Ramzi, the powerful Moroccan who had switched his athletic allegiance to Bahrain three years earlier. Ramzi led the world list with the 3:30.00 he clocked in winning the Golden Gala in Rome.

Webb, however, may have developed his plans for the race in the heady atmosphere that had seen him the most heralded high school star since Jim Ryun. In short, Webb knew pressure, and he knew the weight of daunting expectation. Did it affect his race plan? He got through the heats and semis by running unnecessarily fast times. After his 3:36.07 semi, he told reporters, "Nobody thought I was dumb enough to do it twice in a row."[1]

Said Ramzi, "The weather played a big problem for the athletes, we just could not get the right rhythm. I was hoping we would spread it out a little so I would have more space to run my own race, but I had to wait until the last lap to beat them with my speed."

Ron Warhurst on Webb's Move

It's long been known that Alan Webb and Michigan coach Ron Warhurst did not part on the best of terms. It's a complicated story, perhaps best covered in Chris Lear's book, Alan Webb and the Quest for the Fastest Mile. *However, one aspect that is pertinent to the 2005 Worlds is that Warhurst felt that Webb did not have the tactical experience to compete at the highest level in the 1500m.*

"Now Webb, when he said he was going to go pro and all that stuff, I talked to his parents, and I said, 'You know, he's not ready to do this. He's very immature, and he doesn't understand racing tactics.' I said, 'They're going to eat him alive.' In this next level he's going to go to, he cannot, after 600m, take the lead. Or 800m into the race, take the lead. Because these guys will line up behind him and say, 'Here's our rabbit, man.' Then they'll just jump right on him and follow him around and then kill him with 300m to go."

Results *(10 August 2005): 1. Rashid Ramzi (Bahrain) 3:37.88; 2. Adil Kaouch (Morocco) 3:38.00; 3. Rui Silva (Portugal) 3:38.02; 4. Ivan Heshko (Ukraine) 3:38.71; 5. Arturo Casado (Spain) 3:39.45; 6. Juan Carlos Higuero (Spain) 3:40.34; 7. Alex Kipchirchir (Kenya) 3:40.43; 8. Tarek Boukensa (Algeria) 3:41.01; 9. Alan Webb (USA) 3:41.04; 10. Dahame Najem Bashir (Qatar) 3:43.48; 11. Reyes Estévez (Spain) 3:46.65; 12. Yassine Bensghir (Morocco) 3:50.19.*

2012 Olympic Trials Men's 1500m:
Leer takes the pace

The 2012 Olympic qualifying standards posed a predicament to several of the runners in the Trials field. Only three of the finalists had achieved the standard of 3:35.50 in the year previous. A number of the runners who didn't have it still had a chance to finish in the top three—a finish that would basically be meaningless if it wasn't fast enough to guarantee them a ticket to London. USATF had decided to name the Olympic team directly after the meet, rather than allowing a period of time for athletes to chase A standards frantically, as had happened in past years. One of those men needing the "A" was Will Leer. His race plan was somewhat controversial, but his coach, Ron Warhurst, still stands by it. "That was our decision."

He adds, "In the semi, he just ran, he felt good. He said I can sit and kick and get third and not go to the Olympics, because it's not going to be fast. Or I can just try it and see if I can get some of these people to help me out, and go to the front and whatever." Behind the scenes in the two days until the final, Leer tried to arrange a pace that would give more people a real shot at making the Olympic team.

Says Andy Bayer, "They had asked me to take it at some point because, they were just asking anybody who didn't have A standard. I think at one point they were talking to Coach Ron Helmer about having me try to pace it. I guess no one thought I had a chance to make the team. But Coach Helmer kind of shut them all down. Since you couldn't chase [the standard], a lot of guys were looking to make the race honest."

Jordan McNamara was one such guy. The Oregon alum took it out from the start, with Leer in tow. He passed 400m in 57.6, where Leer took over the pacing. Staying close to the action, Matthew Centrowitz ran third and Leo Manzano fourth at that point. Andrew Wheating ran seventh. Leer had been hoping that BYU's Miles Batty or John Mickowski, the Army runner, would take over after 700m. That didn't happen, and Leer continued to lead past 800m in 1:57.6 and stayed there for another 100m. That was when Mickowski, who had the slowest PR in the field at 3:38.39, finally made it to the front with his ungainly stride.

Leer leading McNamara.

Centrowitz went to Mickowski's shoulder, effectively boxing Leer. But rather than building a strong pace that would give Leer and company a shot at making the team, Mickowski let it slow. With 400m left, Centrowitz took over with David Torrence at his side, and Manzano putting himself into the mix. Leer shot out the back of the pack in the next 50m.

Centrowitz hit 1200m in 2:55.9. Teammate Torrence challenged him on the backstretch, then fell back. Robby Andrews made a great backstretch move as well but didn't get to the front of the pack before the last turn. Coming off it, Centrowitz charged into the homestretch with Manzano in hot pursuit. The two pulled away from the pack, Manzano's kick ultimately prevailing by 0.09, his last lap, 53.08.

The race for third resembled a free-for-all, with five different runners in contention at 50m to go. Wheating's long stride on his 53.58 closer carried him to the final coveted team position, while Bayer snuck through with an inside pass in lane one to grab fourth. Mickowski and Leer faded to the last two spots, while first-lap leader McNamara finished seventh.

Said Leer in his post-race press conference, "John said his plan today was to drive it from 700m out to get away from the kickers... John was supposed to come around me between 700-800m, and when that didn't happen, I was like, 'Aw shit, I'm going to be hung out to dry here for the next 700m or until everyone blows by.'

"Our idea was to get out, get it within reach, and really wind it up with 700m to go to give ourselves an opportunity. Going out super hard, more likely than not, especially in the wind, you're just going to die."

Says Warhurst of the failed plan, "Well, the pace wasn't right. It didn't happen. The tactics were good, if other people were going to help [Leer] do it. But once again, he's a kicker, he's not a leader. Somebody was supposed to take it at the half and nobody took it, so Will jumped on it at 400m and they were lined up behind him. In hindsight, I probably would have said, 'You know what, Will? You're probably not going to get it here. You're not going to get in the top three if you take it out. It doesn't work that way. So just race it, so if you run 3:36 and you just miss it, you're third, that's it, you're third in the Olympic Trials.'

"He said, 'I'm going to go for it.' I respect that too. I'm not a babysitter. 'You're 26 years old, you've been here before.' That was the mentality that went into it."

They took a shot and missed. Arguably, the three best runners prevailed in the end, so perhaps any other strategy would have yielded the same result.

Results (1 July 2012): 1. Leo Manzano (Nike) 3:35.75; 2. Matthew Centrowitz (Nike) 3:35.84; 3. Andrew Wheating (Nike Oregon TC) 3:36.68; 4. Andy Bayer (Indiana) 3:37.24; 5. Robby Andrews (adidas) 3:37.45; 6. David Torrence (Nike) 3:37.70; 7. Jordan McNamara (Nike Oregon TC) 3:37.79; 8. Craig Miller (New Balance) 3:37.81; 9. Jeff See (Saucony) 3:38.81; 10. Miles Batty (Asics) 3:43.58; 11. John Mickowski (unattached) 3:44.17; 12. Will Leer (Nike) 3:46.75.

Andy Bayer's strategy for the race

"Looking back, it may have been better to be at least a few spots up [before the last lap]. But going into the race, we didn't really have an idea what to expect. Coach Helmer was like, 'You made a final, just try and beat as many guys as possible. You do that by being relaxed early and finishing well.' I think I was in last after 200m. I got off the line pretty bad but at that point I didn't want to make any unnecessary moves the whole early part of the race. And so I just kind of let the race come to me and slowly passed guys as they fell off a little bit, and then kind of made a big move the last 250m. Really, 150m is where I passed a lot of guys. At the end, the inside just kind of opened up for me and I took advantage of it."

About that inside pass near the finish: "I actually remember I was just about to swing out wide because I didn't think it was going to open up, and then I think David Torrence moved out and it all opened up and I got pretty lucky that I could just stay in lane one all the way to the line. I went in wanting to finish in the top half of the race. It was my first Olympic Trials, and I definitely wanted to be as close to top three as possible. I was probably one of the only people at the Trials who was happy with a fourth place finish. Everyone else was probably devastated."

The Mid-Race Move: What They Say

Sarah Brown, explaining how slow-paced races have inspired her to be more gutsy in the middle: "I leave races like that feeling disgusted. Those are always races that I wish I could redo. If you go with the pack, you're doing what everyone else is doing. But things always jumble up... To let a race go like that and get knocked around with 300m to go so you really can't get caught back up, it's just one of those things where literally you leave the race feeling disgusted. Just embarrassed. You're hearing boos from the crowd. If I could just go back I would've taken off, knowing what I know now. Who cares if people beat me, at least I make them run.

"Everybody at this level has a kick at that pace... We can all run a sub-60 last 400m. Everyone can. And then it's just who has the best position going into that final 400m. You have all the jockeying, and people hitting each other trying to stay in that best position, because now it's not a matter of who's the best, but who's got the best racing tactics and can be where they need to be. And you just can't guarantee that kind of thing. So for me I don't think that's the best way to go."

Renato Canova on high speed endurance: "We prepare in training the 'kick' according to the characteristics of the athlete. For example, Bernard Lagat had a real 'kick,' the ability to quickly change speed, increasing the frequency of the action, reducing the length of every stride (such as a car going in a lower gear), and in this way creating the conditions for a change of speed in case of a tactical race. This attitude doesn't depend on pure speed, but on the running technique and on the nervous system.

"In many cases, athletes get confused between 'speed for the kick' and 'high speed endurance,' making big tactical mistakes. One of these, in my opinion, was Alan Webb. He had exceptional speed endurance, and this made it appropriate for him to attack progressively with 700m-500m to go, to kill the ability of the real "kickers." Instead, after he ran 800m in 1:43, he started to think he was fast, and ran his next races waiting in the pack, thinking he had a 'kick.' For that reason, he never won any medals.

"Silas Kiplagat is in the same situation. He is able to finish the last 300m in 39.5 during a 3:27.47 race (as in Monaco in 2013), but he cannot finish faster while running a 3:39. Why? Because he is an 'aerobic runner,' with great relaxation and elasticity, but not the technical action (and the nervous system) valid for a quick and sudden change of speed. So, in his case, the training we use is more connected with the idea to develop fast and long progression, not to develop the maximal speed."

Chapter 5: The Long Kick

"Everybody puts up with pain.
So pain, that doesn't matter."

—*Don Paige*

When a good runner is faced with an opponent with a better finishing kick, there are really only two viable options. To lead from the gun, or to go for the long kick to try to burn out that finishing sting. Both are difficult, but if the alternative is certain defeat, it's a simple choice.

One doesn't have to look long to find examples of this strategy being successful. It is one of the most basic of strategies, one that should be utilized by the strength runner. Athletes who have logged their training miles and built a strong aerobic base should consider this carefully, especially if they don't have the quick turnover that can generate a successful kick in the closing stages. Still, there are no guarantees. A strong competitor can follow and still outkick the leader. Of course, in that case, odds are that would have happened no matter how fast the leader pushed the pace.

The trick with the long kick is that a runner who uses it successfully must be supremely fit. There's no faking; no way to hide behind another runner's pace and hope you can bluff a kick. Luckily, it's a move that can and should be rehearsed in training. If you're going to kick hard from 500m or 400m out, you had better have a very good idea of just what speed you can handle without croaking.

The Long Kick: Race Histories

Herb Elliott (right) leads medalists István Rózsavölgyi and Michel Jazy as he begins his long finishing drive that would produce the last world record run in a men's Olympic 1500m.

1960 Olympic 1500m:
Elliott finishes unthinkably hard

Herb Elliott never was beaten in a mile or 1500m race during the six years of his short career when he trained seriously. His incredible kick had been trained by Percy Cerutty, an eccentric coach who spent much time developing a killer instinct among his runners. "You kill yourself rather than be beaten," he once said.[1]

Elliott revealed that he had a mid-race internal debate about strategy: "This guy in a blue singlet [Michel Bernard] charged out a million miles per hour.... He ran like a crazy man for about a lap and a half, and I knew the pace he was setting was faster than I would have been comfortable with if I had been setting it myself. So when we got to the halfway mark, I felt pretty tired. And this was the point where I was going to make my move. Because I felt pretty tired, my positive attitude was being challenged. I expected the voice to come up in my head saying, 'You've been training for four years, you've made huge sacrifices, this is the time for you to move and show the rest of the world what you're made of.' That wasn't the voice that came up in my head at all. This voice came up and said, 'Herb, you're bugging.' So there was a negative voice that emerged so powerful. It advised me very quickly to change my strategy. It said to me... 'You're an idiot if you go to the front right now. Hang back here in second or third place, and just see how you go over the next three-quarters of a lap. Don't take the risk of going to the front.' Because in my training, every day that voice was talking to me, and in my training I had learned to totally ignore it.... I instinctively ignored it in the race." [2]

Indeed, Bernard took it out hard, perhaps to act as a rabbit for his teammate, Michel Jazy. He hit 400m in 58.2. Elliott stayed back, clocking 58.6. By 800m, Bernard clocked 1:57.8, with Elliott just 0.2 behind. He moved alongside Bernard, and 100m later, he moved into the lead. Bernard folded, and was also passed by István Rózsavölgyi and Jazy, along with Swede Dan Waern. Elliott's relentless drive continued. He covered the stretch from 800m to 1000m in a mere 27.4 and passed 1200m in 2:54.0. The next 200m took him only 27.2, and he actually slowed to a 14.4 for his final 100m.

His 55.6 final 400m was impressive enough, but at the time, a final 800m of 1:52.8 was unthinkable. Elliott's fitness level was so much higher than his competitors' that he was never challenged. He crossed the line in a stunning world record of 3:35.6, breaking his own 3:36.0 standard.

How would the race have ended up had Elliott listened to his personal demons and hung back longer? No worries, mate. He still would have crushed the field with a last lap of 52 or 53. The world record, though, would not have happened.

Results *(6 September 1960): 1. Herb Elliott (Australia) 3:35.6; 2. Michel Jazy (France) 3:38.4; 3. István Rózsavölgyi (Hungary) 3:39.2; 4. Dan Waern (Sweden) 3:40.0; 5. Zoltan Vamos (Romania) 3:40.8; 6. Dyrol Burleson (USA) 3:40.9; 7. Michel Bernard (France) 3:41.5; 8. Jim Grelle (USA) 3:45.0; 9. Arne Hamarsland (Norway) 3:45.0.*

1971 Dream Mile:
Liquori and Ryun's ultimate showdown

The build-up to the original Dream Mile at the Martin Luther King Jr. Freedom Games probably saw more hype than any other middle distance race in American history. Jim Ryun, coming back to competition, had run the fastest mile in the world that season at 3:55.8. Marty Liquori, three years younger, had won the fateful race two years earlier that marked the end of Ryun's first career, where he walked off the track and hung up his spikes. In the time since then, he had emerged as the world's top miler.

"He was everybody's hero, and he had every right to be," commented Liquori. "I guess my knocking him off made me sort of a villain."[3]

In the weeks leading up to the race, the nation's newspapers piled on the coverage. Who would show? Who would win? How?

Liquori's coach, Jumbo Elliott, told longtime track reporter Jim Dunaway, "Marty's a competitor. He never runs for time, but only to win, so naturally his times aren't as fast as Ryun's. But Marty's in the best shape of his life, and he's really ready for this race. Remember, he beat Ryun the last two times they raced, and he's two years older and stronger now."[4]

Philadelphia's Franklin Field was packed with 23,000 fans as the two lined up with their competitors. The two stars showed no urgency to lead— they spent most of the first two laps at the back of the pack. It looked to many like Liquori was pursuing a foolish strategy by playing to the feared kick of Ryun. They hit halfway in 2:03.2. Liquori went. Ryun chased.

Would Liquori be able to run Ryun's kick out of him? He covered the next lap in 56.7, building up a slight lead over the world record holder. As he passed three-quarters, he heard the 3:00.0 split and panicked. "I thought I was dead. It was much too slow for me to win the race. I was trying my hardest."[5]

With Ryun gaining on him, Liquori eked out everything he had. He started kicking on the last turn, knowing that a stride behind, Ryun was unleashing his legendary sprint. Finally, Liquori made it to the line a half-stride ahead as the fans stormed the track. His last quarter took 54.6, his last half 1:51.3.

"We were both dead tired at the end," he said. "But I was lucky to hang on. I expected to have him flying by."[6]

"Marty ran a brilliant race and I just followed him. I didn't underestimate his strength," explained Ryun. "He knew I always was strong in the last 200 yards and with 100 yards left I saw him a bit heavy. Then I got a bit heavy myself and he held up."[6]

Marty Liquori in a 1970 race.

Results *(16 May 1971): 1. Marty Liquori 3:54.6; 2. Jim Ryun 3:54.6; 3. Byron Dyce (Jamaica) 3:59.6; 4. Reggie McAfee (Brevard) 4:00.0; 5. Keith Colburn (Sports International) 4:01.1; 6. Morgan Mosser (West Virginia) 4:02.7.*

1979 AAU 1500m:
Steve Scott's epic battle with Don Paige

Just two weeks before, Villanova senior Don Paige won his historic 800/1500m double at the NCAA meet, the first to do so since Ron Delaney in 1958. He won both races with a devastating kick. Steve Scott, anxious to defend his national title at Walnut (Mt. SAC), figured he would have to try something new to burn the kick out of the young upstart. "He [Paige] was just going to run the 15," remembers Scott. "He had run 1:44 for 800m, so he had superior leg speed. But to win the 1500m at the USA track & field meet, he has to have strength as well. My coach and I set up a race plan. That we would let the pace just happen over the first 800m."

The early lead went to Tom Duits, a journeyman miler from Western Michigan who had more potential than his times indicated. Indeed, just a week later he ran on an American record-setting 4 x 1500m relay, and produced the fastest relay leg in history to that time, a stunning 3:34.6. Duits led the field through a steady opening 400m of 61.1. Scott ran a step behind at 61.5, with Paige a little farther back at 62.0.

Scott as a UC Irvine athlete.

Remembers Paige, "Len Miller was Steve's coach, and he was right past the 400m split. He is down on his knee, and he leans in and yells as loud as he can to Steve Scott, 'You've got to go now!' And I'm like, 'Oh crap, I'm in trouble.' Because Steve is very, very strong. I knew his strengths and weaknesses. At least I can outkick him. And he took off."

Scott began his big gamble. He made his move early, much earlier than anyone expected. He hit 800m in 2:01.2, a 59.7 circuit. His next lap was a stunning 54.9. Most of those who tried to go with him felt serious pain. "That extended kick went on for two-and-a-half laps. Steve had to get me tired, and by golly, he did."

Says Scott, "Every hundred meters, I would make another move. It was almost like a fartlek, but it was continually getting harder and harder."

Paige knew he had to stay close, and at 1200m (2:56.1), he was positioned on Scott's shoulder ready to unleash his kick. Though for the last year, he had worked on becoming a stronger miler, he knew that at that pace, he did not have much kick left. Still, he pulled nearly even with Scott on the homestretch. His last 400m took 54.7. Scott ran his in 53.9, with a final 800m of 1:50.1. "Coming around the last turn," Scott says, "he came up on my shoulder. But I burned his kick out of him in the previous 700m. He couldn't catch me down the homestretch."

Says Paige, "When I went to kick in the last 100m, Steve had gotten me tired and he beat me. It was a great race, a great tactical race. There was a lot riding on it. He was a West Coast miler, I was an East Coast kid. But we were good friends. He was one of the toughest competitors you could compete against. He did what he had to do. It was phenomenal. The pain level was very high. It hurt.

"You have to know your competitors. Steve knew me. I knew him, and there was only one way he was going to beat me and that was to get me tired. I was hopeful that I was strong enough. But I obviously think when I evaluated it a week afterward, and really thought about it, that I hadn't fully recovered from the NCAA double and running five races in three days and having that tough double on Saturday. Yeah, I would have liked to have beaten him, but it didn't happen that day."

"I think that was one of the tactically superior races that I had ever run against an individual competitor," concludes Scott.

Results (17 June 1979): 1. Steve Scott (Sub 4) 3:36.40; 2. Don Paige (Athletic Attic) 3:37.33; 3. Todd Harbour (Baylor) 3:40.20; 4. Tom Duits (U Chicago TC) 3:40.22; 5. Steve Lacy (Wisconsin TC) 3:40.8; 6. Ross Donaghue (St Johns) 3:41.9; 7. Dan Aldridge (Maccabi TC) 3:42.4; 8. Phil Kane (Athletics West) 3:43.0; 9. Andy Clifford (Bay Area Striders) 3:44.3; 10. Dick Buerkle (NYAC) 3:47.4; 11. Mike Durkin (U Chicago TC) 3:53.0; 12. Mark Belger (Athletic Attic) 3:58.6.

1984 Olympic Trials Women's 1500m:
As told by Ruth Wysocki

If you weren't alive and watching this race back in 1984, you really missed a hell of a competition. Mary Decker Slaney was the World Champion at 1500m and 3000m. She held every American record from 800m to the 10,000m. She was the undisputed queen of American running. She had not lost a track race to anyone in nearly four years. And Ruth Wysocki, whose biggest claim to fame was winning the U.S. 800m title in 1978—had the nerve to pass her. Her own words tell the story best:

"To tell you the truth, that race turned me into a true 1500m runner, because that was the one where I ran it the right way. I did it more technically, not trying to control the whole thing, and obviously gained a whole boatload of confidence because it worked. Maybe it was sort of the perfect storm. You set the stage. You have Mary coming off the world championship year, could have walked to win it. It was hers to win, there is no doubt. And then Kim Gallagher, who at the time was running so impressively. [*Gallagher had won the 800m earlier in the meet, 1:58.50 to Wysocki's 1:59.34.*]

"I mean when Kim decided to move it was all over. That acceleration she had was amazing. And so Kim was bold enough go into that race after predicting that she was going after Mary. To be honest, it was my husband, Tom, who sat back and said, 'Run for third. I mean you made the team in the 800m, you're already on the team. So what's the worst thing that happens in this race? You're already on the team. You are in a real nothing-to-lose situation.' No one was looking at me expecting me to be the one, you know, to make something happen.

"I was tired. I broke two minutes for the first time in the semis of the 800m, and then again in the finals. I ran a PR for the 1500m in the semis (which was kind of feeble, because after what I ran in the 800m it was obvious I could run that fast). So coming through it was my sixth race in nine days. Basically I had absolutely nothing to lose. And I knew I could run a 1500m way faster than what my PR was showing and so I thought, 'You know what, I could just get towed to a nice PR here. Go run the 800m in the Olympics, and live happily ever after.' And so going into that, Tom set down with my coach, with Vince [O'Boyle], and said, 'You know what, we run for third. Mary is going after it. There's going to be 12 people on the starting line. Somebody's going to run out of their head, and blow-up or whatever. Kim's going to go after Mary, and has boldly said publicly that she's going after her. And so Kim and Mary duke it out to the death, some people try to hang on, and if you just run smart and hang on for third, you could make an Olympic team in a second event.'

"Basically the plan was just to sit back in fifth place until 500m to go and use that homestretch if I needed to, to get up into some kind of decent position, and with 300m to go, just run like there's no tomorrow, which, believe me, we had practiced. Normally in a race like that I don't think I would've relaxed enough in fifth or sixth. I think I would have been trying to win the race or really do something. In my antsiness or whatever, I would've set up closer to the front. The second thing that happened was that we got absolutely no splits along the way. If there were splits, I didn't hear them and I didn't see a clock. There wasn't a Jumbotron there with every second in-your-face. I had no idea what pace we were running.

"Mary went out and actually set a fairly sane pace instead of going out 62 or something like she usually did, she went out in like 65-point. All the little pieces came together. And then the funniest one to me was just at the point that I was supposed step on it, [high jumper] Dwight Stones cleared the height that put him on the team, so all of a sudden there was this big eruption of cheering right when I was supposed to go. It just unfolded that way. And then having competed against Mary from the time that we were kids, there were so many times, I had been told by so many people that, 'If you are with Mary with 200m to go, you could beat Mary.' The problem, of course, was being with Mary with 200m to go, because the first part of her race was so fast and she had such a lead. So at 200m to go I just had this thought in my head like, 'You could beat her,' and I'm like, 'Yeah, right, you can beat her. You know she outsprinted the Russians last year at the World Championships. I'm just going to hang on here the best I can and hope that nobody else comes up.' And everything fell into place.

"The surprise was that the pace seemed comfortable. I was tired and my hamstrings were tight and all that. And I was surprised that Kim blew up with a lap to go. She went to an instant nonfactor and that was the end of her. The biggest surprise was that Mary didn't have another gear, and now I realize why—because we were actually running that fast. And secondly I had absolutely no idea that we had separated ourselves from the field. So part of my fight, so to speak, in the last 200m—I mean there were 12 people in the race, I figured that there were five more sitting right there running for that third-place spot. And I thought, 'Gee, I've made this bold move. If I back off at all, I am not going to get third.' So I had these conflicting thoughts of, 'If you're with her with 200m to go you can beat her.' But part of me was like, 'Man, it's going to be embarrassing if I don't finish in the top three after I made this big move.'

"Especially in American races, Mary got away with a lot on the intimidation factor, and, of course, on the confidence factor. She just never lost. She went to the starting line. I think she had a somewhat healthy respect for her competitors in that strange things could happen. But at the same time when you're on the starting line and your PR is 3:57 and the next PR is 4:06

Wysocki shocked the world with her Olympic Trials triumph.

or something, you can take off pretty comfortably. Obviously I was surprised to beat her. But my first thought was, 'Oh my gosh, I just won the Olympic Trials;' secondly it was, 'Yeah but what was the time, I mean, it was probably slow.' So when I saw the time, I was stunned.

Of course from there, all of a sudden, I was like, 'Oh my gosh, I'm a four-flat 1500m runner, I'm a two-flat 800m runner. I don't have to control the 1500s. When I decide to go with 300m to go, there aren't a whole lot of people who can keep up. Finally after all those years it gave me the confidence to know how to run it properly. Properly for me, I guess I should say."

In one race, Wysocki had chopped her PR from 4:12.85 to 4:00.18, the second-fastest American performer ever. Slaney had led with splits of 65.2, 66.3, 64.7, with Wysocki 0.3 behind at 1200m. Wysocki closed with a 43.7 last 300m, 59.3 last 400m, and 2:05.1 last 800m. After she crossed the finish line, she turned in shock to a crowd of reporters, and said, "What have I done?"

Results *(24 June 1984)*: 1. Ruth Wysocki (Brooks) 4:00.18; 2. Mary Decker (Athletics West) 4:00.40; 3. Diana Richburg (Gazelle) 4:04.07; 4. Missy Kane (adidas) 4:06.47; 5. Sue Addison (Athletics West) 4:06.91; 6. Darlene Beckford (Liberty AC) 4:07.42; 7. Louise Romo (Cal) 4:09.29; 8. Chris Gregorek (Athletics West) 4:09.43; 9. Kim Gallagher (Puma) 4:13.99; 10. Regina Jacobs (Puma) 4:22.47; 11. Jill Haworth (Athletics West) 4:25.87; 12. Lee Arbogast (Athletics West) 4:35.77.

1987 World Champs Men's 1500m: Bile crushes field

This race featured Abdi Bile at his best. In the weeks leading up to Rome, the Somali NCAA champ had clocked PRs of 1:44.47, 3:31.71 and 3:50.75. In case anyone doubted his fitness, he cranked off a championship record 3:35.67 in the semis. He says, "I was just playing, I was just jogging. I could feel it—'I am ready. This is it. Tomorrow is the final. Whatever it takes I am just going to be right there.' Nothing is guaranteed, but I was very confident. I didn't want anybody to surprise me. My coach, John Cook, he used to say, 'Don't let anyone surprise you.' "

Bile faced Steve Cram, the defending champ who won the Euro gold the summer before. Cram didn't appear to be in his best shape, but on the clock he was faster than Bile, with marks of 3:31.43 and 3:50.08 before the championships.

Both men had serious kicks, and it's hard to imagine everyone else in the field was deluded into thinking they had a chance to pick up anything but crumbs in a kicker's race. Yet still the pace went off at a relaxed jog. Jens-

Peter Herold of East Germany had the lead by the time they got to the first turn. He brought the pack through 400m in 63.46, as Bile sat comfortably at the back of the pack.

Bile after his historic win in Rome.

"My only concern when I figured it was going to be a tactical race," Bile said, "was not to be spiked by staying out in front."[1]

Cram decided he needed to pick up the tempo in order to avoid an anyone-can-win sprint finish. He went wide and took the lead at 500m. Kenya's Joseph Chesire made a move from the back and moved to the lead as the pack hit the 800m-to-go mark. As he approached the 800m mark (2:03.90), Bile escaped from his box at the back and started moving into position. By the end of the backstretch, he was up to fifth place, just ahead of a struggling Steve Scott.

As they approached 1000m (2:32.09), Cram challenged Chesire on the turn and Bile moved to fourth. That's when José Luis González moved into the mix. By the time the bell rang, Cram led by a stride over González and

Bile.

Bile says his position with 400m to go was crucial, and he was panicked then. "Gonzáles was in front of me, behind Cram, almost one step, and I didn't even want to take that one step. Gonzáles was right there. I didn't give him an inch. Because, you know, giving a world champion one step, or just relaxing behind him. It doesn't work. You just have to be right there. You have to be ready to strike."

The Briton led through 1200m in 2:57.74, a 53.8 lap for him. That's when Bile started to really unleash his stride. He caught Cram halfway through the last turn and didn't hesitate to go past. "When I passed Cram, I knew I didn't have to look back for him anymore."[7] González also caught Cram coming off the turn, and though he had a furious kick, he could only watch as Bile delivered an otherworldly finish that gave him a 10m win.

Cram, the dispirited defender, jogged home in eighth place. "I did everything I could, but there was nothing there. I was very, very tired at the finish."[7]

Bile had finished his romp with one of the finest long kicks ever, hitting 2:16.6 for the last 1000m, and 1:46.0 for the last 800m. His final lap took 51.4. His was the first World or Olympic gold ever won by a Somali.

Results (6 September 1987): 1. Abdi Bile (Somalia) 3:36.80; 2. José Luis González (Spain) 3:38.03; 3. Jim Spivey (USA) 3:38.82; 4. Joseph Chesire (Kenya) 3:39.36; 5. Omar Khalifa (Sudan) 3:39.81; 6. Jens-Peter Herold (East Germany) 3:40.14; 7. Mike Hillardt (Australia) 3:40.23; 8. Steve Cram (Great Britain) 3:41.19; 9. Han Kulker (Netherlands) 3:42.16; 10. Rémy Geoffroy (France) 3:43.02; 11. Kipkoech Cheruiyot (Kenya) 3:44.54; 12. Steve Scott (USA) 3:45.92.

1993 World Champs Men's 1500m: Morceli's long drive

In every sense this should have been a great match-up: Olympic champ Fermin Cacho, 1987 World champ Abdi Bile, 1991 World champ and world record-holder Noureddine Morceli, plus a cast that included a few possible upstarts.

Instead, it had all the looks of a European circuit race, except that the rabbit wasn't as fast as usual (this despite hints from the Morceli camp that he was looking for a world record). Jim Spivey found himself in the lead (slowly) just before the 400m. Then Mohamed Taki took over, passing the pole in 60.85. Morceli dropped into second, and the race sped up. Taki still led at 1:59.32. Cacho and Spivey ran in third and fourth, keeping their wary eyes on Morceli. After 900m, Bile moved decisively from seventh to fourth. The field bunched as Taki began to slow.

Morceli moved to the fore at 1000m, and over the next straightaway, Bile moved up to his shoulder. On the turn, however, the Algerian stretched out his stride and began jetting away from Bile. With 200m left, Cacho made his way around the Somalian and put a secure hold on silver.

It was speculated that Taki took the lead as a favor for teammate Rashid El Basir, who had won silver the previous year in Barcelona. But El Basir never made an impact on this race. Instead, it appeared that Morceli was the likely benefactor.

Results (22 August 1993): 1. Noureddine Morceli (Algeria) 3:34.24; 2. Fermin Cacho (Spain) 3:35.56; 3. Abdi Bile (Somalia) 3:35.96; 4. Mohamed Suleiman (Qatar) 3:36.87; 5. Jim Spivey (USA) 3:37.42; 6. Matthew Yates (Great Britain) 3:37.61; 7. Rashid El Basir (Morocco) 3:37.68; 8. Mohamed Taki (Morocco) 3:37.76; 9. Simon Doyle (Australia) 3:38.04; 10. Rudiger Stenzel (Germany) 3:38.66; 11. Manuel Pancorbo (Spain) 3:39.68; 12. Gennaro Di Napoli (Italy) 3:47.38.

1993 World Champs Women's 1500m: How O'Sullivan survived the Chinese

The year 1993 marked one of the more bizarre periods in the history of women's distance running. Under the direction of coach Ma Junren, a cadre of young Chinese women all from the same rural province suddenly debuted as the greatest runners the world had ever seen. Controversy exploded over just how they gamed the system, but it was widely agreed that something seemed rotten in the province of Liaoning.

The longer races set the stage for the 1500m in Stuttgart. On August 16th, favored Sonia O'Sullivan was left without a medal as three previously unknown Chinese swept the 3000m. Qu Yunxia won in 8:28.71 after a blazing long drive that staggered the imagination. On the 21st, Wang Junxia won the 10,000m in 30:49.30, part of a Chinese 1-2. Notably, she ran her final 3000m in 8:42.42, a world-class time in itself.

Says O'Sullivan, "I definitely went to the 1500m thinking that I had to get a medal no matter what. I didn't really go in there thinking I had to win the race. I thought I've just got to get a medal from this because up until that point, I was the fastest in the world at 3000m. I was kind of favored to win two gold medals, and I was fairly confident that I could do it, running as fast as I was. I was still quite young, so I wasn't scared, or nervous, I was just ready. I think the 1500m, for me, was a way to put the disappointment of finishing fourth in the 3000m behind me, and to straightaway focus on something else."

The next day, O'Sullivan lined up against Hassiba Boulmerka, the defending champion from Algeria, and three Chinese, led by world junior champion Liu Dong. After getting shellacked in the 3000m, O'Sullivan adopted a very brave game plan: to stay on the shoulder of Liu for as long as possible.

Liu grabbed the lead at the start, mainly to control the pace. She slowed it to 68.20. Boulmerka ran next to her. O'Sullivan stayed right on them, generally in third or fourth place. After 400m, Lu Yi sprinted up from the back and forced O'Sullivan back a bit. Liu still led, with Boulmerka alongside her on the rail. When the third Chinese, Yan Wei, moved up on the outside, the crowd, showing its suspicion, erupted in boos and whistles.

At 800m (2:17.58), Liu started sprinting. O'Sullivan at that point ran sixth. The field immediately elongated, and by the next turn the order was Liu, Boulmerka, Lu, and O'Sullivan. As Liu's acceleration continued—the race for the gold clearly over—the others engaged in a tight battle for silver. Lu passed Boulmerka halfway down the final backstretch. O'Sullivan, making a major move of her own, got past Boulmerka with 200m to go. "Liu had such a lead, and I was in third position and clear, with just Lu in front of me. I could quite easily have just settled for that, and then all of a sudden I realized, hang on a second, there's still a race going on here."

O'Sullivan continued her acceleration into the turn and soon passed Lu to take over the second position. Boulmerka passed Lu back to secure her claim to bronze coming off the turn.

Liu had run her last circuit in just 57.48. O'Sullivan had sprinted hers in 60.0. She could have easily lost heart anytime in the previous week with all the intimidating news about the Chinese and their ungodly training (reportedly a marathon a day at high altitude). Instead, O'Sullivan ignored any misgivings she might have had and competed her very best.

Results (22 August 1993): 1. Liu Dong (China) 4:00.50; 2. Sonia O'Sullivan (Ireland) 4:03.48; 3. Hassiba Boulmerka (Algeria) 4:04.29; 4. Lu Yi (China) 4:06.06; 5. Angela Chalmers (Canada) 4:07.95; 6. Theresia Kiesl (Austria) 4:08.04; 7. Anna Brzezińska (Poland) 4:08.11; 8. Fabia Trabaldo (Italy) 4:08.23; 9. Violeta Beclea (Romania) 4:08.57; 10. Yan Wei (China) 4:09.05; 11. Carla Sacramento (Portugal) 4:09.15; 12. Mayte Zúñiga (Spain) 4:10.79; 13. Lyudmila Rogachova (Russia) 4:12.14; 14. Leah Pells (Canada) 4:13.87; 15. Oksana Mernikova (Belarus) 4:18.93.

1995 NCAA Indoor Men's Mile:
Only following orders

Even before the runners took to the track, this shaped up to be a battle of the Canadians: Kevin Sullivan, running for Michigan, and outdoor NCAA champ Graham Hood, running for Arkansas. Sullivan had handily won the Big 10 mile over 1993 NCAA champ Marko Koers (Illinois/Netherlands) in a kickers' race, 4:09.07-4:11.02. Graham Hood did much the same at the SEC, beating Andre Jakubiec 4:06.27-4:06.98. Sullivan had the world leader going into the race, a 3:55.90 victory on Notre Dame's big track over one of the likeliest challengers, Paul McMullen of Eastern Michigan (3:57.34 in second). But Hood had run a 3:56.79 on his home track, plus he won Millrose at 3:57.08 in a squeaker over Marcus O'Sullivan (3:57.11). All the numbers indicated a titanic battle in the offing.

Both Canadians won their heats easily. So when they stepped to the starting line, expectations still ran high. Brian Hyde of William & Mary led through the 440y in 62.1. Hood ran third, while Sullivan and McMullen lurked farther back. Little changed as Hyde passed the half in 2:03.4. With three laps to go, it happened. McMullen, in third, blasted past Hood and Hyde and took the lead. Fifteen seconds later, he had a six-meter lead on Hood. He hit three-quarters in 2:58.3, still well clear of the field. Sullivan, caught in mid-pack by the move, was still in fourth at that point, another five meters behind Hood.

The chase began in earnest, with Hood running down and passing McMullen with a lap to go. Then on the backstretch, a confident Sullivan finally made his move. He passed McMullen coming off the penultimate turn, and faced a seven-meter gap ahead. Not until halfway through the last turn did that gap evaporate, as Sullivan turned on the jets and passed his countryman 10m before the line.

Said Hood of McMullen's surprise move: "I was expecting a move from someone early, but he went so strong I had to cover it. He's a legitimate runner and you can't let him get away. Unfortunately, he really slowed down on the last lap and put me in a position I really didn't want to be in."[8]

Sullivan, who set a meet record and narrowly missed the collegiate record at the time (Tony Waldrop 3:55.0), covered the last half of the race in a stunning 1:52.7. He now says, "It was such a big move that Paul made. I wouldn't say I was in a great position to respond to it, but I was in a good enough position that when Paul made that move, it just felt too aggressive for how far out it was. One of the things, with Paul being at Eastern and me being at Michigan we raced each other all the time. I probably raced Paul more in the first two years of college than I raced anybody else. And up to that point I had never lost a mile or 1500m to him, so I was pretty confident that even though he made this big move, we were going to reel him in. Really I think at that point, my bigger concern at that point was making sure that I maintained contact with Graham than it was with Paul."

Was Sullivan being supremely confident in waiting until the last strides to catch Hood? He explains, "It just happened to happen that way because that move that Paul made strung things out so much and it was such an aggressive move, it was really going to be a battle to the finish with me and Graham. I would have loved to have gone by earlier, but I wasn't close enough, but maybe if he hadn't have chased Paul as aggressively as he did, maybe he would have held on a little better in the homestretch. I think I laid back just enough that I was keeping contact without redlining things. I just had an extra gear coming off the last turn. My preference would have been to have a much more comfortable lead at that point."

Nearly 20 years later, McMullen is glad to share the backstory on his big gamble. "That's called being a good athlete. What I mean by that is, you don't think. You rely on the 30 years of experience of your track coach, Bob Parks, who says, 'I've been watching you run this season, and this is what I want you to do. I want you to go at 600m. If you're going to win this thing, it's going to be from a long kick.' Sullivan, Graham Hood, they finish these races with 200m to go faster than you and I don't think you can beat them. What I think is, if Sullivan sits too far back and you catch him off guard, then I think Hood and Sullivan might wait for each other to chase you and you might steal it.'

"That's hard to hear, as an athlete. You have to be humble and embrace a new strategy in the biggest mile race of your collegiate career. That's what that was, a risk for victory against two runners who had beaten me every time I had raced them up until that moment.

"In Coach's words: 'Paul, with three laps to go, I want you to start your kick and I want you to hammer it all the way to the finish. I think you're going to catch some people off guard and you might win it. If you wait and sit there you're probably still going to finish third or whatever, but you won't know if you could have maybe won it, if you had taken it from a long ways out.'

"As an athlete—these are my words to athletes—turn your brain off and surrender to your coach's experience. He has the privilege of watching you from a distance and can engineer a unique strategy that caters to your strengths giving you the best probability of success. So we have to surrender. I had implicit trust in Coach Parks and I didn't allow my strategy to get in the way of his strategy. That's what that long kick was all about.

"In hindsight, it was strange to have so many people come up and congratulate me on my move that didn't win. In hindsight, I said, 'Coach, we went for it,' and he responded, 'You sure did. In your first 200m of that last 600m, you ran about 26. I said go hard, but you ran a little too hard, and that caught up with you on the last lap.' That was often my mistake, and that's how the more patient runners could beat me. They knew when I went, I went a little too hard. Going to 100% or pretty close to it before the final stretch left me vulnerable in the last 100m to those who saved 5% for the final 50m.

"That's what I learned from Ron Warhurst: 'Oh no. You don't go 100%. You just go fast enough so they don't pass you. Then with 100m to go you take it to 100%. Or maybe only 95% and then 100% with 50m to go, then no one can beat you. You go too hard too early, it doesn't work.' I was able to learn something from two different coaches, which is kind of neat."

Sullivan triumphing over Hood at the finish.

Results *(11 March 1995): 1. Kevin Sullivan (Michigan) 3:55.33; 2. Graham Hood (Arkansas) 3:55.72; 3. Paul McMullen (Eastern Michigan) 3:58.21; 4. Passmore*

Furusa (LSU) 3:58.77; 5. Brian Hyde (William & Mary) 3:59.16; 6. Louis Quintana (Villanova) 4:01.15; 7. Ken Nason (Villanova) 4:04.51; 8. Andre Jakubiec (Florida) 4:05.06; 9. Matt Holthaus (James Madison) 4:05.20; 10. Sammy Unberhagen (Texas) 4:08.27.

2000 Olympic Trials Men's 1500m: Lananna proved right? Or wrong?

Prior to the Trials, Stanford coach Vin Lananna gave plenty of indications that his guys would do best in a fast race. In fact, he even hinted that Gabe

Earlier in the season, Gabe Jennings (center) and Michael Stember (left) had joined teammate Jonathan Riley in a sweep of the Pac-10 1500m.

Jennings and Michael Stember, his prize pupils, would create a fast race. To a local reporter, he said of sit-and-kick races: "That's why we have all the problems that we have in the 1500m."

Lananna's prize pupils had finished 1-2 at the NCAA the previous month. Of the pending Trials race, Lananna predicted, "I think if they [the competition] want to be in it, if one of our guys takes the lead, they better be able to go with it or they're not going to make the Olympic team... What I'm saying is that I think we have enough young athletes in that event right now, that I think there can be a mindset to change."

David Krummenacker took the race out in a solid 58.63. He stayed out there until Cal grad Richie Boulet took over before 800m in 1:56.95. Behind him, Jennings stayed close, leading Jason Pyrah and Seneca Lassiter, both strong kickers. With 600m to go, Jennings took over, and poured on the steam. He passed 1200m in 2:53.2, a 55.8 lap. He continued his torrid pace on the backstretch and then started to tie up on the final turn. He still managed to hold on for the win in 3:35.90.

Pyrah got past Lassiter on the final turn, and Stember pulled together a solid kick to grab the No. 3 spot just ahead of Jason Lunn.

Said Jennings, who later revealed he had been sleeping on the roof of his house in the weeks leading up to the Trials, "I've been doing that all season, running from my heart and running from the gut. I didn't see any reason why I should change my plan in the biggest meet of my life."[9]

In the end, Lananna was absolutely right. Staying with the Stanford guys was the key to making the 2000 Olympic team, and that was the plan that worked for Jason Pyrah—and nearly so for Jason Lunn. Yet a full appreciation for the "courage" of a fast race has to really center on the two men who sacrificed themselves as pacemakers—early leader Krummenacker, who finished a distant last, and 800m leader Boulet, who ended up second-to-last. Without them, odds are the race would have been nowhere near as fast, and the team composition could have been a bit different.

Of the American team at the Sydney Olympics, only Pyrah made the final, where he finished tenth.

Results (16 July 2000): 1. Gabe Jennings (Stanford) 3:35.90; 2. Jason Pyrah (Nike) 3:36.70; 3. Michael Stember (Stanford) 3:37.04; 4. Jason Lunn (unattached) 3:37.24; 5. Steve Holman (Nike) 3:37.36; 6. Andy Downin (WiR) 3:38.36; 7. Seneca Lassiter (Nike) 3:38.81; 8. Matt Holthaus (Reebok) 3:39.85; 9. Karl Paranya (Asics) 3:40.72; 10. Michael Ryan (Reebok) 3:41.14; 11. Richie Boulet (New Balance) 3:43.88; 12. David Krummenacker (adidas) 3:50.50.

2010 NCAA Men's 1500m:
To go or not to go with the 600m sprint

The set-up for the 2010 NCAA race was nothing unusual. For the host Oregon, it meant maximizing team points (the Ducks would eventually finish third in the team standings, 10 points away from the win). With three entrants in the race—all of them solid kickers—a slow pace would be favored by the Duck coaches.

Something of a prodigy, A.J. Acosta had won the U.S. Junior title twice.

He made it to the Olympic Trials as a sophomore, the same year he broke Steve Prefontaine's school record for the indoor mile. He came into the meet with a best of 3:39.44 from the Oregon Relays six weeks earlier.

Matthew Centrowitz at this point had not won any international medals, but he knew how to race. The previous year, he had clocked a 3:36.92 at the Payton Jordan meet. He hadn't raced much in 2010, but in four finals he had been undefeated, winning the Pac-10 crown in 3:41.16.

Andrew Wheating, a 2008 Olympian at 800m, was the big horse in the Oregon stable. The night before, he had won his second NCAA 800m crown. If he triumphed at 1500m, he would be the first since Oregon's Joaquim Cruz to win the 800/1500m double. He ran his PR of 3:37.52 in winning the West Regional.

Early leader Lee Emanuel of New Mexico.

No one else in the final had any real stake in the team race, so it's natural that no one considered sacrificing the pace in order to blunt the Oregon kickers. The most likely challenger was Great Britain's Lee Emanuel, running for New Mexico. A 3:37.25 performer, he had beaten Acosta at the Oregon Relays.

The Oregon coaches couldn't have wished for a more relaxed early pace. Emanuel and Acosta led through the first lap in 66 seconds. Acosta took over sole ownership of the lead for a 65.9 second circuit. Halfway down the backstretch, Emanuel moved out of seventh place to make his big move. The next 400m took only 54.6. In fact, Emanuel's stretch from 900m to 1300m took only 53.0. It shook the race up, to say the least. Said Wheating, "It went out real slow. I was kind of surprised because if it had gone out faster I wouldn't have had anything left.... I kind of knew that either at 1000m out or 600m out it would go, so at 1000m I put myself in position. At 600m I saw a movement happening and I put myself on the back end of it. I saw Centro take off and I knew he was going to have a great finish."

Centrowitz covered the move well and stayed on Emanuel's shoulder, while most of the field was gasping after the blazing lap. Centrowitz finally edged ahead after the last turn. "When I took the lead," he said, "I looked up at the scoreboard and saw there were a couple of other people left there. I was just trying to get to the finish line as quickly as possible."

Jack Bolas of Wisconsin finished well and pressed him down the homestretch. Meanwhile, on the outside, the big story happened, as Wheating and Acosta both swung wide and powered down the straight to give Oregon the first-ever 1-2-3 sweep of the event.

"I came in the last 100m," said Wheating. "I could see Centro on my left, and I felt the presence of someone over my left shoulder. I did not know it was A.J. I thought it was someone else. And the crowd erupted when I started moving. I thought, 'Oh God!' It got even louder when A.J. got there and I thought for sure I would get caught... If it was three or four meters longer I would have gone from first to maybe fifth."

Said Centrowitz, "I knew a certain runner in the race was going to go at a certain point, and I needed to be right on his shoulder. When the guy made the move, I was dead last... I just went outside and passed the whole field. I seriously went from dead last to second place in 100 meters. If you're not the world record holder, that's something you shouldn't be doing."[10]

For Kyle Merber, just a sophomore also-ran, the race was a wake-up call. "I was the youngest guy in the field. There were a lot of really good runners, and 600m to go, they took off. Even though I was feeling good, I didn't believe that I could take off so hard with 600m. And I ended up eventually kicking maybe from 300m out. I thought I could close pretty hard, but even though I had one of the fastest last 400s in the field, I gave so much room up so early that I didn't even give myself a shot at finishing higher up than I did. That's something that I think about a lot. And now [the concept] I'm trying to apply tactically is that you have to see the race to even be in the race, instead of watching from afar. It was a while ago, but I still kick myself for it."

Results *(12 June 2010): 1. Andrew Wheating (Oregon) 3:47.94; 2. A.J. Acosta (Oregon) 3:48.01; 3. Matthew Centrowitz (Oregon) 3:48.08; 4. Jack Bolas (Wisconsin) 3:48.21; 5. Jeff See (Ohio State) 3:48.37; 6. Lee Emanuel (New Mexico) 3:48.61; 7. Craig Miller (Wisconsin) 3:48.85; 8. Mark Matusak (California) 3:48.91; 9. Dylan Ferris (Stanford) 3:48.95; 10. Kyle Merber (Columbia) 3:49.75; 11. Riley Masters (Maine) 3:51.37; 13. Daniel Clark (Notre Dame) 3:51.87.*

2012 Olympic Trials Women's 1500m:
Uceny makes people hurt

The names on the line indicated that a team berth would not come easy to any newcomer. Morgan Uceny had won the USA title in 2011. Jenny Simpson had won the World Champs gold. Shannon Rowbury had won the bronze medal in the same race. All of them had splendid kicks, yet they also had the tools to run fast. Uceny had a 4:00.06 best and had cranked a 4:01.59 a month before the Trials. Simpson had a PR of 3:59.90. And Rowbury had a best of 4:00.33. All had shown ample fitness in the races leading up to Eugene.

The smart money said that no one would be outrunning them from the front. The only race they would be vulnerable in would be a slow, kickers race. That, of course, does nothing to explain why Brenda Martinez and Treniere Moser tried to take it out fast. The answer to that has more to do with the Olympic "A" standard of 4:06.0, which neither had hit yet.

Moser took it out early, but Martinez had caught up with her by the 300m. Together they passed 400m in 66.0. Then Martinez took over, aiming for a 2:11-2:12 at 800m. She got a good stride ahead of the field, but was only able to hit 2:14.1. On the next turn, Uceny, Simpson and Rowbury went past. That's when Uceny started winding up her long kick. As the three pulled away, she kept it safe until she got the signal from her coach—her mission was to land a team spot first, and then go for the win if possible. Said Uceny, "Terrance [Mahon] was telling me, 'Make sure you've got the top three down. Don't do anything stupid.' " She led them past 1200m in 3:19.6—and she kept applying more pressure.

Uceny came off the turn with confidence and dashed to the line the victor. Rowbury and Simpson, as expected, grabbed the remaining team spots. Gabe (Anderson) Grunewald finished fast in fourth, more than two seconds back.

Watching the video, it's hard to say that the chasers—Grunewald, Anna Willard, and Sarah Brown—made any mistakes tactically. They were simply outrun by superior athletes. Grunewald notes, "I don't think there's too much I would do differently. I think the biggest step for me to have made that Olympic team was maybe just to have had a little more experience, and maybe run just a little bit faster in the season leading up to that point. The top three broke away fairly early. I didn't really go with that move. When they broke away, I kind of ran for fourth place. I don't think I did anything wrong, but I didn't really put myself in the mix. It had more to do with confidence, more so than tactics. Had I put myself out there I [still] might've finished in the same position."

Results (1 July 2012): 1. Morgan Uceny (adidas) 4:04.59; 2. Shannon Rowbury (Nike) 4:05.11; 3. Jenny Simpson (New Balance) 4:05.17; 4. Gabe (Anderson) Grunewald (Brooks/Team USA Minnesota) 4:07.38; 5. Anna (Willard) Pierce (Nike) 4:07.78; 6. Sarah (Bowman) Brown (New Balance) 4:08.25; 7. Margaret Infeld (NYAC) 4:08.31; 8. Alice Schmidt (Nike) 4:09.64; 9. Katie Mackey (Brooks) 4:11.46; 10. Nicole Schappert (NYAC) 4:13.51; 11. Treniere Moser (Nike) 4:15.84; 12. Brenda Martinez (New Balance) 4:17.41; 13. Sara Vaughn (Nike) 4:30.89.

2014 World Indoor Women's 1500m:
Another reason to leave early

Coming into the World Indoor Championships in Sopot, Poland, only one female distance runner on earth was seen as unbeatable: Genzebe Dibaba. The Ethiopian shattered the world indoor record with her 3:55.17 on the first day of February. It would be the first of three records at various distances that she would take down over the next two weeks. However, at Sopot, Dibaba chose to run only the 3000m, one of her other record distances.

That left the 1500m gold wide open, but only for Abeba Aregawi. The Ethiopian-Swede, in Dibaba's absence, presented just as formidable a prospect for the competition. She had blasted a 3:57.91 European record, a mark that would have been a world record itself had it not come five days after Dibaba's mark. No other contender in Sopot had a 2014 time within seven seconds of that.

So maybe the gold was spoken for, but the other medals needed necks. Treniere Moser took second at the USA Champs to Mary Cain, who had withdrawn from the team for Sopot. Moser's kick could make her a threat in any race. Another possibility would be Axumawit Embaye, who had a 4:05.16 outdoor best.

For Heather Kampf, expectations were low. She only made it to Poland because of Cain's withdrawal, and she was still better known as an 800m runner. When the gun went off, Kampf shot into the lead—an unplanned, but bold, move.

"That wasn't my game plan or intention for the final race," she says. "I was hoping to just get into a position where I could just ride the pack and not really go about having to push the entire way for myself. And then the first few steps off the line were quick, and I thought, 'Great, this is going to be a fast honest race,' and then it just seemed like somewhere the brakes went on. And why would you spend more effort to put the brakes on to stay out of the lead when you're just in it already. And you're racing against the eight other fastest 1500m runners in the world at that moment. You know someone's going to take it at some point."

So Kampf, running from the front, waited for something else to happen. Her pace could not be described as fast—she hit 34.09 for the first 200m lap. Canadian Nicole Sifuentes took over a half lap later, and passed 400m in 67.05. Aregawi joined her at the front. She stayed with Sifuentes for 100m, took a look around, and decided that riding coach was not her thing. She left the field behind with a 62.3 second 400m.

No one in their right mind would chase after Aregawi in those circumstances, given her superior credentials that season. By taking off, she put the lock on her gold. She also protected herself from traffic mishaps, which are sometimes a bigger threat in women's races than in men's. Her next 400m took 63.9, and she capped her golden run with a 47.2 final 300m, winning by over six seconds, the biggest winning margin in WIC history.

Kampf illustrated the pitfalls of pack running not long after Aregawi moved up to first class. Coming around the turn at 550m, she went down hard and fast. "I've watched a million times over to try to figure it out," she says. "I honestly couldn't tell you [why I fell]. The thing I can say is that that track was so banked that every time we went around the curves, the race condensed just a little bit. Everybody fell into the inside, and I was racing right on the rail on the inside. So my best guess is somebody kind of came down and bumped me. I don't really remember feeling any sort of contact or having any fair warning that I was about to hit the track. It just seemed like I was running one second and then I went to take another step forward, I think with my right leg, and then, what it felt like to me, was that my leg was gone. I rotated through with my hip, but my foot was stuck somewhere. So I just felt like I stepped in a hole."

Sweden's Abeba Aregawi avoided traffic problems to win in Sopot.

Video replays showed Moser on the outside of Kampf, so perhaps they made unintentional contact. In any case, the results were immediate and devastating to Kampf, who picked herself up and finished with a 4:21.78 in last place. In an insult of irony, she was also disqualified, not for the fall, but for stepping inside the line earlier in the race. She wasn't the only one. The original third-placer, Rabab Arrafi of Morocco, also earned a lane disqualification.

Kampf's crash could just as easily have happened to Aregawi had she been running on the inside of the pack. By avoiding pack running almost entirely, the champion protected herself from crashing. However, such a strategy is only possible for athletes who clearly have a huge edge on the field to begin with.

Results *(8 March 2014): 1. Abeba Aregawi (Sweden) 4:00.61; 2. Axumawit Embaye (Ethiopia) 4:07.12; 3. Nicole Sifuentes (Canada) 4:07.61; 4. Siham Hilali (Morocco) 4:07.62; 5. Treniere Moser (USA) 4:07.84; 6. Luiza Gega (Albania) 4:08.24; 7. Svetlana Karamysheva (Russia) 4:13.89;...dq—Rabab Arrafi (Morocco) 4:07.53; Heather Kampf (USA) 4:21.78.*

2014 NCAA Men's 1500m: Other Outcomes Possible?

When the script for a race has already been written, how much flexibility does an athlete still have? We're talking about the NCAA Final, and everyone involved seemed to act as if the top two already had their names set in stone: defending champion Mac Fleet vs. eight-time NCAA champion Lawi Lalang. According to the script, Lalang would lead from the gun and try to burn Fleet's kick away. The previous night, Lalang did just that to Fleet's teammate, Edward Cheserek, to win a historic 5000m. Lalang had been able to use that race plan successfully in the 1500m as well, winning the Pac-12 race against Cheserek a month earlier, 3:36.34-3:36.50.

As formidable an opponent as Lalang was, it was hard to be surprised with the outcome of the final stretch match. Remember that Fleet had many months to prepare for this race, and it went exactly as he had visualized, with one exception: "It was a little bit slower than what I expected the first K [kilometer] to be," he said. Yes, battling to the wire in a fast 5000m takes something out of a man's legs, and Lalang's limbs lacked a bit of zip. His 1500m pace of 58.0, 1:58.3 and 2:59 was not fast enough to burn anyone off. In fact, a disciplined rabbit could have done no better for the field. Not to dismiss Lalang's kick—he was a true master at kicking off a fast leading pace—but that 13:18 had an inestimable effect.

The script almost seemed too easy for Mac Fleet. Follow, kick, lean. Perhaps the only thing easier would be memorizing Hodor's lines in *Game of Thrones*. Fleet followed the formula for victory, his 3:39.09 beating Lalang by 0.04 on the lean. Note that he was prepared for the lean, as he made clear in the post-race press conference. He never expected that getting by Lalang would be easy. In fact, the only surprise was the aforementioned slowness of the pace. (Not a bit slow by NCAA Championships standards, but a bit slow for Lalang.) Said Fleet, "When we came through 800m and the race was what it was, I was pretty excited because my chances from there got better. I knew we weren't going to drop the field at the pace we were at."

Fleet's observation is spot-on. The slower Lalang's pace, a greater variety of runners that had a chance on the last lap. That generates the real question here. Did some of the other runners, by believing the pre-race hype that this race belonged to Fleet and Lalang, throw away their own chances to win?

The next two finishers bear a much closer look. It is possible to imagine scenarios where either of them could have gone down in history as the biggest upset winner in recent memory.

Loyola's Sam Penzenstadler is a curious case. Looking at his season record going into the NCAA meet, the typical prognosticator can be forgiven for not noticing him. On the surface, with a best of 3:43.25, he had no business in the finals. Hence *Track & Field News* left him out of their final top 10 picks, and *LetsRun* gave him short shrift as well. Says Penzenstadler, "My goal was to get top eight. That would be first-team All-American. And then a spot on the podium. Anything above that would've been great." Realistic stuff there.

But a post-race look at Penzenstadler's numbers makes one wonder if maybe he could have challenged the favorites. He ran his last lap in 54.76, just faster than Lalang. And his last two laps took 1:54.87, faster than anyone else in the race. His last three took just 2:55.96—faster than both Fleet and Lalang. (Note that sixth-placer Grant Pollock produced similar closing numbers.)

How did those numbers not bring him closer to the win? It's not that he went out too slow. At the 300m, he ran a reasonable sixth. However, over the next 200m he lost contact and allowed several others to pass him. At 600m, he had fallen back as far as ninth. Finally, at around 800m, he seemed to engage again, tightening the gaps and running more aggressively. He recalls, "I think I was falling off a little. Then they slowed down just a little bit, which helped me and some other guys catch up. It was like a big pack again with like 600m to go. We were all back in the race."

Maybe it was that he had slipped to 10th place and Number 11 was knocking on his door. He stuck to the rail, passing one on the inside, and then bumping with another. His move to position himself for the kick at the 400-to-go mark brought him to the outside of the pack in eighth place. Then more contact. On the backstretch, Penzenstadler found his rhythm just before Peter Callahan blasted past. "I was moving and that got me going because he just flew by me, and I used his momentum. He kind of left an alleyway for me to go through and I got behind him. It helped a lot. It did catch me off guard, but it was a good thing." On the turn, Penzenstadler got up to fifth. Though Callahan got ahead, the Loyola junior continued his steady drive to the line, finally nailing him in the last 20m.

After the race, the Loyola coach, Randy Hasenbank, said, "We had a plan, based on how the field would go out, and the race unfolded just how we thought it would. And Sam executed that plan to perfection." No doubt he did, if Penzenstadler was aiming for All-America status. After all, who would have thought he could have won? Yet, if he had run for the win from the start, he might have kept better contact over the first lap, and certainly been in better position once the kicking began. While we don't know how Fleet would have reacted to being side by side with Penzenstadler on the final 100m, the race would have been infinitely more interesting, particularly because Fleet was only focusing on Lalang.

Now that he's had some time for it to sink in, Penzenstadler reflects, "I think that if I was up there with Fleet and Lalang, those two wouldn't have wanted me to win. And they would've pushed even harder. It would've been close, though, and would've been interesting to see how that would have played out. Fleet looked very relaxed in the video. He looked very good."

As for his amazing improvement that year, the former 4:18 high school miler says, "It's still kind of unbelievable to think about. It still hasn't sunk in fully. Now our next goal is I've got to go for the national title."

Peter Callahan: "It is important to take risks."

The other upset candidate, Peter Callahan, came into the race highly regarded, even tabbed by some as a dark horse favorite. The New Mexico junior had improved steadily all season and clocked a 3:40.50 in taking a narrow (0.05) second to Lalang at the West Regional. So while Callahan surprised no one by being in the mix on the last lap, what many will remember is his unfortunate fade-out over the last 100m. While fourth place in the NCAAs is not an embarrassing result, take another look at that last lap. If not for bad timing, Callahan might have won. He delivered an incredible 200m stretch in the midst of the last lap, from 1200m to 1400m. From the available videos, it looks like he may have split about 25-flat from post-to-post, even while running on the outside of the turn to pass traffic. Compare that to Fleet's 26.4 for the final furlong, and Fleet's sprint was close to the rail for most of the curve, until he ran wide to hold off Callahan and chase Lalang.

Says Callahan, "I actually kick myself. For me, I know what works usually. Usually around 200m I'm able to make a big strong push and kick it into another gear and go, and right before NCAAs, I was feeling strong and comfortable and hoping to have a good race. And someone says, 'Save something for the home stretch.' I usually don't think about that, but I am like, 'That makes sense, I do want to save something for the home stretch.' And so it came to 200m to go, 150m to go, I started to move out and kick up in the final gear, and I was right on Mac Fleet's shoulder. I was like, 'Shoot, this might be a little bit early, I need to save this for the home stretch.' And then I tucked in again, and the home stretch comes around and I didn't have that final gear because I touched on it a little bit and then I backed off.

"I kind of lost faith. When I make my move, I make my move—that's what I've always done, and here I had made a move and then backed off, and then tried to go to it again and then that final gear had all been used up. So I was very, very happy with my first 1350m of that race. I felt like I'd covered position, I had been in the different phases of the race, I'd been there mentally and I'd been focused on what I needed to do. And just in the last 100m which is usually where I feel comfortable, it's where I usually thrive, I second-guessed myself a little bit: 'I shouldn't make my move now I should wait a little later.'

"That was an example of letting outside things influence me in a negative way, as opposed to motivating me to really finish and run to the tape. I was like, 'I am going to back off and try something new this race.' It is important to take risks, and it's important to try new things, but I think that was a time that I misjudged and backed off instead of staying with what has always worked. I learned from that race, definitely."

It's true that if Callahan had been closer than seventh at the beginning of the final 400m, he would have avoided some of his traffic problems. Yet his self-assessment is right on the mark, and it is a fantastic lesson to all runners. To win, you've got to believe.

Results (14 June 2014): 1. Mac Fleet (Oregon) 3:39.09; 2. Lawi Lalang (Arizona) 3:39.13; 3. Sam Penzenstadler (Loyola/Chicago) 3:39.77 PR; 4. Peter Callahan (New Mexico) 3:39.90 PR; 5. Jordan Williamsz (Villanova) 3:40.25; 6. Grant Pollock (Virginia Tech) 3:40.41 PR; 7. John Simons (Minnesota) 3:40.57; 8. Michael Atchoo

(Stanford) 3:40.66; 9. Rorey Hunter (Indiana) 3:40.75; 10. Sam Prakel (Oregon) 3:41.04 PR; 11. Thomas Joyce (California) 3:41.08 PR; 12. Brannon Kidder (Penn State) 3:44.30.

The Long Kick: What They Say

Abdi Bile – The race begins at 800: "I had one problem. And that problem is long legs. I'm a tall guy, so physically I had a hard time running in the middle. And always I used to fall, or something happened because I needed space. So the middle has never worked for me. So it was either I stayed in front, or I stayed in back, just to stay out of trouble. At the same time I learned through years of running that in the 1500m, all you need is the last two laps. The first 700m it doesn't mean anything where you're at. And for me by running way in the back, I saved so much energy. I just relaxed and flowed, no pushing, no changing. Really very little happened in the first 700m. But at the same time, the other most important thing I used to do at the time was, starting the race. You plan about how you're going to run, or your expectations of the way it's going to go, but it's always different when it starts. The first lap, when I'm running in last place, that is where I'm not using my legs, but just my computer. It's calculating everything, how the first lap goes, who is leading, who is there, who is looking like, this is what they want to do. So I get a complete picture of what this race is going to be, because I'm just watching the race. Like a spectator. And then that is when I make my decision about when to make the move. You know, what the winning time is going to be roughly. You know who has a fast kick too, what do I need to do. So that was a very important time. And the last lap, you're just right there. It doesn't matter where you are, you know, the first lap and a half."

Thomas Wessinghage on why the long kick was crucial to his success: "I jeopardized my chances when I decided to sit in a race, and not take it out. Some revelations come late. And looking back at my races now, I found that whenever I took out hard, maybe not from the start, from the halfway point or the last 500m, I ran good races. When I waited too long, sometimes I ran a race that left me disappointed. So looking back I would say that once in a while I should've raced more aggressively than I did. If you would ask me what I would change looking back, it would be mostly that. The other big parameters of my racing and my medical career, I would probably perform like I did. I don't think there was very much that I could improve. But concerning the racing strategies, as of now I would say, yes I could've run a little more aggressively here and there."

Jim Spivey winning the 1985 USA title over Tim Hacker and Steve Scott.

Jim Spivey on coach Mike Durkin's advice before the 1992 Olympic Trials: "The night before the final, Mike told me: follow to half a mile to go. Run the next quarter in 56. And then with 200m to go, I want you to visualize people breaking into your home, and their names are Steve Scott, Joe Falcon, and Terrence Herrington. What are you gonna do? Are you going to let these people come in and steal everything out of your house, or are you going to defend what's yours?"[11]

Mike Scannell on where the mile race actually starts: "Somewhere between 500m and 300m to go is the start of the mile race. It is not when the gun goes off. It is not the starting line of a race to me. It is not when you line up on the waterfall. So we need to get you to the start of the race. The question is, how do we win that race? The starting line isn't 1600m or a mile from the finish line. The starting line is 500m to go."

Jeff Atkinson on why the long kick isn't always a winner: "There is always somebody who thinks they can draw it out of people longer, which they can't. Anybody who can kick is going to be able to hang and outgun those guys. The guys who win the big kickers races, they run exactly that way: run as little extra distance as possible, rest as long as possible, kick as late as possible, and don't get caught in any weird little boxes or in bad positions at trick points."

Don Paige on why a kick is more about strength than speed: "A kicker, his speed comes from his strength. You have to be very strong to have speed at the end of a race. He who is less tired will have the best kick. I already had natural speed. We worked on my speed. Rarely did I think I didn't have enough speed. Rarely did I think I would be outkicked. The thing that I feared as I was training was I needed to be strong enough to have that speed at the end of a race. To be a great kicker, you have to be very fit, you have to be very strong. I'll give you a point. Do you think I could beat Carl Lewis at 800m? Who's faster, him or me? And young athletes or people don't understand kickers. You have to be very strong and very fit to have your kick at the end of the race. And obviously, put up with pain, but everybody puts up with pain. So pain, that doesn't matter."

Ray Flynn on Steve Cram's championship style: "You would notice in championship running, he would go from 600m out. And one of the great things about Steve was when he went from 600m out, which is a long way to go, we would imagine that it would be easy to pass him as he got tired, but he had that self-belief and had pre-decided that this was where he was going to go from. But with 200m left, he had already taken the legs out of them.

"I think different athletes have different styles but one has to respect the athletes who really knew what they could do and carried their plan through. I think one of the greatest disappointments is saying, 'Oh I should've done this, I should've done that, I should've gone from 600m out, I should've made a move first.' You don't want to finish a race and as its outcome you're regretting what you did or did not do. You want be able to say, 'I gave it my best shot whether I won or not.' I guess what I'm really saying is, I respect those athletes who knew what they wanted and went for it."

Sarah Brown on playing to your strength: "If you want to win a race you're going to have to lead at some point. And I think it's just that kind of attitude, taking it a little farther, and not coming down and relying on that kick. All of us at the level we're running, at some point have a decent kick and can outkick each other—it depends on the race. But sometimes you don't know what's going to happen when you leave it to a kick. There's a little less guaranteed. So if you can, you play to more of your strengths... We need to play to our strengths and the fact that we can finish strong, but we can finish from farther out. It doesn't have to be this 200m kick. So we can take some of the people who like to sit and kick out of the game."

Dave Wottle on the simple kick: "We just weren't that sophisticated back then, in my opinion. Well, let me say this: I wasn't very sophisticated back then. I didn't have a diet like they have nowadays, I didn't train quite as hard as some of the runners are training nowadays, not saying that we didn't train hard, but I just didn't think a whole lot about it. I saw each race as an individual race and I just ran against the competition: the way they were feeling, the way they were breathing. We didn't have the research back then to look at the runners and know their styles so you were just reacting a lot of times to the runners. You know I was a kicker. To me it was a very basic strategy. All I had to do was hang with them for three laps and put myself in position to win on the final lap."

"I ran to win." – Marty Liquori on his first victory over Jim Ryun, in the 1969 NCAA mile. He followed coach Jumbo Elliott's instructions to be ahead of Ryun when the kicking started. His time was a meet record 3:57.7, to Ryun's 3:59.3.[12]

Chapter 6: The Short Kick

"All milers think they're kickers. It's just that some are better than others."

—Ron Warhurst

It is the classic way to win a four-lap race, the most common in any championship setting. The athlete conserves energy, stalks the leaders, chooses the best point of attack, and moves in for the kill. Nothing could be more natural in the world of racing. Even going back to the sport's early days, the kick was omnipresent. Edwin Flack of Australia and Arthur Blake of the United States stalked leader Albin Lermusiaux of France in the 1896 Olympic 1500m, gunning him down in the last straightaway, Flack prevailing for the gold. Critics disparaged the race because of the slow time, 4:33.2, in a period when the world record was 4:16.4. Lermusiaux himself would run a 4:10.4 later that summer.

And there's the rub. It all boils down to values—what is more important, the victory or the time? I remember during one Olympic Games sitting near *Track & Field News* founder Cordner Nelson, a giant of the sport who was one of the world's great experts on the 1500/mile. Cordner would grow disgusted—almost personally offended—when it became apparent that a championship race would turn out to be a slow, kicker's affair. He believed that the race would be diminished if the athletes did not run up to their physical potential. I still respect Cordner's feelings on this—he had earned them, having been to 15 Olympic Games starting with 1932. He had seen Herb Elliott decimate the 1960 Olympic field with a world record on a dirt track. He had written *The Jim Ryun Story*.

Yet I respectfully disagree with Cordner on this point, and the many who would vilify the kicker. These would include Steve Prefontaine, whose tussles with kicker Harald Norpoth left many fans wanting to punch Norpoth in the nose. Remember Pre's famous quote? "I don't have any respect for a runner who'd let a kid do all the work and then go by at the end."[1]

How many times have we heard—even from athletes I interviewed for this book—the phrase "honest pace," as if there were something inherently dishonest about kicking to a win?

There are no style points in racing—no judges holding up cards to rate the way an athlete achieved victory. On the track, there are no "primes," as there are in cycling, giving a bonus to athletes who lead at intermediate points during the race. Only one measure of victory exists—the finish line, and the owner of the torso that hits it first is the victor.

Who is inherently dishonest? The athlete who leads much of the distance, and then complains that somehow the athlete who outkicked him was less than virtuous. The hypocrisy is that the complainer would surely trade places with the winner if he could. Who wouldn't rather win than be the griping loser? To put it in even stronger terms, what kind of idiot would intentionally throw away the victory to pursue a strategy they know will lose? It's a race! A gun fired at the start and a winner crossed the line at the end. The mission of the competitive athlete is to race in a way that is most likely to assure victory.

What about the fans? The ones who boo a slow pace, who think that athletes owe them a record every time? Are they being cheated when they don't get what they want? Really, if they feel that way, they need to stick to Diamond League races, where there is a rabbit hired for virtually every middle distance and distance event these days. Glorified time trials, with money on the line. Sometimes—usually after record hopes have died—an actual race breaks out. Real racers don't owe the fans a time; they can only hope to offer what they're actually gunning for: victory.

Ray Flynn, a journeyman miler himself and now one of the sport's most respected agents, says it well: "As time has gone on, I really now relish watching championship races. They're so much more attractive as a spectator, and so much more exciting to watch than paced races. I really enjoy, of all the events at a championship, I love watching the 1500m races that are tactical… As a spectator, I kind of get tired of talking about how slow they're running. I'm like, 'Look guys, it's a race.' And when you were a kid racing it's the first past the finish line or the top three if you're qualifying or going for medals. I think it's easy to get too caught up in the times. That shouldn't be the important part of it."

Another point that needs to be considered from a developmental perspective is that the more our athletes become accustomed to time trials behind rabbits, the less prepared they will be to handle championship racing. It's one thing to have virtually every Diamond League race in Europe guided by rabbits, but now the trend is percolating to invitationals farther down the food chain, and we are seeing college and even high school races with rabbits. If we truly want our runners to win medals, we might want to give them more experience in tactical races.

The Short Kick: Race Histories

1958 Australian Championships Men's Mile: Elliott waits… and waits…

Herb Elliott won his Olympic gold in 1960 by charging to the front immediately, and running a world record pace that crushed his opposition. That and his famous quote ("the only tactics I admire are those of do-or-die") might give one the impression that such an all-conquering hero of frontrunning would never soil his career with something so demeaning as sit-and-kick tactics.

Flashback to 1958, a Sunday afternoon at the Australian Championships in Brisbane. Elliott lined up against his arch-rival, Merv Lincoln. Over 8,000 fans had come in hopes of seeing a four-minute mile. Elliott claimed later that he didn't have a plan in mind when the gun went off. Starting from the outside, he immediately dropped to last place. Lincoln, on the inside, ran the first stretch of the race anxiously looking around and slowing until he and Elliott were well behind the pack.

According to a reporter on the scene, "the pair almost walked the first 300 yards in a struggle for last place." The leader, a man named Denis Wilson, passed the quarter in 61 seconds, with the superstars seven seconds behind. Lincoln ran slightly ahead of Elliott and seemed nervous about when to make a move. This continued until halfway through the third lap, when Lincoln tried to go.

Elliott immediately flew past him—"in a few strides he was four yards clear." By the time he passed three-quarters in 3:16, he still was more than 40 yards behind Wilson. Astoundingly, he took the lead halfway down the backstretch, Lincoln chasing him still. Before the finish line, he slowed, later claiming because there was no tape he was worried he had to go another lap. He crossed victorious in 4:08.8, as the newspapers called it a "fiasco."

Said Wilson, "I was all keyed up in my first senior championship race and started very fast, finding myself in the lead. Unbeknown to me Elliott and Merv Lincoln were dawdling at the rear watching each other and apparently I ended up about 50 yards in front of the pack. Unfortunately I ran out of puff and three runners passed me in the last 200 yards."

Elliott ran his last lap in an unprecedented 52.8, his last half mile in 1:52.8. Lincoln said, "I probably would have been wiser to have moved earlier, but the race was a final sprint and I must have run my fastest quarter mile anyway."

Elliott's coach, Percy Cerutty, had a celebrated lack of tact. His comment: "Herb went out to win and prove he is the best miler in Australia. He made mince meat of him."[2]

Results *(15 March 1958): 1. Herb Elliott 4:08.8; 2. Merv Lincoln 4:09.9; 3. Terry Sullivan 4:14.0; 4. Denis Wilson 4:14.0; 5. Pat Clohessy 4:19.3; 6. Geoff Legge 4:19.8.*

1964 Olympic 1500m:
When you're the fastest, patience pays

In 1964, Peter Snell was considered the overwhelming favorite to win the gold medal, despite the fact that he had never actually run a 1500m final in his life. He had, however, built up significant experience in racing the mile since adding the longer distance to his repertoire after his 1960 Olympic gold in the 800m. In 1962, he set the mile world record of 3:54.4 in Wanganui, New Zealand, winning with a strong kick: 54.8 for the last 440, 1:53.3 for the last half.

Over the next few years he came to the United States several times in search of tough competition, so his North American rivals were well aware of his usual style: to hang with the pack until the last backstretch, then make an overpowering move with a half-lap to go. Some, like American Dyrol Burleson, hoped to anticipate that move in time, and somehow outkick Snell. In fact, Snell's coach Arthur Lydiard even gave interviews tabbing Burleson as the favorite (possibly to put more pressure on him).

Burleson seemed confident after the first two rounds, telling reporters fatefully, "I've managed to get in the positions I sought in most instances. I have not been boxed in yet, and you can bet I won't Wednesday."[3]

Burleson's coach, Bill Bowerman, opined that Burleson had a chance, on one condition: "Burly must get a six-yard lead on Snell as they enter the final 100 meters if he expects to win."[3]

Bowerman knew that Snell was the superior miler of the time, and his finishing speed was unmatched. Even though he didn't have the benefit of surprise, he didn't need it. No one could touch him. In this situation, the most important caution is to not screw it up: stay in contact, be in position to kick when the time comes.

Snell didn't waste time or energy battling for the early lead. At 200m, he was tied for seventh. At 400m, he was 58.7 in fifth, 0.7 behind the leader, Michel Bernard of France. For the next two laps, Snell basically glided along. He hit the 800m in 2:00.9 (a 62.2 lap), running fourth behind the leader, his teammate and training partner, John Davies (2:00.5). Over the next lap, he moved up a little, to third place in 2:59.7, a 58.8 lap.

Down the backstretch, Snell exploded into the lead. The move was not unexpected, but the power of it was stunning. His 200m stretch from 1200m to the 1400m mark took only 25.0 seconds—a 12.7 on the straight and a 12.3 on the turn. By the time he hit the stretch, he had destroyed his competition. He even eased up before the finish. His last 200m clocked at 25.9, his final 400m an unheard of (at that time) 52.7.

Burleson, who had hoped to kick in with Snell, found himself boxed on the backstretch and many observers said it appeared he gave up. He finished fifth. After his return home, he said philosophically, "I had a beautiful view over their shoulders of Snell's finish. When you get in a box, that's it."[4]

Results (21 October 1964): 1. Peter Snell (New Zealand) 3:38.1; 2. Josef Odlozil (Czechoslovakia) 3:39.6; 3. John Davies (New Zealand) 3:39.6; 4. Alan Simpson (Great Britain) 3:39.7; 5. Dyrol Burleson (USA) 3:40.0; 6. Witold Baran (Poland) 3:40.3; 7. Michel Bernard (France) 3:41.2; 8. John Whetton (Great Britain) 3:42.4; 9. Jean Wadoux (France) 3:45.4.

1973 NCAA Men's Mile:
Wottle burns a 1:52 last half in the heat

The history buffs will tell you that the mile in Baton Rouge produced a collegiate record for David Wottle with seven others breaking the four-minute barrier behind him. Sounds like it must have been ideal conditions for a fast race. Hardly.

"I think the pace was slow because of the heat," said Wottle to reporters afterwards. Actually, the Olympic 800m champion was referring to the early pace, which dawdled a bit. So how did a record emerge from the race?

Says Wottle, "I do remember it must've been 98 degrees with 95% humidity. I was raised traditionally; you warm up with your sweats on. But that was one of the few times in my career I remember I had to take my sweats off during the warm-up. It was extremely hot and humid. I can remember just struggling through the race. I just didn't feel good."

At the time, Wottle told reporters that he had no awareness of just how slow the pace was: "I really didn't know because everybody was sitting back and relying on his kick." He was also worried about his back, which he strained in the heats.

The early lead fell into the pedestrian category, with BYU's Paul Cummings taking it through 440 in 61.2, with Charlie McMullen of Missouri at his side. The two hit 800m in 2:04.4. On the backstretch, McMullen went to the lead and started hammering. Says Wottle, "With [kickers] Tony Waldrop in the race, and myself, Charlie didn't probably have quite the kick that some the other runners had, so he was pushing. Kind of the old Liquori versus Ryun 1971 Penn Relays mile where Liquori did a long sustained

600m drive to take the sting out of Ryun's kick. I think that's what was happening in 1973."

The next lap took only 58.2, with McMullen leading Ken Popejoy and Hailu Ebba. Wottle still lagged behind the pack.

"And I was pretty much just hanging on until that last 200m or so and I made a move to the outside. I was fine on the home stretch coming into the lead moving toward the finish line. In hindsight I think I let up a little bit. Tony Waldrop of North Carolina was coming up on the outside." Wottle's last lap took only 53.3. Waldrop's was even faster, 52.8.

"It ended up being a fairly good race. I can remember almost seeing bright lights afterwards. I was probably seriously dehydrated, well spent. It took just about everything out of me that last quarter.

"I still was amazed why he didn't beat me. I don't know. I talked with Tony afterwards. I was at a camp with him in 1973. I just didn't think that he believed in himself enough. I think he could beat me, to tell you the truth.

"I always think milers have to know their strengths and their weaknesses and I always looked at my strength as being able to come off of any pace with the kick, so I had a lot of confidence in my kick. I usually just sat around and waited, just dying to get the last lap, the last turn, the last 150 yards or so of the race to use my kick. I was almost never in the lead, I was a follower. I used my kick."

Results *(June 9, 1973): 1. Dave Wottle (Bowling Green) 3:57.06; 2. Tony Waldrop (North Carolina) 3:57.29; 3. Reggie McAfee (North Carolina) 3:57.88; 4. Hailu Ebba (Oregon State) 3:57.88; 5. Ken Popejoy (Michigan State) 3:58.6; 6. Mark Schilling (San Jose State) 3:58.7; 7. Knut Kvalheim (Oregon) 3:58.7; 8. Charlie McMullen (Missouri) 3:59.6; 9. Paul Cummings (BYU) 4:01.3; 10. Mark Feig (Oregon) 4:03.0; 11. Brian Mittelstaedt (Stanford) nt;... dnf—Willie Eashman (Hay State).*

1976 Olympic Men's 1500m:
Walker's gamble paid off... by two feet

John Walker was every bit the favorite in 1976, perhaps not as overwhelming as Snell eight years earlier, but the strength of the field had been whittled down in previous months, as Marty Liquori was injured, Rod Dixon opted for the 5000m, and rival Filbert Bayi—who would have guaranteed a very fast pace—was kept out by the African boycott.

Yet despite the fact that he won, the race did not develop to Walker's advantage. Consider that the heats were extraordinarily fast. According to Cordner Nelson, in previous Olympic history only nine runners had ever broken 3:40 in the heats. In Montreal, 25 would, led by Steve Ovett, who ran the fastest prelim in history, 3:37.9. Walker upped the ante with a 3:36.9. By the time the final came around, the surviving runners had dead legs. Thus, they were happy for a slow pace in the final, especially the four in the field who had solid 800m credentials.

However, for distance types such as Ireland's Eamonn Coghlan and world record holder Walker, the slow early pace was not so bright. Coghlan had few options, knowing that the early leader rarely medals, and knowing that he wasn't strong enough to outrun the New Zealander. Walker, though, had no excuses. "I was in a dilemma. There were six guys faster than me for 800m," said Walker. He knew unless the early pace was fast, he would have to deal with them on the last lap.

Jim Ryun's Montréal predictions

Ryun wrote his thoughts on the upcoming race in mid-July for a newspaper. He did not know at the time that Filbert Bayi would be kept out of the Games by the African boycott. Still interesting, his thoughts on a match-up that was never to be:

"Bayi will, as always, try to lead the race from the starting gun. Walker will lay back and try to finish off the field with his late kick.

"I think Walker's strategy will work, and Bayi's won't. I think Bayi will find you can't kill off an Olympic 1500-meter field as easily as he's handled other fields in other races.

"Walker will win, and his time could be under or about 3:30, which would be the equivalent of a 3:47 mile. I look for a very fast race.

"One aspect of the Olympic 1500-meter competition that I feel has been overlooked is the necessity of running trial heats. Bayi will run his usual style ahead of the pack, and possibly waste himself before the final. Walker, on the other hand, will be more content just to qualify from one round to the next and hold back his best effort for the final."[5]

Yet, perhaps tired out from his too-fast heat and his 3:39.7 semifinal, Walker dawdled. He and coach Arch Jelley had worked out three different strategies for the race. It would be up to Walker to decide during the first lap how he would proceed. The pack hit 62.5 for the 400m (Walker in eighth). The pace sped slightly over the next lap. Coghlan made a move to the front and Walker covered him by moving up to fourth; they hit 2:03.2 at 800m. With a little over 400m to go, Walker made the move that won him the race—he made his way to the lead, and led at the bell. That ensured that when the furious kicking began, he would have a virtual head start on the field. On the next turn, the field began to bunch up behind him, as they readied their kicks.

They passed 1200m in 3:01.2, and Walker took off with everyone chasing him. He hit top speed early—he had been planning on a 300m kick, so he gained a real advantage on the backstretch. It looked as if the half-milers in the field all wanted to wait until the last 200m to kick. Still, Walker saved his best for the last turn, a 12.2 for that 100m. For the last 100m, it was all about hanging on. He could only manage a 13.2 as kickers Ivo Van Damme and Paul-Heinz Wellmann chewed into his lead. At the finish, Walker held on to win by about two feet. He had gambled and won, though the argument could be made that had the early pace been faster, he would have won by a bigger margin with much less drama. That was perhaps a sure thing had someone

John Walker, here winning an indoor race.

else pushed the pace early. Had Walker himself driven the early pace, he likely would have made himself a sitting duck for the kickers in the field, and would not have been able to produce that 37.9 final 300m (compare it to Snell's 38.6 in Tokyo).

Rick Wohlhuter might have made a difference in the race given his normal kicking skills. The world record holder for 880y, he had won the bronze medal in the 800m a few days earlier. When he lined up for the 1500m final, it was his sixth race in seven days. "That was a bit too much for me at the time," he says. "The first two rounds I ran a 3:38-3:39 or so. My tactic always was to get into the automatic qualifying spot. You don't want to gamble waiting for your time to get you in. So to do that, you have to run a little faster. By the time I got the final, I was just too exhausted."

"I remember coming around [the last lap], and thinking maybe I get a medal out of this, too. But I was just too tired. I didn't have a strong enough finish. If I had run the race earlier, and everything else equal, I'm sure I would've had a higher place finish, but that didn't happen."

Results *(31 July 1976): 1. John Walker (New Zealand) 3:39.17; 2. Ivo Van Damme (Belgium) 3:39.27; 3. Paul-Heinz Wellmann (West Germany) 3:39.33; 4. Eamonn Coghlan (Ireland) 3:39.51; 5. Frank Clement (Great Britain) 3:39.65; 6. Rick Wohlhuter (USA) 3:40.64; 7. Dave Moorcroft (Great Britain) 3:40.94; 8. Graham Crouch (Australia) 3:41.80; 9. Janos Zemen (Hungary) 3:43.02.*

1979 NCAA Men's 1500m: Paige's Historic Double

If any one meet characterizes Villanova's Don Paige at his absolute best, it is the 1979 NCAA Championships. From his fourth-place in the 1500m the year before, Paige had developed into one of the nation's top middle distance guys. One of the most powerful tools at his disposal was the kick that he honed to perfection under the coaching of Jumbo Elliott and Villanova assistant Jack Pyrah.

"You got to realize," says Paige, "I was really mad at myself for not being properly prepared for the [1978] NCAA. I dedicated August to really getting strong and fit, putting in more mileage, more basework, and we had a great cross country season. We had a great cross country team that year. We trained really hard. I was injury free. Having good teammates really helps push you and make you better, because you can never do it alone. It started in cross country season, went into track, and I stayed healthy, felt stronger, faster. I'm a year older, a year more mature. I learned my lessons from 1978.

"By the time we got to the national meet, the NCAA, in Champaign, Illinois, [teammate] Sydney Maree was really fit, I was really fit. You've got to understand, three weeks before that, at the IC4A Championship, we went 1-2-3-4 in the 1500m. I remember getting the phone call from Jumbo. Monday before the meet, and he told me that he had entered me in both events, and I said, 'Mr. Elliott, you can't do that. They set the schedule. You can do it for the trials and the semis, but the finals, they're too close together.' He said, 'Well. I've entered you. We can't take you out, so we have to leave it at that.' Then he said, 'Champ, you'll be okay. Don't worry about it.' And that was it. So we hung up, and a few minutes later, there was a knock on my door. And it's our assistant track coach, Jack Pyrah. And Jack says, 'Hey, did you talk to Mr. Elliott?' I said, 'Yeah, I did.' And he said, 'Don, he honestly believes you can win both. He knows the schedule. This is the year before the Olympics. He wants to see how tough you are, and he would not put you in both if he thought you would lose one.' I said, 'Alright.' That boosted some confidence, but I was still scared to death. I'm like, 'Nobody's done it with five races in three days, and two being back to back so close.' The 1500m first. That's the only way I could have done it. I could not have done it the other way. For me the 800m is so much easier than the 15.

"The 1500m went out at a modest pace, because Todd [Harbour of Baylor] and I both kicked quite well. I remember Mr. Elliott giving me just a little advice which he rarely did. 'You just win by this much,' and he's holding his fingers apart. 'You win by this much. A foot, six inches. Don't expend any more energy than you have to.' The 1500m was very easy for me."

Paige ran as if he were in no hurry to win it. He ran in eighth place for the first half, and passed two more after hitting the 1200m in 2:59.6. It wasn't until the final stretch that he dashed past the leaders. His final 200m took only 26.2, his last 400m, 53.7. Behind him, Todd Harbour also produced a stunning kick.

Results (2 June 1979): 1. Don Paige (Villanova) 3:39.20; 2. Todd Harbour (Baylor) 3:39.27; 3. Kip Koskei (New Mexico) 3:39.64; 4. Ross Donoghue (St John's) 3:39.76; 5. Dan Aldridge (Cal Poly SLO) 3:40.72; 6. Andy Clifford (Cal) 3:40.84; 7. Richie Harris (Colorado St) 3:40.9; 8. Paul Becklund (Arizona) 3:42.9; 9. Mike Bollman (North Dakota St) 3:43.3; 10. Geoff Cooper (Memphis St) 3:44.7; 11. David Rafferty (Murray St) 3:45.5; 12. Mike Quigley (LSU) 3:46.5.

Don Paige tells how he completed the NCAA double:

"The hard part was, I finish the 1500m, hands down on my knees, I'm breathing, I'm sweating, and I hear the announcer up there, 'Second call, 800 meters' and I look over on the backstretch, over on the field next door and these guys are doing their final strides. I'm like, 'Oh my god.

There's no way I can run 800m right now.' My goal was to finish the 15 at the finish line and walk back down the straightaway and go down where the start of the 100m was. I was going to sit there, lay down on the track there, and rest. And the other competitors in the 1500m that I had just beaten, all came over and patted me on the back, and said, 'Great race, good luck, you can beat them, you can win both.' I found that really strange. These guys are my competitors and they're wishing me well in this 800m. I didn't get it. These guys, they really wanted me to win both. I'm walking down the track to the start of the 100m thinking, wow, that was a nice touch for those guys to say that to me, but why would they do that? I thought as I walked down the track, 'Oh my god, that 800m is going to be a very long race.'

"And there's some things you need to know, like Mr. Elliott never coached on the weekends. He coached Monday through Friday, so at a track meet, you never saw Mr. Elliott on the track. Never. So I lay down, I found a little chair and I put my feet up on this chair. And I'm sitting there with my eyes closed, thinking what am I going to do in the 800m, and all of a sudden somebody kicks me in the bottom of my foot. It hurt like heck. I almost opened my eyes and swore at whoever it was. And it was Mr. Elliott standing down there. This is my fourth year at Villanova, and this might have been the first or second time I had seen him down on the track during a track meet. Ever. I opened my eyes, and said, 'Oh Mr. Elliott!' And he says, 'Champ, Champ, did you bring your sticks?' He was teaching me how to play golf. And I said no, 'I left my golf clubs at home. I thought it best that I concentrate at the NCAAs.' 'Yeah, good idea,' he says. 'Here's what we'll do. Let's see, tomorrow? Tomorrow's Sunday. Monday, the golf course is closed, but the driving range and the clubhouse is open. We can get a sandwich there. Here's what we'll do. I'll come by the dorm. I'll pick you up right before noon, we'll grab a sandwich, and then we'll hit some balls on the range.' I said, 'That sounds really good, Mr. Elliott. That would be great.' He turns around, walks straight back up into the bleachers. I'm sitting there thinking to myself, this guy just came down here to talk about my golf game? And at that moment, I had to get down and tie up my spikes at the starting line. I go down to the starting line, and the 800m race. We go for the first 100m and we break in, and I go, 'My gosh, you've got to be kidding me. This is going to be a long, long two laps.'

"The first 400m was a daze to me. I'm like, 'Wow, I'm not sure if I'm going to make it.' It didn't go out too fast, I could tell because the pack

Paige winning the Jumbo Elliott 800m in 1984.

was tight together at 400m, and wasn't strung out. We go round the turn after 400m, I say, I'm going to see what I can do. As we hit the backstretch, I'm now in sixth or fifth, just weaving my way up on the outside. I said, you know, fifth place. Everyone would think fifth place is pretty good at the nationals, after the mile. Wonder how many points fifth is. I say the guy up in front of me is in fourth, I bet I can catch him. By the time we get to 200m, we're working our way around the bend. My mind is wandering, which it normally does not do in a race. And I'm like, 'Hey, I can get that guy in third. Third will be pretty good, you know?'

We hit the homestretch, and I think I'm in third or fourth. And I look up and I can see the finish line. Now, I'm a natural kicker. Kickers love the finish line. When I catch the guy in second, I then did not say, 'I think I can catch this guy in first.' I didn't say that. You know what I said to myself in my mind? The sooner I get to the finish line, the sooner I can lay down. And I passed the guy in first place, and I laid down on the track. I was exhausted. It was mentally a very tough race."

Paige won the 800m in a PR 1:46.18, the first man to complete the double in 21 years. He did it with 200m splits of 27.3, 27.0, 26.4, 25.5.

1983 World Championships Men's 1500m: Timing is everything

A cast of legends lined up for the first-ever World Championships 1500m in Helsinki. Steve Ovett was the world record holder; Saïd Aouita held the fastest time in the world that year at 3:32.54; Steve Cram had won the European Championship a year earlier. Steve Scott had dominated the world the previous year, recording a 3:47.69 American record. The American TV commentators hailed him as the "strong favorite" in their introductions to the race.

Some observers say the race was affected by the loss of several likely frontrunners in the semis—Sydney Maree and Ray Flynn among them. Another story emerged, after the race, that the Cram camp had been tipped off that Aouita was planning a big move with 500m to go.

In any case, the race became a waiting game, and the pace went out brutally slow: 64.98, 2:07.73. Cram wrote later, "I just hovered at the back, watching what was going on. In those situations you get nervous; you just want things to get going because you're not sure where you should place yourself in the pack. But even though I was as anxious as everyone else, I was still reasonably calm because I knew it was going to be a race over the last 700m."[6]

All of the contenders stayed away from the lead until Aouita began positioning himself at 850m. Cram responded, moving to his shoulder, and Scott likewise, moving to Cram's shoulder. A move at 500m to go is not exactly a shocking development in a slow championship 1500m, but it almost seemed as if everyone but Ovett got the memo about Aouita's move in advance. They ran five abreast at the 1000m mark, with Ovett trapped in a box behind.

Aouita took off, and Cram and Scott followed closely. They passed 1200m in 3:02.83, and on the backstretch, both Cram and Scott made big moves. Cram took the lead with 200m to go, and Scott passed him coming off the final turn. As they raced down the homestretch, Scott looked like he might be able to tag Cram, but he fell short by 0.28.

Said Cram, "I knew if Aouita was to beat all three of us–me, Ovett and Scott—he was going to go hard from 600m out, which played into my hands. He led us out and I clung onto his coattails, as it were, and kicked with 200m to go."[6]

Explains Scott, "I was waiting for Cram. The two of us were the two guys in the race, so we were kind of watching each other. That was a very frustrating race, because we went out slower than the women's 1500m. So what that does, everyone has the same strength, everyone has the same finishing speed, so whoever runs the smartest race is going to be the one who wins. The mistake I made was after Aouita went by with 500m to go, both Cram and I go after him. On the start of the backstretch, Cram made his move just a fraction before I did. He got around Aouita. I got stuck behind him. I went around Aouita on the homestretch and I just couldn't run Cram down. So, had I made the first move, and got around Aouita, and Cram had to then get around him, things could have been different. So, I was just a fraction late on the outside. 'Okay, I'm going to make my move right... boom.' He already made it."

He adds, "If you're confident, you win. You've got to run to win, and not run to try not to lose. In the Worlds, I think I was running to try not to lose, instead of going for broke. Could I have gone early? Yeah. I ran just a little bit cautious. I didn't make my move early enough."

For his part, Ovett later wrote that he was simply in the wrong place when the sprinting started. "I was trapped anyway, which I should not have been, by a wall of runners and there was no way of going around the outside. With 300 metres remaining I was waiting for a gap to open up, but with everyone running fast that was not going to happen. Meanwhile the real contenders were getting away. I kept to the inside track and when there was a clear space I accelerated and tried to get through on the inside lane, something which, just as on a motorway in Britain, you should not do. I came alongside Jan Kubista of Czechoslovakia going very fast and he moved to his left and hit me—it was my fault—and being big and heavy he knocked me to the infield. I stepped back on the track and ran round him thinking that this was one of the most bizarre races in which I had ever run... I had made an absolute mess of things and I was out of the hunt."[7]

Results *(14 August 1983) 1. Steve Cram (Great Britain) 3:41.59; 2. Steve Scott (USA) 3:41.87; 3. Saïd Aouita (Morocco) 3:42.02; 4. Steve Ovett (Great Britain) 3:42.34; 5. José Abascal (Spain) 3:42.47; 6. Pierre Délèze (Switzerland) 3:43.69; 7. Andreas Busse (East Germany) 3:43.72; 8. Dragan Zdravković (Yugoslavia) 3:43.75; 9. John Walker (New Zealand) 3:44.24; 10. Ján Kubista (Czechoslovakia) 3:44.30; 11. Uwe Becker (West Germany) 3:45.09; 12. Mike Boit (Kenya) 3:46.46.*

1988 Olympic Trials 1500m:
A slow race means anyone can win

According to the formcharts, this race should have gone to other people. But that's the problem with races where so many people run so much slower than their best: the door swings wide open and just about anyone with a great finishing kick can win. In these sorts of races, it almost doesn't matter who can run a great four laps—one is all it takes.

In the hot, steamy conditions of the 1988 Olympic Trials in Indianapolis, veteran Steve Scott figured to be a lock, as did wunderkind Joe Falcon, who had run a 3:35.84 earlier that year. Three straight days of racing apparently had most of the field thinking that a fast pace would be a suicide wish.

Deady, in third, surprised everyone.

Tim Simpson went for it, figuring he didn't have what it took to outkick the stars, and that a fast pace might be his only shot. He went perhaps a little too fast on the first lap: 56.2, and no one followed. Scott was back at 59.7. Simpson produced a second lap of 63.9, but still ran all alone. He hit 800m in 2:00.1. Jeff Atkinson, who had never broken into the top three at a national meet, led the second pack at 2:03.7, with Scott a step behind. Falcon still seemed to be in the hunt at that point, but a few strides later he came unplugged, and jogged disconsolately into the finish.

By 1200m (3:01.5), former Clemson runner Terrence Herrington pulled alongside Atkinson (Simpson had fallen apart on the third lap). Jim Spivey—another likely member of the team—stumbled as elbows flew in the tightly packed bunch of runners. Steve Scott described it as "the roughest race" he'd ever been in.

Going into the final turn, it was a mad dash where a blanket could cover the first seven runners. Scott led with Spivey and Tim Hacker closing fast. Once they hit the straight, Scott began to pull away, but Atkinson surprisingly finished stronger. His 53.3 final circuit brought him the win. Scott ran his last lap faster, in 53.2, but he had started from farther back. Collegian Mark Deady shocked everyone by finishing fastest of all—53.0—and claiming the third and last team spot.

Hacker, a legit team hopeful who ended up in seventh, said, "It was just slow, and people were ansty, real nervous. They have their race plan set in their mind and they don't want to deviate from that, so if that means pushing to get into their favorite running lane, or whatever, that's what they'll do."

Said Scott, "This would have been the absolute last combination I would have come up with for our Olympic team."

In a faster race, Deady wouldn't have been there at the finish, and Atkinson likely would not have won. The results were as much an indictment of the slow pace as they were of the three-day selection process that took the strength out of their legs.

The race from Atkinson's point of view...

"Tactically it was very similar to every other event I'd been running for the previous two years, which was to absorb the first two-and-a-half laps as easily as possible, run as short a distance as possible, and then put myself in position to strike, which for me was always from the 700m to the 600m-to-go mark. I specifically chose that stretch because it is usually where the race lags just a bit. I moved—not a dramatic move—because I was taking advantage of the lagging field. Everybody heats up at the bell; some people heat up with 500m to go. But at 700m you have one more little lap of rest before you go, so it's kind of a soft spot in the race.

"At the Trials I just tried to do the exact same thing.... I moved into position with 600m to go, into my usual spot which was about third from the front on the outside shoulder. I felt pretty confident that what I was at least in the right place to handle anything coming up from the outside and match whatever was happening from the front. Other than that, I was just being as patient as possible and guarding the position. With 400m to go, Spivey came up on the right. He was trying to get his way on the rail but there wasn't any space there, so we kind of bumped elbows a little bit. But I was just holding my position trying to wait as long as possible. With 200m to go, I pretty much couldn't wait any longer. I knew I had to stretch the speed longer than the superspeed kickers would have so I could draw it out more.

"Yeah, I didn't expect to win it all. I did expect to make it. I thought I would get caught going down the stretch, but not lose all three spots. So when I came off the turn I was pretty much in full flight. Scott came up on the right, and he was also kind of cutting in slightly in front of me. I yelled, 'Stay wide!' and I don't even know if he heard me or if I even said it out loud, and I hit the stretch getting up on my hams and my tippy toes as much as possible. I stayed technical as much as possible. I was surprised that they weren't drawing on me. So I got halfway down the stretch, and nobody was still drawing on me, I started to think, 'Oh my God, I can take this all the way to the line.' "

Results *(23 July 1988): 1. Jeff Atkinson (Nike North) 3:40.94; 2. Steve Scott (Tiger) 3:41.12; 3. Mark Deady (Indiana) 3:41.31; 4. Jim Spivey (Athletics West) 3:41.52; 5. Richie Martinez (Reebok) 3:42.67; 6. Maurice Smith (Reebok) 3:42.90; 7. Tim Hacker (Athletics West) 3:43.31.*

1989 World Cup Men's 1500m:
Boom, boom, and boom!

"That race was just me and Sebastian Coe," remembers Abdi Bile. "That year, you know, I ran 3:30.55 and 1:43.60 and 2:14.51 for the 1000m, and I was winning." But the oft-injured Bile had other concerns. "I pulled my muscle, the iliopsoas. That is, a deep muscle that was really painful. And I was not able to sprint, I was not able to train every day. I was training one day, and I was taking some days off. Train one day, and then two-three days off. The biggest problem was I could not sprint 100%. So even when I came to the World Cup, I had so much pain. The day of the race I even told the reserve guy to warm up. I told him, 'Listen, just warm-up. I will see how I feel, I will do a few strides, and hey, if I can't do it, I will tell you to go.'

"But I really just wanted to run with Sebastian Coe, one of my big idols for a long time. You know, I had run with him and beat him before. But he is still Sebastian Coe. Somehow I got so excited, and forgot the pain."

Edgar de Oliveira took it out hard for the first 300m, then reconsidered and moved to lane 2 to encourage anyone else to take over. Australian Dean Paulin moved up to join him at the 400m (57.67). Sebastian Coe ran a stride back, while Bile stayed near the back of the pack. Shigeki Nakayama soon took over and took the small field through 800m in 1:58.68, Coe in third, Bile in sixth.

Despite the fact that the pace was not too fast, no one went with Nakayama, and he built a 5m lead. The likely truth is the main contenders didn't regard him as a threat, and simply ignored him. With 500m left, Bile brought himself to Coe's heels. He wasn't looking for a long kick here. Rather, he simply had to keep his eye on Coe, running in the last major 1500m of his career.

Coe began his drive from just over 300m out, taking the lead and passing 1200m in 2:57.74. Bile dogged his steps. As Coe's acceleration stretched out the field by the time they entered the last turn, Bile turned it on. The fight between them was furious, and several times they made contact. Coming off the turn, Bile moved so quickly into Coe that he nearly drove him over the rail.

On the stretch, Bile produced the strongest kick, but just barely. Coe was a stride behind in second, just edging Jens-Peter Herold.

Says Bile, "The last lap, I was just right there with him. You know, Sebastian was just a great runner. That guy, even that day, at his age, there weren't that many guys who could beat him. I could only beat him myself. Because the last lap, especially the last 300m, he shifted like three times. When you're already going all out, already you are going 100%. Just *boom*! He just puts a little extra. And boom! And boom! It was incredible. It was incredible, and I stayed with him. I was confident that at the end I would have more power and speed. It came through."

As for the contact coming off the last turn, Coe said, "It was obvious we clashed at the beginning of the home straight, which is obviously not the best place to come to grief, when you`re approaching top speed. No doubt it threw me off stride, and at that point in the race it was a problem, but I don`t want to say much more than that."[8] The British team filed an official protest, which was denied.

Bile says that the British had it all wrong. "What I remember is when I passed him he grabbed my singlet, and just pulled me back. All I remember is he is holding my shoulder, and, pulling me down and I was really lucky just to survive and not to stumble or anything, and maintain my pace and get that win, and just finish the race. So that's all I remember. I think the guy just wanted to win at any cost. But when we finished the race, you know, the British protested that I cut him off. I don't remember any way of cutting him off. But it's possible you know, when the two of you are running side by side, and you come so fast from the curve, maybe you will go to the edge of his lane. Something like that. But there was no indication, nothing that I remember like that, no."

Results *(9 September 1989): 1. Abdi Bile (Somalia) 3:35.56; 2. Sebastian Coe (Great Britain) 3:35.79; 3. Jens-Peter Herold (East Germany) 3:35.87; 4. Gennaro Di Napoli (Italy) 3:36.65; 5. Dean Paulin (Australia) 3:38.84; 6. Fermín Cacho (Spain)*

3:42.78; 7. Terrance Herrington (USA) 3:40.88; 8. Edgar de Oliveira (Brazil) 3:41.59; 9. Shigeki Nakayama (Japan) 3:43.23.

1992 Olympic Men's 1500m:
Cacho avoids the *yuyu*

As Olympic finals go, Barcelona stood out as a wide-open contest. World champion Noureddine Morceli was not at full strength, due to injury. World record holder Saïd Aouita, though entered, chose not to run because of his own injuries. Kenyan veteran Joseph Chesire showed up next on the Track & Field News formchart, but Spain's Fermín Cacho had no worries about him. "The truth is that Chesire was not very fast. You could get him at the end of the race and always win. It was not hard sprinting faster than him," he said. "If you were with him at the end, surely you'd win."

Chesire is the one who went to the lead, but it certainly wasn't because he wanted a fast pace. He jogged through the first two laps in 62.25 and 64.58, with the pack tightly bunched behind him. Cacho, who always preferred running on the rail, stayed tightly inside. American Jim Spivey maintained good positioning on the outside. "My coach told me, 'In a slow race, you got to be in front,'" said Spivey. "But I thought I was right where I was supposed to be, fourth."

With 500m to go, Chesire started upping the ante, and the pack began to string out. Jens-Peter Herold stayed right on his shoulder, with Spivey on the outside in third, basically running alongside the badly-boxed Cacho. The third lap took just 55.62, but the race broke open on the backstretch.

Cacho found himself in a bind. He clearly had the energy to sprint like crazy. His route was blocked, though, by Chesire and Herold ahead, and Spivey to the side. To get out on the outside, he would have had to deck Spivey. Meanwhile, some of the best kickers, Mohamed Souleiman, Morceli, and Jonah Birir, started passing people on the outside. Cacho had to make a decisive move, and he saw a narrow path to the inside of Chesire. He muscled his way past the Kenyan before the turn, and went into full sprint once he got a clear track.

"I remember I was in the pack on the curve, and I knew that everyone would begin to take off on the straightaway [with 300m left]. Then, when we got there, everyone went to the right and let me through in lane one. Two hundred meters from the finish, when I saw the gap, I said, 'What happened here?...' I did not think I would win until I got to sprint the end."[9]

On the homestretch, Cacho kept turning his head in disbelief, expecting one of his competitors to come up on him. Then it dawned on him that no one could match his 50.3 finish. "With 80m left, all I could think is that something very bad had to happen for me not to win. I had to fall and have a *yuyu* [freak-out]."[9] He raised his arms in victory well before the finish line, and his win in front of his home crowd was more dominant than the half-second margin would seem to indicate.

Results *(8 August 1992): 1. Fermín Cacho (Spain) 3:40.12; 2. Rachid El Basir (Morocco) 3:40.62; 3. Mohamed Suleiman (Qatar) 3:40.69; 4. Joseph Chesire (Kenya) 3:41.12; 5. Jonah Birir (Kenya) 3:41.27; 6. Jens-Peter Herold (Germany) 3:41.53; 7. Noureddine Morceli (Algeria) 3:41.70; 8. Jim Spivey (USA) 3:41.74; 9. Graham Hood (Canada) 3:42.55; 10. David Kibet (Kenya) 3:42.62; 11. Manuel Pancorbo (Spain) 3:43.51; 12. Azat Rakipov (Belarus) 3:44.66.*

2008 Olympics Men's 1500m:
Ramzi kicks to infamy

The focus here is not so much on the original winner, Rashid Ramzi, who was disqualified for doping. Rather, it is on the athletes who kicked for medals on the final stretch, and how they got to that position. And while there is a certain justice in erasing Ramzi's name from the historical record, it is impossible and completely misleading to write about the tactics involved in the race without mentioning the man who crossed the finish line first.

When the gun went off, long-striding Asbel Kiprop moved to the fore. Ramzi hung back in mid-pack. The pace moved at a good clip for a championship: 56.48 at 400m. Betal Mansoor Ali of Bahrain (the former John Yego of Kenya) challenged the lead then, but Kiprop held him off.

At 800m (1:56.06), Kiprop's teammate, Augustine Choge, moved to the front. Abdalaati Iguider of Morocco accelerated to his shoulder, and others moved as well, boxing in Kiprop at about fifth place. Even farther behind, New Zealand's Nick Willis ran on the curb in tenth position.

With a lap to go, Ali made a move to challenge for the lead. That, combined with Britain's Andrew Baddeley moving up on the outside, boxed in Ramzi. He gave his teammate a hard shove from behind in an effort to get out of the box before the sprinting began.

Willis's coach, Ron Warhurst, was not thrilled that his charge ran in last place with 400m to go. "He got pushed to the back. Tactically, it looked like he did a good job but he didn't. He was not supposed to be there. At the bell, he got pushed from fifth to eleventh. He was on the inside, and they slowed right at the bell, and four guys went by. Then everybody—they didn't go till 300m. If they had gone at the bell, Willis would have never caught them. He was so trapped."

With 300m to go, Ramzi began his final drive, taking the lead halfway down the backstretch. Kiprop used the backstretch effectively as well, moving into second as they entered the turn. At that point, Willis, sticking to the rail, ran in sixth place, breaching the gap between the top five and the trail pack. "He moved right at 300m to get back into it."

On the straightaway, Kiprop gained on Ramzi and very nearly won. Meanwhile, Willis ran to the outside and stayed ahead of the mass of sprinters gunning for the bronze medal.

Says Warhurst, "His tendency many times was to come off the curve and stay on the inside and hope it opened up enough on the straightaway for the finish. This time he came around the turn; I was right at 100m to go. I could see him coming around the turn, and I'm going, 'Outside Nicholas, outside, outside, outside!' And he started drifting out of lane 1 into lane 2. And I said, 'You've got to go outside, outside!' And he went outside, and he ran down the straightaway past those three guys. The kid from France came up on the inside, stayed on the inside, and it didn't open up until about 40m to go and he made a little surge in the end but he didn't catch him; Willis outleaned him for the medal."

Mehdi Baala of France, who was edged by Willis at the line, said, "I was really tired at the end. I was dropped by the pack and then I gave it my all."[10]

Said Willis, "I've never had the one perfect race and I seriously believe that, considering it was my third race in five days, it was the best race I could've done. My legs were dead before the race started."[11]

Results (19 August 2008): 1. Rashid Ramzi (Bahrain) 3:32.94 (DQ 15 months later); 2. Asbel Kiprop (Kenya) 3:33.11; 3. Nick Willis (New Zealand) 3:34.16; 4. Mehdi Baala (France) 3:34.21; 5. Juan Carlos Higuero (Spain) 3:34.44; 6. Abdalaati Iguider (Morocco) 3:34.66; 7. Juan van Deventer (South Africa) 3:34.77; 8. Belal Mansoor Ali (Bahrain) 3:35.23; 9. Andy Baddely (Great Britain) 3:35.37; 10. Augustine Choge (Kenya) 3:35.50; 11. Daham Najim Bashir (Qatar) 3:37.68; 12. Christian Obrist (Italy) 3:39.87.

2011 NCAA Women's 1500m:
Reid best in traffic

Oregon's Jordan Hasay ruled the collegiate ranks during the 2011 indoor season, capturing the NCAA Indoor mile crown as well as the 3000m, in which she held off the kick of Villanovan Sheila Reid by a mere 0.15 seconds. Earlier, Reid had topped Hasay on the anchor of the distance medley relay. Hasay had a solid outdoor season as well, and improved her 1500m PR to 4:10.28, a bit better than Reid's 4:11.85 at Mt. SAC.

Reid didn't start the race like a sit-and-kick artist. The previous night she had beaten Hasay to win the collegiate 5000m crown, sitting on her until the closing stages. In her attempt to become the first ever to win the 1500/5000m double at the NCAA meet, it might have made sense for the Canadian to again hang back and let someone else do the work. Instead, Reid went immediately to the lead, which she shared with Brittany Sheffey for the first 300m. It was Hasay, the Oregon soph, who hung near the back of the pack.

By 400m (70.1), Sheffey had taken the lead, and Reid had slipped to mid-pack. She recalls, "I actually didn't sleep a wink the night before. I kind of felt like a zombie during the race." The pace continued to slow, and they hit 800m in 2:21.7. By any reckoning, the other competitors in the race were doing Reid a favor. Not a sure thing by any means, but the one hope they had was to run hard, and hope that her legs hadn't recovered from her 5000m win.

At 1000m, Reid and Hasay both were in fifth or sixth place, with one key difference. Hasay was running wide on the outside. Reid, on the rail, was completely boxed. Over the next 100m, the picture changed completely. Virginia's Morgane Gay accelerated down the homestretch to take the lead, giving Reid a bit of daylight to get out of the box. It took some bumping, but approaching the bell, Reid ran in second place. Hasay responded, and cut in front of Reid at the bell.

It seemed as if Reid had broken out of a box only to jump right back into a box. Yet she explains there was a difference: "Something clicked right before the final lap. I think one of the most important things is to know your competitors in a 1500m race. And when I knew that I was behind someone who was not a contender, and I saw the contenders moving, [I got out]. So while I got boxed again, I was behind people who were speeding up (Lucy Van Dalen and Jordan Hasay). These were people who I knew had the potential to win. I knew that I had to go with them. And while I don't quite remember who I was behind right before the lap, I knew they weren't speeding up. That's the biggest thing–you can't get trapped behind people who aren't going with the move."

The situation got frenzied on the final backstretch. Hasay fought her way into the lead. Reid found herself boxed again, and struggled to get out. First she tried to move outside, but there was no path. Hasay, running wide probably to maintain her lead into the turn, went a little too wide. Reid, thinking quickly on her feet, saw the opening Hasay had created on the inside and shot into it.

With 200m to go, Reid had the lead and the momentum. Gay came past Hasay on the outside, as Kate Van Buskirk and Lucy Van Dalen followed Reid on the inside. Hasay's race crumbled.

Coming off the final turn, it looked as if Reid might have a fight on her hands, but the Villanova junior delivered a stunning kick that destroyed her chasers. Her last lap took 62.93 seconds; without traffic issues in the first half, it likely would have been faster. In comparison, Hasay produced a 66.11. Reid exhibited such power that in any game of "what-ifs"—what if she hadn't passed Hasay on the inside—the answer would always be the same. Reid wins.

She says, "If that lane hadn't opened up, I would have waited longer just so I didn't have to run the extra steps on the outside. But obviously if you see

Sheila Reid capped her NCAA double with a stirring sprint in the 1500m.

an opportunity like that where you've been given enough room on the inside… Which you have to be careful of—if there's not enough room, you can't make it for yourself on the inside. That's for sure. You're going to get DQed for something like that. But in my mind I was just waiting, and thought if I don't get an opportunity with 200m to go, I'll wait till we're around the curve, around the bend and I'll make a move there. That's the thing. You're at a little bit of a disadvantage because you're behind someone.

You want to make up that extra ground and presumably run the last 200m quicker than they can. You definitely don't want to have to run extra steps while you're doing it. If that lane hadn't opened, I suppose I would have tried to wait until 100m to go before I kicked. I definitely felt that I had that extra spring in my legs. At least that's the way memory serves. I think we kind of paint these situations a little romantically; at the actual time I'm sure I was in a lot more pain than I remember.

"I mean it was a brilliant opportunity for sure, but you either have the potential to win a race or you don't. I don't know if it can be seen as my stealing the race or something, by going on the inside, but I think I had enough of a cushion once I did go by on the inside. I feel pretty confident that I would have had the speed to go anyway. I knew going into that race that I was maybe a little tired from the 5K the day before, but I knew if I were there from 200m to go, that's where I'm strongest. That's where I'm most dangerous."

Sheila Reid on coming back from another event

"After winning the 5000m [2011 NCAA], I kind of said, 'Okay, whatever happens the next day is gravy.' But competitiveness kicks in. I certainly would have been disappointed if I hadn't won the 1500m the next day. When it starts to hurt in a race, if you don't have anything, you're going to ignore the hurt and you're going to go for it. I think it's easy [for the doubler] when the pain sets in, to kind of be complacent and say, 'Okay, well I already have won one. Why not just make this easier on myself?' At some point, you just have to shut your brain off and let your legs do it.

"I was fit enough. It was just a matter of getting on the line. I was sore, and that kind of creeps into your mind. I'm surprised. I think that other girls are capable of doing that double. It's not really a question of strength. There's enough time between the races. The tiredness from the 5K wasn't really a factor—especially since it wasn't a fast 5K. I think if the 5K had been all out, it would have been a different story, but that was another sit-and-kick type of affair. It wasn't much of a factor."

Results *(11 June 2011): 1. Sheila Reid (Villanova) 4:14.57; 2. Lucy Van Dalen (Stony Brook) 4:15.33; 3. Kate Van Buskirk (Duke) 4:15.37; 4. Renee Tomlin (Georgetown) 4:16.17; 5. Becca Friday (Oregon) 4:16.76; 6. Hannah Brooks (Florida St) 4:16.81; 7. Morgane Gay (Virginia) 4:17.40; 8. Jordan Hasay (Oregon) 4:17.67; 9. Lea Wallace (Sacramento St) 4:18.73; 10. Cory McGee (Florida) 4:19.18; 11. Kristen Gillespie (Arkansas) 4:21.75; 12. Brittany Sheffey (Tennessee) 4:22.50.*

2011 World Champs Women's 1500m: Simpson's kick perfectly timed

Many eyes were focused on Morgan Uceny. Not the strongest of favorites, but she had produced some solid races. Her fastest, a PR 4:01.51, came behind Maryam Jamal and Btissam Lakhouad at Monaco. In contrast, Jenny Simpson was regarded by many as the No. 2 American. She was noted for her kick, but in her first year away from the steeplechase, she lacked experience in high-level four lappers.

Jamal, the two-time World champ, took the early lead. Uceny bided her time in mid-pack. Simpson floated to the back, then shot up to join the leaders on the turn.

"I'm not very quick off the line," admits Simpson. "I had not run many 400s or 800s at that time in my career and so I always have this understanding that the first 100m I'm not really in the fight. That race was funny because everybody did get off the line really fast and settled in coming around the turn, and really slowed down. [With] their dramatic slowdown, I went around and up to the front, and it looks like I'm picking up speed. It was more that group slowing down, than it was me speeding up."

She adds, "That moment really set the mood for the race for me. I think even that early and very brief contact with the lead group helped me to kind of stay in mental contact with the lead group throughout the race. It set the mood for me not to lose touch and put me in a good position, then close the last 400m and get right back up there."

Mimi Belete moved up and took over from Jamal as they passed the first lap in a lackadaisical 68.78. Simpson had floated back again through the pack, with Uceny confidently running a couple places ahead.

Belete started applying some pressure over the second lap, but places remained relatively stable, the two Americans running behind the bulk of the pack. After 800m (2:13.94), Uceny started working her way up on the outside. The star-crossed Natalia Rodríguez then came into the mix; the Spaniard had crossed the line first in the 2009 championships, but was disqualified for causing another athlete to fall. Here she exploded down the backstretch and made a fast move to cut into the lead pack on the turn.

Suddenly Uceny was boxed. Then it happened—Kenyan Hellen Obiri fell and took Uceny with her. Jamal got spiked in the melee, and fell back.

With a lap to go, Rodríguez led at 3:03.47. Perhaps there wasn't much awareness among the competitors who had fallen, but they ran the last lap as if they all realized the gold was wide open. Rodríguez hit 1200m in 3:18.89. At that point, Simpson seemed out of it in seventh.

Recalls Simpson, "I remember that the previous two rounds I had run really wide on a lot of the turns, and so with 400m to go I didn't expend a lot of energy trying to pass people, and instead I just thought I would stick on the rail and stay smooth and strong. Everyone freaks out with 400m to go. Just be in contact and stay on the rail. Making that decision turned out to be such a perfect decision because then, of course, on the backstretch things really opened up. I was able to freely and without combating people, really just move up smoothly."

Morgan Uceny on the fall in Daegu

"With 500m left, people are trying to get fancy. Someone brushed me at the wrong place and at the wrong time and I got cut off. I had no time to react... It's no one's fault. It's the nature of the beast. When you get in these big races you have to learn to get in a different spot."

With 200m to go, Simpson had barely edged into sixth. She ran a hard turn, and made progress, but was forced to the outer edge of lane 2. With 100m to go, she was still only fifth, with Rodríguez desperately trying to hold onto her lead. As her momentum built, Simpson, from lane 3, charged into the medals, running down Kalkidan Gezahegne and then Rodriguez. Behind her, Hannah England gave chase. Simpson hit the line first in 4:05.40.

She describes the things going through her head in those moments: "As we came around the turn I remember there was this huge group of people and I so vividly remember thinking about counting the number of people that were there. What would it take to be top three? What are my odds? I remember thinking that, and in the same moment, thinking, 'You can't think that. You can't think that, because you just have to focus on finishing. Just finish and the places will sort themselves out.' And so I think that suppressing that desire to wonder what my odds were in that moment, that was what really, really helped me, later on, focus on the finish.

"Then as more and more people started fading in my peripheral vision, I think was that last 50m when I realized, 'I'm going to win.' It was just unbelievable. That's one of the few races of my life that I think I really knew, where I really thought, 'I'm winning this,' while I was doing it. Usually I don't think a lot about place until it's over with. I don't think a lot about time until it's over with. I just do it and see how it all shakes out. It's so funny too, because with my expression at the end everybody was like, 'Did you not realize you had won?' No, it was so much more, and it was already settling in on me. I knew the last 20 or 30m that no one was going to catch me. That wasn't happening. I was kind of expecting somebody to catch me, and nobody was. I was like, 'Now I don't know what to do.' You win and... I never even dared to dream about this day. I just didn't know how to react."

The key for Simpson had to have been the timing of her kick. She did not panic at the bell and she did not fight for it. She calmly stayed close to the rail and worked on smoothness, and getting into position for a terrific last 200m.

Jenny Simpson on her gold medal mindset

"I don't know that I very seriously thought that I could medal. I definitely wanted to do as well as I could but I don't think I entered that race thinking, 'Tonight's the night I'm going to come home with a medal.' Especially because history had really proven that that wasn't likely to be the case. I really treasure that race because there are things about it that because it was really an unexpected win for me and for everyone. I remember it better because it wasn't like, I was super honed in and focused on something that I felt I had to do. Instead the development of realizing how well I was doing sort of changed mid-stage. I think I remember the race a lot better. I can run with 400m to go, and it's great because I think that I learned a lot just in that week while I was there. I didn't have a ton of 1500m experience and I had zero championship experience. And so I really took very seriously that I was going to be at a disadvantage experience-wise. That left me open to learn a lot while I was there and so I got better as I went through the rounds."

Results *(1 September 2011): 1. Jenny Simpson (USA) 4:05.40; 2. Hannah England (Great Britain) 4:05.68; 3. Natalia Rodríguez (Spain) 4:05.87; 4. Btissam Lakhouad (Morocco) 4:06.18; 5. Kalkidan Gezahegne (Ethiopia) 4:06.42; 6. Ingvill Måkestad Bovim (Norway) 4:06.85; 7. Mimi Belete (Bahrain) 4:07.60; 8. Tuğba Karakaya (Turkey) 4:08.14; 9. Nataliya Tobias (Ukraine) 4:08.68 (later DQed for doping); 10. Morgan Uceny (USA) 4:19.71; 11. Hellen Obiri (Kenya) 4:20.23; 12. Maryam Jamal (Bahrain) 4:22.67.*

2012 Olympics Men's 1500m: Kicking for medals

Much of the pre-race prognostication centered around the three Kenyans who had already broken 3:30 that season: defending champion Asbel Kiprop (3:28.88), Silas Kiplagat (3:29.63), and Nixon Chepseba (3:29.77). Many experts thought a Kenyan sweep was a "legitimate possibility." Curiously, there was not much focus on Algeria's Taoufik Makhloufi, who had run his PR 3:30.80 for fifth in the same Monaco race as Kiprop's world leader. However, he jumped on everybody's radar after he blasted a 3:35.15 in the first round. Makhloufi trained under Jama Aden, who coached Abdi Bile the year of the Somalian's World Cup win (1989).

Whether Makhloufi legitimately had a place in the race is another question. A few days earlier, he jogged off the track after less than a lap of the 800m. The lack of "bona fide effort" should have banned him from further races in London. However, the Algerian team doctor produced a medical certificate saying that Makhloufi had a bona fide knee injury that kept him from completing that 800m. A day later, the injury healed completely. Amazing... and he didn't even fly to Lourdes.

At the gun, Taoufik Makhloufi powerfully jetted to the lead, but before the turn Abdalaati Iguider shot ahead of him. The pack bunched on the first turn and Belal Ali took over (58.03) with Nixon Chepseba at his side. At 800m, Chepseba led in 1:58.63. Makhloufi (1:59.0) stayed comfortably in the top six while Leo Manzano lagged in tenth. At 1000m, the pack got crowded again, with Ali fading and Nick Willis and Matthew Centrowitz moving up to Chepseba's shoulder. Farther back, Kiplagat made a big move but was immediately pushed away by Makhloufi, who had made a move of his own. Kiplagat recovered, and approaching the bell, three men ran abreast: Chepseba, Centrowitz, and Kiplagat. Makhloufi elbowed his way past Centro and Kiplagat and put himself on Chepseba's shoulder. Kiplagat came back on him and actually edged into the lead at 1200m (2:54.72).

That was where Makhloufi made the move that ended the speculation. He exploded at 300m to go, clocking a 12.6 on the backstretch. Chepseba melted. Kiplagat gave chase, and Mekonnen Gebremedhin moved up strongly from the back. That was the order with 200m left, as Iguider ran fourth and Manzano way back in eighth. With 100m left, the gold had been sealed for Makhloufi, but it looked like Gebremedhin would get silver. He had pulled alongside Kiplagat with just the final straight remaining.

That last 100m saw some crazy position changes that no one could have predicted. Iguider dashed into the silver position. Kiplagat died painfully and came home seventh. Gebremedhin didn't fare much better, his 14.3 closer giving him sixth. The two Americans charged brilliantly, Manzano zipping past Iguider and Centrowitz nearly catching him as well.

This was the ultimate kicker's race, not just for the win but for all the medals. Makhloufi finished with a 52.8 final circuit, highlighted by a 25.4 blazing half lap from 1200m to 1400m. His final 800m took 1:50.2—not quite Abdi Bile territory, but impressive. Manzano produced the fastest final 100m of the race, 13.1 to pass four men. The defender, Kiprop, jogged home in last, later revealing that he had injured his hamstring before he left Kenya.

What really stood out here was not so much the powerful 300m drive that gave Makhloufi the gold. John Walker ran similarly in 1976, albeit with a much faster finish off a slower pace. What actually stood out more was the way the tiny (5-5) Manzano negotiated the traffic on the last lap, seeing how he was only tenth at the bell and owned a silver medal at the finish line.

Makloufi didn't hesitate when the gun fired.

"With 400m to go I find myself between a rock and a hard place," said Manzano. "My lungs were fixing to explode, my heart was just not there. And the next thing I knew, I just had to start making moves."[12] In another interview, he remarked, "I just started moving; my arms started moving. I start making moves, and the next thing I know, I start passing people. I remember a particular instance with 200m to go, I'm passing this guy who has a very good kick, and I'm passing him on the outside of the track, on the curve.... So, as I'm passing him, it's like I'm gaining momentum. With 100m to go, I was probably still in about fifth or sixth place. About then it was almost like I was in a praying type mentality, where I was asking the big man upstairs, 'Come on, give me the strength.' But at the same time I was talking to myself. The next thing I know I'm pushing myself. I was like fourth, third, and I'm like, 'I can get one more, I can get one more!' "[13]

"I can't really tell you how I came from tenth to second," said the silver winner afterward. A few days later, Manzano said the key was that he knew he would get a medal if he "was the last one to kick."

Warhurst on Willis

"Tactics were perfect for the final. He was in third at the bell, I told him it doesn't matter who goes. It might be the Kenyans.... I said if you're there, someone's going to break at 300m, and you're going to go or else you're not going to get a medal. I think Willis was fourth at that point. And the kid went, and they all started to go. Willis was still fourth halfway down the straightaway, and then they started going by him. I thought, when he was fourth with 300m to go, he was still going to get a medal. He usually finishes like crazy. His legs went out on him, because he overstretched himself that day. Four or five times he stretched himself for 10-15 minutes. It's like a rubber band. You stretch it, it comes back okay, you stretch her good. He stretched himself too much and the rubber band was all flaccid. He had nothing in his legs. That was that day. He should have gotten a medal."

Results (7 Aug 2012) 1. Taoufik Makhloufi (Algeria) 3:34.08; 2. Leo Manzano (USA) 3:34.79; 3. Abdalaati Iguider (Morocco) 3:35.13; 4. Matthew Centrowitz (USA) 3:35.17; 5. Henrik Ingebrigtsen (Norway) 3:35.43; 6. Mekonnen Gebremedhin (Ethiopia) 3:35.44; 7. Silas Kiplagat (Kenya) 3:36.19; 8. Ilham Tanui Özbilen (Turkey) 3:36.72; 9. Nick Willis (New Zealand) 3:36.94; 10. Belal Mansoor Ali (Brunei) 3:37.98; 11. Nixon Chepseba (Kenya) 3:39.04; 12. Asbel Kiprop (Kenya) 3:43.83.

2013 Ivy League Men's 1500m:
Patience pays for Callahan

Sometimes it's best for the kicker to wait for the perfect moment. It can be hard to keep calm when other runners are flying by, but for some, it works best to pick a spot, and wait until then to surge. Peter Callahan displayed that patience well in 2013 at the Ivy League 1500m.

The last lap of this race was a marvel to behold and a great lesson in patience. With 400m to go, Callahan ran in third place, directly alongside fourth. The two leaders had already begun their kicks. At 300m to go, they started pulling away and got several strides ahead of Callahan. Halfway down the backstretch he was passed by another big kicker and fell to fourth. Then, with 200m left, nearly seven meters behind first place, Callahan checked his steps and exploded. He moved into the lead before the top of the turn and powered away to a five-meter win.

The time, 3:49.74, may not have been something for a national class runner to write home about. Callahan's last lap took only 53.8. That last 200m sprint took 26.2.

Says Callahan, "I had a stress fracture. I didn't run many races. That was my first and last outdoor meet of the year. It was weird, specially going into that, not having many races in my legs. I was a little bit rusty. I wasn't comfortable. But with that race—with any race—patience is really important, and having faith in your training and faith in your race strategy is important. Any coach will say, 'You can only control yourself in a race.' It's important to respond to other athletes when the time comes. But especially for me in that last 400m of the race, I had a lot of faith in my training, a lot of faith and trust in my final move. I have been working on increasing that final kick a little bit farther back, moving down the back stretch to get in a good position. But in that race it's about being confident, comfortable in what you know works, and actually speaking to that and I think sometimes when you move away from what you know works, other people kind of spook you into different types of moves, that's when you mess up."

The Short Kick: What They Say

Paul McMullen on the lesson learned: "My sophomore year, 1993, I got into a footrace with a Bowling Green Falcon by the name of Todd Black. The toughest lesson I ever learned. Todd Black was a good 800m runner. He was a senior. We were running the 1500m in very high wind as it always is down in Bowling Green [at the Mid-American Championships]. And I waited way too long and didn't start my kick in earnest until probably 125m to go. Just started to speed up coming off the corner and started to pick it up and Todd was a tall lanky runner with good 400m speed and I found myself sprinting for my life, which I had done a couple of times before, but I was simply outmatched. He stayed right with me, even though I had gone through some pretty good acceleration. And he was able to pull even with me. [Black won, 3:55.02 to 3:55.03]

"Coach [Bob] Parks was on the line, and he had a different version of things, but the lesson was, it didn't need to be that close. At the time I had run 3:40 for 1500m, and allowed a race with a 1:47 800m guy to come down to 100m. That is a tactical mistake. Coach Parks reprimanded me pretty handily. He was not gentle with his words. That never left my mind. That particular race, that experience I had, equated into me really finishing strong later in my career coming down the homestretch in big races where sometimes there were just a couple hundredths of a second—the one [USATF] in 1995, there was a thousandth between me and the winner. I would really dig in and know that that memory had gone through my head before about not finishing strongly enough and I didn't want to repeat that experience." [*Black eventually ran 1:46.00 for 800m in 1996, and finished eighth in the Olympic Trials. His lifetime best at 1500m was a 3:43.33, nearly 10 seconds slower than McMullen's.*]

Andy Bayer on being the last guy to move: "When I got to college, Coach [Ron] Helmer actually had me move down to the 1500m. It was kind of a tactic that he instilled in me. And he always taught me that the last guy to make a move is normally the guy who wins, which is what I went by."

Ruth Wysocki on kicking as strength: "Me as a kicker is sort of different than some other people kicking, I guess. I knew that I was playing to my strength as my strength. So I don't think I really ever or rarely ever counted on the last 200m or 150m or 100m. I knew that I was strong enough, and really worked on being strong enough to go from 300m out. The idea of being longer legged and everything else was to really use that backstretch, because everyone uses the last hundred, you know? So I think part of my thing always was to take the sting out earlier and not really count on that flat-out leg speed at the last part of the race."

Steve Scott on strength: "The kick is kind of a misnomer. Really, it's that you're so strong you can maintain a fast pace at the end. Because that's all the kick is. A person can have superior leg speed but if they don't have the strength to get to the fourth lap okay—and still have a lot left—then they're not going to finish strong. So it's a combination of still having good leg speed, and being able to use it at the end. I was always a very strong runner, so I had plenty left at the end. But someone like Sydney Maree, who did not have a lot of leg speed, more often he would have to employ other tactics to try to beat you. Like run hard from the start, or start his move from quite a ways out."

Renato Canova on aerobic power as a must: "For winning a championship, a runner needs to have high speed endurance. Speed endurance is not pure speed, which never can decide a competition for some title. Don't forget in the World Championships and Olympics, athletes have to run three times, and the ability to recover is a fundamental quality. That's the reason, without a high level of aerobic power—in direct support of the specific speed endurance—it's not possible to win any championship. Also athletes coming from 800m (such as Makhloufi), to be able to win at 1500m, developed a lot of endurance, running in winter with 5000m specialists and working on the track with long repetitions (1000m - 1200m - 1600m - 2000m), for creating the fundamental support to the specific training of speed."

James Li, coach of Bernard Lagat: "If a runner can cover the last 200m in 25 seconds, he'll dominate the 1500m. Well, most college milers can do 25 easily when they're fresh. But in the last 200m of a 1500m, it's not your absolute speed, it's your ability to kick when tired."[14]

Jack Lovelock, writing to his coach in 1933: "I cannot understand why it is, but these days when I am fit I find I have a most lovely sprint at the end, and it is on that that I am relying now to 'kill' my opponents in the last 80 yards, and it's only this year that it has come."[15]

Gene Venzke, describing how his increased strength led to a better kick: "I'm no faster than I was last year, but I'm a lot stronger... have more endurance to draw upon when the pressure is applied. Hoodoos and jinxes have never bothered me. I used to lose because I didn't have the reserve energy needed for a strong finish. Now I seem to have recovered the drive I had back in 1932 when I ran that 4m 10s mile. It's a matter of physical condition and tactics. I follow pace now, instead of setting it, and time my spurt at the end."[16]

Leo Manzano on the kick that gave him the silver medal: "I've been blessed with a talent for a solid kick. And because I've kind of developed it over the years I have learned to use it to my advantage against other guys. As you know, championship races are very tactical, and you have to have very good foot speed, and usually the last 600m to 200m you have to be able to move in different ways, and I've been able to use my kick to perform well on the track."

Abdi Bile on kicking: "When I was running a championship race, I was always confident with my kick. That way I knew I didn't need to run any other way, as I know I'm confident to win if it comes anywhere down to the last lap, 300m to go, 200m to go. I had more kick than anybody else. So that was the easiest way. I had good speed at the end. It was so much more natural. I also trained my mind like that. If I was doing 800s, I would change the pace the last 200m. Always a little change. Not just running the same pace. Still, as a coach, I do those kinds of training things, I train my athletes like that. Really the kick has a lot to do with the mind also. You know you don't want to lose, and whatever it takes to change that last 100m or 200m, it works. It works. The mind is also very important. You need to know that even if you're dying with one lap to go, you're going to kick. And you put it in your mind, you know, '300m to go I'm going to kick.' So I always had some kind of mental preparation. 'I'm going to kick today at 300-350m.' 'Today I'll try something fast in the last 100m.' It depends."

Andrew Wheating: "There is nothing more fun than jumping first and going all out the last 200m."[17]

Richie Harris leading Don Paige in his heat in the 1980 Olympic Trials.
"Guys like that, they knew they couldn't kick,
so they were going to make you pay."—Todd Harbour

Todd Harbour on looking back: "The first big one I remember was conference my freshman year against Mike Clark of Arkansas. I had only run 3:47. I wasn't one of the favorites by any means in the 1500m. I was doubling back from the 800m. I wanted to go out in a 60, and [Clark] throws in a 56 and a 1:56. How many races do you see run like that today? Nobody's got that kind of guts. You watch all these USA and NCAA finals and nobody runs like that anymore. I mean we always had somebody to lead almost every championship race, like Richie Harris. Guys like that, they knew they couldn't kick, so they were going to make you pay. And I guess we weren't too far removed from the Pre era, and those guys all looked up to him. Anyway, Mike took it to a 1:56, and the rest of us came through with two flat. He came through in 2:56 and we came through in three flat. Then he made the mistake of looking back on the back stretch. At that point I didn't think I could catch him, I was just running for second. He made the little mistake of looking back and I started thinking, 'Oh God, maybe I *can* catch him,' so I started going after him. I think I was the only one that did, and I caught him right at the tape, and that was my first unofficial sub four (3:42.53). But that one hurt. That wasn't a sit-and-kick, that was just trying to go get someone that was way out there."

Francie Larrieu Smith on kicking: "In the men's 1500/mile, [the trend toward championship races going to kickers] started back with rabbits, in my personal opinion. The big meets in Europe back in the 1970s started bringing rabbits to help people run fast, so those guys never ever had to take the lead in any big race in Europe. And then they get to the Olympic Games and half the time they were running the first lap slower than the women would run. That is how that evolved. Now they get rabbits for women. And no one wants to take the lead.

"One of my early coaches, Preston Davis, who coached me to my PR in the 800m and 1500m, said to never go to the front until you're ready to win. He was talking about championship events primarily. When I talk to my kids I tell them I want them to experiment and figure out what their strengths are, but when it comes to a championship, I don't want to see them in the front of the race until it's time to win. So if you can run from the front, go for it. But if you can't, don't even think about it. And very few races are won from the front."

Grant Fisher on the buildup to the kick: "Usually, everything leading up to the kick is all prep for the kick. The kick is what is anticipated in everything. Sometimes I feel like the entire race is just preparation for a kick, and it just keeps me in contention so the kick will be effective. When I do get into a position to kick, it does feel pretty good, as I'm pretty confident in how I can close a race. Coming in with usually two laps to go, I know I'm feeling fresh. And even if I'm not feeling fresh, I know that even if I can get to just 200m out, I know I can kick with the best of them. When I do kick, there has been anticipation for that moment. It's not exactly an explosion, because you can't explode off an already solid pace, but it definitely is a shift of gears and a different mindset once that hits. The whole race is conserve energy, conserve energy, get into position to kick. And the kick is just the pinnacle that you look forward to."

Don Paige on being born to it: "Why do all the work if someone else can do the work for you? It came natural. I was a born kicker. It just sort of evolved and I became a fast finisher as I went through high school and into college. Either you're born to be a kicker or you're born to be a leader or some people can do both, but it's rare."

Wottle rightfully earned a reputation as a ferocious kicker himself.

Dave Wottle on kicking: "I was a very selfish runner. One thing that I admire about the runners nowadays it that they will go out and say they'll lead for little while. I never had that mentality. My philosophy was I'll go out there to win; I wasn't going to help with the pace. To me it was always to my advantage to have someone else do all the hard work, and I would simply kick in. And that came across to me, and again I'm not proud I was that way, it's just the way I was. I'm trying to be honest."

Jeff Atkinson on the physics of racing: "I was always cognizant of the physics of racing from the get-go: never lead, run as little distance as possible, draft when possible, save energy for when you need it most. So I ran that way in high school pretty much all the time. If it was a dramatically less competitive event, then I would run away from the front."

Chapter 7: How to Beat a Kicker

"Only athletes who could muster the stamina and strength to stay with my pace… could pose a challenge to my ability to win."

—*Kip Keino*

True this: most of the time, the superior kicker will win. Yet no superior kicker, at least since the days of Herb Elliott, goes through a career undefeated. They can be beaten.

However, there is no surefire strategy to beat a superior kicker. As we have explored in previous chapters, driving a hard early pace is one way to sap a competitor's kick, though it is also fraught with danger for the runner who is driving the pace. A mid-race burst can also be effective at times.

Sometimes, though, beating kickers will come down to simple luck—for example, by catching them off-guard with a race that unfolds in a way they hadn't imagined. Or by beating them on the kick itself, a feat that usually involves a precise knowledge of the opponents' racing style and timing, and either going just before they go, or even going after. That's how Leo Manzano described his silver medal sprint in the 2012 London Olympics: "I knew I could get it if I was the last one to sprint."

In the 1937 K of C Meet, Glenn Cunningham's kick beats Archie San Romani as 1932 Olympic champion Luigi Beccali of Italy trails.

1937 New York Knights of Columbus mile:
San Romani tries something new

Glenn Cunningham was unbeatable on the circuit the winter after his Olympic disappointment. Archie San Romani wanted to take it to him, but San Romani was not only also from Kansas, he was also a kicker. So he needed to try something different. At the New York K of C meet, he decided to shock everybody by leading. He hit the first quarter in 61.0, and managed a 64 for the second.

As a local sportswriter put it, "It's the first time I recall [San Romani] running in front. It probably will be the last. Somebody evidently 'steamed' Archie up to make the effort of a lifetime probably with the idea that he would nip the record and he almost did. He led every stride of the way until the last 150 yards, at which point the faultless Cunningham stepped up the pace through the backstretch, led at the turn and went away to win."[1]

San Romani, who didn't respond on the backstretch, came to life again in the final yards and went after Cunningham. The four-time champion responded, and San Romani gave up, almost himself being caught by Luigi Beccali. The last quarter took 59.6, the last half 2:03.3. The final times were quite notable, as Cunningham missed his own world record by 0.3, in the fastest mass finish in history.

"Archie ran a really great race," said Cunningham. "He was in perfect condition. I was not surprised that he set the pace, though everybody else seems to be."[2]

Give San Romani kudos for trying something different against a famed kicker. While he didn't get the win, he could pride himself with having crafted one of the greatest races ever. It was worth the shot.

Results *(17 March 1937): 1. Glenn Cunningham (USA) 4:08.7; 2. Archie San Romani (USA) 4:08.8; 3. Luigi Beccali (Italy) 4:09.0; 4. Gene Venzke (USA) 4:11.1.*

1968 Olympic Men's 1500m:
The Kenyans team up against Ryun's kick

Jim Ryun was still just a boy in the 1968 Games, though it was his second. At age 21, he had experienced the best the sport could offer: world records, victories and adulation. However, the suffocating weight of public expectation was thrust upon the Kansas college student as well. He had not lost a mile or 1500m final in over three years. In the months leading up to Mexico City, however, he had dealt with mononucleosis, a kidney ailment and a pulled hamstring. Still, he had bounced back with a win in the U.S. Olympic Trials, and in the first two rounds in the thin air of Mexico City (elevation 7,350 ft/2240m), he appeared strong, finishing a step ahead of Kenya's Kip Keino in the semi.

Kip Keino was an international celebrity even before his Olympic win.

No man on earth had a more feared kick than Ryun. At that point in his career, he stood as invincible. Consider the following: In 1967, he finished his world record 3:51.1 with a 53.7. That same year, he crushed Kip Keino in a 1500m, breaking the world record with his 3:33.1. His last 300m took about 39.3, his last 880y 1:51.3, his last 1000m 2:18.7, and his last three-quarters 2:48.7 (faster than the world best for that distance). At a 1500m race in Düsseldorf, Ryun capped a 3:38.2 with a 50.6. His last 300m took only 36.4 and his 100m on the backstretch was timed at 11.6.

Ryun's primary rival would be Keino, who also competed four years earlier without distinction. In the time since, Keino had developed into one of the world's best, and in 1965 had broken the world record for the 5000m at 13:24.2. Yet the 28-year-old, who lived and trained at high altitude, had never defeated Ryun. His PR of 3:36.7 was well short of Ryun's world record 3:33.1. One of his greatest feats was his 3:53.1 mile at altitude, then the third-fastest mile ever. He won a three mile later the same day.

Ryun had won the Olympic Trials at altitude by closing with a 50.8 and a 1:50.8 (for yards). He seemed to recover his peak shape at just the right time. Keino had experienced some off races and furthermore handicapped himself by coming to Mexico City to attempt a distance triple. Running with the leaders in the 10,000m, he left the track with horrible cramps. In the 5000m he ended up with silver after what Cordner Nelson called a "tactical blunder" on the last lap. Then he wasted energy by bizarrely hammering the middle of his 1500m prelim and winning by five seconds.

Months before the race, John Velzian, an expatriate coach for the Kenyans, forecast that the high altitude would play a critical role. "I don't think we can overestimate the psychological and physical advantages high altitude acclimatization will give a runner in Mexico City. Competing against East Germany's Jürgen May at Nairobi's 6,000 feet, Kip ran him into the ground. May just couldn't get his breath… Kip may pull off a big surprise. Ryun runs to the clock and knows exactly where he should be at any given time. He's a superbly-trained athlete. But that kind of runner may not be able to cope with high altitude conditions against men who have lived in the clouds, so to speak, all their lives."[3]

Many of the races—including the 1500m semis—at Mexico City had been sit-and-kick affairs. Many of the low-altitude runners worried that a fast pace would destroy them. However, Keino had plenty of experience racing at altitude, and his 3:53.1 had proven that he could handle a fast pace. Faced with the prospect of racing the fastest kicker ever, Keino had no problem coming up with the only logical race plan. He even had the added benefit of a rabbit, as his younger teammate Ben Jipcho would sacrifice his own medal prospects to ensure a Kenyan gold.

"Before the final, Ryun was the fastest and Keino was only the third-fastest," recounted Jipcho. "Kenyan officials called us together the night before the final and we talked it over… I was not really willing, but they convinced me. They said that I was young and Kip was getting old. So it was arranged for me to set the pace."[4] At the time, Jipcho was 25, Keino 28.

Ryun had the confidence that told him he could outkick anyone. One wonders what was going through his mind when Jipcho ran his first lap in 56.0. Keino followed in 56.6, and Ryun ran at the back of the pack in 58.5. Keino continued the pressure after Jipcho yielded the lead, passing 800m in 1:55.3. Ryun lagged even farther behind, a stunning 10 yards behind the main pack. Keino continued the pressure, hitting 1200m in 2:53.4—faster than Ryun had split in his world record. Ryun, in fourth, passed in 2:56.0, actually gaining a little bit, but not enough.

Keino sped a 55.9 final lap and won gold in 3:34.91, the second-fastest time ever. Ryun, who had thought a 3:39.0 would be sufficient to win, jogged in once he saw that the best he could get would be silver. His fabled kick had been blunted by the altitude and Keino's brave pace. He told reporters, "If I had tried to keep Keino's early pace, I wouldn't have won any kind of medal."[5]

Keino said that the race went completely according to plan. "I knew Ryun had a great kick. I just figured to get out so far in front that his kick wouldn't be enough."

Results *(20 October 1968): 1. Kip Keino (Kenya) 3:34.91; 2. Jim Ryun (USA) 3:37.89; 3. Bodo Tümmler (West Germany) 3:39.08; 4. Harald Norpoth (West Germany) 3:42.57; 5. John Whetton (Great Britain) 3:43.90; 6. Jacky Boxberger (France) 3:46.65; 7. Henryk Szordykowski (Poland) 3:46.69; 8. Josef Odložil (Czechoslovakia) 3:48.69; 9. Tom Von Ruden (USA) 3:49.27; 10. Ben Jipcho (Kenya) 3:51.22; 11. André De Hertoghe (Belgium) 3:53.63; 12. Marty Liquori (USA) 4:18.22.*

1977 World Cup:
Could Ovett's kick be beaten?

The World Cup race in Dusseldorf a year after the Montreal Olympics remains one of the greatest races in the history of the event. The video, even nearly 40 years later, still grips, and invariably when fans watch it for the first time—or the tenth—they are astonished by the finish. That day, the IAAF brought together an amazing assemblage of milers: John Walker—the reigning Olympic champ; Steve Ovett, the up-and-coming 21-year-old from England, who had upset Walker already that season; Thomas Wessinghage, the West German medical student who had won the European Indoor title and the World University gold two years earlier; Steve Scott, the NCAA champion from UC Irvine who was just beginning his international career. Also notable were Abderrahmane Morceli, the older brother of Noureddine, who would later rewrite the world records in the event, and Jürgen Straub, the East German who the next summer would stun both Ovett and Sebastian Coe to win the European 800m title.

Walker and Wessinghage stood as the veterans in the field, and they had seen Ovett emerge as a kicker to be reckoned with. Recounts Wessinghage, "John Walker came up to me and said, 'Thomas, Thomas we've got to talk. Thomas, we have to run the kick out of Steve Ovett. I think you should take the first lap. I will take the second and third lap.' And that's what happened."

The gun fired. Straub, not part of the conspiracy, shot to the lead, but soon Wessinghage overtook him and set a vibrant pace. Ovett did not hide in the back, but reacted quickly to stay near the front. On the first turn, Walker brought himself up to slip between Wessinghage and Ovett. Game on. The German burned a first lap of 56.48 ("Right as we had planned to make it"). That's when the first sign of trouble emerged. Walker had fallen several strides behind on the second turn, and worked hard to catch up so that he could lead lap two. "The only thing was, John was way past his peak for that year," admits Wessinghage. The New Zealander managed well on the next lap, hitting a 58.48 (1:54.96). However, it took too much out of him. He began to struggle on the backstretch, and the field started to bunch up a bit as the pace slowed.

Steve Ovett, shown here competing in the 800m in the 1984 Los Angeles Olympics, had the most feared kick of his era.

At that point, Ovett showed amazing tactical brilliance. Before Wessinghage, running second, could respond to the slowdown and take over the pace again, Ovett shot up beside him and boxed him in. Walker continued to tire and slow even more, and no one in the race responded. That gave the Briton the opportunity to rest and prepare for his final lap. From the back, Dave Hill of Canada sensed the slowdown, and over the turn began his attack after nearly going down in a collision. He brought himself to the lead with 400m to go, but that move itself was probably all he had. Hill still led at

1200m (2:54.91—a 59.95 for the lead, but a 58.3 for Hill).

Three minutes into the race, both Walker and Wessinghage crowded Ovett, who held second behind Hill. Ovett looked over his left shoulder to check on Walker. A few strides later, he looked over his right to check on Wessinghage. Then he took a breath and exploded in a ravaging sprint. His dash from 1300m to 1400m took only 11.8! Walker was so stunned that he actually stepped off the track and quit. Wessinghage gave the best chase, to no avail. Ovett led by an insurmountable margin off the turn, and pumped his arm in the air in celebration with 50m left ("his usual imperious disdain for the opposition," according to one Scottish paper[6]). "When I reached the straight and looked round, I was surprised to see I was 10m ahead," said Ovett. He cruised to the finish, breaking the British record.

Ovett's account of the race

"... It was a fast pace, yet I did not really appreciate it as my mind was preoccupied with thoughts about positions: not getting boxed in; not tripping over Dave Hill again. My mind was too busy to absorb the speed at which we were running.

"As we went past the bell, Hill was still in front and I eased on to the shoulder of John Walker who was then in second place, with Thomas still in touch a close fourth. It was the perfect position for me and down the back straight with the speed increasing I sensed that Walker was preparing for a sprint, but was still trapped. So at 200 metres I thought 'Go, now' which acted like a trigger and I was away. I kept repeating 'Keep going, keep going' but I could not resist taking a look back—I was stunned at what I saw for they were 20 metres down on me and I only had 80 metres to go. I could not believe that I had gone that far away from them and my thoughts were, 'I've won, they can't make up that.' What I did not realize at that point was that Walker had dropped out..."[7]

So much for the Walker-Wessinghage plan. Says the doctor now, "The second lap was slower. And the third lap was even slower. So the race that started out a fast race became a slow race. Everyone else caught up, and then Ovett kicked devastatingly." His last 200m, eased up, took only 25.1.

Said Walker, who claimed he had been pushed, "I just lost my momentum, and that was it. So I just quit."[8]

British international runner Tim Hutchings watched the race, and Pat Butcher quotes him as saying, "[Walker] must have just gone, 'Jesus, what the hell is that?' when Steve kicked, because he was operating at a different level. That must have been a huge shock for Walker."[9]

Results (3 Sep 1977): 1. Steve Ovett (Great Britain/Europe) 3:34.45; 2. Thomas Wessinghage (West Germany) 3:35.98; 3. Jürgen Straub (East Germany) 3:37.5; 4. Abderrahmane Morceli (Algeria/Africa) 3:37.8; 5. Takahashi Ishii (Japan/Asia) 3:38.2; 6. Dave Hill (Canada/America) 3:39.2; 7. Steve Scott (USA) 3:44.0;... dnf—John Walker (New Zealand/Oceana).

2013 USA Championships Women's 1500m: Being faster helps

If ever a race unfolded as a kicker's feast, this was it. Without Jenny Simpson present, the milers dawdled. The top three would go to Moscow to represent the United States at the World Championships (as defending champion, Simpson had a bye). Among the favorites—Mary Cain, the high school junior from New York who had wowed the running world with her galloping running style and ferocious kick.

Cain's speed seemed ready for the championships. She had run an American Junior record (AJR) of 4:04.62 at Eagle Rock a month earlier, just an eyelash behind Katie Mackey's 4:04.60. Two weeks later, she set another AJR, this one at 800m with her 1:59.51. There were even reports of her ending hard workouts with a 55-second 400m.

The early pace was all that and less. Cain and occasional training partner Treniere Moser went straight to the back. Shannon Rowbury jogged alongside Gabe Grunewald and Amanda Mergaert. They passed the first lap in a stunningly slow 85.1. Grunewald and Mergaert sped up a little—just a little—on the second lap, which passed in 75.4.

That's where Cain started putting herself into position, in her somewhat awkward way, bouncing off her competitors here and there. She went outside and came up just behind Mergaert. Moser, meanwhile, stuck to the inside rail, trapped on all sides.

With 400m to go, everyone remained in contention. The field actually spread out eight or nine across just before the bell. None of those faces was Moser's, as she was still boxed on the inside. Cory McGee had eased her way up and led at the bell, with Cain on her shoulder and Grunewald behind. Panicked and buried, Moser fought her way from the rail to the outside of lane two, cutting off Stephanie Brown badly.

"Once I saw [Cain] go," said Moser, "it just gave me the strength, like I know I have another gear.... So I was just digging to get that other gear.... I knew I could close very hard."

McGee and Cain passed 1200m in 3:44.9 for a 64.4 lap. Mackey ran in third, and Moser caught her about halfway down the backstretch, as Cain took over first. Moser's momentum carried her well past McGee with 200m to go, as Rowbury also turned on the jets and moved into third on the turn.

Coming into the finish, the 17-year-old led her 31-year-old teammate. Cain tried frantically to maintain her stride to the finish, but she showed signs of fatigue as Moser caught her with 15-meters remaining. Behind them, McGee regrouped, and sprinted past Rowbury for the final team spot. Said Moser of her ultimate sprint, "Alberto [Salazar] told me to get ugly the last 100m, and I did that."

Without Moser there, Cain would have crushed the field with her kick. Moser simply had more in the tank: more strength, more speed. She started from farther back with 400m to go, had to fight through traffic problems, and ran on the outside for most of her final drive. And she still produced a faster last 400m than Cain, 57.45 to 57.86.

For Mackey, being third with 300m left didn't guarantee anything, as she was passed by six more runners before the finish. "I wished all year that I could rerun that race. I think that really helped me this year, because sometimes you have to learn mistakes the hard way for them to really hit you, to really learn from them. It was way more of a tactical race, and we were all just running so slow and I started to get really antsy about 600m out because I really wanted to be within a stride of those girls going into the last 400m. But I kind of let my emotions take over and I really didn't think of a smart way to do that. So I just went out into lane two and made a huge move on the curve to get around everybody, and it was really aggressive, and then that put me into a pretty good position. But then when I got to the last 200m of the race, I had nothing left, and I was just getting passed by everybody. I really wish I hadn't made such an aggressive move. I probably could have moved earlier in the race and it would have been a more gradual move that didn't take the explosive energy out of my legs the way that move did."

Grunewald, who found herself leading early on, looks back on the race with nothing but frustration. "That was a really strange race, and for some reason I found myself in the lead. It was really clear that nobody wanted to take it. I did take it for little bit but I did not commit to throwing down the pace. Part of it—that affected the decision to sort of be in the front, rather than do whatever I needed to do and not be in the front—I heard people starting to boo us. Then I think I made a little bit of an emotional decision, that this is ridiculous and someone needs to lead, even though I didn't really pick up the pace. I don't know, I just think that it was a strange feeling to hear us being booed and I made a quick decision that probably wasn't the best."

McGee recalls, "We went out so incredibly slow, far behind five-minute mile pace, and about halfway through, I think we were being booed by some people in the stands, and I remember hearing that, and having this moment of realization where I thought, 'You know, I could win this race.' I was just going to go in and run the race and compete, but then we went out so slow it was that moment when you realize anything can happen, we've evened the

The battling kickers: Moser topped training partner Cain in the final strides.

playing field. That was unexpected. That was my first USA final, and I expected it to be incredibly difficult from the start. When you're young, that's just what you expect, when you're running with all these women who you've always looked up to. That was unexpected."

Grunewald also had visions of pulling an upset. "Once I was in the lead, I was trying to tell myself that it was a fine position to be in, and it's not one that I typically find myself in. And I just thought that there's a chance if I try to stay in control of the race, that I try to be in control when we start kicking, I'll be on the inside and can kind of react if people are coming up on the outside and go with people. It didn't work out that way. Unfortunately I ended up stuck in the middle of the pack and I couldn't really move. I think some of the psychological issues with leading when I didn't really plan to, caught up with me by the time that it was time to kick."

With a lap to go, one of the panicked runners gave Grunewald a hard shove from behind (it can be clearly seen on the video). "That just kind of threw me off because I felt like it was a critical point in the race," she says. "Mary Cain was starting to go right outside of me. And when everyone starts to go, there's definitely panic within the pack, and you feel that. I definitely remembered after the race, that shove from behind. I'll never know if it affected my momentum. It felt weird, and I think it was a critical time in the race, and I didn't have a lot of room for error at that point. It may have thrown off my timing a little bit."

Results (22 June 2013): 1. Treniere Moser (Nike Oregon Project) 4:28.62; 2. Mary Cain (Nike Oregon Project) 4:28.76; 3. Cory McGee (Florida) 4:29.70; 4. Shannon Rowbury (Nike) 4:30.09; 5. Kerri Gallagher (New Balance) 4:30.56; 6. Sarah Brown (New Balance) 4:30.99; 7. Amanda Mergaert (Utah) 4:30.99; 8. Morgan Uceny (adidas) 4:31.32; 9. Katie Mackey (Brooks) 4:32.10; 10. Heather Wilson (unattached) 4:32.62; 11. Gabe Grunewald (Brooks) 4:32.93; 12. Hillary Holt (College of Idaho) 4:33.49.

How to Beat a Kicker: What They Say

John McDonnell: *At the 1983 NCAA Outdoor Championships, Arkansas senior Frank O'Mara faced a tough field that included Marcus O'Sullivan, Joaquim Cruz, and freshman Earl Jones. The latter two would win medals at 800m in the next year's Olympics. Concerned about Jones' speed, O'Mara's coach gave him the following advice:*

"Frank had really good top-end speed. I just told him to try to be behind [Jones] if he could, but it didn't happen that way. So I told Frank, if he is behind you with 350 meters left to start really cranking it up. He did that, and Jones tried to come back on the final straightaway, but Frank had taken quite a bit of the steam out of his legs."[10]

O'Mara won the race in 3:50.51, just 0.13 ahead of Jones.

Steve Scott on kickers who are nearly impossible to beat: "A lot of the outdoor races, I could win, but it was with my finishing kick. There were some people I had trouble with, and Steve Ovett was one of them. I raced him at 1500m 10 or 12 times, I guess, I think I only beat him once or twice. Outdoors, he had just an amazing finish. It didn't matter if I pushed hard from a lap to go, two laps to go, 600m… he would just annihilate me in the last lap. So you can try different tactics, but they're not always going to work. It depends on the strength of your competition."

"For me to beat somebody like that, you have to do something. It's been proven it's pretty hard to outkick him."
—Steve Prefontaine
discussing the prospects of a 1971
race against legendary kicker Jim Ryun[12]

Kip Keino on his racing style: "When I ran, I liked to 'front-run.' European athletes, on the other hand, used to pace themselves with the aim of saving themselves for a final lap sprint finish. On the contrary, I started slowly and gradually wound up the pace. If you had the strength, you would live with my pace… As far as I was concerned, it was only athletes who could muster the stamina and strength to stay with my pace who could pose a challenge to my ability to win."[11]

Andy Bayer — is kicking a macho thing? "I think it is. I think everyone feels that way, and they think if they go to the front early, they're just sacrificing themselves. So a lot of people are probably too confident in their kick. 'I've outkicked this guy before so I'll do it again.' That's kind of how it goes."

Todd Harbour on the pitfalls of being a kicker: "At the Trials in 1980, I got stuck in a box and I came after Mike Durkin and almost caught him right at the tape, got fourth by a tenth of a second in that race… Sydney [Maree], my junior year at Austin [for the NCAAs], he got out on me. Don [Paige] was on the infield, actually. He saw me in a little bit of a box, and he told [Sydney] to go. Sydney had enough respect for me he felt like I could probably beat him in the last 100m or 200m. He got out on me, he opened up five yards. When I got out of the box, I came after him, but he was so strong. You couldn't make that kind of mistake with Sydney. It cost me there."

Chapter 8: Running the Rounds

"You've got to run every race like it's a final, until you're absolutely sure that you're getting through."

—*Steve Scott*

Not many young runners have to worry about surviving qualifying rounds in order to make it to the 1500m or mile final. However, once the athletes advance to the collegiate level and beyond, surviving the rounds becomes a crucial skill. And for rookie athletes who advance to the biggest of stages—the World Championships and Olympics—the qualifying heats can be the toughest and most crushing part of the entire experience.

That's because any first-time international team member probably is so exceptional a runner that any previous experience with qualifying heats has seemed quite easy. For instance, running collegiate qualifying heats at 1500m against 3:43 runners shouldn't be too stressful for a 3:37 man. However, on the world stage, that 3:37 doesn't shine so brightly when on a starting line where it seems everyone else has a PR of 3:32 or better. The athlete needs to quickly rethink any previous ideas of qualifying heats being something he could just cruise through.

Suddenly, that mundane little qualifying heat becomes a race that must be run as if *everything* depends on it. Because it does.

The 2013 World Championships in Moscow perfectly illustrates the challenge of qualifying for the finals. The top five automatically qualified in times from 4:04.82 (Zoe Buckman, second from right) to 4:05.23 (Genzebe Dibaba, third from right). Two more qualified on time: Nancy Langat (4:05.30, third from left) and Siham Hilali (4:05.32, fourth from left). Missing by 0.04 was Svetlana Karamasheva (second from left).

In most championship meets, there are two ways to advance to the next round: as an auto-qualifier, or as a time qualifier. The meet organizers might have a field of 24 runners in the 1500m. They need to cut that number in half for the typical 12-runner final. So they set up two qualifying heats. The first five in each heat will automatically qualify for the final.

That leaves 14 runners battling it out for the last two spots in the final. The two fastest will get in as the time qualifiers. Usually, they will come from the same heat. Which heat, though, will be the fast one? Research shows that in a competition with three or more heats, the fastest will generally be the first and the last. That information is not much help in a two heat situation.[1]

In effect, what happens is that sometimes the competitors in a heat will decide that a faster pace will yield more qualifiers for that heat, and they will contribute to that pace because it will be advantageous to them individually. The opposite happens as well, where the stronger runners feel quite confident of finishing in the top five, and have no interest in pushing the pace because they are hoping to save energy for the final.

In the fast heat situation, the decision of the marginal athlete is quite simple—go along for the ride, knowing that a top seven finish just might yield a spot in the final. In the slow heat situation, the marginal athlete faces a real quandary. An attempt to try to make the pace faster would weaken the athlete for the finish, when they will be overwhelmed by the stronger runners. The alternative is perhaps the best choice: to simply sit and kick with the faster runners, hoping that one of them has a bad day and can be picked off at the end.

A study from the 2012 Olympics showed a strong correlation between positions at intermediate points in the race and whether or not the athlete qualified for the next round. Translation: it pays to be near the front throughout the qualifying race—dawdling in the back and relying on a kick is a fool's game.[2]

Running the Rounds: Race Histories

1972 Olympic Men's 1500m Semi-final: Dave Wottle's experience

Dave Wottle today is remembered as the man who won the upset victory in the 1972 Olympic 800m. What many younger fans don't know is that Wottle spent most of his career as a miler and had big hopes of winning a medal in the 1500m. "I've always thought of myself as a miler," he says, "except for three months of my life, right around the [1972] Olympic Trials and the Olympics."

Of his Munich experience he say, "Well, I just ran a dumb race in the Olympics in 1972. I was cocky. It was after the 800m. Actually the interesting thing about the 1500m in the 1972 games was in the semis, I felt the best of any of my Olympic races. I felt very sluggish in the half [where he won the gold]. I have my training log where I have a code system for how I felt. For the finals of the 800m I think I put down that I was 'fair.' (I was either 'poor,' 'fair,' 'good,' or 'very good'.) I was kind of really sluggish. I was good or fair through most of the stuff. I felt very good for the 1500m semifinals. That combination of feeling very good coming off the 800m, feeling very confident, 300m to go, maybe 250m, I'm sitting back in probably fifth or sixth place, and feeling like, 'Geez, I can give these guys a little bit more. You know, I'm the 800m champion, I'm feeling really great. I can run them down, and not have to put much energy into the semis.' And I had given too much distance, and I couldn't catch them. [Tom] Hansen from Denmark inched me out, probably by about the distance that I won the 800m. Just a fraction of a second, hundredths of a second, I'm sure. He was third, I was fourth. I didn't proceed to the finals, which probably was my biggest disappointment because my goal—if you look at my workout sheets—my goal was to win the 1500m in the Munich Olympics. It wasn't to win the 800m. I did change to the 800m probably after tying the world record in the

Trials, I switched. I thought that I probably had a shot in 800m since I had the fastest time going in, but my biggest disappointment was not making it into the finals of the 1500m. I don't think I could've beaten [eventual winner Pekka] Vasala. But I probably had a shot at medaling. I wasn't in the greatest condition. I had come down with tendinitis six weeks before the Games, so I just wasn't in the kind of shape I needed to be to compete in at 1500m the way I would've wanted. That was the biggest disappointment. So I had one of the biggest thrills and one of the biggest disappointments of my life within a week of each other."

1996 Olympic Men's 1500m Semi-final: McMullen's two mistakes

This is the race that American Paul McMullen looks back to with regret, where he made mistakes that cost him a spot in the Olympic final. Flush with confidence after winning the Olympic Trials on the same track, the Michigan native had a legitimate shot at the final, having finished 10th in the World Championships final the previous year.

The pressure jumped up a notch in the first semi, which looked an awful lot like an Olympic final. Noureddine Morceli ran the fastest ever qualifying time in history, a 3:32.88. He needed all of it to edge the all-stars behind him: Fermin Cacho, Abdi Bile, William Tanui, and so on. For the second semi, McMullen lined up alongside Hicham El Guerrouj, Stephen Kipkorir and Reyes Estévez for starters. McMullen's own words tell the story the best:

"I made two big mistakes. They were just what I would call freshman mistakes, it being my first Olympics. And I think this is the mistake that most runners make, and [Eastern Michigan coach Bob] Parks coached us not to make that, is when you make your move, be committed to the rest of the race, and don't second guess or hesitate. And I made two moves when I went with about 500m to go with that race, on the homestretch. This is a lot of times what some runners do, is when they're coming around on the homestretch, and they're getting ready to hear the bell ring. You really start to get into position so that you are on the front or in second or third with the bell, and you usually have that homestretch to do that because everyone is kind of in limbo waiting to hear the bell. That's sort of the Pavlovian trigger for all of those runners to begin to start to kick. And what you want to do is have all the gaps closed and be in perfect position when you hear that bell, because getting into position at the corner and down the backstretch, significant position, on other good runners, is impossible. It just doesn't happen. I mean, you can do it, but it better be real slow if you're going to do it.

"So I think I did two moves in that race against those guys. It was really a matter of insecurity. Lack of confidence. There's a moment in everybody's

Paul McMullen, seen here running a relay for his Eastern Michigan squad.

career, where it's best to be ignorant of what actually is happening, because if you really ponder the moment, it can be just crushing. To say, 'I have trained for eight years for this season, for this moment, and now two of those laps are gone. I'm in front of 80,000 people in my home country, and they are screaming bloody murder for me to [do it], and I can feel the shock waves from the stands urging me to perform well and make it to the next round, and into the final, and I cannot meet those expectations. I can't fathom what I'm really doing here.' That in a nutshell is what can happen, I guess. And that's one of those races I wish I could take back.

"Two moves of hesitation. One was moving into position after 700m, so that when I came down the homestretch I knew I would be in a good spot. And then coming down the homestretch, it's really good to use that momentum. That if you build it up a little bit, you can pass right into second or third as the bell rings, and you can make it very difficult for people to pass you the whole final lap. And at least hold that position at fifth or sixth [the final qualifying spot]—that's what you're trying to go for. I hesitated and watched that moment slip away."

El Guerrouj won in 3:35.29, and the last qualifier for the final was Marko Koers of the Netherlands in 3:36.06. McMullen finished in ninth at 3:37.81.

2001 World Champs Men's 1500m Semi-final:
When you really have to run the semi like a final

McMullen points to the semis of the 2001 World Championships in Edmonton as one of the races in his career where everything went right. The trouble was, the race was a semifinal. "The reason I say that is we go back to the positioning that you need in a 1500m championship-style race. You have to be in position with 700m to go, you really do. Anything after that, you're really rolling the dice if it's slower. If it's fast, and you have slower people ahead of you that are going to die, it's not a big deal. But if you're in a tactical race, 700m to go is really sort of the marker in a race where you have to be in position, or be very close to your final position where you're going to execute your final kick."

The field was stacked: Hicham El Guerrouj and Laban Rotich had both broken 3:30, and William Chirchir would do so in a few weeks. Another four men had run bests in the 3:31s. Altogether nine of his 11 opponents had run faster than McMullen's best of 3:33.89. "We came through very, very slow [62.61]… 700m to go, get in the right position. And what I sensed as we're coming around the bend there with two to go, then you get your feedback of your 800m split, which typically incites a panic. El Guerrouj is in the lead, and sees we're going to be as slow as all get-out [2:06.17 actually]. He starts to extend his stride, and I am right with him. I sensed that this is what he was going to do anyway. What that guy can do, is he starts to speed up in the smoothest, most powerful way you've ever seen for a guy and he extends his stride so much, that—I was right behind him and his spikes came up to my shin and cut it open. That was when I knew, okay, this is game on. This guy can really fly on the last two laps. And if I hadn't have been there, the result would have been what happened to Sullivan.

"Hicham El Guerrouj starts running at such a pace that he finished in 1:47.9 or 1:48 over the last 800m, because we went out in 2:06. And I was sitting in third place as we went past the 800m mark, and it was a blast getting down the backstretch. Doesn't look that fast, but we just start flying, and we run a negative 800m. I think it went 54 and then it went 53, over the last 800m. And I'm sitting in third and there's nothing really changing, other than the fact that people in the back are realizing that this race is about over, because he just keeps running faster and faster and they're not in position. It just creates this really long expanse. And I come around with a lap to go, and I think I'm still holding onto fourth—I don't know if I went by some people or some people couldn't get by me, but the really fast Kenyans couldn't match that speed down the homestretch, and here I place sixth in that semifinal, and I recorded I think it was 1:49 over the last two laps. And that's fast.

"I looked down at my leg, and it was bleeding pretty good. The blood was just black, it was so full of lactic acid, I literally had gone to my maximum. And here's Kevin, who placed fifth in 2000 for Canada in Sydney, and he wasn't able to get out of the semifinals, a devastating race for him. And I felt horrible because there we were both training partners at the time under Ron Warhurst... It was a couple of tough training weeks after that."

El Guerrouj came across the line first in 3:39.54. McMullen clocked a 3:40.57 to grab the last qualifying spot by 0.12 over 3:29.91 man Rotich. Sullivan finished ninth in 3:42.30. The predicament for McMullen was that he had to use everything he had to simply qualify in a brutal race with the shots being called by the world record holder. When the final came 42 hours later, it was all McMullen could do to come home tenth in 3:39.35, nearly eight seconds away from a medal.

2012 Olympic Women's 1500m semis: For Simpson, it was about fitness

"In the first round, I barely got in by the skin of my teeth. I barely got into the second round. So I think that's kind of where the story begins. Looking back, I don't even know 100% what it was. Was it the pressure of having won the year before? Was it just all the incredibly high level expectations surrounding the Olympics? Or was it my preparation going into there? I think it was a combination of all those things. I just wasn't in four-minute race shape and I was running really, really hard the last bit of the first round to make it. And I don't even remember what my time was in that race [4:13.81]. It's something that I should be able to run on the track by myself with nobody there. It shouldn't have been as hard as it was, but I was running as hard as I could.

"I think in the rounds that one of the tricks to being able to get through, and *still* be prepared for the final, is that you can't be running all out every single round. If you're running all-out every single round, you are at a distinct disadvantage compared to people that aren't. And so my memory of 2012 was just how hard the races felt. And that I just felt like I was running as hard as I could.

Simpson learned from 2012 and returned a year later to win silver.

"[In the semi], I felt like I put myself in a good position. And I said, 'All right, don't ever not be in the top five. I think that I had really been frightened by the first round where I almost didn't make it. I just kept telling myself to just keep fighting to stay in the top five. And don't ever *not* be in qualifying position. And that turned into me just fighting so much throughout the race that I just had nothing left at the end. I look back and I think that rounds can be so painful when you don't make it because sometimes it is just as simple as a tactical mistake. And all of a sudden you find yourself too far back and you're fighting your way forward, and you're not making any ground. I painfully watched Leo [Manzano's] experience [in 2013] in Moscow. Leo found himself at the back and just never made any ground throughout the entire semi-final. He went towards the front and was never in position, but he had never had a chance. He just had a really, really difficult time. That's exactly the opposite of how I felt in 2012. I felt I had put myself in a good position. I just was not prepared to make the final. And I was running as hard as I could and I really believe that if I had had it in me to run faster than I did that day that I would have. I was last in that semi but my time was 4:06.89. The fastest I ran that entire year was 4:04.07. And so for me it was at least as painful, because it wasn't a mental or a tactical mistake. I think I wasn't as physically prepared as I should've been and I think that's a mistake over the course of months. Not a mistake over the course of one instant in that race."

Running the Rounds: What They Say

Katie Mackey — you need to respect how important your brain is: "Championship situations can be really hard going in your first time. Especially in an Olympic Trials year, you have three rounds. In the other years you have two rounds of the 1500m. And getting really amped up three times in a few days, you have to learn how to come down from that, and not run the race a million times in your mind before you actually step to the line. You need to feel fresh and really respect just how an important of an organ your brain is. It needs to be fresh going into the race as well, because flooding it with cortisol every time you think of the race is going to hinder recovery, especially between rounds."

Sheila Reid on staying calm: "Just know where everyone is with a lap to go. And be confident with where you are. You can't make sudden movements, all of a sudden, and realize, 'I'm in seventh and only the top six move on,' and make some crazy move to the front, because it's a waste of energy. The biggest thing is conserving energy and making the right moves, whatever those are. At some point I think it just comes down to your instincts. You can't really be told specifically what to do in a prelim. You have to kind of feel it out."

Sonia O'Sullivan on being near the front: "Always be in the automatic qualifiers. I had no problem finishing off the last 200m in winning the race in the rounds. I wasn't someone to sit back and say, 'I'm going to get through easy here.' I didn't believe it took too much out of you to run fast the last 200m of anything. I think it kind of gave me a bit of confidence, and it felt good when I came on the track and went into the next round."

Abdi Bile — expect the unexpected: "Really, it depends on who is in the race, because crazy things happen. Like my semi final in Rome [1987]. It was [like] the final—all the top guys. *Everybody* was in the semifinal. We were asking what had happened, and they said, 'Oh, just the computer.' What computer did this crazy thing, you know? So I mean number one, you should check who you are running with. So if it happens to be [like] a final, then you're running a final. It is no longer a semi final. But if it is a normal semi final, the main important thing is just to make it. You're not thinking of winning, you just have to be smart and stay out of trouble and make it. If it's top three who make it or top five that make it finish fourth or fifth but just make it. And save energy as much as possible at the same time."

Francie Larrieu Smith on time qualifiers: "I can't say that I made it through every time because I didn't make it through in '72 or '76 for that matter. One thing that happens when you're running rounds is that the first heat is generally the faster heat because people don't know [how the later races will unfold]. They know they have to be in that automatic position. And not have to wait around for all the rest of the races to see if they got in. In heats two and three, depending on how many there are, the race might be a little slower, and then you find yourself in these kicking positions, and then the times are slower. Because the times are slower, the people who qualified on time come out of the fastest heat."

Cory McGee on sending a message: "If you don't [run the round like a final], you're making a big mistake. It's very important to go to every race, whatever it is, a prelim, a final, a fun run, whatever, with that mindset, because otherwise I think you're giving your competitors a false impression. Coach and I actually argued about this at the SEC meet this year, in the prelims. With 250m to go, there was a little bit too much elbowing and whatnot, and I took off. I mean, my times shaped up pretty well against the competition, and I didn't want to burn myself out in the prelim, but the second that I was getting pushed around, I just was like, 'Forget it. I'm not going take any risks here, I'm not going to fall.' And I kicked with 250m to go. And after the race, he told me, 'Cory, what are you doing? It's a prelim for SECs. You don't need to make this big move when you have two more races this weekend.' But I told him, 'Coach, I think that in a prelim or not, if I gap the competition, I'd rather them see that I'm capable of doing that, and be a little worried, than jog it in with them and give them the false impression that I'm not ready to race.' I don't want to give someone else that kind of confidence. I'd rather feed my own confidence, I think. The point is, I'm going to go into every race with a competitive mindset. I don't like to take it easy. I like to keep it honest."

Ray Flynn on paying attention: "1500m heats are some of the most tantalizing races that you will ever run; you get 10 guys coming off the bend together sometimes. And there's a lot that can go wrong. Certainly I think that one has to be paying attention to what was going on in the earlier heats if you happen to be in a later heat, if there is an opportunity to avail and statistically have a better chance because there are more places available… However, if you want to do any damage, you've got to get to the final first."

Amanda Eccleston on running the heats at the 2014 USA Championships: "I got out pretty well, and basically just didn't let any space form between me and the leaders the whole time. I think the biggest thing is we went out a little bit relaxed for the first 800m, and then I know that Jenny Simpson started really pushing the pace and going. Deciding to go with that, I felt like I was sprinting from 700m out, and I was a little worried. But you don't really have a choice but to stick with the pace and go with it. The other thing for me personally in running the prelim was I have to treat it like a final. I think that I have to go all out at this point to make it. And not come in relaxed: 'Oh, this is a prelim, you need to save it for a final.' At this point in my career, to make a final at the USA level, I definitely feel like I have to go all out and leave everything there, and not think that it's going to be easier than it is. That's one of the biggest things mentally for me."

Steve Scott on keeping it relaxed: "Every race is a final. You can't go into a race thinking, 'I'm going to go through with the least amount of energy possible.' You've got to run every race like it's a final, until you're absolutely sure that you're getting through. You're in the last 100m of a round and you have a five-meter lead, okay, you can shut it down. But you certainly can't get complacent early on in the race and think you're going to catch everyone that's ahead of you. And you can't be too tense in the early rounds. You know, the people who are kind of uptight and utilize a lot of energy. And then you have the other guys who cross the finish line and don't even look like they're breathing hard. It is advantageous to run relaxed in the rounds, because the final is hard."

Heather Kampf on keeping your focus: "You have to run a prelim like a final, even if you're a favorite, to make sure you're in that final. If you make it to the final stretch and there's 50m to go and there's plenty of room between you and the next possible auto-qualifier, then sure, you can pump the brakes a little bit. But for the most part, I think that in this day and age in the United States there's really little opportunity for you to pump the brakes and still make a final automatically. It's almost more that mental aspect of not thinking of saving anything for the next day because I think that's something that a lot of athletes think about, 'I want to make the final, but I

Amanda Eccleston: "I definitely feel like I have to go all out."

want to use the least amount of energy possible so that I'm fresh for that final.' So I try as much as possible to focus on today and the here and now and worry about the rest later."

Kyle Merber on the ultimate qualifying mistake: "My sophomore year at nationals indoors in the prelims, the race just went out kind of slow and I just took the lead and I had never done that before. I never lead races, and whenever I think about that I kind of kick myself because I don't think nationals is the time to start learning about how to lead a race."

Jeff Atkinson on making it count: "Number one is every race is a final. Don't ever think you can conserve or save and get to the next race. Every single thing you run, it's as if it's the last race of your life. You only ease it or shut it down after you're certain that you're in. So as long as you approach every race as if it's the whole enchilada, you're not going to make any dumb mistakes.

"Number two, know that everybody else has to run the rounds. It's no big deal to run several days in a row, especially in a shorter event like the 1500m. So that's not a big deal. The third thing is that the rounds have, by necessity, watered-down fields. If you're used to running international races, then you know that by the third race you're running against the best in the world. But in the rounds there are one or two of those top eight guys and there are a bunch you never heard of. Sure they got great marks and so on, but there's a reason you haven't heard of them. They're not going to get to that third final with you. So if you're in the Olympic Games or the World Championships, the rounds are clearly watered-down fields compared to the final or perhaps to a big international race that you might have been in before. So you have to go in there and say, 'I can race all of those guys, they're on the same playing field as me.' As far as going day after day after day, you do a little recovery jog, you eat well, sleep well and it's no biggie until the next day.

"The biggest thing is you run it as if it's the final, as if it's the last race you will ever run. And if you find yourself pulling away, you can look around. If you're in the top six and seventh is 50 yards back, of course you're going to shut it down. It's much easier to run a full speed race and in the last 50 shut down, than it is to run a moderate or slower speed race and have to use the last 150 to blaze your way up into it. That way, in the former, you feel that the race was easy, shutting down before the end. But in the latter you sense that the race was hard because you had to work your way into the top end. Now physiologically, one race might be 3:36 and the other race might be 3:38. Two clicks of the clock isn't anything physiologically, but emotionally, your sense of how it went is dramatically different. You always want to set yourself up. The emotional part is by far the most important piece. Your physical strength is going to be what it's going to be, based on your training. You were lucky or not lucky in how you prepared. But the emotional part is a gift or an outcome; it's the thing that most affects how you feel. Your confidence level is entirely generated by your tactical and technical and intellectual approach. So if you try to control your emotions you're screwed. All you control is your tactical and intellectual execution of the event; if you do that properly, the reward is this great emotional feeling about how you feel you can carry it into the next round. It's sort of an important distinction that I don't think most coaches or most athletes really understand. They all think you got to get really hyped up for this next one, it's the big show and you've got to do it! blah blah. Or you're going to do it because your mom died two weeks ago, and you're going to do it for her, or you're going to do because you're the kind of person that gets up for a big event. Focus on the technical bits and the execution of it and all the rewards of being hyped up or running for your mom or whatever, they come flowing to you at the conclusion of a technically masterful performance."

Katie Mackey on staying out of trouble: "I think a lot of the reason that I've had more success in making finals is that I shifted my training cycles, because I was changing my outlook from doing well at the NCAAs to, 'Hey, there's a ton of the season left.' Now as an elite, the track season goes until September. I need to not be peaking—I need to obviously be running well at those times, but now I am on a different racing schedule at the next level. I also started to take more ownership over my training, learning about training cycles and respecting the fact that I'm human and can't go 100% in every workout all year long without burning out. I've learned a lot since being coached by Danny Mackey. I needed to have an outlook on how am I going to last in my racing all season, so shifting my outlook a little bit has helped me to feel better at the championships which has helped me to make more finals.

"But I also think, as far as going into semifinals, I like to just stay near the front and stay out of trouble. That's an approach that I bring with me, because most of the time in the semifinals, you're running kind of slow, and then it can turn into a kickers' race. So if you're already a couple seconds back, that's a couple seconds that you don't have on somebody when you have 400m to go. So I like to stay really safe and stay near the front in a semifinal."

Kevin Sullivan on the challenge of qualifying at the highest level: *Over his long international career, the Canadian star had mixed experiences getting through qualifying rounds:*
"It's a tough situation, especially when you're at that level, and there are so many guys who are so closely bunched together in terms of personal bests and talent. I think there were a couple of championships where positioning was definitely an issue for me, where I found myself too far back in the race to really respond to big moves. I think in a couple of those races, it was more of a luck of the draw situation. I got stuck in a slow heat at a time when I

didn't have the kind of leg speed I had when I was younger and I would have fared much better had I been in one of the heats that had gone a little bit more aggressively.

"To that extent too, I didn't take it upon myself to go to the front and lead those races either. In hindsight, maybe I should have gone to the front at least to get the pace going. Or if you see one heat go a certain pace and you think, 'Oh someone's going to be aggressive enough to take the pace,' and everybody kind of thinks the same thing and it ends up being tactical. There were a couple situations where it was bad positioning on my part, and a couple situations where I think the race just did not play to my strengths at that time of my career. And I had one where I just completely blew up. Where I didn't make it out of the first round, and that was Seville in 1999. That one still baffles me to this day. I had run 3:34 ten days before in Zurich, and then I went in there and ran 3:44 in the prelims and just got my doors blown off. It happens sometimes, and sometimes you can't put your finger on what happened."

Andy Bayer on easy ones versus close calls: "It's about getting yourself in a good position early so you can be relaxed. At least in the NCAAs and the Big 10s, Coach Helmer, he would a lot of times prefer me to control the race, so I would just get to the front and make it decently honest, a 60-second pace. We knew I could run sub 3:45 anytime we kind of needed to in a prelim, and so we'd make it fast enough so that no one would have a 51-second quarter in them. But I could stay relaxed enough that I wasn't taking all my energy away from the future rounds or the final.

"The [Olympic] Trials was a little bit different because I had been hurt the couple previous years outdoors. The NCAA, there's obviously a lot of good guys, but it's a different level when you get to the Olympic Trials. Everyone in the race has run a PR as fast or faster than you. That was the situation I was in in 2012. We were a little more conservative there and just made sure we were right at that top five or whatever with the automatic placement, make sure we had that in our sight. Make sure we had one more gear that last 100m to put myself in the right position. I made it by the skin of my teeth in the Trials. I think I was the second-to-last one through both in the first round and the second round."

Peter Callahan on moving on: "Really just to run to the tape. That's one that all the coaches across-the-board say, just run to the tape. When you're in the home stretch, if you are very much on top, you can let it up a little bit, but don't take the prelim lightly.

"Two is, once the prelim is done, just get it out of my head. I just got to get it out of there. Once you start saying, 'Oh, the other prelim went much smoother, they're going to be fresh.' Once it happens, you've just got to put it out of your mind and focus on the next round. Because once you start to overanalyze how hard you raced, or how much energy you had to use or things like that, then you're really wasting a lot of mental energy. I like to treat a prelim as very important when I am going in. I'll go through the mental steps, I'll be pretty meticulous about my preparation for it, but as soon as it's done, I act if it was just another day of practice, so I can mentally regroup for the next race. Because it's exhausting if you put too much mental stock into it after the fact. But get through it, and stay calm. If you need to run hard, run hard, if you don't need to run hard, don't run hard. Get to the tape, do what you need to do to get through, and then move on. Cross it off the list and move to the next round."

Ron Warhurst on making it through: "You got to get to the next one, or else you're not going to run any farther. I like to run the rounds like finals. We experimented with Nick Willis in London. Not experimented, but we did two things. Let the first one go, sit back, and let it go. And then kick like hell like you always do. In the semis, I said, 'You've got to run the semis like you're going to run the final. You've got to be in it the whole way. You've got to be there. You can't lay back, you can't be on the curb in traffic. A quarter to go you've got to be in the top three or four. You can't be ninth or tenth like you usually are. You got to have free rein. And you got to kick with them when they go at 300m. You've got to wait for 100m, and then you surge down the straightaway, and then you relax and look around.'

"In that race, from 600m out, Willis ran a 54-second quarter, and then he sprinted the curve and the straightaway. And that's how the final was going to go."

Ruth Wysocki on qualifying and rocket science: "Tom Sturak was the first person that ever pointed out to me. He said, 'Ruth do you realize, you have always made the final?' And I'm like, 'What are you talking about?' He said, 'Championship races, you never *don't* make the final.' Now the only time I didn't, that I remember, in 1976 I made the final of the [USA] 800m, and I ran the 1500m, and I didn't make the final there. But he said, 'You always make the final.' And I said, 'Yeah, but I bombed a good bit of finals, too.' And he said, 'Yeah, but you're always in it.' And I started thinking, 'Holy cow, I do make the finals.'

"I don't think it's rocket science. I truly, truly believe that in the 1980s and 90s, there were too many women that really thought they were that fast and that they would save it for the final. Way too many people try to run that semi final saving something. I think Suzy Hamilton and Regina Jacobs are classic examples of it. They would play games in the semi, trying to get through it as easily as they could. And from the time I started training with Vince O'Boyle, his advice to me every time was, 'You run the semi like it's the final. You don't save anything, because if you do you might not be in the final.' And deep down I knew that I was strong enough. Most of these races you run the semi then you have a day off before you run the final. You've got to go for it or you're not going to be there.

"I think sometimes the Americans, again, I think Suzy [Hamilton] had some amazing wheels—her 800m speed proved that. She was very, very quick but I think there were too many times in qualifying races – and not to just pick on her, she was just an example of this – these gals would run these races and they would sit back thinking, 'Boy, I'm so fast I can outsprint people all the time.' But there's a difference between outsprinting people with a 62 or 63 last lap and all of a sudden being in an international race where everyone on the starting line can do that. If you're holding out for that 100m or 150m, it's a pretty equal playing field. And so with Vince, we practiced this, using the backstretch and moving from 300m out, and not playing games and waiting for that last home straightaway bid. We tried to have it decided before that."

Gabe Grunewald on keeping your eyes locked on the prize: "When I'm running rounds, I'm generally not going to control the race entirely but I try to stay close to the front. It's really easy for me, because it's just a matter of focusing on where I need to be, whether I need to be in the top two or whatever. It's really simple. I try to stay close to the front, and if I'm not close to the front, I have to make up as much as I can over the last 200m. If you have your eyes locked on what you need to do to make the final, I think then it's actually a bit easier to mentally prepare yourself for that situation.

"There was a time when I would always go for second place in my prelim because I didn't feel I always needed to win it. That's not really the best habit to get into. I'm definitely one that has counted in the last 100m and made sure that I know which place I am in, absolutely. My college coach always told us – in college, so it was a little different – to run our prelims like the final. That's kind of what I aim to do, outside of the needing to win part."

Ron Warhurst, on being in position to respond to the leaders: "Ninety-nine percent of the prelims aren't going out in 1:55. They'll be between 1:57 to 2:02. 1:55 to 2:02 is a hell of a difference. If it's 2:02, you're dealing with a cluster. Everyone's there. And then you better be in the right position or you better wait. If you're at the 800m mark, by the time you get to 500m-to-go you better find your butt out of trouble and on the outside, ready to run. If you're there with 500m to go, coming down the homestretch and heading for the bell, you better be on the outside and cranking it. Or be in position to know where the leaders are.

"When you get stuck behind people and you're going down the straightaway, you can't see what's happening up front. It's a mess. There's 3-

4-5-6-8 guys in front of you. All you see is backs and heads. There might be three guys in front that have made the break down the straightaway, and you don't know it. You head into the turn and then you see they are 15-20 yards up on you.... You've got to be out to see what's happening. If you come down the straightaway and you're in ninth place, there are three guys up front. By the time you get down to the end of the straightaway, you might be trapped on the curve, but these guys might have opened up 30 yards. You don't know that, because you're in the back. If you're on the outside with 500m to go, you can see them make that break. And then you go. If you're in a cluster, not looking, and you're looking the wrong way, you come out of the next straightaway and these three guys have got 30 yards on you. And then you're going, 'Oh crap,' and you're still stuck on the inside.

"When you're looking at their shoulders, if guys are making a break, you can see it. If you're on the outside, you don't have to worry about running into a mess. You know you've got free range. Nobody's going to jump out on you.... You've got to be looking; you can't run blind. If you're involved in looking to win, being in the top two, those are the things that you have to be aware of. Always find out where other people are. It doesn't matter who they are, but it's *where* they are. If there are three bodies up front, and they make the break, it doesn't matter who it is."

Andy Bayer on making mistakes: "Last year [2013] at US champs in the 1500m, I felt like I was really dumb the last 10m. I had kind of taken it out a little bit in the beginning just to make it honest. But I think Lopez Lomong won and Ben Blankenship was second. And I was right on him in third, and maybe 5m to go, I was like,'Oh sweet, I'm third,' that was automatic [qualifying]. I kind of eased up, and Miles [Batty] caught me with less than half a step left. He beat me probably similar to how much I beat him at NCAAs. I didn't make the final. I would say, had I run through the line, I think I likely would have made it through for sure. I was stupid."

Bayer was running in the third of three heats. The three time qualifiers made it out of heat one, with 3:41.70 being the last one. Timewise, the third heat was very close to that pace, but this isn't horseshoes. Lomong (3:41.52), Blankenship (3:41.66) and Batty (3:41.69) grabbed the three automatic qualifiers. Bayer's 3:41.77 missed out on a time qualifying position by 0.07.

Sarah Brown on saving it for the final: "It's not like you have to win your round, but you have to be prepared that it's not going to just feel like a walk in the park. At the level we're running, anything can happen. You're almost more nervous for a round, because in the final you're there and you just have to execute. In the round I think you can overthink things, and all the different scenarios, so I think you're little more on edge going into rounds.

"Why save it if you don't even make the final? So I am not afraid to go for it.

"You know it's funny what you can do on the home stretch, because I have counted runners, I have thought, 'I need to get this person.' I don't know if I have ever been in the scenario where I could necessarily let up."

Ruth Wysocki on when she looked around: "Home straightaway. Last 50m, usually, you're kind of taking a glance around. Let's say I'm in a race where five go on, I'm not going to just sit there in fifth place, but if I'm in third, and I can sense that nobody is there, I don't care if I win, as long as I move on. But that would come in the last 30-40-50m. It was just as the last two steps are taking place. I don't care from third or fourth, as long as I am getting in."

Peter Coe's advice to son Sebastian for the 1980 Olympic 1500m heats: "Be in touch with the leader, no more than a stride down going into the last bend, and run wide almost into the second lane, so that if anybody tries to go past they have to run really wide, and you still have the space to respond and go past the leader if you need to."[3]

The finish of the faster semi at the 2012 Olympic Trials. Seven made the final, the last qualifier being Jordan McNamara (third from left). Daniel Clark (not seen in picture) missed by 0.08. Garrett Heath (left) missed by 0.18. Two other runners who were in the top four with a lap to go failed to qualify, as the top seven all produced a last lap of 54.06 or faster.

Chapter 9: Racing Indoors

"There is a great difference between running indoors and outdoors. I can't run the same way indoors as I do outdoors."

—Filbert Bayi,
after the LA Times indoor meet in 1975,
where he let Steve Prefontaine
do most of the leading

Racing indoors can be a different art entirely than racing outdoors. Certainly, in decades past, one could say this with great conviction. Many indoor tracks were small, 160 or 176 yards in circumference, making milers run 10 or 11 laps. They were usually banked, made out of wood, with nothing on top but the occasional layer of paint. They bounced under the runners' feet. Figuring out how to run on such a track was a real challenge for the neophyte.

These days, the small board tracks are virtually gone. In their place, the pros run on banked 200m ovals, with a wooden base often covered in synthetic materials that make the grip more sure. Still, the runner has to become comfortable with the energy return that the somewhat bouncy surface can give, as well as the challenge of running on banked turns. It's not as dramatic a transition as the long sprinters face indoors, but it's still important for distance runners to master.

Most college facilities feature flat 200m tracks that tend to be much easier to handle for the young runner, though they still pose some challenges.

Passing can be tougher than outdoors because the straightaways are shorter. Running wide could add more distance than outdoors because there are twice the number of turns. The turns, though shorter, are tighter. The runner needs to think carefully about how to time a kick. Obviously, going with a lap to go is an entirely different experience than using that same plan outdoors.

More and more, we are seeing colleges install 300m oversized ovals, both for economic reasons and their advantages vis-à-vis NCAA qualifying. Nothing really could come closer to racing outdoors, with the biggest challenge facing runners being the awareness of just where they are in the race, since the 200m and 400m marks are not in the same place every lap. Since so many runners are used to thinking in those units, it can be a little confusing when implementing a race plan.

However one slices it, indoor racing does raise some different considerations for the miler. It can pay to have an awareness of what they are before the race, instead of after.

Racing Indoors: Race Histories

2001 L.A. Invitational Men's Mile:
Lagat guards the lead

The importance of being in the lead with a lap to go is seen in many indoor races, and was perhaps even more essential back in the days of the smaller tracks (10 and 11 laps per mile). One such case came in 2001 in an indoor match that showcased Bernard Lagat (still a Kenyan then) and one of the top Americans at the time, Jason Pyrah.

Lagat, who had won the Olympic bronze the summer before, followed rabbit Clyde Colenso for the first half, passing through in 1:58.8. Pyrah ran right behind him. Said Lagat, "Jason is a great runner. And he is very strong on the last lap, so I didn't want to have to outkick him."

With three laps left (160y track), Lagat took off. Turned out that Pyrah had also been planning a move for that point. The American tucked in and made a split-second decision to wait until the last lap. Said Pyrah, "My coach will probably kill me for that, but we were moving pretty fast. I waited until the last lap, but Bernard wouldn't let me by."[1]

Results *(20 January 2001): 1. Bernard Lagat (Kenya) 3:57.61; 2. Jason Pyrah (Nike) 3:58.20; 3. Jonathon Riley (Stanford) 4:04.30; 4. Ryan Hall (California HS) 4:09.46; 5. Ricky Ethridge (unattached) 4:17.89.*

2009 NCAA Indoor Women's Mile:
Brown's persistent kick

Sally Kipyego captured her ninth NCAA title the evening before with a win in the 5000m. The Kenyan fully expected to make it No. 10 with the mile. With all the confidence in the world she set out on a strong pace, hitting 440y in 67.6 and halfway in 2:16.3. Sarah (Bowman) Brown lurked a step behind, just thrilled that the pace was hard. "She took it out," says Brown. "At that point I knew I was in shape, and I just wanted to run fast. I was really excited that she was going after it because I was like, 'Wow, she's going to pull me through to a good time.' "

Brown tried to pass Kipyego numerous times over the last two laps.

Brown's margin at the finish was a mere three-hundredths of a second.

With two laps to go, Bowman started challenging for the lead as the two left the field behind. Kipyego ran wide where she needed to in order to maintain her grasp of the lead. The last lap was a knock-down, drag-out battle. "I just remember thinking, 'I'm just going to hold her off and outkick her at the end.'" Some of these races, you just know you feel good. But she definitely had a little more of a kick and started running wide, and I had to do a little more to get around her."

Brown kept chasing, and amazingly, never seemed to lose heart. She summoned all her strength on the final stretch and edged Kipyego at the line by inches. "I was able to get around and get the win, but looking back, I might've needed to start kicking a little bit earlier, because I waited a little bit too long for indoor track. Indoors is definitely a lot different. It's a lot harder to get around, and you have to sometimes make the move a little bit earlier. Once you get around, the other person then has to work to try to get around you. So it sometimes plays to your advantage on an indoor track."

Brown had spent at least the last lap-and-a-half trying to get around Kipyego. "I'm sure I was testing the waters, in indoor track you do that sometimes just to see if you can get around," explains Brown.

Results (14 March 2009): 1. Sarah (Bowman) Brown (Tennessee) 4:29.72; 2. Sally Kipyego (Texas Tech) 4:29.75; 3. Kellyn Johnson (Wichita St) 4:34.41; 4. Pilar McShine (Florida St) 4:36.87; 5. Brie Felnagle (North Carolina) 4:37.00; 6. Lennie Waite (Rice) 4:38.60; 7. Brenda Martinez (UC Riverside) 4:39.58; 8. Charlotte Browning (Florida) 4:40.25; 9. Sheila Reid (Villanova) 4:40.99; 10. Natalie Sherbak (Virginia Tech) 4:41.40.

Racing Indoors: What They Say

Don Paige on running the boards in the 1970s: "We trained on a board track at Villanova. So when we raced indoors, it was a piece of cake. We were very used to the boards, the banking, how it all worked. The beauty was, when we went indoors, we took off two layers of clothes and ran in shorts and a singlet. We had been wearing double clothes training outside. So I think we had an advantage in racing on a board track. The key is to stay healthy. And so you have to really work on that when you're training on a board track. I trained through the whole indoor season. It was all part of my training. I never backed off."

Heather Kampf on fighting back: "You get in the front, it's really hard for other people to pass you. Because as long as you push just before you enter and exit each curve, nobody's going to get around you. So that was our strategy going into that prelim is just get in front, control the pace—you don't have to go crazy, just make sure that every time somebody challenges you, you fight back."

Eamonn Coghlan on the difference between indoors and outdoors: "The tactics are totally different running indoors and outdoors. Indoors requires a lot more acceleration to get by a runner very quickly because of the short straightaway. Outdoors you don't have that problem. Your speed can be more sustained."[2]

Sheila Reid on liking indoors: "I really like indoors. I feel like my running style—my gait—is conducive to it. I just like running around an indoor track. I find it easier to even run from the front that way. I mean I love outdoors, but indoors is different. I'm more willing to be in the front of an indoor race than an outdoor race. Plus I think 400m to go on an outdoor track seems a lot more than two small laps to go indoors. I don't know if there's any psychological research behind that, but going at 400m indoors doesn't seem as scary as going at 400m outdoors."

Actually, Reid is absolutely correct. One of the fundamental dictums of applied behavior analysis is that difficult tasks become more manageable when broken into smaller steps. So yes, to most people, running two consecutive 200m laps seems somehow easier than running one 400m lap.

Ron Warhurst on indoor high school miles: "In the mile, you've got maybe two kicks. You see kids, they break out of the pack, and they're behind a little bit, they make a big run to get back in second. That's fartlek; you can't run 64 for 400m, and then run 29 for 200m, and come back in 36, and then come back to 30. You're done. You're cooked. You've got to be 64-64-63-62. It's much easier to do it that way. I just think they have to be taught to be relaxed. Position is important. You can't be too far back. Indoors, you can't run in lane 6 around the curve. You need to be in the front or in the back until it thins out. It always thins. It never has occurred in a high school race after 800m that it doesn't thin down. It might start off the first lap or so with four across, so either be at the front part of it or behind. I look at it like this: the best place to be is either up front, or right behind the pack, because after three laps, it just thins down. And then you can just move the way you want. The point of it is not to panic. Folks say you've got to get out and get into position. If you get out and get into position but you're stuck on the outside, that's not position. You're better off to stay back and practice coming from behind. Unless you're a 4:05 [high school] miler, go up to the front and burn them off."

Todd Harbour on the indoor difference: "You're expending more energy running indoors even on the great tracks they have today compared to when we ran on 160y and 176y [tracks]. Watching Eamonn Coghlan run—it was a thing of beauty to watch him run indoors. Or Marcus O'Sullivan – those guys were just so talented and so good at it. I was in [Coghlan's] race where he broke 3:50 and I was back running a PR at 3:56.48. I hated indoors. It didn't feel the same. It didn't even feel like you were running. Almost like it was a different sport but that's just how I look at indoors. That's still pretty much how I look at it, as far as coaching it. We try to take it, and get what you can out of it, making sure they're training and staying strong for the outdoor season. But to me it's a whole different animal, I mean, how you race indoors. There are some people who are great indoor runners, but aren't necessarily great outdoor runners."

From left: Steve Scott, Ray Flynn, Sydney Maree, and John Walker running on an oversized flat track in the 1980s.

Amanda Eccleston on racing the 300m track: "I actually race a lot on 300m tracks, and I honestly haven't raced very much Division 1 at 200m, which I would say is a little more intense just because of how close everyone is. I do think it plays into your tactics a little bit, especially when trying to make your final move. A lot of times in outdoors, milers will make it with 100m to go coming off that last turn. But when you're indoors, sometimes that last straightaway is only 30-40m and you don't have a lot of room, so you sort of have to make moves a little bit earlier. I know when I'm on a 300m track, I actually like it, because making a move with one lap to go is a little bit easier because it's only 300m. It seems like when you're racing that's just a very natural point to go. You can usually carry your kick around a lot better. The fields are generally smaller, I think that helps. In general, sometimes I prefer indoor. I don't think it's that much slower. I know Nick Willis has said that too. Especially the 300m tracks, because those turns are not that tight, there's no wind, and really no weather to worry about. Sometimes I think you can run faster on the indoor tracks."

Kyle Merber on the indoor challenge: "Outdoors, so much can happen in the last 100m on the straightaway, but indoors, the final straightaway is maybe 50m long. So you don't have as much time to get around people and move around. I think that whoever's leading with a lap to go has a lot more of an advantage than would be the case outdoors. It's harder to get around and you have to force someone up into lane 2. So it's always been my strategy getting to the bell first as opposed to waiting a bit longer like you would outdoors. Additionally, tactical races can be really, really brutal indoors. Jogging in lane three on a banked track, that takes a lot more out of you than being just on the outside of lane 2 on an outdoor track. You're running up higher on the bank and running a lot further outside. With double the turns, it just adds up."

Steve Scott, on trying to beat Eamonn Coghlan indoors: "When there were times when I could not beat somebody with my kick, then I would have to try to utilize a different tactic, like with Eamonn Coghlan, of course. He was such an exceptional indoor runner with a short stride length, so he could handle indoor turns a lot better than me with my longer legs. I would try different tactics with him. But he did have that superior acceleration. He would just accelerate really quickly, get by you, get into the lead, and then basically hold you off.

"So I did have to try a lot of different tactics to beat him. I would try to take off early, or try to take it in the middle. In Ottawa in 1981, I was in the lead, and I was feeling good. I was pushing pretty hard. And I knew he was in trouble. And he came up on me, and he had that acceleration. He actually fouled me, he cut in on me on the turn, and I had to break my stride. I was holding him off; he should've run wider on the turn. That became very tactical for me, because I knew he had that quick acceleration. I pushed on the straightaway, knowing he was going to make that move, so I would hold him off. But no one is going to disqualify Eamonn indoors. He cut me off, I wasn't able to chase him down, and he won the race. I was quite upset with it."

Coghlan won that Ottawa race in 3:57.9, and Scott protested publicly. Afterward, Coghlan said, "I apologized to Steve afterwards and he told me the next time he'd make me eat the track. He doesn't like to lose."[3]

Thomas Wessinghage on the adjustment from small board tracks to 200m banked ovals: "I spent many winters in California, starting in 1978-79, for training and indoor racing. And I experienced those small tracks, 11 laps to the mile. With those small tracks it is quite essential to be up front in the last lap, or shortly before the last lap. Which quite rarely happened to me because normally there were the likes of Eamonn Coghlan or Steve Scott to prevent that. When I got back to Europe the 200m banked tracks were somewhat between those American wooden tracks, and the outdoor tracks. But of course it was quite important even on the 200m banked tracks to not leave it too late with your kick. So the tactics were a little different. My aim normally was to be in the front at least before the last bend. Maybe going into the last lap and taking the lead or taking it on the back straight. That worked out well quite often."

Katie Mackey on being aware: "You just need to realize that there is less room to move, especially when you're used to having a whole 100m to really dig in, and it can feel kind of weird to be kicking in on those indoor tracks where you know it's 100m to go, but you still have a whole curve. It feels different, so I think indoor races, just realizing that there's less room, and the straightaways are shorter. You really have to recalculate when you're going to make your move. There are more bodies, it's a little bit smaller, getting boxed in can be a little more of a problem. So I would say, just be a little more hypersensitive to everything that you would be already sensitive to on an outdoor track."

Andy Bayer on the effect of banked tracks: "Indoors you only have a 50m homestretch, so you can't save your move for it. If I'm going to sit on someone and outkick them, normally I would go earlier, like 150m to go on the backstretch, rather than saving it for the homestretch. There's normally not enough room for you—even if you're flying—it's not a whole lot of room to get around a guy and ahead of him in that short period of time. So I would make my move a little bit earlier. Other than that, [racing indoors] is not a whole lot different. It's a lot better to stay on the rail indoors at least early on, because running up those banks can be a little tiring, if you're out in lane 2-3. I feel like the bank just kind of sucks you into the rail anyway. It's hard to stay up there when you're not running a sprint race or whatever."

*Steve Prefontaine, running the banked boards in Portland in 1974,
where he clocked an American record 8:22.2 for two miles.*

Cory McGee on the fun of indoors: "I think that you approach indoors differently, in a sense. Maybe tactically, I put myself into a different mindset in terms of being competitive and making sure that I put myself in position. And I don't run timid. All those things just stay the same… But I find indoor to be a lot of fun. I think that the atmosphere and the setup are really exciting, and it's a fun time of year, and the places and locations you travel for indoor are always great. In that sense it's a different approach. I guess I have a little more fun indoors. I don't take it as seriously as I do outdoors."

Paul McMullen on being a big guy on a banked track: "The only place I could run fast was Notre Dame, where it was five exact laps to the mile. I ran against Laban Rotich, he was 5-4 and weighed 98 pounds. We ran in the Garden in 1998. I was second place and ran 3:57. I'm weighing 180 pounds. That guy weighs 98 with a lot shorter stride, lower center of gravity, and you're running on the outside of a basketball court. There's a significant disadvantage for the tall guy. That was the last time we got to run on the boards. We were running on painted plywood. It wasn't Mondo rubber on top of plywood. And I figured out how to run those corners, by changing my stride as we went into a corner. I practiced that at a gym in Kalamazoo so I could figure out how to do it, so I could run very fast, and sort of chop my stride a little bit as we went around a corner and figured out how to use the spring in the wood to sort of launch down off the banked corner onto the backstretch, and kind of get a little pop. And once you're in position on an indoor track, and I'm in front of you, it's almost impossible. You can't even get by me. My shoulders are too wide. There's no space. You'd have to go way up on the outside, but at that point, no one is passing me."

Grant Fisher on his plan to win the New Balance mile in 2014: "Conserve energy, and 1200m, get into the lead. For one lap, defend the pole position, and with a lap to go, just go into all-out, because a lot of times the mentality is still that you're on a 400m track, but it goes by pretty quickly. More quickly than you think, being on the 200m track. So the key was to have the pole position with a lap to go because we discussed it and we thought that if I have the pole then no one can pass me with a lap to go. That was the plan, and it was kind of defense for a lap and then offense for a lap."

Filbert Bayi on indoors being better than nothing: "I like the indoor meets because they are better than staying home in Tanzania doing nothing. But running indoors is completely different than outdoors. The Americans are usually the better indoor runners because they have a more compact stride and handle tight turns better. I prefer to stretch out more and that's why I'm a better outdoor runner."

"I know the corners. They're really tight, but I know how to run them. He'll have to see how they run them by following us... He's going to be playing in our field."
—Bernard Lagat, on his 2006 match-up at Millrose against 5000m/10,000m world record holder Kenenisa Bekele. Lagat won in 3:56.85, nearly five seconds ahead of runner-up Bekele.[4]

Kevin Sullivan on aggressiveness as an advantage: "In general you've got to think things through a little more indoors. There is typically closer proximity, more jostling, it's tougher to make really decisive moves—or I should say—it's tougher to respond to decisive moves. I think it's easier to run away from somebody indoors if you make a good move, just because it's harder to accelerate and keep that acceleration on the tighter turns of the indoor facility. Indoors can certainly play to your advantage if you're an aggressive runner."

Gabe Grunewald on the difficulty of passing: "It's harder to pass people on the indoor track and it's hard to make that really late move on an indoor track. It's harder to time that kick. So I think that you want to probably be in your position a little bit earlier than you would on an outdoor track. I think that front running indoors is going to work out probably a little better. It's probably smart indoors, because it's hard to get around people. And if you're leading indoors, you're not dealing with wind or conditions or anything like that, so it can be really smart move to lead more often indoors than you would outdoors. Moves are harder to pull off indoors, because it's a little different timing your kick, and those straightaways are shorter, the turns are tighter. It condenses those moves at the end of a race."

Sonia O'Sullivan on indoors being like any other race: "I don't think I ran indoors regularly enough to really have figured it out. To me, I just treated it like any other race. You're always a bit worried that you're going to get boxed in coming off the top bend. I know when I ran in the World Indoors in Paris in 1997, I was in the lead and came off the last bend and ran wide and got beaten because I did that. If I had done a lot of indoor races, I would've been a bit more tactically aware and not run wide. It seems indoors, that the inside lane is a lot shorter than the outside one because you are also throwing yourself up a little bit of a hill."

Chapter 10: Racing Behind Rabbits

*"It's not fair to the rest of the runners in the race
if someone is running
to set a record pace just for a few."*

—*Filbert Bayi[1]*

Personally, I'm not a big fan of rabbited races, though the directors of the Diamond League circuit are convinced fans love them. Rabbits make every race a record chase—and while it can be great to see a fast time, rabbited races yield few surprises. Throw away the stopwatch and just look at the race, and most rabbited races look similar. First couple laps, the rabbit will be a few strides ahead of the rest of the field, leading with a pace that's usually a hair too fast (sorry, unintended pun). Then, if the director has arranged for a second rabbit, that one takes over after the first one peels off, and carries the field to around 1200m. Then that one stops and the designated winner, no hand holding now, sprints to a fast time.

I always wonder about that second rabbit. I mean, 300m to go and they drop out? Aren't they curious what they could do if they just tried to finish?

I maintain that if you need the clock to tell you that you just watched a good race, it wasn't much of a race. And a rabbited event is more of a time trial than a test of racing skill. The argument has also been made that runners who run regularly in rabbited events have not built the skill set they need to do well in non-rabbited, championship events. Over the years we have seen a number of top runners who show extreme discomfort or even fail miserably in championship races that are slower than they are accustomed to running.

All the same, sometimes there are rabbited races that can be quite interesting from a tactical point of view. Usually, it's when the race fails to follow the script. Occasionally there are rabbited races where tactics come into play ever so slightly because the designated winner has a real challenger. And rarer, but not unheard of, are championship races where certain favorites have—perhaps unethically—arranged for rabbiting services. We'll look at all those situations here.

Racing Behind Rabbits: Race Histories

1980 Koblenz 1500m:
A mistake leads to a world record

Very often in the rabbiting game, there are missed cues that affect the efforts of the athletes involved. Ironically, sometimes there is a very big upside to this. Following the Olympics in the year 1980, the rest of the season was about breaking world records. Both Sebastian Coe and Steve Ovett were at their zeniths, and in the tit-for-tat battles that record chases were in those days, the last major 1500m race of the year offered an opportunity for Ovett to grab sole ownership of the 1500m world record that he shared with Coe because of an odd rule technicality. (The FAT on Coe's 1979 performance was 3:32.03, while Ovett's from July 1980 was a slower 3:32.09. However, at IAAF rules at the time rounded both marks to 3:32.1)

Thomas Wessinghage had to stay home while the British fought for medals in Moscow; the West Germans had joined the United States in its boycott. As he recalls, "Later in the season when I was always in my prime, there was that traditional meet in the small town of Koblenz on the Rhine. Steve Ovett and Andy Norman came up to me again and said, 'This is the last race of the year, so why not try again for a hard race?' And Norman brought that 800m runner, Gary Cook. He was supposed to take the first two laps and then, 'You should take over, Thomas.' That's what we did. But because I had some experience that it was not so easy to run just behind the pacemaker and then take over for yourself, I made the suggestion that Steve Ovett would run the first two laps behind Gary Cook and I would sit in the third position and take over after 900m or 1000m."

Cook ran on target, hitting 400m in 55.6 and 800m in 1:53.0. Five runners ran in his wake, tightly packed in single file. "Cook left the track at right about the 900m mark, and Steve Ovett was in front, which he didn't like. He looked down and looked around his shoulder and so I took over on the bend before the 1000m mark (2:23.9) and then hit it hard in order to catch up with the schedule. We thought we were too slow in the beginning. The splits that we heard were not quite correct. There was a little discrepancy between the splits we heard at the 400/800m marks and those we'd get from 200/600/1000m [on the other side of the track], so I thought we were too slow. And that's why I ran quite hard from the 1000m mark on."

Wessinghage led through 1200m in 2:50.69—slower than the 2:49.5 that Coe ran in his record, and about the same as the 2:50.6 that Ovett had split in July. Four men remained in the front, Omar Khalifa having just dropped off the furious pace. Wessinghage, though glad to hammer the pace to help out Ovett, his friend, was never expected to drop out. He held the lead through the last turn, forcing Ovett to work hard to pass him. Perhaps the most surprising aspect of the final stages is that Wessinghage's two countrymen, Harald Hudak (PR 3:36.1) and Willi Wülbeck (PR 3:36.05), ran right on Ovett's heels.

In his autobiography, Ovett later admitted that because so many people were together on the last lap, he was sure it must have been a slow pace: "World-record thoughts poured out of my mind as fast as the Rhine flowing alongside the stadium as I concentrated on how to beat the four competitors who should not have been there."[2]

With 100m left, Ovett finally made it to the lead. Wessinghage did not fold; he kept pressing. Hudak ran wide in an attempt to sprint to his own upset victory. Ovett, stealing glances toward Hudak on his right, had to fight for every step. With 15m left, Hudak faded a bit, but Wessinghage kept the pressure on, finishing less than a stride behind Ovett. All three had broken the world record. That Ovett had done so—not a surprise. Wessinghage—not inconceivable. Hudak—a shocker by any definition.

Results (27 August 1980): 1. Steve Ovett (Great Britain) 3:31.36; 2. Thomas Wessinghage (West Germany) 3:31.58; 3. Harald Hudak (West Germany) 3:31.96; 4. Willi Wülbeck (West Germany) 3:33.74; 5. Omar Khalifa (Sudan) 3:34.11; 6. Dave Moorcroft (Great Britain) 3:39.70; 7. Klaas Lok (Netherlands) 3:40.16; 8. Ingomar Falk (West Germany) 3:41.40; 9. Hans Allmandinger (West Germany) 3:41.49; 10. Henning von Papen (West Germany) 3:42.07; 11. Kip Rono (Kenya) 3:42.46; 12. Peter Belgar (West Germany) 3:42.82; 13. Jón Didriksson (Iceland) 3:43.37; 14. Joost Borm (Netherlands) 3:42.82; 15. Herbert Wursthorn (West Germany) 3:45.30;... dnf—Gary Cook (Great Britain).

1981 Oslo Dream Mile:
Harbour waits for the kick

Todd Harbour wasn't even supposed to be in the Dream Mile. He was supposed to race somewhere in Germany. The Dream Mile at the Bislett Games in Norway is the race where world records had fallen the two previous years. *The* gathering of the world's elite milers. Harbour, at the time, was a 22-year-old senior from Baylor University with a best of only 3:57.3. "I was the slowest guy in the race. I was the last person they let in." And even that took some doing.

As Harbour recalls, his friends in the Santa Monica Track Club went to bat for him. "I was not even going to go to NCAAs that year [he ended up going and placing second]. I was hurt. I had a calf tear. I was going home to take a break. [SMTC manager] Joe Douglas talked me into going. I ran down in Milan, a decent race, 3:38.28. So then Carl Lewis and Billy McChesney both called the meet director in Oslo. I had run 3:35.87 [at Oslo the year before], but I still wasn't good enough to get into the Dream Mile. They called the meet director behind my back and they told him if he didn't let me in, they weren't coming. We had pretty good little team. Johnny [Gray] was pretty young at the time. Carl still had not won his four gold medals, but he was pretty well-known. And Billy had broken Pre's records in Oregon. So they did that, and Joe comes in the room and tells everybody to leave and says, 'Todd, you're not going to Germany. You're going to Oslo.' I said, 'No.' He said, 'Yes, you're in the Dream Mile. So I was excited, and scared to death. I knew who was in that field. It was loaded. I don't think there was a better field ever.

"And here I am. I am kind of relatively unknown in this group. So I was just praying I wouldn't be last. That was my prayer."

The race had been set up as a record attempt for Steve Ovett, with the target being his own record of 3:48.8 from the previous year. Bob Benn, a friend of Ovett's, took the early pace. Ovett ran on his heels. However, after 200m, the only athlete close to Ovett was Harbour, clearly ahead of the rest of the field.

"I see where I got out, I was so pumped, I got out a pretty good. Then I said, 'Wait a minute, what am I doing up here?' Because I knew Ovett was going for a world record. What happened was, I relaxed just a little bit. My thought was I would just fall back into the pack."

Then Harbour found that a little relaxing had a huge effect. "The next thing you know one guy passes me. And then it's an endless stream. One guy goes past you, then the whole field goes past you." At the quarter, Harbour found himself in dead last. "I didn't want to be in last place running like that, because that would cost me too." Yet at halfway, he still ran in last. At the front, Tom Byers had taken over the pacemaking for Ovett.

With 400m left, Harbour finally moved out of last. "I had too much left. It was almost perfect splits—57, 1:55, 2:54. When I started to go with a quarter, Robson died at 350. He just died. And so I kind of had to slam on the brakes, so I could get past him. I got back going again, I was on the backstretch and I was moving pretty good. And then Coghlan died with about 150 to go. He hit the wall. So I had to stop again, and I lost a little more momentum. When I was coming on the home stretch I was moving on everybody. I'm closing, and pipping guys at the end, I wasn't that far behind Steve [Scott]. I ran 3:50.34, he was 3:49.68, which was the American record at the time. Joe came out and said, 'You broke the American record, but

*Harbour's big break into rabbited Grand Prix races
came thanks to his teammates on the Santa Monica TC.*

Steve got there first.' "

Harbour had run faster than Jim Ryun's legendary American record of 3:51.1. He had closed the race with a 55.2 final 400m, faster than anybody, Ovett included. He had beaten some of the sport's greatest legends: Steve Cram, Eamonn Coghlan, and Thomas Wessinghage. It would be the fastest race of his life. However, Harbour still has his regrets. "I just didn't run smart enough to put myself in a position to do a little better job on the last part of it... Instead of relaxing and taking my foot off the gas a little bit when I got out and looked at what I had actually done that first 150m, I would've said, 'Hell, I'm just going to sit on it a little bit, I'm going to go with it.'

"My confidence wasn't very high, I wasn't in good shape. I finished dead last in an all-comers meet the week before my conference meet that same year. I was in terrible shape. In my mind I was just not where I needed to be. I had missed six weeks of training. My race confidence wasn't very good. I was just getting through it, kind of just hooking it up and doing it. The Lord was really stepping up in a big way for me, but in certain situations I knew I wasn't at my very best. That's probably some of the why I backed off that first 150 like I did. I got in other races in Europe where I put myself up there, and ran a little smarter, ran more in the middle of the pack, but that one I didn't, I just went straight to the back, thinking, 'Okay this is where I'm supposed to be.' That's what it looks like."

Results (11 July 1981): 1. Steve Ovett (Great Britain) 3:49.25; 2. José Luís González (Spain) 3:49.67; 3. Steve Scott (USA) 3:49.68; 4. John Walker (New Zealand) 3:50.26; 5. Todd Harbour (USA) 3:50.34; 6. Steve Cram (Great Britain) 3:50.38; 7. Thomas Wessinghage (West Germany) 3:50.91; 8. John Robson (Great Britain) 3:52.44; 9. Eamonn Coghlan (Ireland) 3:56.50; 10. Tom Byers (USA) 4:07.72;... dnf—Bob Benn (Great Britain).

1983 AAA Championships Men's Mile:
The foul that backfired

This wasn't a "big" race in terms of payday or honors. For Steve Scott, it was a chance to prove his fitness and stamp his claim to being a favorite before the World Championships opened in Helsinki a few weeks later. For Brits Sebastian Coe and Graham Williamson, it was about testing themselves while vying for a spot on the British team for Helsinki. The race itself was a special invitational event that had been added to the British AAA Championships.

Perhaps because Williamson was seen by many as being in the second tier of British milers, after legendary world record breakers Coe, Steve Cram, and Steve Ovett, he was willing to take more chances. A solid 3:34.01 runner, he had covered the mile in 3:50.64 a year before in Ireland.

Despite the work of veteran rabbit Bob Benn, the race turned tactical early. No one followed Benn but Craig Masback, who would be a non-factor on the last lap. The real race, more than 20m behind, was led early on by Coe and Mike Boit. On the second lap, Scott took over, hitting halfway in just under 1:57. Benn dropped out, leaving Masback at the front, but moments later Scott put himself alongside the leader. Boit began to fade, and as they passed 1100m, Scott ran outside of Masback in the lead. Coe ran behind Scott, and Williamson behind Masback.

Williamson decided then to impress the British selectors. Even though he had no pathway at all to the lead, he charged at Scott and Masback and shoved his way between them (in his defense, there was perhaps four inches of daylight between the two Americans). Williamson took off sprinting like he had just robbed a liquor store. Masback, stunned, immediately dropped back.

Scott describes his reaction: "Instead of going around, Williamson plows right between us and pushes us both literally out of the way. It did kind of startle me. I was pissed. My first inclination was probably to go after him and push him over, but after I caught up to him, I thought that would be stupid. Honestly, it was such a ridiculous foul. It was dumb. It gets your adrenaline going when somebody does that. The first reaction was to go after him, and it actually helped me, because it got me going."

Williamson hit three-quarters in 2:58.37, with Scott a stride behind. Scott crushed him on the backstretch, and Coe followed past coming off the final turn. Coe, despite his credentials, had no hope of catching Scott on the final stretch—the man was on fire. He finished off his 3:51.56 with a 53.1 final 440y.

"I think [the Williamson foul] helped in beating Coe because it forced the pace to really get going from 500m out, close to when I was going to make my move. The longer that you drove with Coe, the better your chances. He had more 200-800m speed. He didn't have 3K or 5K speed, as I did.

"That's a perfect example of the roughness of European racing. If he had done that in America he would have been disqualified."

Results (23 July 1983): 1. Steve Scott (USA) 3:51.56; 2. Sebastian Coe (Great Britain) 3:52.93; 3. Graham Williamson (Great Britain) 3:53.96; 4. Eamonn Coghlan (Ireland) 3:57.61; 5. Craig Masback (USA) 3:58.02; 6. Mike Boit (Kenya) 3:58.57; 7. Wilson Waigwa (Kenya) 3:59.79; 8. Tom Byers (USA) 4:02.35;... 10. Chuck Aragon (USA) 4:20.97; 11. Brian Theriot (USA) 4:30.81;... dnf—Bob Benn (Great Britain).

1989 Golden Gala Men's 1500m:
Abdi Bile's world record lost

As the world's best runners converge upon Europe for the remainder of the Diamond League season, much of the focus will be on records. Especially in the middle distances and beyond, records are forged on the fastest European tracks more through careful orchestration than brute competition. Indeed, if competitive fire was needed to make distance records happen, fans would see far more of them in the Olympic Games. Rather, most distance records happen with a rabbit leading the way, and no medals on the line.

Abdi Bile seemed always stymied in the chase for Olympic gold and records. The Somalian great certainly had the talent for both. In 1987, he captured the World Championship title in the 1500m with a stunning 1:46.0 final 800m. Two years later, he outlegged Sebastian Coe at the World Cup in the British great's final 1500m race. Yet his Olympic history played out unfortunately. In 1984, as a relative unknown with two years of running behind him, he qualified for the historic Los Angeles Olympics 1500m final against Coe, Steve Ovett and Steve Cram—this despite having fractured his leg at the NCAA meet. However, he was disqualified after Brazilian Agberto Guimaraes failed to finish due to a bumping incident. Then, in 1988, when he should have been near his career peak, he missed the entire season because of injury. In 1992, the injury story all over again. Finally he made it back to the Games in 1996, but by then, he no longer had that killer kick; he finished sixth in the final.

Similarly, his chase for records, even behind the pacing of friendly rabbits, was equally unlucky. After his world title in 1987, he felt stung by some people saying that José-Luis González, the silver medalist, was actually the better runner and would have prevailed if the initial pace had not been so slow. So he aimed for a world record attempt in the 1500m at the Van Damme Memorial in Brussels. "I just wanted to show those people that I could win either way."

Trouble was, the weather didn't cooperate. Temperatures were below 60 Fahrenheit (16°C) at racetime and wet and windy. "That day it was raining, it was cold, it was freezing, and when I got there, I just said, 'Oh my goodness this is crazy. Maybe you just have to change your mind.' I thought if I could run 3:40, I would win. 'That's all you need!' And I just said no. I don't care if it's raining. I don't care if it's freezing. I'm going to go.

"I went to the front. I did and González followed me up to 800m, and he just died badly. I mean, I destroyed him." Bile's 3:31.80 indeed demolished the field. Jim Spivey of the U.S. salvaged second place more than five seconds back. Steve Scott was even farther behind (3:38.25 in fourth), and González finished sixth in 3:41.60. "That shows you how bad that day was," says Bile. "But I ran a time that showed that I could run in the cold and the rain and the sun." But had the weather gods smiled on Bile, that 3:31.80 might indeed have been a world record.

Two years later when he lined up at the Golden Gala 1500m, in Pescara,

Italy, he still had his eyes on Saïd Aouita's world record of 3:29.46. Bile's best was 3:31.71 from two years earlier, but he had just come off a victory in Oslo's Dream Mile in 3:49.90, a 1:44.68 in the 800m two days later, and then a PR 2:14.51 in the kilometer. He felt ready, very ready.

The Pescara race had been orchestrated for a record. Briton Ikem Billy and another would do the early pacemaking, and Tony Morrell would then take the field to 1200m. It started well: 55.52 at 400m, and 1:52.94 at 800m. "I was feeling so good, and the pace was just right on," recalls Bile, who passed those posts at 56.0 and 1:53.6. Then, with more than 400m left in the race, Morrell started slowing. At the same time, Bile wanted to stretch out his long legs and unleash a long kick. He passed the 1100m mark in 2:35.8, and would need a 53.6 finish to get the record, a split that seemed very achievable given his history as a kicker.

"With one lap to go, the pacemaker was slowing down, and I tried to tell him, 'Get out! Get out! Get out! Move out!' But he didn't move out. He stayed there. And I'm trying to pass him from the outside, the inside, push him, saying, 'Move! Move! Move!' and he didn't move. I think he was thinking he just wanted to get to 1200m to get his money." Bile couldn't begin his kick because of the obstruction, and his frustration grew throughout the penultimate turn.

That's when Bile, worried that the record would slip away, decided to get more aggressive. He launched a major drive to get past Morrell as they came off the turn approaching the 1200m mark. But when Morrell hit 1200m, he slowed and veered to the outside of the track, putting him on a collision course with the World Champion. Says Bile, "When I tried to pass him on the outside, he tried to move out. So he pushed me, and we ran together all the way to lane eight. I [had to] stop."

It had all happened quickly—the snafu can be seen in the video, though somewhat obscured by the discus net. Yet it is clear that Bile suddenly found himself out of the race, at a near stop, and out of world record contention. "By the time I ran all the way out to lane eight, the people who were behind me already came and passed me."

Kenya's Wilfred Kirochi had gotten well ahead of Bile, with Italy's Gennaro Di Napoli now running even and New Zealand legend John Walker a step behind. It took 80 meters for Bile to get back into the lead: "I came back again, and I caught the people, and I passed them." He stormed around the turn and to the finish as the clock ticked away. At the line, he led by nine meters in clocking a PR 3:31.20 ahead of national records for Kirochi and Di Napoli. He missed Aouita's global standard by 1.74 seconds. His final lap took 55.4, a split that included the bumping out to lane 8 and the loss of his momentum. "Still, I ran 3:31.20, which took a little bit with all the stopping... and chasing people—a very bad race."

That Pescara race is almost lost to history. Though Bile would run a faster time later in the season—3:30.55—he probably never had a better chance to break the world record than he did in that Italian city by the sea. He would end his season, and his career, without a world record. The reporter from the Italian paper *La Stampa* recognized something special in the 26-year-old's performance that day: "Bile always remained close to the leaders, deciding to produce a performance of great historical magnitude. And when he stretched, majestic as ever, in the last 250 meters, he created a vacuum no one could fill."

Long ago, Bile, now a coach for the United Arab Emirates, made peace with the lost opportunities in his career. "There were always some problems and some confusion, but still I managed to run some good times and still win."

Results *(7/19/1989): 1. Abdi Bile (Somalia) 3:31.20; 2. Wilfred Kirochi (Kenya) 3:32.57; 3. Gennaro Di Napoli (Italy) 3:33.33; 4. John Walker (New Zealand) 3:35.96; 5. Alessandro Lambruschini (Italy) 3:37.25; 6. Branko Zorko (Yugoslavia) 3:37.74; 8. Davide Tirelli (Italy) 3:38.29.*

2000 Olympic Games Men's 1500m: El Guerrouj and his rabbit

Back in 1993, world record holder Noureddine Morceli, who did not like to run in traffic, was accused by some of arranging for a rabbit in the World Championship final. Fellow North African Mohammed Taki led with splits of 60.85 and 1:59.32 before Morceli took over. Whether or not that was planned cannot be established. The splits weren't really very fast, and it doesn't look as if the course of the race was affected dramatically.

Six years later, though, the track world saw a real case of rabbiting at a championship meet when Hicham El Guerrouj, Morceli's heir to the title of the world's fastest miler, successfully managed a rabbited race to win the World Championships in Seville with a 3:27.65.

So it was no surprise when El Guerrouj planned another rabbited race for the Olympic final. Says Kevin Sullivan, "We were pretty confident in exactly what was going to happen, particularly the way El Guerrouj had been running his championship races for the last few years. As soon as one of the other Moroccans made the final, we were pretty sure where it was going to get set up where Baba would take the pace for El Guerrouj. And sure enough, that's exactly what happened.

"It's funny. Actually we were standing in the tunnel waiting to walk out on the track in the final, I'm lined up beside El Guerrouj and he turned to me before they walked us out and said to me, 'Kevin, first 100 meters, no shoving, okay?' And right there that pretty much told me that he was getting out as hard as he could. At least that's how the first 600m played out."

The only ones to get in the way of the two Moroccans were the two Kenyans, who tangled with them in the early going and made sure they also got away with the rabbit. Showing mixed potential at rabbiting, Youseff Baba got out a little too fast with his 54.14. He followed that up with a 60.62 (1:54.77), then ran out of steam. "Baba actually relaxed too much in the next 400m. The way you see the video, it's actually pretty strung out for the first part of the race, and then all of a sudden the field kind of comes back together till 500m to go, when El Guerrouj was finally at the front, and then he started to crank up the pace and string it out again."

El Guerrouj had hoped he would have the strength to take it from the 800m. He led through a 56.90 lap (2:51.67), but was unable to shake the Kenyans and France's Mehdi Baala. Coming off the final turn, they went for the kill, and Noah Ngeny gradually edged ahead on the final straight to score the upset.

Did El Guerrouj blow it by using a rabbit? Perhaps not. In a tactical elbows-out race he might not have even finished in the medals. That style of racing had never been comfortable for him, as he was weaned and weakened on the safety of rabbited races on the European circuit.

Sullivan: "I just let a couple of guys put too much room between me and the medalists."

For Sullivan, who ended up a respectable fifth, the lesson learned was one that would serve anyone well in a Diamond League race: "I knew going into the final it was going to be fast, and it was going to be a matter of getting in line and holding on.

"The one mistake I made, I was in pretty good position when the field bottled up again, and when El Guerrouj made his move, I let two guys get by me, so I was back in seventh by that point. By the time I got back past them, there was such a big gap to the medalists that it was almost impossible to get close enough to take a run at Bernard—at that point, Lagat was probably the one guy that I could have caught. I had already beaten him a couple of times that year. That was probably the tactical mistake I made. I just let a couple of guys put too much room between me and the medalists. It was tough after running two rounds, the pace isn't going out at 3:32 pace, and it's tough to get yourself in there at some point."

Results (29 September 2000): 1. Noah Ngeny (Kenya) 3:32.07; 2. Hicham El Guerrouj (Morocco) 3:32.32; 3. Bernard Lagat (Kenya) 3:32.44; 4. Mehdi Baala (France) 3:34.14; 5. Kevin Sullivan (Canada) 3:35.50; 6. Daniele Zegeye (Ethiopia) 3:36.78; 7. Andrés Manuel Díaz (Spain) 3:37.27; 8. Juan Carlos Higuero (Spain) 3:38.91; 9. John Mayock (Great Britain) 3:39.41; 10. Jason Pyrah (USA) 3:39.84; 11. Driss Maazouzi (France) 3:45.46; 12. Youseff Baba (Morocco) 3:56.08.

2002 World Cup Men's 1500m:
Another rabbited championship

Just two years after the Sydney Olympics, though, the track world saw another case of rabbiting at a championship meet. At the World Cup in Madrid, Bernard Lagat—still a Kenyan then—represented the Africa team. Hicham El Guerrouj had been the original African entry, but he withdrew, handing the spot to Lagat. At the start, American Seneca Lassiter—Lagat's training partner—sped to the front, and led Lagat through world record-worthy splits of 53.42 and 1:50.20 before he moved out and slowed to a jog.

That broke Lagat, Estévez, and de Souza away from the chase pack. When de Souza imploded, it became a two-man race. On the final go-round, Lagat accelerated and left Estévez floundering. He broke Steve Ovett's World Cup record by 3.25 seconds.

The most interesting part of the race took place over the next 24 hours, with all sorts of indignation and accusations flying. The infraction was serious because this wasn't a typical European circuit race. The World Cup (since replaced by the IAAF Continental Cup) was set up as a team scoring competition between continents and countries. Lassiter's obvious assistance to Lagat, followed by his last place jog, cost the United States points (the

U.S. finished fourth overall, seven points behind the Americas team).

Lagat, who earned $50,000 for the win, admitted the pace was arranged. "There was nothing financial involved; he is my friend." Lassiter initially denied being a rabbit, but admitted and apologized the next day. According to British reporter Simon Turnbull, Steve Ovett watched from the stands and said, "What was that about?"[3]

Results *(20 Sep 2002): 1. Bernard Lagat (Kenya/Africa) 3:31.20; 2. Reyes Estévez (Spain) 3:33.67; 3. Mehdi Baala (France/Europe) 3:38.04; 4. Youcef Abdi (Australia/Oceana) 3:41.01; 5. Franek Haschke (Germany) 3:41.58; 6. Michael East (Great Britain) 3:41.88; 7. Abdulrahman Suleiman (Qatar/Asia) 3:42.27; 8. Hudson de Souza (Brazil/America) 3:42.58; 9. Seneca Lassiter (USA) 4:05.82.*

2010 Commonwealth Men's 1500m: Team Tactics or Accident?

Given recent history, it perhaps seems sensible that the Commonwealth field in New Delhi deferred to the Kenyan contingent as pacemakers. Silas Kiplagat had the fastest time in the world that year at 3:29.27. James Magut, only 19, had run a stunning 3:36.8 at altitude. And Gideon Gathimba had run a 3:50.53 for third in the Bislett mile. As has happened before and since, the presence of three well-credentialed Kenyans in the final created the impression that team tactics would play a factor. While the race certainly may appear that way to the viewer, the real question here is what affected the outcome of the race more—the tactics the Kenyans used, or the perception among their opposition that they were going to use team tactics?

At the gun, the Kenyans went to the fore, and ran three abreast for the first lap, a slowish 59.89. Behind them, defending champion Nick Willis tucked next to the rail. A 62.32 second circuit brought them around in 2:02.21. Kiplagat had slipped to third, running comfortably next to Willis; the Kenyans still controlled the race. That control of the race boiled down to the pace being slow to benefit the kickers, and perhaps keeping the most dangerous runner (Willis) boxed in.

Yet is that even a valid assessment? When the vast majority of championship 1500s are run at a slow early pace, how hard did the Kenyans have to try to make it that way? Was anyone present who didn't want it slow and was willing to work toward that end? As for Willis, he's a man who loves to run along the rail behind the leader, which generally makes him a poster boy for being boxed in.

At the bell, Australian Jeremy Roff had moved to third. The pace sped slightly to 1200m (3:03.27), as Roff applied pressure to the leaders. Kiplagat, coming off the turn, found himself in a box behind Gathimba, with Willis on his left and Roff on his right. He decelerated just enough to get to the outside of Gathimba's feet, then bumped off of Roff on his way to the front. With

Kiplagat racing in Berlin.

250 to go, he exploded—that was the game plan he had been prepared for by coach Moses Kiptanui.

Roff and Gathimba faded around the final turn as Kiplagat stretched his lead out to win by 0.49. Willis never left the curb, and finished well for third behind Magut. Britain's Andy Baddeley finished only sixth, but was brutal in his self-assessment to the BBC: "I ran like an idiot. There's no excuse for that. I don't know how I ended up where I was."

Perhaps what threw the Brits off was the perception that the greatly faster Kenyans would set a burning pace. As Tom Lancashire said, "I couldn't believe it was so slow for so long. It sort of lulled me into a false sense of security."

James Thie added, "The race never kind of happened. We thought it might have gone out faster with the three Kenyans in it."

Kiplagat didn't give any indication to reporters that the pace was planned and that the presence of the three Kenyans at the front was anything but coincidence: "The pace was slow, so I wanted to push the pace. I started sprinting at 200m. Usually I sprint at the 50m but they went slow." Perhaps Kiplagat would have been unbeatable that day no matter what the pace. His final 400m took 53.0, his last 200m, 25.2.

Results (12 October 2010): 1. Silas Kiplagat (Kenya) 3:41.78; 2. James Magut (Kenya) 3:42.27; 3. Nick Willis (New Zealand) 3:42.38; 4. Chaminda Indika Wijekoon (Sri Lanka) 3:42.93; 5. Gideon Gathimba (Kenya) 3:43.11; 6. Andy Baddeley (Great Britain) 3:43.33; 7. Jeremy Roff (Australia) 3:43.53; 8. Tom Lancashire (Great Britain) 3:43.58; 9. James Thie (Great Britain) 3:44.25; 10. Andrian Blincoe (New Zealand) 3:44.47; 11. Mitchell Kealey (Australia) 3:44.57; 12. Alastair Hay (Great Britain) 3:44.61.

Racing Behind Rabbits: What They Say

Filbert Bayi on setting his own pace: "Whenever I run, I'm not out to break a world record. I'm there to have a good time and to win a race... and I don't like those rabbits, those pacemakers.... My feeling is, if you're going to run in the front like that, at the pace, then you've got to be prepared to stay there. It's not fair to the rest of the runners in the race if someone is running to set a record pace just for a few. How can you keep a pace for someone else? If I run, I keep a pace for myself.... I like to set my own pace—but I don't like it when people call me a pacemaker.... What I know is what everybody knows. And what everybody knows, I don't know."[1]

Francie Larrieu Smith on whether rabbits make a runner a weaker competitor: "I think that on the international level it's a whole different thing. They even do the rabbits for the women now. I think that when you put the rabbits in the race, it changes the race. In my day there was only one person they put a rabbit out there for and that was Mary Decker Slaney. We never had that dynamic in a race, and so I don't know how having that would affect things. At the same time if every guy goes to the line knowing who's going to be taking the lead, for how long, and at what pace.... So they just sit back, find their position and wait for the first guy to drop out, and wait for the second guy to drop out and then it's a free-for-all on the last lap. When you don't have this situation at a World Championships or an Olympic Games, nobody's practiced how to run without a rabbit. So you go to the line and it's who's going to be the sacrificial lamb? Who's going to take out the race?

"It's very rare what happened in the 800m with David Rudisha— somebody runs from wire to wire in the lead and wins. And that was a truly amazing performance. But it's very rare that that happens. Nowadays in the middle distances at the international level, they're not practiced at how to run that way in big meets."

Jeff Atkinson on wasted energy: "In my day if Morceli wanted a rabbit, you would just hang on, that's the first thing. In my fastest race the opening lap was 57, which is very fast by modern standards but I was at the tail end of the pack. The rabbit was 53 or 54. I was hanging on for dear life. I just went 58-58-58 after that, and it just felt like a real drill-down the whole way. So in that sense, yeah, you're basically hanging on the whole way. There are three things: stay on the inside as much as possible next to the rail, draft as much as possible, and be as even-paced as possible.

"You know, people talk about tactics. There are no tactics; there's only one correct way to run a race, and anyone who says otherwise isn't paying attention. It's straight physics. If you want to fire a cannon ball as far as you can, the barrel of the gun, the cannon, has to be 45° – not 46, not 42. That's the physics of it; that's the math. All that crap. Running is the exact same thing. The idea is to draft the whole way, to run on the rail the whole way, make no extra effort any which way, and run even pace the whole way with a slightly faster last lap, and that would be the best you could do. If you look at any sort of time trial in cycling, it is exactly that way. It's the straight physics rules that can't be broken. So if tactics mean anything, they should try to approximate the ideal physics of the event, and anything else is wasted energy. So all that going out fast, going out slow, doing a surge, all that's just a big waste if it doesn't serve, like I said, trying to replicate the physics."

Paul McMullen on dealing with rabbits that aren't hitting the pace: "These rabbits, they get in the way, but they got their contracts. [When the pace slows] I'm like, 'Dude, you didn't do it, get out of the way.' "

Kyle Merber on racing behind rabbits: "I think for some guys it's just about getting out there, sticking with the rabbit, and kicking. I don't necessarily like getting out very fast. I'm a big fan of negative splitting, so in all of my races it was about getting out a little slower and working up into the field a little bit, taking advantage of the straightaways. Going wide and just passing the guys one or two at a time and just clicking them off. It's a little bit different of a strategy because it's not bunched up. If you're up with the rabbit, maybe you're going through at 56 seconds, but if you're in the back of the pack, maybe you're running 59-60. It's less positioning and more your personal choice of strategy."

Sheila Reid on the pros and cons of rabbited races: "I'm a racer, I'm not much of a time trialer—at least I've never run a decent time trial in my life. So I'm kind of biased to enjoying racing, pure racing, more so than running in rabbited races, but there are some benefits to rabbited races. Of course, I benefited from a rabbited race at Prefontaine [2013, when she ran a PR and made the World Champs A standard], especially since the pace was so quick that it strung everybody out. We had enough space to run as fast as I could. And I obviously see the benefit in terms of chasing times or standards or records or what have you. But at the end of the day you need to learn how to race because that's what the championship races are all about. That's what every single prelim is about. I much prefer racing and I see a lot more value to that than chasing a time."

Jenny Simpson on her 2009 breakthrough to 3:59.90 in a rabbited race: "It's funny because I always said that was kind of a perfect storm; it was a lot of things coming together at once. Two or three years later I appreciated it even more. Because the 1500m is super-tactical, and is an incredibly variable race, depending on the personalities of the competitors and the mood of the race as it kicks off the first 200-300m. But to be so inexperienced and naïve, it could not have turned out better for someone like me in that race, someone that had a high-level of potential ability but a very, very, low level of experience. I think we went through with 400m-to-go at 2:57. I don't think that I was ever on the outside of somebody for more than just the time it took the pass. And that's really, really unusual and I think it's fair to say that tactics were not really an issue in the 2009 Prefontaine race. I think one of the reasons I ran really fast was that it didn't require technical knowledge."

Steve Scott on the downside of rabbited racing: "That is kind of the sad thing about [Diamond League] racing these days. They're all world record attempts. Tactics go out the window, there's a rabbit. There's a 55-second first 400m, and then they go through in 1:50 or 1:51. Get a new rabbit or a second rabbit, and then one or two guys are trying to get the record. I think it hurts a lot of people because that's all they're used to, and then they get into a world championship or Olympics and don't know how to race.

"The only tactic that comes into play [in a rabbited race] is going out and getting the pace that is optimum for you. I remember there was a race in Germany and Sydney Maree, he did the first lap in like 53. God, that was suicide for me. I was back. I went through in 57 or 58, somewhere around there. He had four or five seconds on me in the first lap. The field was all spread out. If I were to hold it together mentally, I would have run him down at that pace. You have to have patience. You're not going to catch him until the last lap, so don't even try. What happens is people start getting impatient. They start getting tense and start tightening up, running a pace that really shouldn't get them tired. And then if you do go out with them, you're racing

Simpson upon realizing she broke 4:00 at the 2009 Prefontaine meet.

at a pace you're probably not prepared to run. I mean, I've never prepared to run 53 for the first lap of a mile or 1500m. So I think that's the only tactic in a rabbited race, going out in a pace that works for you, and also, making sure that you have patience to know that you can still run them down in the end."

Leo Manzano

Leo Manzano on his 1500m PR in 2014 at Monaco: "In these types of races, the pace just goes out screaming. For me, I was just trying to stay as relaxed as possible, knowing that I was going to be running faster than I've gone before. The key to my record was to just stay as calm as possible and don't make too many moves so that you are conserving that energy and being more efficient about your tactics."[3]

Jenny Simpson on the bother with rabbits: "Rabbits are a really strange phenomenon in racing. I don't think that they're a bad thing because they certainly serve a purpose. But they can be [a bad thing]. And you don't know until the gun goes off and oftentimes we're in racing situations and the rabbit is somebody we don't know. It seems that there are very few 1500m races for the women that are rabbited well. I'm especially nervous when we're standing on the starting line and the rabbit doesn't have a watch. It just seems to me that if you're practicing splits, then you're doing it with a watch. And if you're not doing it that way today, it just makes me nervous that you're not going to do it right... The task is so simple, to see who can run the fastest from this point to this point. And [the rabbit's] presence has the potential to really politicize something that should be seemingly so simple. Because you have to go too slow, or somebody asked for a fast pace, and agents are involved, and the meet director, and oh my gosh. It's funny. It's interesting to me because I never in my career, all the way through World Championship and Olympic experiences, I never ran with a rabbit until a few years ago as a pro. There are moments when I'm so grateful for them. And the Prefontaine Classic [2009] is a great example of it. We had a perfect rabbit that did a perfect job of it. And then there are times I think, why do we bother with this? It makes our life so much more complicated; it's not worth it."

Gabe Grunewald on how to handle European racing: "There are some situations with a women's field where it doesn't even go with the pace, and that's when it does get tactical. Like in Monaco in 2013 where I ran my PR. It was a superfast track and good conditions, but I don't think our pacer went out as fast as anybody expected, so at that point it became sort of a long, long kick to the finish rather than just a long pace type of PR situation where you're just hanging on at the end. It's just a mixed bag. You're in so many rabbited races and you expect the field to go with them; you think if you go out toward the middle or the back of the pack you'll be okay. But sometimes it just doesn't work out for whatever reason and that it's tough to get around all those people again on the third lap. I've started to learn that being a little closer to the front is generally going to work out better regardless.

"In my experience, most athletes will view the European races as opportunities to PR, and not worry as much about race tactics or where they finished. You can see people get 10th place in a race and they are happy that they PRed still. They don't care that they got 10th. So I kind of see it that way, and as a place to do things outside of your comfort zone.... I think winning is always good, but I do think there is little more of an emphasis on running fast in Europe."

Katie Mackey on bad rabbits: "One of the things, when I was in high school, when I was in college, and my first couple years as a professional, is that I didn't really realize what percentage of energy you can save by drafting. In cycling it's as extreme as 30 percent; in running I've heard that it's 6-7% energy that you actually save by drafting off of somebody. The rabbits become more important because you want to try to save that 6-7% for the first couple of laps whenever the rabbit is in there.

"But I think the thing I would say about rabbits is that I haven't actually gotten into that many races where the rabbit has run the pace they said they were going to run. It's almost always slow, especially in women's races. At least at the level of races that I am running, the IAAF challenge meetings and down. Even the rabbits I have run with in some of the Diamond League meetings have run really uneven splits, for example, out too hard the first lap and really easing off the pace on the second lap to make up for it... Everybody is depending so much on the rabbit, and if they don't do what they say they're going to do, then the difference between going through 800m at 2:10 and 2:14 is the difference between maybe a 4:03 race or a 4:07 race. And it can be really difficult. This year I missed getting into some of the Diamond League races that had really good pacing, and so it's been kind of hard to run some of those faster times because the races haven't been fast or the rabbits have been a little slow the first 800m. Obviously, that's not only the rabbit's fault. I mean, everybody in the race has a responsibility to make the race how they want it to be. But with the rabbits, and knowing that you can save a little bit of energy, and knowing that sometimes you have a better chance to win if you don't go out and put it all out there. It all kind of blends together and plays in.

"Even in some of those Diamond League races, the pacing can be really off. The men rabbits, I will say, generally do tend to run more close to what they say they are going to. There's a guy on our team, for example. Matt Scherer, who has been an amazing rabbit over the last years he has been doing it. He has decided to retire and not do it anymore this year, but he could get it down to a tenth of a second. There are not really any women rabbits out there, that I know, that can regularly be relied on to get it to a tenth of a second."

Katie Mackey competing indoors.

Kyle Merber on the challenge of even getting into a rabbited race in Europe: "Getting into the right race makes such a difference. There are only a few opportunities—if that—each year to set your PR. My 1500m is 3:35, but the fastest 1500m that I was in this year [2014] was won in 3:38 and was won by myself. So there aren't always opportunities to run. It's not like the 100m where as long as the weather's good you can run a fast 100m. It's a lot more dependent on how a race is set up and getting into the right race. I think that's something that a lot of people forget about in the 1500/mile, is there are a lot of variables that need to be controlled in order for a race to go as fast as people would like. It's not only competitive once you get into the race, it's competitive to *get* into the race itself. That was something that was really interesting in Europe that I had never really realized before. In college, if you run a good enough time, you get your chance at regionals and nationals, whereas in Europe and on the pro circuit, it's hard to prove you're good enough to even get the opportunity to try to get good enough."

Kevin Sullivan on the predictability of circuit races: "When I was on the circuit, especially with El Guerrouj, you knew every time. He was going to ask for 1:49, 2:46 maybe quicker through 1200m, and you were just going to get in line, wherever you slotted, and were going to run as hard as you could. There wasn't a whole lot of tactics behind it. You were either on or you weren't."

Thomas Wessinghage on the event's dependence on rabbits: "When I was brought up as a runner, I only knew sit-and-kick. I was brought up as a runner who really didn't care about times that much. I liked to run a good time, but I never went out to run a fast time as a youth. Only after having been with the [senior] men for a few years, did I develop the feeling for fast paces. That went according to a change in TV commentating, I believe. Because whereas in former years, in a race with a close pack, the commentators said that, 'The tension is building now, everyone is still in contention for the last lap.' That attitude changed, and I had a few races with the national team where the leader started out with a lap of 58 and the commentator said, 'Well that's quite a mediocre split for the first lap and more or less forget about the race, it won't be very interesting.' That was quite disappointing for me at that time because I always found races with a close pack more interesting. So even during my time the concept had changed.

"In 1981, Steve Ovett and Sebastian Coe broke the world record for the mile and that was a completely different [type of race]. They had a rabbit. They started out behind the rabbit, and they took it out hard and never saw anyone during the race but the rabbit. And we had to adapt, of course. But then again before those days the rabbits were somewhat illegal. The executive director of the IAAF, Adrian Paulen from the Netherlands, found that having a rabbit in the race changed the course of the race. That is why he declared that rabbits were more or less illegal, so in those days we usually had to run without rabbits. [In 1980-81] the meet promoters tended to bring rabbits again into the races and then the course of the racing changed again. We would have three rabbits who would take turns: one would go for one lap, and lead for the second rabbit. And [the second] would go to the 800m mark. And then the third rabbit would run the third lap. So really, perfect strategies for a fast time.

"If you're adapted to that and you've been brought up like that, then a championship race with no rabbit is a complete change. You, of course, will be quite unaccustomed to those slow races, and I would think that is the problem right now. There are only two solutions for a runner who knows that he can go fast with a rabbit. First solution: he takes it out himself hard from the beginning or from mid-point or wherever. Second solution: he gambles and sees what happens. And you never know what happens in a slow race with a fast kick in the end. What we live to see now has been experienced by former generations of runners. We see perfect runners who present themselves perfectly in championship races like Hicham El Guerrouj or Noureddine Morceli before him. And then we have top runners lose the gamble of the slow race with a hard kick."

Kyle Merber on racing on the European circuit: "I had heard from so many former teammates and friends about how you go to Europe and you don't necessarily know where you're going to go next or what heat you're going to be in. You don't know what's going on even. You race multiple times each week and you just jog in between. It's kind of chaotic. One of the big reasons I wanted to go over this year was to get that experience and figure it all out. For me, luckily, I got into a bunch of good races and it was in a few week period when I was feeling great. It was, you know, just exciting. Every time you had a race, you turn around and look at a calendar and it's two more days until your next race. It's kind of different, because you're not really working out at all. The weather is good and there are tons of fans there. The races are faster and it makes it fun. You don't really get nervous anymore. By the third race, the pre-race jitters are gone, let alone by the fifth."

Chapter 11: Tools in the Toolkit

"One never knows with Filbert."

—*Erasto Zambi*
coach of Filbert Bayi

One of the biggest differences between high school and higher level competition is that athletes must get comfortable with running in a more crowded pack.

The most dangerous runner in a championship race is the one who can win from the front or the back, or any number of strategies in between. Being unpredictable enough to keep your opponents guessing can be a great advantage. Not only that, on occasions when you are in a race and you are not the favorite, you may have to adapt to a certain strategy that is most effective against a certain competitor. Therefore, in addition to preparing your body to compete, you should also prepare your mind for various approaches to the race. The more tools you can put in your toolbox, the more effective you will be in competition.

In addition to being tactically versatile, the successful competitor should have at their disposal a number of racing skills that can help them in the heat of competition. The list below is by no means complete, and some of the entries may seem obvious.

Learn to use a variety of tactics. As indicated above, an athlete who can only kick, but is incapable of leading a race at a solid pace, is handicapped. The all-conquering racer is one who develops the confidence and skills to handle any type of race, and therefore be more unpredictable to the opposition.

Learn to start from the curved line. In high school in some states, you started 1600m races from a safe box, with a safe lane that you had to run in for the first 200m or 400m. Not so in college and beyond, where you start on a curved line, and cut in as soon as you can find an optimal path. Yes, it gets a little rougher. However, unless you want to start all of your races behind everyone else, it makes sense to get comfortable with sprinting at the start until you find your best position.

Get out hard for the first 40-50m. It's free. Research shows that whether the runner starts fast or slow at the gun, the amount of lactic acid building up in the legs at the start of the race remains basically the same. After that first 50m, it makes sense to settle into position in the pack and find a more sustainable race pace. Continuing that hard pace beyond 50m will lead to problems, so it is wise to practice this maneuver before the big race.

Learn to run in a crowd. For the younger runner, any opportunity to run in a crowded track race is an opportunity to practice essential traffic skills. And it's better to learn those skills in the leisure of relatively unimportant races than it is to hope to master them in an important race without adequate preparation.

Be careful about looking back during a race. Your competitors might take it as a sign of weakness, and gain new motivation from it.

Only make one big move. Your creatine-phosphate system is your gas tank for a burst during a race. It can recover from your opening sprint—that first 50m. However, later in the race, it is not capable of regenerating after a burst. So if you hit the gas pedal hard more than once later in the race—to catch up to the leaders, to break out of a box, to shake your pursuers— remember that you will most likely have nothing left in the tank when you hit the gas on the final stretch.

Use the stadium scoreboard. If you are running in a big meet that has a live feed of the race showing on a Jumbotron-style screen, it's not a bad idea to look up at the screen occasionally to see where everybody is in the race. This can be especially crucial if you are in the lead and otherwise are running blind.

Move out on the final stretch... or not. This is one of those cases where it helps to have eyes in the back of your head. If you are on the last straight sprinting to the finish, and someone is trying to pass you on the right, it can be advantageous to drift to the right a bit without fouling or cutting the opponent off. However, drifting to the right can be dangerous if someone is running on the rail behind you. You are potentially leaving a clear path for them to the finish by allowing them to pass you on the inside.

Always look for a clear passing lane—and take advantage of it. In a crowded race when it's time to kick, the competitor needs to be incredibly aware of the traffic patterns among the runners ahead. Is someone drifting to the right and opening up an inside passing lane? Are people accelerating from behind and causing you to be boxed in?

Learn to have faith in your race plan, and learn when to throw it out. The greatest attribute of many champions is their ability to stick to the plan. However, we also know that sometimes a race unfolds in an unexpected way, and the winning athlete is the one who can confidently switch to Plan B. Even in a matter like when to begin the kick, say an inside passing lane opens up that represents a golden opportunity. Do you stick to your plan slavishly, saving your kick for the planned point even though you may be boxed in then? Or do you jump early and take advantage of the opening?

Tools in the Toolkit: Race Histories

1996 Olympic Trials Men's 1500m: Was it settled in the semis?

On the surface, Paul McMullen's win in the Trials 1500m over heavily favored Steve Holman might look like a typical kicker's race. The dynamics of that win, however, were engineered much earlier in the rounds and even had their roots in the indoor season leading up to the Olympic year. Call it a grudge match. Steve Holman was the fastest man in the field and the darling of the media. A Georgetown grad, he was a favorite of TV commentator and former miler Craig Masback, who would later be the CEO of USA Track &

Field. McMullen was a Midwest guy, a former football player who had a reputation as a man who said what was on his mind.

The slight came when USATF set up the mile field for indoor nationals that year. McMullen had only run 4:01 that indoor season, missing the standard. Still, he hoped to run at nationals. The standard, after all, was not ironclad. According to McMullen, Holman was paid $5,000 to run, even though he hadn't even run a mile that season. And two foreign runners also were paid $5,000. But McMullen, the defending outdoor 1500m champion, could not get in. "I was shocked that I was not permitted to run my own national championship in the indoor mile. That made me very angry. I boycotted all the big races leading up to the Olympic Trials."

As Masback said in his NBC commentary before the final, "You can be sure that this is not a friendly rivalry."

So the Eastern Michigan grad did more overseas running than ever in preparation for the Trials, only paying attention when someone would hand him a quote by Steve Holman to tweak his focus. When he ran his prelim race in Atlanta, he felt decent, finishing a close second to his friend Jason Pyrah. "I recognized that Jason was in very good shape and he was going to be there in the final stretch, for sure."

Then came the semifinal, a race that put fans of McMullen and Holman at each other's throats. Says McMullen, "There is kind of a backstory related to the way I conducted myself down the homestretch with one Steve Holman. That race was in itself the final—mentally—for me and Steve.

"It was just a semifinal, but at the time I was able to mentally size up a race knowing all of the personnel there and being certain that my speed and tactical positioning would prevail no matter what happened. I can say there were only two times it ever happened in all the races I have run, where I visually saw all the race variables in my head and still could see myself winning. To me it was hard to do and until that day I didn't believe it was possible.

"So tactically how the race happened, in the first 100m I allowed someone else to take the lead, then I sat right on their outside shoulder running on the line of lane one and two. This allows you to police who goes to the front. If someone comes around you, just accelerate to their outside shoulder and repeat as needed. In this race Brian Hyde, who was also from Michigan, was leading. We weren't training partners or even friends as it was ironically the third time we ever raced each other. His pace was relatively honest, and with me on his outside shoulder, a box was created for one unfortunate runner right behind Brian."

That runner happened to be Holman. McMullen points out that Hyde probably didn't know all that was going on behind him because he was leading. But McMullen knew. "I peeked to the inside and I started to see Steve really panic as we rounded the 800m mark. Down the backstretch the panic spiked as Steve attempted to claw his way out. He literally ripped off Brian's hip number... to try to get out of there. And he ran into me a couple of times, but you can't really see this in the race because I don't break stride or shift laterally as he tries to push me.

"Most of the race that's going on and it was exactly what I wanted to do, to test him. At one point he asked me to get out of the box, but no one was cooperating because with just two guys in the front, you can usually get out.

"The conditions on the track that day were above 100-degrees [Fahrenheit] and no one wanted to let him out of the box and have him unduly tax everyone with a much faster pace. So it's not that you have something special against someone where you're going to have a fight after the race like in NASCAR. It was simply the goal set forth by my coach to demonstrate that I had the ability to control the race. And if we were successful in our demonstration, the final would go easier, so that's what we did."

Snell did it too

McMullen certainly wasn't the first to try to crush an opponent's spirit in the semi. Peter Snell described planning with his coach, Arthur Lydiard, to do exactly that in the 800m in the 1960 Rome Olympics:

"The real strategy began now. The heat was coming on. Arthur and I had heard it rumoured that [Roger] Moens had psychological problems, and, in fact, had never won a really big race. Largely on the strength of this, we decided that my tactics in the semi-finals, in which I was drawn against him, would be to attempt to win the race. On the psychological basis, that should put paid to Roger."

McMullen continues: "I literally just sat there and no one came around. Steve's final tactic was to hit the brakes until he found an exit in the back of the field and go all the way around. By the time he got back around, there was only 100m to go. As Brian naturally accelerated off the turn, I responded as well, and then, out of the corner of my eye, Steve appears. Up on my toes now, ready to drop the hammer should I need to, I look over at him and he is not relaxed, but in a sprint with a grimace on his face. At that moment I could see that he was afraid to lose. I could see the pressure to win the Olympic Trials was heavy and I was able to beat him if I wanted to.

"Then the monster that was created back in February raised its ugly head and I displayed terrible sportsmanship by raising my hands in the air with a smirk of arrogance some 50m to go in the race. I have regretted it every day since."

As they raced down the homestretch, McMullen, pointedly watched Holman's frantic finish and let up before the line, allowing Holman to win by 0.08. The incident led to controversy and confusion among fans of both.

McMullen thought back to his not getting invited to indoor nationals: "Steve had become sort of my totem as it related to my anger toward USATF. In retrospect I would have changed my behavior as I feel it tainted my performance. I worry now my kids might come across that video some day and ask questions."

The final: The runners waited under the hot sun for what seemed like 10 minutes as NBC broadcast its profile of Holman, the favorite. Then the officials took over, and the gun went up. The rest in McMullen's words: "Everybody goes off as they normally do. Nothing's too noticeable. I moved right into second place [behind Michael Cox], just kind of cruising along, and at one point—the people who are with it start to gain their position around 700m. Then they're going to hold that as long as they can. And the only moves that happen after 700m are relatively small to gain position. And so Jason Pyrah and I are on the front and we come into 400m to go, and I'm still holding that position and if you look at the tape, Steve Holman is in perfect position. He is in third place right behind me. Pyrah's on the rail and I'm in second. The bell goes off and that sort of Pavlovian response, where here-we-go kicks in and Jason is not allowing me, even though I ran 25.7 sec for 200m, he's not allowing me to get to the rail. He's that strong. Even though I accelerate and take it up to almost—finishing kick speed—I think the temperature on the track is 111 or something with around 85% humidity. I'm from Michigan and haven't even trained in this kind of stuff, I took a risk. At some point in the race, you have to risk all of it, almost... If you can stay with me, then I'm going to lose. But if you can't, it's too fast, too early, you're going to believe you can't make it. And so that was my tactic at that point, and then as I go down the backstretch, knowing that Pyrah is not going to give up the rail, I'm going to have to go past what he can go. And really expose myself to getting walked down on the homestretch, so I go one more time, almost up to 99% of what I had, into the rail, and let that momentum around the corner carry me onto the homestretch. Now there's no room for looking back.

"There is no sound that I experienced that I can recall, even though there are 40,000 people in the stadium and everyone is going to finish within .3 seconds. I can't hear them, I don't look back, I am simply a 100m runner from the end of the curve to the line, and it seems to take forever. And thoughts of 'That risk was too much,' and 'You're not going to make it' and 'A whole bunch of people are going to go by you' come into your head. 'Do I really deserve to make the Olympic team?' comes into your head. My grandfather somehow made his presence known in the last 100m, but he always believed in me and was the first person I told my secret to when I was about 20 years old, that I wanted to go to the Olympic Games. I didn't tell anyone else that. And then there is almost certainty at about 15m to go that you are not going to make the team. Because Jim Sorenson, who had trained in 110 degree weather, suddenly appears in my peripheral. I'm not even looking over at the guy, he's just that close to beating me. That memory of what happened at Bowling Green comes back again—that you're going to get beat by Todd Black again and your coach is going to be really mad at you. And you know what to do at that point and you shift your hips forward and prepare for that final 10m just like every sprinter does, where it's going to require a lean, and it's going to come down to a picture. You had better get all your weight forward on your toes and up on your feet to really create as much of a lean as you can and try not to fall. And it's difficult to do when you don't have that momentum, and those negative thoughts start creeping in, and all of a sudden the silence goes to a roar and you can sense that you were the first to break that plane. But you still don't want to believe it yet because it was so close.

"And then Jason Pyrah, he dove and hit the ground as well after the end of the race, and he ended up placing third. Jim Sorenson was second, and I was fortunate to win. And Steve [Holman] who was actually in the best possible position with one lap to go, faded to 13th. I believe each person is responsible for their performance, but I didn't help him at all, and certainly didn't believe in encouraging his confidence. I did my best to make the argument that I wasn't going to be beaten by anyone that day, especially by him. And that's tactics. That's what Steve Prefontaine did. He would make an argument against everybody he was competing against—that 'You do not have the ability to suffer, or take the risks that I'm about to take. Therefore, you will be with me for a while, then you will be with me no longer. Because I'm going to a place of hurt, which you're not mentally capable of.' You usually do not think that 1500m runs are that painful, but that one in particular hurt really bad, just because it was so hot."

McMullen, who ran 53.9 for his final 400m and 1:52.9 for the last 800m, ended up winning by only 0.02 over Sorenson, who was the real surprise of the race. Holman, who held third place into the final turn, appeared to jog in after he realized he would not make the team. His final 200m took 31.1; the previous one, 26.3. Asked on live TV what happened out there, Holman could only say, "I don't know." (NBC interviewed Holman after the race, and ignored McMullen.) This race—in perhaps extreme fashion—showed the psychological side of racing. What some have called "head games" are very real, and an effective racer should be sharply aware of the psychological component of competition.

Results (*23 June 1996*): *1. Paul McMullen (Asics) 3:43.86; 2. Jim Sorenson*

(Athletes in Action) 3:43.88; 3. Jason Pyrah (Mizuno) 3:44.03; 4. Erik Nedeau (New Balance) 3:44.11; 5. Brian Hyde (William & Mary) 3:44.13; 6. Andy Downin (Georgetown) 3:44.25; 7. Paul Vandegrift (unattached) 3:44.94; 8. Mark Sivieri (Georgetown) 3:45.35; 9. Jamey Harris (Reebok Aggies) 3:46.01; 10. Mark Dailey (PowerAid) 3:46.29; 11. Derek Treadwell (Maine) 3:46.38; 12. Matt Holthaus (Reebok Enclave) 3:46.98; 13. Steve Holman (Reebok Enclave) 3:47.44; 14. Michael Cox (Nike) 3:51.72.

1998 NCAA Men's Indoor Mile:
Two big, basic lessons

Every race yields its lessons. And while perhaps the winner might be able to say, "Yeah, that went perfectly," for everyone else in the race, a lesson stands to be learned. Even though Kevin Sullivan won this race, he acknowledges that he learned a big lesson in doing so. The previous June at the NCAA outdoor meet, he lost in a kicker's match with Seneca Lassiter of Arkansas. Still comebacking from Achilles surgery, Sullivan felt the real culprit was a lack of conditioning. However, that didn't stop him from wanting to serve Lassiter a taste of his own medicine.

In his pre-race planning and visualization, Sullivan focused almost exclusively on Lassiter. In the process, he neglected to think much about the rest of the field, which included Bryan Berryhill. Not that anybody can be faulted for overlooking the Colorado State runner; this would be the fourth mile race of his college career. Only a sophomore, he had just started running the mile, after a freshman year that saw him hit just 1:51.79 for the 800m. "I really didn't know much about Bryan Berryhill at the time. It was a breakout year for him," says Sullivan.

When the race got off, Berryhill put himself at the front of the pack immediately. "In the heats, he just went for the front, and then he did the same thing in the final, and instead I just kind of discounted him because I didn't know much about him and my focus was on Seneca," remembers Sullivan. Berryhill was joined by the looming figure of South African Clyde Colenso, all 6-2 (1.88m) of him. Colenso went to the fore and hit the 440y in 61.7. Lassiter ran sixth and Sullivan stayed right on his shoulder.

At the halfway point (2:05.2), Colenso moved outside to let Berryhill run alongside him. The two ran at the front as if they had planned it, side-by-side with no tussling over the lead. Sullivan, meanwhile, kept his eyes glued on Lassiter. Over the next lap, the Arkansas junior moved up to a position just behind the leaders. With two laps to go (3:08.6), Phil Price made a bold move for the front. That jarred Lassiter, his teammate, into action. Lassiter started to inch past Berryhill, with plenty of bumping between the two. Then the expected failed to happen. Berryhill, the rookie, neglected to get swallowed up by the pack. Having missed his cue, he fought his way back into the lead, passing Price with a lap to go.

Suddenly the kicker's match between Sullivan and Lassiter looked perfect, with one exception—Berryhill still ran at the front, and he wasn't letting up. "I figured that I was just going to sit on Seneca and let him make the first move, and every time we tried to go, Berryhill would just inch the pace up and inch the pace up and inch the pace up, and then you realized with 200m to go that this guy's not going away. It was almost a bit of a panic at this point, because you want to get past Seneca to get at the next guy, and neither one of us could get past Bryan."

With a half-lap left, Sullivan and Lassiter sprinted alongside each other, still a stride short of the upstart. On the final turn, Lassiter found himself boxed with Sullivan on the outside. "One of the things indoors, I always like to accelerate down the backstretch," explains Sullivan. "If you can get a jump on your competition into that last turn, it's pretty tough to come back on somebody with only a 50-60m straightaway. At that point, I was in a little bit of a panic because I wanted to get past Seneca to get to Bryan, because it was obvious at that point that he wasn't going away. He wasn't going to crumble." On the brief homestretch, Sullivan (on his way to a 26.3 final lap) still ran a half-stride behind his rival, with Berryhill looking like he would pull off one of the event's biggest upsets.

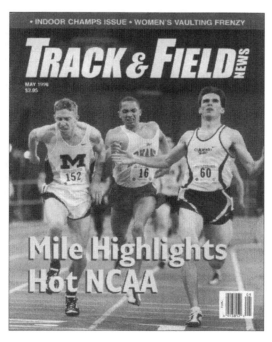

Berryhill's early celebration made the cover of Track & Field News.

Big Lesson Number Two: Remember we referred to Berryhill as a rookie? With five meters to go he still had a winning margin. The sprinters were gaining fast. With a meter to go, Sullivan and Lassiter began to lean. Berryhill, overcome with the emotion of the amazing race he had just run, began to lean also... backward, a look of victorious relief on his face. Sullivan's torso got to the line first, his eyes watching Berryhill in disbelief as the premature victory celebration cost the rookie the win.

"He eased up a touch before the line, thinking he had it won, and that's the great shot on the cover of *Track & Field News*," says Sullivan. "I'm leaning in there, and you don't know who won the race. You almost think Bryan won. That was a mistake. Bryan obviously made a mistake by not running through the line, but I made a mistake by not knowing my competition as well as I should have."

Results *(14 March 1998): 1. Kevin Sullivan (Michigan-Canada) 4:03.54; 2. Bryan Berryhill (Colorado St) 4:03.56; 3. Seneca Lassiter (Arkansas) 4:03.60; 4. Jonathan Riley (Stanford) 4:05.03; 5. Daniel Kinyua (Mt St Mary-Kenya) 4:05.28; 6. Clyde Colenso (SMU-South Africa) 4:05.79; 7. Phil Price (Arkansas) 4:06.61; 8. Todd Davis (Portland) 4:07.40; 9. John Jordan (Georgetown) 4:08.21; 10. Shane Bingham (Utah St) 4:09.76.*

2010 NCAA Women's 1500m:
The importance of maintaining contact

Emotionally, the pressure of this race at Hayward Field fell upon Jordan Hasay, though the favorite in non-Duck eyes had to be Florida State's Charlotte Browning. The Brit ran on the rail for the first three laps, and though she did not pursue a pure run-from-the-front strategy, she always made sure she was darn close. She took the initial lead off the start, but let Katie Follett (Mackey) edge ahead on the first turn. Though Mackey held a clear lead over the next 400m, she never got ahead enough to cut in to the rail. A bold move there might have changed the course of the race. Over the next lap, Mackey slowed the pace, seemingly inviting anyone else to take over. They bunched up so badly that Villanova's Sheila Reid tripped up and nearly fell. Approaching 1000m, the field got antsy, and Hasay made a move to the lead. Browning covered it, and remained on her heels as the field stretched out again. Well-positioned earlier, Gabe Anderson (Grunewald) had fallen back to seventh.

With 400m to go, Mackey started to fade, and Browning moved confidently alongside Hasay. The Oregon freshman gave her best on the backstretch—pulling away to the beat of fan noise—but with 200m to go, Browning had caught up again, edging her way into a clear lead for the first time in three laps. For the most part unchallenged, Browning sped to a solid win over the field.

The biggest story on that last stretch came from Grunewald, who came off the turn in fifth and still ran two strides behind Hasay with 50m to go. She ignited the final strides, leaving Sheila Reid behind and passing both Pilar McShine and Hasay, finishing a couple of strides behind Browning. Had she been closer or started sooner, the ending could have been very interesting indeed.

Says Grunewald, who produced the fastest last lap at 62.33, "I knew that my kick was pretty powerful. I was prepared for both types of races, but I think it was a situation where nobody really wanted to lead and push the pace and I was okay with it. I remember thinking, with about 600m to go, that I just needed to be calm and relaxed and stay towards the front. There was a little bit of traffic on that last lap because everybody was kicking at a different pace. I remember starting to get around people. I went from fifth to second in like the last 100m. So it was important to me to get off the final bend, and have that space open up so I could kick into the second position. I think if I positioned myself a couple of places higher in the third lap, I might've had a chance to actually win the race. The way that it played out I was coming from a little bit farther, more middle of the pack, and I think second place was the best that I could finish, given where I was."

From left: Jordan Hasay, Keri Bland, Pilar McShine, Gabrielle (Anderson) Grunewald, Katie (Follett) Mackey, and winner Charlotte Browning.

Results *(12 June 2010): 1. Charlotte Browning (Florida) 4:15.84; 2. Gabriele (Anderson) Grunewald (Minnesota) 4:16.25; 3. Jordan Hasay (Oregon) 4:16.43; 4. Sheila Reid (Villanova) 4:16.66; 5. Pilar McShine (Florida St) 4:16.72; 6. Karly Hamric (West Virginia) 4:17.78; 7. Lauren Bonds (Kansas) 4:18.06; 8. Lucy Van Dalen (Stony Brook) 4:18.42; 9. Keri Bland (West Virginia) 4:19.98; 10. Katie (Follett) Mackey (Washington) 4:20.19; 11. Alex Kosinski (Oregon) 4:20.93; 12. Brenda Martinez (UC Riverside) 4:25.60.*

2013 NCAA Women's 1500m:
Don't box me in

With no clear favorite in the race—none of the top three from the previous year were present, and indoor mile champ Emma Coburn was concentrating on the steeplechase—it's no surprise that this race boiled down to tactics. Specifically, boxes.

The first 1100m can be summed up fairly easily. Arizona State's Shelby Houlihan ran from the front, leading through steady 69.1/69.1 laps. At 2:18.2, it was a respectable pace that didn't shake up the field at all. Then, Houlihan made her gambit on the third lap with a 67.6. A bit of an increase, but not enough to break the race open.

Behind her, Cory McGee of Florida ran steady. Oklahoma State's Natalja Piliušina ran in the middle of the pack, seemingly unconcerned with positioning. At the bell, Houlihan drove harder, creating enough of a gap behind her to free McGee—on the rail—from the box she was in. McGee chased hard, passing Houlihan halfway down the backstretch, and building a lead convincing enough that it just might hold.

With 200m to go, McGee had a stride on the fading Houlihan, and another stride on the pack of five that had effectively blocked off Piliušina. McGee maintained that margin, while at the top of the curve, Piliušina seemed more hopelessly boxed than ever. With 100m to go, it looked as if McGee would be victorious, as Piliušina still was trapped behind a wall of runners. But Amanda Winslow, running in lane 1, started to fade. Amanda Mergaert shot past her and moved to the rail for a clear path to the finish. Piliušina wasted not a moment, following Mergaert through the gap and then weaving back out to lane 2. She passed McGee with 30m to go, closing with a 14.7 final 100m (McGee finished in 16.1).

"Probably with 150m to go, I thought, 'Well, I guess I'm going to finish fifth or sixth,'" said Piliušina. "I didn't think there was any way... I didn't even feel like I could win at that point. It was just that I had nothing to lose."

McGee says, "It still kind of hurts a little bit to think about. I've watched it time and time again, and I just don't really know how she got out because when I watch that race, I can still convince myself that I'm going to win it. She's just in the worst spot. Natalija, she's so strong, and obviously has her

800m speed, and she just, she found that little space, and she pushed her way through. It was aggressive."

Natalija Piliušina shocked many by breaking out of her box.

Results *(8 June 2013): 1. Natalija Piliušina (Oklahoma St) 4:13.25; 2. Cory McGee (Florida) 4:13.94; 3. Amanda Mergaert (Utah) 4:14.30; 4. Rebecca Tracy (Notre Dame) 4:14.42; 5. Amanda Eccleston (Michigan) 4:14.56; 6. Stephanie Brown (Arkansas) 4:14.58; 7. Shelby Houlihan (Arizona St) 4:14.95; 8. Amanda Winslow (Florida St) 4:16.00; 9. Linden Hall (Florida St) 4:16.42; 10. Emily Lipari (Villanova) 4:18.68; 11. Becca Friday (Oregon) 4:20.85; 12. Anne Kesselring (Oregon) 4:28.17.*

Tools in the Toolkit: What They Say

Peter Snell on how he got out of a box with a lap to go in the 1964 Olympic final: "I decided I wasn't going to go again through my 800 metres performance of dropping back to the tail of the field, and running right round the outside to regain the initiative, so I set about extricating myself by the direct route. Fortunately, it wasn't necessary to use the discourteous elbow-jolt so common in races of this kind. I merely glanced back to see who was behind me as we rounded the bottom bend and then extended my arm, rather like a motorist's hand signal, to show my intentions. I breathed a sigh of relief when the athlete on my shoulder, John Whetton, with the manners of a true Englishman, obligingly moved aside. As simply as that, I was out."

Snell won that Olympic race in 3:38.1. It's fair to note that on occasion he would box in a rival intentionally. Earlier in his biography, he described doing that to American star Jim Beatty. For Snell, all ethics were situational.

Gabe Grunewald on what to do when the hometown favorite is getting all the cheers: "It definitely can be intimidating sometimes… I hear those cheers for other people and take that energy and use it for myself too, even though they're not cheering for me directly."

Sonia O'Sullivan on practicing tactics subconsciously: "Whenever I was doing a training session, I always felt that no matter how tired I was, or what I'd done before, that the last rep would be the fastest. It was always the same at Villanova; when it came down to the last rep, it was nearly a race. And people were always saying, 'It was a race in your mind, but to no one else it was a race.' You were practicing tactics subconsciously, without even knowing it. But it just came down to the last rep, and you were so happy that the session was going to be over that it turned it into a bit of a game and said let's play around here and have some fun."

Steve Scott on getting stuck: "I learned a lot about getting boxed in in my senior year of high school in the state meet 800m. That was a race where we were all pure 800m runners. I was stuck in the pack, I mean, I had nowhere to go. [John Musich] had already taken off. He was going to win the race. But in the battle for second, I'm stuck in the pack, I have no way out. So I just stayed on the inside. In that particular race, they were going into the outside of lane 1 or even into lane 2 down the homestretch. It opened up a path for me straight on the inside of lane 1. So I went by all of them and made it to second place.

"The same thing happened at the USA Championships one year. I've got nowhere to go. I purposely stayed where I was and did not try to go wide and did not try to slow down. I knew people would go wide. Sure enough they did, and I was able to go by on the inside and I was able to win the race."

Sonia O'Sullivan on rough running: "I ran wide, because that's where I was more comfortable. I'd rather be wide than boxed in—you feel like you're getting punched all around the place. I didn't think it made any difference if you weren't running that fast. If you can run much faster, and you're running five to six seconds slower, then it should not make any difference if you're running wide."

Cory McGee on patience: "I think for me the hardest part is about 600m left when I usually feel fantastic and I'm getting frustrated and I want to take off, but I have to remember that with 200m to go I'll probably regret it."

Heather Kampf on a race where she was forced to the back at the very start: "I sort of remember feeling like the athletes that were on each side of me just went diagonal across my plane of running right at the starting line. That's something that I still need to work on is being a little more aggressive at the start because similar things happened to me later this year. Athletes are going to be aggressive off the line, and I'm such a polite person. I always think I run best if I don't touch anyone. So I just kind of got boxed off right away and shot to the back because I wasn't interested in muscling my way through at that line. Especially in international competition that's something that I'm just going to have to get rid of and be more aggressive about."

Jenny Simpson on breaking out of a pack: "I guess the word that comes to mind to me is 'abrupt.' There are things I was doing, ways I was running [in 2011], that were really abrupt. I wouldn't say it was necessarily a really bad thing but I think that it showed a little bit of inexperience, because you are still kind of figuring out what you need to do and then doing it. And those two things are not synonymous. When you haven't had to run in a really aggressive pack like that, there's certainly a learning curve to the finesse of getting to the front. Or when someone fights their way out of a pack and then doesn't go anywhere. It's funny to me how often I hear people say exactly that, especially coaches talking to athletes: 'You worked so hard to get yourself out of there and then you did nothing with it.' It takes everything out of you just to get out and then by the time you've done that, you're exhausted, and your ability to make the next move has been expended. I mean, if I was coaching someone tactically I think that's one of the things I would mention and teach is that you have to think of where you are and where you're going as one fluid movement. If you are put in a position where you have to put up a fight, you can't break it into stages, otherwise you're not to get to the last stage."

Cory McGee on waiting: "I'm really confident in my strategy and I think that as I get older and explore different training methods that I'll be better at those kinds of moves with 300m to go and maybe even earlier in the race, because there have been times at 400m to go I'll feel incredible, and then those last 50m get me. So I don't question that method and I don't think it's foolish. I just think I'm not entirely prepared to race that way yet."

Paul McMullen on getting out of a box: "It's such a subtle thing that I think a lot of the high school kids that I demonstrate it to are amazed at how well it works. That's when you're running in a pack, and it's not a push, more of just a gentle tap that no one is actually going to see. The person you do it to might not even know that it happened until a stride later, and that is you drop your one hand down if you have a runner to the outside of you. And you need to get out of a box, or you need to find some space, where you think everyone is just crowding in. You're ready to make your move, and it's now, in the sense that your opportunity is closing. I'm not sure who taught me this, it might have been Steve Scott. You take your hand, and drop it down near your side. You still kind of have that running motion. But then what you do is you put your hand on the runner to your side, and when they leave the ground you just gently sort of tap their hip with your fingertips. Not a palm thing or anything. It's very subtle. And when they're in the air, they'll shift over just like a foot. Most people think it's some sort of stiff arm or elbow or something like that, but all it is is the fingertips on somebody's hip. It will open up a gap so you can get out of a box. Tactically no one will ever see it. The only people who will know about it are you and the other guy, about two strides after you magically escape from the box you were in."

Abdi Bile on being sure you'll always have a kick: "I did some training for the kick. As a coach, I still do those kinds of training things, I train my athletes like that. The kick had a lot to do with the mind also. You know you don't want to lose, and whatever it takes to change that last 100m or 200m, it works. The mind is also very important so that you know that even if you're dying with one lap to go, you know you're going to kick. You put it in your mind: '300m to go, I'm going to kick.' So I always had some kind of mental preparation. 'You know, I'm going to kick today at 300-350m. Today, I'll try some fast in the last 100m.' It depends."

Marty Liquori on race plans gone bad: "I may have spent a week carefully plotting an attack, but the gun goes off, and someone steps in front of me, and suddenly that plan is no longer viable, and I must be calm, I must settle back and let matters unfold and make adjustments along the way."[5]

Steve Scott winning the 1982 USA title over Sydney Maree and Ray Flynn.

Steve Scott on whether being a gifted tactician is the key: "It has more to do with confidence, not with tactics. If you have somebody who's extremely confident, it doesn't matter. Take Brett Campfield. He ran for me for a couple years. He was a Princeton guy, and he came back home, and wanted to keep running for me. A very talented guy. He was very confident. He could spot somebody 15 yards and know that he was going to get them back. So he'd just wait till he was ready and then he would just go through and blow by everybody. But that really wasn't tactics as much as it was confidence. And then I have other people who just are so capable, but because they have no confidence in themselves, they let people go. There are those times when people are fit, are confident, and they just get stuck on the inside. Three or four people will move and they'll be stuck in the second pack. Once you've lost contact, it's really hard to get it back. Especially for someone who is marginal in athletic ability. They tend to hang back from the leaders, like they're not part of the same race. And that's the thing. I keep telling my athletes, you have to be aware of your surroundings and be conscious of what's going on around you. If you feel like a break is going to be made, you've got to get out. I can't tell you how many times I've screamed at the top of my lungs, 'Get out, get out, get out!' "

Todd Harbour on his transformation into a kicker: "It was crazy how my racing tactics changed. I looked at it, tried to analyze it. In high school, I did not face much competition in those days. I didn't run the mile but a couple of times maybe in my whole career. In the 800m I would just get out. I led almost every race, I'd never sit back. And just would lead it, come through in 52-53. That's what I did at the state meet.

"I got to college, and I moved up to the 1500m, and all of a sudden I discovered that I could kick. It didn't have anything to do with my speed. I think it was because I started off running cross-country. I never had run cross-country in high school. I played football and basketball. I had good leg speed, I was 48 in the quarter. But the strength came, and as I got stronger, and all of a sudden this big kick started coming. I learned how to run like that, I had this big weapon. But looking back on it, it would let me down sometimes. When you learn how to be a front runner, you don't ever have to worry about tactics sometimes. You just go out and control it. A lot of people do that. But for me, once I saw that I could outkick someone in a pretty convincing way, I could sit way back in races, and just come up with a big last 200m, 300m, and sometimes 400m. It just became who I was. I tried to run some races from the front for Joe Douglas of the Santa Monica Track Club, but I just couldn't do it. I never felt comfortable. I could sit in the back and run relaxed. I knew, okay, I had to hurt at some point, but if I didn't have to do any of the work early, I was in the good, I was going to be fine."

Abdi Bile on passing on the turn: "I did it to Sebastian Coe, and I did to Steve Cram also. I feel when you follow a person when he is going, you want him to go as hard as possible, so at least you are keeping the other people back. But when you feel maybe the guy is just slowing down just a little bit, and that maybe will bring back the other group that is behind you. They will get little bit confidence that, 'oh, maybe we can challenge those two guys.' I didn't want to wait and give them hope."

Gabe Grunewald on staying near the front: "I feel that my tactics often hold me back in races and that's something that I've really had to work on as a professional. I ask myself, why is it so hard for me to stay close to the front on the third lap? For someone like me, it's fundamental to go for it on the third lap, and I'm always wanting to save something for the last 200m but it ends up not working out that well. I do think it's interesting, because every athlete, every miler, has a part of the race that's the tough part, whether it's sprinting on the last lap, or going to the next gear over the last hundred meters. For me it's always going to be the third lap."

Sonia O'Sullivan on how she learned to lead: "[Early in my career] I typically would've went and hung around at the back, and come flying home on the last lap. Often, I gave a lot of people a head start, and in the 1500m it's very difficult to catch up. [Coach] Kim McDonald said to me, 'No matter what, I want you to get out there in front of the pace. It doesn't matter what the result is. Just get out and see what it's like.' And I went out and finished fourth in the race. So at least I gave it everything I had… I knew it was likely to go at a really fast pace. And I think some of the [younger] athletes should experience that, to be able to to go out, and not think that everyone's going to come past you. I was expecting everyone to come past me, because I was alone out there. But at least I was learning something about doing that."

Joe Falcon on using team tactics while at Arkansas: *Team tactics rarely seem to work in the 1500m. For every 10 big races where we hear that the Kenyans are going to use team tactics, it only seems to pan out once or twice. However, Falcon, America's top miler in the late 1980's, describes a time that coach John McDonnell had his milers run a team plan to maximize points at the NCAA Indoors:*
"John felt like I could dictate the pace, so he asked me to go really slow through 600m and then really hard for 400m and then back off again. By doing that, it was going to allow my teammate Matt Taylor, who knew the strategy, to run an even pace while everyone else was running and up-and-down pace, and gain a tactical advantage to sprint at the end. So after being the last to qualify, Matt sat back like Coach said and sprinted like the dickens at the end. I won but he got third which was huge."[3]

Both Matthew Centrowitz (right) and Leo Manzano (left) have earned international medals thanks to their command of tactics in the closing stages of the race.

Matthew Centrowitz on the importance of being flexible: "Coming into this race, we knew it was going to be slow. I entertained the idea of me being last the first few laps. We didn't have a set plan coming into it. I just wait for everything to unfold. I had a few strategies coming into it."

Jim Ryun on being flexible: "A strategy is real important to have and to think through, but also to have the flexibility that if something happens in the race that no one had expected, you can adapt to it while the race is developing."[4]

Kevin Sullivan on the need to be cool when the heat is on: "Some guys definitely, as soon as they get jostled or as soon as the race plan doesn't go to form, they mentally collapse. It affects people differently."

Chapter 12: The Unexpected

"You have to be able to learn to handle whatever gets thrown at you."

—*Sarah Brown*

Not every race can be visualized in advance. Not every plan works. Perhaps the opposing runner shows up in far better shape than anyone could have predicted. Perhaps the weather presents conditions that have a huge effect on the outcome. More often than not, the conditions and circumstances aren't quite what the athlete has visualized. The best advice might be what coach Joe Vigil told Brenda Martinez before a 2014 meet in Croatia: "Learn to be comfortable being uncomfortable."[1]

Sometimes, however, things happen in a race which are absolutely unforeseeable, that no amount of visualization could have prepared an athlete for. As 1992 Olympic champ Fermín Cacho says, "There are things you can control, but accidents you cannot."[2] The most common disruption of this nature is a fall. Especially in a tight pack, a fall can have the effect of an explosion, scattering bodies across the track, leaving the survivors to hurdle, step carefully, and refocus on the task at hand, while the victims have to struggle to get up and resume the chase, often with cuts, scrapes and injuries that they haven't even taken into account yet.

World-class runners report other sorts of disruptions as well. Sometimes these disruptions can be awkward to admit. Said one top runner, "I've been peed on in a race. I don't know if I could identify the person, but I just got out of the way. It kind of motivated me to just get up to the front and take the lead. That was a bit creepy. I assume [it was an accident]. That was kind of wild, but honestly, it woke me up a little bit. I was kind of behind almost a wall of people—it was coming up on two laps to go. And I just thought, now is as good a time as any to start making my way to the front."

Anything can happen out there, just as in life itself. To carry the analogy further, sometimes the unexpected can cause us to completely freeze up. In the case of real life accidents, an adverse response can be classified as acute stress reaction. One would hope that events on the track aren't quite that traumatic, but every coach and competitor knows of cases where the athlete is so emotionally invested in the outcome of a particular race that when disaster strikes, it seems as if their world has crashed around them. Old-timers probably recall Mary Slaney's response to her infamous Olympic fall.

When disaster strikes, the successful racer learns to react quickly while staying focused on the task at hand. It's easier said than done, and while experience helps, it's no guarantee.

The Unexpected: Race Histories

1996 Olympic Men's 1500m:
El Guerrouj crashes, as do the Kenyan tactics

Noureddine Morceli, typically used to running with a rabbit at the front, here faced a real challenge. The serious contenders included defending champion Fermin Cacho and Moroccan Hicham El Guerrouj, who came to Atlanta undefeated that season, with a 3:29.59 best a month earlier in Stockholm. Plus, Morceli, an Algerian, faced all three of the Kenyan entrants. This raised the prospect of team tactics—oft rumored but rarely realized in the world of championship racing. "I had 10 different tactical plans in my head before the race," said Morceli.[3]

However, as the racers took off, the three Kenyans went to the front and surrounded Morceli, making it difficult for him to find his stride. They passed 400m in 61.03. Morceli moved to the outside in fourth place, with challenger El Guerrouj on his tail. With 800m left, Abdi Bile made a huge charge to the front pack, bumping Morceli a bit. The Algerian put his hand on Bile's back to steady himself. Approaching the 800m mark, Cacho also tried to pass Morceli, but Morceli accelerated and drove him wide.

The pack hit 800m in 2:01.63, with Morceli edging his way to the lead, as behind him, the race became more and more physical. "When I saw the pace was slow, I knew I could kick in the last lap," he said.[3] Going into the turn, Morceli surged ahead of Stephen Kipkorir, and Cacho made a strong move to run with him. Coming off the turn with 500m to go, El Guerrouj made his bid to challenge, rocketing past Cacho and bumping against Morceli. The Algerian surged ahead before the bell, and that's where El Guerrouj clipped his trailing leg. The young Moroccan went down hard. Morceli, startled, looked back to see what happened before beginning his last lap drive. Cacho had to hurdle El Guerrouj, while Bile swerved around on the inside. The Kenyans ran wide on the outside. The immediate effect of the crash gave Morceli a clean getaway, and he entered the penultimate turn with a two-stride lead on Cacho.

On the last lap, Morceli sprinted furiously, monitoring the stadium video scoreboard to see who would chase him. Cacho had produced a 50.5 last lap four years earlier to catch him, but with 200m left he had only lost ground. Bile held third, but no longer had the finishing speed of his younger days. He was outrun by Kipkorir and Laban Rotich in the stretch, but otherwise the positions didn't change. Morceli slowed dramatically before the line but still won his Olympic gold. He had won with a 53.51 final circuit, surprisingly modest considering the slow early pace and the quality of the field behind him.

Said Morceli of the fall, "He stepped on my foot, and I saw blood coming out. I don't know whether he was pushed or not. It was a tactical race and accidents can happen if you're not careful."[4]

The Moroccan coach, Aziz Daouda, said, "It was an accident," and claimed the contact happened when Morceli moved to the outside to prevent El Guerrouj from passing. He also claimed that El Guerrouj would have won the race by 25m otherwise.[5]

Obviously, El Guerrouj's fall had a major effect on the finishes of Morceli's rivals. Said Cacho, "I was in good position going into the last lap. After the accident, I was too far behind to catch up."[4]

Years later, Cacho's thoughts haven't changed much. "Hicham and I have spoken many times and are convinced that if he had not fallen in that final, Morceli would not have won the gold. You can bet on it. We both wished it had played out between El Guerrouj and me, and possibly I would not have been second… I was well placed to win, but things happen and there is no getting around it. In the end you stand there and you're like, 'What can we do?' We've talked about many times: if El Guerrouj does not fall, Morceli does not win the gold. Neither gold nor silver. It would have been third because he had enough of a lead over fourth; but winning? He would not have won. That's for sure."[2]

El Guerrouj later said, "Atlanta was a black point in my life."[5]

Cacho says, "I don't dwell on it. It happened and that's it. I'm friends with Hicham. I've always gotten along with him better than with Morceli, who has always been more distant. El Guerrouj and I see each other a lot and we have a lot of things in common. Let's leave it at that and say he tripped. He screwed up, he tried to overtake [Morceli], he tripped and fell. And leave it at that. [laughs]"[2]

Results *(3 August 1996): 1. Noureddine Morceli (Algeria) 3:35.78; 2. Fermin Cacho (Spain) 3:36.40; 3. Stephen Kipkorir (Kenya) 3:36.72; 4. Laban Rotich (Kenya) 3:37.39; 5. William Tanui (Kenya) 3:37.42; 6. Abdi Bile (Somalia) 3:38.03; 7. Marko Koers (Netherlands) 3:38.18; 8. Ali Hakimi (Tunisia) 3:38.19; 9. Mohammed Suleiman (Qatar) 3:38.26; 10. Driss Maazouzi (Morocco) 3:39.65; 11. John Mayock (Great Britain) 3:40.18; 12. Hicham El Guerrouj (Morocco) 3:40.75.*

2014 NCAA Women's 1500m: The art of bouncing back

This race would be instructive in a number of respects. First, many had figured that scintillating kicker Emily Lipari of Villanova, the indoor mile champion, would be able to capture her first outdoor crown. Second, the competition didn't know that Arizona State's Shelby Houlihan would switch up her game plan from the frontrunning she tried the previous year. Finally, an extraordinarily rough race would put Cory McGee to the test.

Even the prelims were rough. Says McGee, "This year at NCAA was absolutely the most physical race I've ever been in. I look back on the prelims included. Both races were absolutely out of control. In the prelims, I was essentially run over. And I'm an aggressive runner. I like to hold my ground and like to control the race to a certain degree. I'm not really doing anything too obviously forward, I just hold my ground and make it obvious where I want to be. I was just being completely run over by a girl and that was in the prelim."

In the final, the contact was accentuated because no one wanted to take the pace out. Last year, Houlihan took the reins, and ended up eighth. Surprisingly, it was Lipari who sprinted out to the front on the first lap, but that was only so that she could enhance her chances by ensuring a slow pace. Her teammate, Angel Piccirillo, strode alongside. At 300m, Georgetown's Rachel Schneider went to the fore. The pace still lagged, and after the crowded pack passed 700m, Oregon's Lauren Penney stumbled and veered off the track, grabbing McGee's ponytail on the way. "Kind of where you want to make sure that you're calm and very aware and getting ready for the last bit. It threw me off a little bit and got my adrenaline going. I got pretty angry, because I felt like I almost fell over and I almost went down in my last NCAAs, so it was a close call," explains McGee.

That increased adrenaline may have made McGee more dangerous in the closing stages of the race. The snail pace (Schneider hit 800m in 2:25.0) might have made it anybody's race, but Lipari surely felt confident. However, at about 850m, Houlihan edged her way to the front. McGee started to get pushed back, but smoothly accelerated along the rail and reclaimed her position behind the leaders.

As the tight pack passed the bell, Houlihan had the lead and made the most of it. Lipari, meanwhile, was nearly in last place. McGee found herself battling for third, outside of Georgetown's Rachel Schneider. Then the Florida senior sensed an opening, and made a huge gamble. She accelerated, passed Schneider into a gap that Houlihan had just opened, and passed Houlihan on the inside. "Whenever I see a window, I try to take full advantage of it, and I try to be aware of where everybody is from a tactical

Houlihan (right), shown here in the early stages of the 2013 Pac-12 1500m. She ended up winning this race over Hasay (left), among others.

Hollobaugh

standpoint," says McGee. "I'm sure what was going through my mind was that I didn't want the same thing to happen to me that happened to me at indoor nationals [where she felt she missed her chance because she couldn't get around another runner].... Just a little bit of fear, definitely a panicked feeling, but I think that also you can't let that set in. You definitely have to try to cancel any negative feelings, especially at that point in the race. So once I saw it, I just went for it, took full advantage and didn't really let any other negative thoughts come in."

Houlihan waited patiently to respond, but as she crossed the 200m to go line, she had already begun a scathing kick. McGee chased her to the finish. Lipari, who waited far too long to kick (she was seventh with 100m to go), only managed to nab fourth. She had a faster last lap than McGee (62.67 to 62.69), but started from too far back. Houlihan, meanwhile, finished with a 61.74. Her winning time was the slowest in 15 years. She said, "It really played into my strength that we ran such a slow race. I had to deal with a little pushing, but in the last 400m, I tucked in and laid it all out there."

Results (14 June 2014): 1. Shelby Houlihan (Arizona St) 4:18.10; 2. Cory McGee (Florida) 4:19.19; 3. Linden Hall (Florida St) 4:19.33; 4. Emily Lipari (Villanova) 4:19.60; 5. Allison Peare (Kentucky) 4:19.68; 6. Brook Handler (Michigan) 4:20.45; 7. Agata Strausa (Florida) 4:20.60; 8. Stephanie Brown (Arkansas) 4:20.86; 9. Rachel Schneider (Georgetown) 4:21.15; 11. Molly Hanson (Wisconsin) 4:23.85; 12. Angel Piccirillo (Villanova) 4:27.66.

2014 Weltklasse Women's 1500m: Is the dive at the end really a dive?

Running is not baseball. Let's start there. In baseball, sliding into the plate and diving for the catch are fundamental elements of the game. Players learn those moves when they are children, and they practice them in nearly every game of their lives.

Not so in running. Contact between the ground and any part of your body except the bottoms of your feet is generally to be avoided. Usually it means you have tripped. Often it means you will hurt (in ways that baseball players never seem to).

Occasionally, though, runners might be faced with the finish line dive, when they want to win a race so badly that they are willing to put scabs on their faces to do it. However, maybe the true dynamics of some of the grand finale falls we have seen don't fit into a headline. Maybe what looks like a dive is something else entirely.

For PattiSue Plumer at the 1991 Prefontaine Classic mile, it was, well, more of a fight. Plumer, one of the strongest U.S. distance runners of the era, had a ferocious rivalry with Suzy Favor (Hamilton), who won the USA

Champs that year. Throw into the mix a young Maria Mutola, later an Olympic champ but at age 19 a high school student in Springfield, Oregon, and you had a real dust-up. The three were close and tangled when they began the kick on the last turn. Plumer claimed she was cut off by Mutola and in nearly falling, had to grab Favor's jersey. And that was only the appetizer! At the finish, Plumer recovered her sprint enough to chase Favor down. She lunged at the finish and fell, clocking a 4:33.04 that came just short of Favor's 4:32.99. Fingers were pointed.

"When someone tries to pass you, you try to keep them from passing any way you can," said Plumer. "At the wrong time for me, she gave an elbow in mid-stride and I went flying."[6]

"We try to keep it interesting," Favor said, of her second bumping encounter with Plumer that season.[6]

What happened at the Stadion Letzigrund in 2014 had tongues wagging, since Jenny Simpson and Shannon Rowbury created the most thrilling finish of the year in their clash at Zurich's legendary Weltklasse meet. The race started off with Phoebe Wright doing a commendable job as the rabbit.

Sifan Hassan of the Netherlands (2014 world leader at 3:57.00) repeated her mistake of running directly to the back of the pack and then wasting ghastly amounts of energy in catching back up. Once again, that put her in the position of having to sprint hard several times during the race. With 100m to go, that put her exactly where she wanted to be—a step behind the hard-leading Simpson—but missing exactly what she needed, a sprint.

When they hit the straight, Hassan moved out for the pass. Simpson saw that coming and moved to the outside of her lane to force Hassan into some extra yardage. Meanwhile, behind them, Rowbury had put together a beautifully intelligent race and decided her best line of attack would be from the inside.

Simpson had vanquished Hassan's meager kick with 35-meters to go, but was not aware of Rowbury's inside charge until the last eight meters or so. She moved in slightly, but it was too late to close off the lane. She threw her left arm out a bit wider than normal and made contact with Rowbury, who kept charging.

Pause here to discuss what is intentional and what is reactive. *Intentional* is when a runner makes a decision and pursues it consciously. "Rowbury *intentionally* went for the inside pass with all its inherent risks." *Reactive* is when a runner acts instinctively in response to a situation that they didn't initiate. "Simpson threw out her arm *reactively*." People who attend too many high school meets in the U.S.—as well as certain top coaches—like to speculate about whether or not athletes should be disqualified for "offenses" on the track. I would agree with them, if Simpson had punched Rowbury.

But an arm flailing? That's a normal, reactive response in the world of international racing. The arm is still the key, however. **Unpause.**

When the arm made contact with Rowbury, that initiated Simpson's dive. Or can you even call it a dive? In an email, Simpson herself said no. "Despite the dramatic headlines from Zurich, I did not dive at the line. I fell due to contact in the race. I'm just fortunate that I fell forward and across the line!"

The two tumbled across the line in a tangle, a mere hundredth separating them, 3:59.92-3:59.93. Simpson picked up some stitches and the win (though she didn't realize it for a while). Rowbury, who hit especially hard, seemed dazed and disappointed. Both athletes competed brilliantly and both have every reason to be proud.

Concluded Simpson, "My personal opinion is that diving is not an effective strategy even when the race is close, and I haven't ever done it. If it was truly the fastest way to finish I think we would see sprinters trying it when the races are far closer and usually higher stakes. I think the fastest way to finish is to keep your form and stay on your feet. That's what I'm always trying to do. :)"

Diving? Perhaps you don't want to practice them, unless you're looking for more scars as a conversation starter. Recall our conversation about intent? Maybe the best thing to remember is that a fall is not always a dive; sometimes, in racing, things happen to you.

Results (28 August 2014): 1. Jenny Simpson (USA) 3:59.92; 2. Shannon Rowbury (USA) 3:59.93; 3. Viola Kibiwot (Kenya) 4:00.46; 4. Sifan Hassan (Netherlands) 4:00.72; 5. Meraf Bahta (Sweden) 4:01.34; 6. Brenda Martinez (USA) 4:01.36; 7 Mimi Belete (Brunei) 4:01.63; 8. Abeba Aregawi (Sweden) 4:03.40; 9. Hellen Obiri (Kenya) 4:04.75; 10. Federica Del Buono (Italy) 4:06.80; 11. Eunice Sum (Kenya) 4:10.22; 12. Maryam Jamal (Brunei) 4:18.10;... rabbits—Phoebe Wright (USA), Irene Jelegat (Kenya).

The Unexpected: What They Say

Jeff Atkinson on running in a pack—high school vs. college: "College races are smaller than high school races; in a dual meet there would be six guys in it. In high school races you're used to running with 12 or 15 men in a big event, or even more in an invitational. So by the time you run a couple of dual meets and a couple of invitationals in college, it's not too much different than high school as far as the craziness. It's faster and maybe potentially rougher. But high school is much more crazy and unpredictable because the people involved are less skilled. In terms of safety you would rather run with people who are pros than people who aren't. [To use a cycling analogy] there are more crashes in a category five race than a category one race."

Why women fall more: According to one coach, it's simply about strength. "When women get bumped, in a pack or in a situation, they usually fall. They're weaker and they don't have the rhythm that men do. Men will stumble and get themselves back in. Women get bumped and they'll fall. When you're weaker and you get bumped, you lose your flow and rhythm. In incidental contact, the stronger guy is going to knock the guy who's way weaker off his stride, and that's what happens with women. It's like a bowling alley when they get falling."

Brown: "You just have to react and keep going."

Sarah Brown on falling: "I have – knock on wood – never actually completely fallen on the track, although I have caught myself. That's always kind of annoying because it throws you off. You are in your drive, you're in your pace and someone pushes you from behind, and that's always the frustrating part of it. In the adrenaline of the race, you just keep going. It's kind of a quick thought process — catching yourself, you don't fall, and you just keep on going. I've had some people fall around me, like at USA's, Morgan [Uceny] fell. She was off my right hand side. She fell and you just have to keep on going. I mean, I saw her fall but I didn't think much about it after that. Because those are the things, I think in the adrenaline of the moment, you just have to react and keep going."

Cory McGee on the rough stuff: "At USA's [in 2014], I was in the mix when the fall happened in the women's 1500m, and Morgan Uceny went down. She actually kicked back and hit my knee—I have a scar from it now—and fell over. And that completely threw me off. I didn't know what to do. For a split moment I wondered, was that my fault? And then I considered again and realized again, no, I know that I didn't do anything. I worried for a minute. Yes, that was really unexpected."

Katie Mackey on crashing: *Mackey is well-suited to address the question of reacting to falls. At the 2014 World Relays in the 4 x 1500m, she got the baton and took off, smashing right into an Australian runner who had just handed off and was walking on the track.*

"My first thought is, 'Oh man, I can't believe this is happening.' And then the second thought has to be, 'Okay, it happened, but the race isn't over yet.' Specifically at the World Relays, I had both of those thoughts, and then the thoughts keep going through your head, 'Get up, get going!' And then you just start treating the race as if nothing had happened before. Okay, the people are in front of me, keep your eyes up, focus on them. The World Relays was a little bit hard because there were only four of us in the race, and quite a big gap had formed. It's less racing and more time trialing. I think even in any situation it applies. Anytime that I've ever fallen, I'm like okay, I just get back up. The race isn't over yet. You lose critical seconds and that's obviously a very big mistake, but the race isn't over until it's over. Keep going. You never know what can happen.

"You do obviously get this surge of adrenaline. I find it to be disorienting, more than anything when something like that happens, but learning to stay calm and re-focus is part of learning to be a professional athlete. You have to learn to curb your reactions. I'm a very emotional person and that's something that I've had to do over and over and over and over again the last couple years. Every time you deal with it you get a little better at it. It's not totally different dealing with something that happens to you when you're traveling or in the days leading up to a race than something happening in the race itself in how you approach it mentally. Stay calm, it happened, try to minimize the damage as you move forward.

"The world relays has got to be the strangest thing that has happened to me honestly. Just because it happened right when I got the baton, and you're never expecting to turn around and run into somebody at full force. That's pretty unusual for a 1500m runner who doesn't run relays that often anymore."

Sheila Reid on rough racing: "I've definitely caught elbows before. It doesn't bother me. It's just kind of an occupational hazard. I mean, people are running and you're running right by their elbows. I don't take it personally, and I'm sure that someone has met my elbow before. It's never intentional. I would hate to think that people are doing that intentionally. I get elbows all the time. They've gone into the face even, which can be disorienting, but it's almost an extra adrenaline rush when someone does that.

"Honestly, I think that sometimes women's racing can be just as rough as men's racing. I know a lot of times there are pile-ups. Women go down a lot and I don't know if that's intentional, if people are being too rough out there. Or just, accidents happen. That's been a bit of an adjustment for sure. I actually fell one time at NCAA regional and kind of flipped right on my head. My head was bleeding and all this. I was on the ground for quite a while... I mean it happens, and no one's doing anything on purpose. It can be rough."

Sonia O'Sullivan on the effects of falling: "In 1992, after finishing fourth in the [Olympic] 3000m I ran in the semifinal of the 1500m. Some big powerful athlete came and knocked me totally off. I was away with 100m to go, and when you're new, and quite young, and not very strong, you are quite easily knocked over. So I just got kind of pushed out of the way. You totally lose your rhythm, and the flow that you're going with. You just lose time, and you lose space, and that was kind of the end of the 1500m for me there."

Graham Williamson on losing a shoe: *In 1979, British teenage phenom Williamson ran in the Oslo Dream Mile race in which Sebastian Coe set his world record. On the last lap, he found himself in fourth, and went after and passed legend John Walker. There his rookie skills showed, as he cut in too close to Walker and got a shove in the back. Then he went after Steve Scott on the last turn. On his tail was American Craig Masback, who got too close and ripped off the back of Williamson's shoe with his spikes.*

"One second I was sprinting at Scott, thinking he's not too far away. And the next 'Christ, what can I do?' I kept looking down. I ran a few steps with the back of the shoe tucked under my foot like a carpet slipper. Then I got it off. People began to go by me. My running action was gone."[7]

He faded to seventh place in the stretch, though he set European Junior records for 1500m (3:36.6) and the mile (3:53.15) in that race. Scott ended up at 3:51.11, so the incident might have cost Williamson two seconds or so.

Heather Kampf on patience after falling: "[Falling is] different in every situation. I have learned enough in my experiences of having these things happen. I always want to finish a race no matter what, so my first thought is get up as fast as I can and start moving. And then it's just that mental challenge of looking how far ahead did the field get from me after I fell. At Worlds [indoors 2014], they're not going to be coming back to you. I saw one girl that was sort of falling off the back of the pack and I made her my target and my sort of priority to try to keep myself pushing, just find that one, try and chase after her, try and get one."

Jim Ryun

Jim Ryun on getting bumped off the track during his first sub-4: "Just relax and get back into the race gradually. And [Coach] Timmons had talked about that, not knowing that that was going to happen in that particular race, or at that particular time, but to make sure you're adaptable. So we were on pace in that race, but once I got bumped off onto the infield, instead of getting frustrated or angry, just simply sit back and work your way back up through the pack, adjusting to the circumstances, as the race dictates it to you. Because you don't always have control of the race.

"On the other hand, you need to be ready for the unexpected. And that was one of those cases. I was bumped, stepped off on the infield, fell back to last in the pack. I caught up with them, regained my posture and positioning and just continued to try to make it the race that we expected it to be."[8]

Kevin Sullivan on the unexpected: "Probably the most unusual thing to happen to me was at the 1995 World Championships. I can't remember if it was the first round or the semifinals. We had just passed 600m to go, and were coming off the turn about to go into the homestretch and one of the guys—I don't know if he ended up dropping out of the race, but he just took a tangent across the turn out to lane 6. I was on the outside of him at the time, so I got pushed out to almost lane 5 on that turn, and basically the whole field went by me and I had to recover, get back in the field, and I ran like 51 or 52-point over the next 400m to get myself into the next round. But it was just because some guy decided to take a right turn off the track. Why, I don't know. I have no idea."

Amanda Eccleston on rough racing: "I have not fallen, I've been pretty lucky. I've gotten close and been tripped up. There's been a couple races where I've been pushed around really bad and times where I felt it might have been a foul. For me, it kind of makes me angry, and if anything it gives me a bit of motivation to get going. I mean, somebody sort of blatantly shoves you out of the way, and then you get a little bit upset, and you get a little extra energy then to go after them and try to beat them in the race."

Jenny Simpson on mid-race falls: "I remember jumping over a couple of people [when Morgan Uceny fell in the 2011 World Champs]. Unless it's a situation where somebody's right in front of you and you have been working on that person for a while, you very rarely register exactly who has been taken out, who's going down, who you're jumping around, and who you kind of clawed over to stay on your feet. There is so much of that kind of survival that kicks in when somebody falls in a race. And it's a surprisingly small amount of data that is gathered in those few moments outside of just doing what you can to stay on your feet. And so I didn't know and didn't register that it was Morgan or Hellen [Obiri] that had fallen. I do remember dodging the traffic.

"You have this immediate survival instinct to stay on your feet. You just try to survive the initial rush of the fall. In the next three or four steps I think you have this overwhelming sense of relief and I definitely experienced that at the Worlds. I remember thinking, 'Oh my God, I made it through and I didn't fall!' I think instead of it being something that motivates me in the middle of the race, it's something that I have to really, really quickly move past and get beyond and disconnect from. Otherwise I can easily get through the next 50m or 100m just so happy that I didn't fall, and end up losing contact with the group. A fall is really distracting. It is horrible and upsetting and distracting whether you are in the fall or not. It always changes the race."

Simpson herself was victim to a major crash at the 2013 Diamond League Final in Brussels. Running in a crowded 17-woman field, she was in about fifth place at the bell lap. Then Sifan Hassan, running in front of Simpson, went down, taking four others with her, and scattering the rest of the field. Simpson crashed hard on top of Hassan. She got up to finish 10th in 4:10.70, a stride behind Hassan.

"In Brussels [2013], from actually hitting the ground till 200m to go on the race, I hardly have any memory of that transpiring. I think that when you're so highly focused on a task and you're working so hard, and you're really pushing your body to the edge, I think it's not an exaggeration to say that going through an experience like falling—or surviving the traffic and not falling—is really traumatic because you are pushing your body to an incredible edge. You are in a mental state that you can only sustain for a certain amount of time and then it's traumatic to be interrupted."

Heather Kampf on the adrenaline rush after a fall: "I think it's a risk, but it's also a blessing, because if you didn't have adrenaline, all you would have is that deflated feeling that you have from being taken out of a race like that. So for what it's worth, I would take that over just feeling horrible."

Ruth Wysocki on why women fall more in races: "A lot of times you get in races and you are used to being in control of everything around you. Suddenly you get to a championship race, and you think you have it all planned out, and you think you got it under control, and you don't even realize there's somebody there tangling legs with you. Whereas guys, they've gone from day one, every single race they've run, they're surrounded and they're bumped and jostled and somebody catches their heel. They just have to live with it and move on. I just think women lack that experience, because I don't think there are many women at that level. I don't think they constantly have to deal with it until they get to that very high level, and then they're not used to it."

Sonia O'Sullivan on rough racing: "The one that I got pushed around the most was in 1997 at the World Championships. It was one of those things where one girl tried to come from inside out and pushed everybody out of the way. I got knocked down and grabbed Regina Jacobs' number I think, and her shorts. I did everything possible not to fall down, and so you basically grab the nearest thing to you. This was one of those races where I wasn't on top of my game and fully confident, and when you get pushed around, it can affect you. If you're really fit, and you're ready, those kind of things don't affect you.

"Very early on in my career, in a 1500m race in Lille, France, I did fall. I remember coming off the top bend and whatever happened, I was flat on the track to the point where I don't think I finished. Maybe I got up and jogged down the straight. But in the same race [Hassiba] Boulmerka fell, and I remember she got carried off on a stretcher. And I thought, 'I'm not going to get carried off on a stretcher.' It was all very dramatic and everything. You just get up and you dust yourself off and you go on to the next bend.

"NCAA racing was definitely less rough, and we always had these rules where if they fell in the first 100m, you would get called back and start again. And that did happen to me once. Definitely less rough, and I knew a lot of the American girls, when they first went to Europe, they would always talk about how rough it was. You know athletes, if they want to get through, they will get through. They will find a way, so you need to be ready for it."

Cory McGee on staying aware: "I find myself explaining when I talk with people who aren't that familiar with distance running, as a miler, you have to be aware of your body and just be aware of yourself whenever the race starts to get tactical because so often people end up getting caught up in each other and falling over because they're not aware of themselves. When you have to make a move, it's really difficult to find a gap and get to where you want to go. I think that it was really important in that race to make sure that you covered every gap in time to get up there and finish in the highest place possible."

Peter Callahan on visualizing multiple possibilities: "It was my senior year of high school, and I went to Nike Outdoor Nationals. It was an 800m race; it was my first time at a national caliber meet. I was pretty terrified of the whole experience. The thing is, I had run 1:51 and this was a field, Robby Andrews was in it, Mac Fleet was in it, Casimir Loxsom was in it. This was a really strong group of 800m runners. My coach is convinced that it's going to go out in about 52 seconds. Because [one of the runners] always took it out. Always. Every, every time he took it out hard. And that's what we expected. At least, I'm expecting a 55 or 54, something that's going to get things strung out a little bit. And here, the first lap was like a 58 for 400m, and it's just an incredible pack. One, I wasn't used to running in a pack for 800m. Here we had 15 people in this race and all 15 of us were in a really tight pack coming through the 400m in a 58, and then it just turned into this crazy mad sprint to the finish. People were falling all over the place. Everyone was shocked; everyone was confused about why it didn't go out harder. For me, that kind of stands out as a really unexpected race. Running 58 seconds in an 800m at the national championships was a little bit unexpected. So whenever I visualize races, I go through the first 800m at several different paces. If the mile goes out in 1:55, 'Oh, it's great, I'm happy with that.' And I visualize that. If it goes out in 2:10, 'I'm happy with that. That's great.' I try to visualize that and go through the multiple scenarios."

Andy Bayer on the barrel roll: "I've been involved with a few falls, so maybe it's my own fault. In cross country, I've fallen a couple of times and in track my freshman year at the Junior USA meet. I was coming in seeded No. 1, I was feeling pretty good about my chances to make the Junior Pan Am team or whatever it was. In the final, with 350m to go, I was moving out. The guy barely clipped my heel, but it took me out. I did a perfect barrel roll and ended up on my feet, but it still was enough to cost me six or seven places. I only ended up being able to catch up to eighth. I missed out on making the team, which was probably my first big frustration where it was out of my control a little bit. I felt like I should have been able to make the team but then didn't. I was pretty pissed off, actually. One of our coaches thought I was going to throw punches after the race when he saw me. But I'm not a fighter really. I've got a soft heart."

Shannon Rowbury on the 2009 World Champs final: "I was right with the lead pack of four or five, we were together and I was going right with the pace. Then with 200m to go all of a sudden there was a body in front of me on the track. I was grateful for my dance training and all my years of racing as I was quick on my feet and kind of reacted. I just got around her and kept on moving."[9]

Dub Myers, after being knocked to the infield halfway through the 1987 USA Champs, finishing last: "Somebody just tripped me up from behind. There was a lot of pushing and shoving going on. Somebody must've figured I wasn't there so they ran right into my place... It was just a boxing match out there. I sensed somebody coming up on my shoulder and the next thing I knew, I felt this hand slapping me, somebody trying to get in. By the time I realized what was happening, I was on the grass."[10]

Jenny Simpson on the unforeseeable and inexplicable: *For a competitive racer, running in a championship event is about as stressful as it gets. The stress is like heat that can cause the finest steel to be forged, but it can also cause some to go up in smoke. One athlete at a World Championships won notoriety by getting so nervous waiting in the tunnel for his race that he vomited and left the stadium before even racing.*
In circumstances so highly charged emotionally, the mind can perform some incredible gymnastics. Jenny Simpson candidly shares an odd story from her 2011 World Championships win in Daegu, South Korea:
"I do have one really specific thing that I remember being very, very

strange. Going through one of the rounds in Daegu in 2011. I remember we were coming along the backstretch of the race and there was a cameraman sitting in lane one and I remember thinking, 'Oh my gosh, we're going to trample this guy.' Like he's not paying attention. 'We're going to totally trample this guy or somebody is going to fall, or are they going to call us back or what's going to happen?' And I remember really panicking over that thought of what are we going to do if I get up there and this guy is sitting in lane one. Because, it's not as simple just going around them, right? There is somebody outside of you, there's someone in front of you, what if the person behind you doesn't see him? So I remember for several seconds really panicking, and at the last second he got up and scooched onto the infield. Afterwards I stepped off the track and I was relieved I made it.

"I didn't mention anything until I got through the mixed zone, and I saw my coach, Julie Benson. I told her, 'Oh my gosh, it was so frightening, it was so scary that the camera guy was in lane one.' I kept telling her about this and she was like, 'Okay, okay, whatever.' I made a little bit of a dramatic deal about it. And then we went and watched the race and I told her, 'You're going to see what I was talking about.' And there wasn't anyone in lane one. I'm watching the video and there wasn't a camera person in lane one. And it's one of the strangest, scariest moments of my life. I had this scary and panicked moment. I remember it so well, and I remember exactly what position he was sitting in. The way that the camera was on the race too, there is a chance that there was someone sitting on the infield, even though you don't see them in the camera shot. But there was certainly no one actually on the track.

"It's strange what your mind is capable of when you're in those sorts of situations. In a similar vein there are times when I have felt like something very specific happened in a race, and then I revisit it and see it from a bird's eye view. Your mind can alter your memory and it's fascinating to me how inaccurate some of my very strong memories are. Diamond League races or World Championships, there are things that you go through and things that you see and things you experience. In your first few years of racing overseas, it's just all new and it's at such a high and grand level. I think your brain is like, 'Whoa, major overload.' "

Simpson, after her heat, shows no sign of the scare she experienced.

Chapter 13:
Advice from the Great Ones

*"Every year that you race the 1500m, you start to
break it down a little bit more, and learn more of the
finesse of it."*

—*Katie Mackey*

It is impossible to bring together a project of this scale without running
across scads of great running advice from some of the most experienced
racers on the planet. Yet much of it tended to defy categorization. Here it
is, without any further introduction:

Fermin Cacho on what goes through the mind when the gun goes off:
"You do not think anything. You run and you are seeing what you have
before you. You hear the breathing of athletes, along with the noise they
make on the track with spikes. You try to see how the race is going to be,
whether it will be quick or it will be slow. Run, watch how people breathe,
how if their footstrikes are heavier or lighter. Of course you also hear people
yelling from the stands, but you try to concentrate on what you're doing. But
mostly you're watching. You have an idea of how you want the race to go,
but there are also eleven other people who might be thinking the same as
you, or thinking the opposite of what you're thinking, and want to anticipate
what you are going to do."[1]

Ron Warhurst on being flexible about your race plan: "You can say
here is the plan, but you have to be able to think on your feet. You can't
panic. I'm going to make a move—and you have to be able to say in your
mind—I'm going to see if anybody responds. If somebody responds, and
passes you, you can say okay, he's a player. Okay, where's the next player.
I'm ready to make my next move at 150, instead of saying, oh man, I'm

done. You've got to always have a next move. You've got to be able to respond to what's happening on the track. I told [Nick] Willis, you've got to be able to go from 500m out, you've got to respond from 300m out and you have to save something for 150m to 100m. You say that's a lot of kicks. No, it's a response to tactics. You may have to start your drive sooner than you wanted to. You still have to be able to respond to what happens after that."

Ron Warhurst with 3:52.63 miler Nate Brannen,
one of the many sub-four runners he has coached over the years.

Ruth Wysocki on controlling the race: "One of the big problems I had with running the mile and the 1500m, was I tried to run it like I run the 800m. That's basically trying to control the race too much. You know, I don't think I have the flat out leg speed that most 800m runners did, I was just stronger than they were. So I had to make sure I just hurt them during the race, so that those girls that would just run circles around me in an open 400m didn't have that left in their legs at the end. When I started running the 1500m and the mile, I tried to control those races from the start. That worked for Mary Decker, but that didn't work for me. In her case she got away with it a lot because she was so much better than everyone else, and I didn't have that luxury."

Kyle Merber on mental preparation: "You have to mentally prepare for all situations. That's what I always try to think about. This race might go out in 57 or it might go out in 69. And you need to have some idea of what you're going to do in either situation. And if you practice the different scenarios of possibilities in your mind, if it ever happens, you'll be best prepared and know how to handle the situation properly. So it's kind of that visualization beforehand and just being prepared for the unknown that is important."

Herb Elliott on drawing lane 1 in the 1960 Olympic final: "I don't like this inside lane I've drawn. It means either I must start fast and assume the role of pacemaker or let a few charge ahead and risk being boxed in. I'll take the risk."

Matthew Centrowitz on the benefit of no strategy: "With me, you don't want to give me a strategy because there's a million different things that can happen. So going into a race with a set strategy can only set you up for failure."[2]

Gabe Grunewald on not being used to pack running: "Being from a smaller area, I got a good mix of races in, but [in high school] I still had plenty of those scenarios where I would just go to the front. Sometimes it would catch up to me at the state meet where I wasn't necessarily used to having as much competition. I didn't really learn how to race in the pack until college."

Grant Fisher on not freaking out: "It's important not to make any dramatic moves in the middle of the race. It's important just to stay patient. A couple races, I was really impatient and I made a few surges in the middle, and it kind of cost me in the end. I feel like what I took most from this year is just to stay patient. I think I can stay patient more as I develop my kick. Even if I'm mid-pack with two laps to go, I'm still confident that I have the ability to make an impact towards the end with my kick. A lot of times, my freshman year, I would get antsy and surge to the front and be worried, 'What if my kick doesn't work? These guys all look fresh and I'm already tired.' Now I can relax because I know that come crunch time, I can hang with these guys. I don't feel the need to pull a freak-out and go to the front or get too nervous."

Craig Masback prior to running in the 1979 Spartakiade: "Basically, I'm what you would call a sitter. I react to what other people do, and that's why I've been a loser. I usually have superior speed over the last period of the race, but I don't set the tone. If I want to be a winner on this level, my strategy has to change to take command of a race. I'll think of tomorrow as being a start."[3]

"If you're going to take the lead, you're going to take it for the rest of the race and not let anyone pass you."

—Katie Flood, 2012 NCAA Champ from Washington, reporting her coach's advice

Katie Mackey on getting out from the start: "I do like being on the outside, because I just think it gives you a bit of a better vantage point. What you want to do in the first 100m of a 1500m is cut to lane 1, but you want it to be gradual. This year especially I realized how important that is, the first 100m of the race, because if you really do set yourself up well, or if you get off the line poorly, it can affect the rest of the race. For example, at one meet, I was in the opposite situation. I was one of the first couple people on the inside, and I stumbled a little as we were pushing off and I went right to the back of the pack. Then I spent the next lap and a half—two laps—making a gradual move to the front and that was wasted energy that I wouldn't have had to spend if I simply would have gotten out near the front initially. At USAs, on the other hand, I was on the outside and I cut in gradually over the first 100m. Because of that, I got a really good vantage point. I got right to the front and I didn't have any ground to make up."

Andy Bayer on learning how to race as a college freshman: "I redshirted cross country and indoor track my freshman year, and then my first outdoor race I remember was at Alabama. And there were two Kenyans in the race who were pretty good. Coach Helmer, was like, 'I don't care what happens in the race, I just want you to hang on to them as long as possible.' I ended up third with a respectable 3:51-3:52, for my first 1500m, but I was dying. My last quarter was probably 65 or something like that because I had gone out pretty hard with those guys. From there on, every race I would try to stick longer and longer. That's how I made it through my freshman year."

Katie Mackey on the experience of getting beaten: "In high school, there's an element of talent and natural ability that contributes to winning races. A lot of the races they go into they end up winning. That was certainly the case for me in high school. A lot of the races in which I ran, I would just go out and lead the whole race and then that would be it. I had some really hard experiences in high school as well. I didn't realize it at the time but I was really anemic. I would start out the season, especially cross country, well. And then at the state meet, I got worse and worse and worse each year until my senior year I was in the lead pack with 800m to go but practically collapsed and crawled to 170th-something. When I got into college I figured that out. I started taking an iron supplement, and I stopped that problem. Because of some things like that, I never actually won a state title.

"So I think that in some ways, it wasn't as hard for me when I came to college. I had the experience of just going out there and winning, but I also had the experience of really getting my butt kicked and never winning a state title. I think that made it easier, because when I came into college, I was in a bigger pond, but I was already used to not winning everything. The racing itself was different, because there were fewer races where I would actually go out and lead the whole thing and win it. That didn't really happen that much in college. For the first time, I had to respect the tactical side of it, where you're running with bodies all around you, you're tucked in, you might get boxed in, and you need to be aware of your space. You're racing people down to the line. Even more so at the professional level, because everyone is that much better. You're all within a percent of each other, and if you make a mistake, that can really come back and hurt you."

Heather Kampf – deer in the headlights: When Heather Kampf (née Dorniden) ran at Minnesota under coach Gary Wilson, she was a true 800m runner, strong enough to win the 2006 NCAA Indoor. "That was definitely my main event," she says. "I did the mile or 1500m at Big 10 meets because that was a way to earn more points.

"My coach always said that I looked like a deer in the headlights. I would be out there sort of dazed for the first 2.5 laps, and then, when I could smell the finish, that's when I would start doing my kick in."

Herb Elliott, the Anti-Tactician: "I rarely go into a race with any preconceived tactics. If I do, that means I'm not particularly hopeful of my chances. Athletes who resort to tactics have no real confidence in themselves and lose as many races as they win. Dr. Roger Bannister apparently didn't train too well and needed tactics, as did Christopher Chataway. If tactics are going to be used they are best determined after the race starts, because no one can be sure how a race will be run. For instance, say you decide to sit on a certain runner for half a mile and he withdraws after a quarter of a mile. You must then consciously change your tactics, thus disturbing your concentration and unsettling yourself. The only tactics I admire are those of do-or-die. A runner must approach a race determined to win in any circumstances that exist."[4]

Ruth Wysocki on trying too hard: "I think between the [1984] Trials and the Games I trained a little too hard. In the Games themselves, I tried a little too hard. I started to feel the pressure of going from, 'Wow, I'm lucky to be there,' to people believing that, 'Gee, you have a chance to win a medal.' I just don't think I raced with that same relaxation and confidence that I ran with in the Trials. It was a matter of trying too hard, and there was a little too much stress, a little too much tension, and when you go to unleash it that last quarter, that last 200m, you know, you've sapped yourself more emotionally and physically, and it just wasn't there. In some ways it was heartbreaking, because tactically that was like the *perfect* race for me. That was the one I think I could've taken to the bank. I can't say I would've won it. But I could've done better than eighth place. It was heartbreaking. Then to go to Europe after the Games, there was that nothing-to-lose mentality again, beating everybody who beat me in the Games. Sometimes in slow tactical times, but just realizing that if I decided to go, I could run with anybody in the world."

Kevin Sullivan, here winning over David Krummenacker, himself a 3:31.93 man over 1500m.

Kevin Sullivan on how his experience helps him coach: "One of the things I always tell my athletes is you never lead a race until the point you think you're going to win it. That's something I struggled with in international competition was being confident enough to run from the front early on in a race, which is a little bit ironic because that's the way I had run when I was younger. I always ran from the front. But you think, who am I just setting the race up for? It's harder to lead a race, that's a fact. But am I just setting myself up to have six guys come past me on the homestretch? And I do all the work and I miss out on a spot in the final. In hindsight I wish maybe I had taken more chances. I don't really have a lot of regrets in my athletic career. I achieved most of what I wanted to do, but certainly those are learning experiences that as a coach I can take forward and explain better to my athletes, because those are situations that I was in. I know what it was like to not make a decisive move and how that affected the outcome of a race. So hopefully some of my athletes will be better for some of the mistakes that I made racing."

Kyle Merber on being well-rounded: "It's easy to overthink things when things aren't going well, and when things start just clicking you can kind of relax and not worry about it. But for me, you know, you just got to learn to control your thoughts. If you do have a lot of time to think and you're the thinking type, then you just have to direct yourself more toward the positive route than the negative route. I don't like to sit around and wait for the next time I run. I like doing things, I work, and have a life outside of just running and practice. So it kind of allows me to become well-rounded and having more exciting things going on in your life between each run. It's a distraction that's really helpful."

John McDonnell on being prepared: "When it came to racing, I always felt like if you were prepared that it was important to lead a race or take control of it. Don't run a race and try to win it cheap. That's how you get beat. Have a plan if you cannot outkick a guy over 600m or 800m to take it far enough out to finish them off. Always save your best weapon for a big meet. Never show your hand so you can surprise your competition."[5]

Sonia O'Sullivan on running in the NCAA: "The American college system, the best thing it does, particularly for 1500m runners, is the racing. You run so many races in a year. It's not all time trials, and you practice racing. If you look through particularly some of the more recent results, the last 10 years or so, there always seem to be girls coming from the NCAA one or two years out, and they're always making it into the finals. They know how to race. It's a very good system to get athletes to practice racing."

Peter Callahan on the importance of competition: "For me, track's all about competing. My high school coach, Patrick McHugh, really emphasized that it's not about time trialing, it's not about going and searching for a specific kind of race, it's just getting out there no matter what kind of race it is, and really fighting to get to the finish. For me that meant, when you can see the tape, really make a move for it, really try to finish strong."

Heather Kampf on the hardest part of a race: "I guess I'm considering myself more of a miler because I sense that's where my future lies. But at the same time, I love the 8, and I really want to break 2:00 since I've gotten so close to that barrier. So I don't anticipate putting that down anytime soon. I feel that the speed I get from training at 800m is helpful for me in the mile and 1500m, so they really complement each other well.

"Any running coach would tell an athlete that the hardest part of the race and also the most important part of the race is just after the half, so the third quarter of the mile or the third 200m of an 800m. But I think having moved up from the 800m to the mile, that [third section] seems more manageable for me to start pushing and driving forward and knowing what that feels like, and how to be able to finish well. I can really see that translate into better races. So I think having started with only 200m of that to focus on, and then moving up to the mile, where I know that full third lap is going to be a grind, is sort of a graduated experience for me to push for that much longer."

Amanda Eccleston on the learning curve from high school to the pros: "I was seventh place in the state meet my senior year, and it was only Division 2. A lot of it was trial and error, racing in high school. I'll be the first to say that. A lot of times I would just try to go out too hard at first and had no concept of racing other people very well. When I got to college, for me it was actually very good going into a less competitive D2 school [Hillsdale] because I was racing people a little closer to my range. I wasn't getting destroyed out in these races. I think a lot of it was just getting into races and realizing that I wanted to win them. At first I was sticking to the fast girls until I fell off. And then as I got more and more fit, starting to realize more of the tactics of sit-and-kick, and wait for a little bit. You need to conserve more energy… Racing by instinct was a lot of it. I think the last several years especially, just watching races on TV, watching them online, seeing how other people race, and how they won races tactically. I still think I have a lot to learn. Just watching the best milers out there has been really helpful.

"Now, I probably run a little more tactically. At the professional level, I don't really consider myself as much of a strong kicker. I don't have a 60-second close and a lot of these milers do. Right now I am honestly trying to work on that. And we spent a lot of this year working on improving my finish. If anything, I think I'm a pretty strong runner from more like 700m out and I'm good with pushing the pace from that point. I'm just maybe not as quick with the sprint gears at the very end."

Heather Kampf running for Minnesota.

Gabe Grunewald on shoving: "Every time there's bumping in a race, it's not ideal, and you kind of have to calm yourself and try to expend as little energy as possible to get back and engaged with the race."

Grunewald, who was disqualified—and then reinstated—after winning the USA Indoor 3000m title in 2014, says that she has been in many races where the contact has been rougher than the relatively minor bump in that race: "I've been in a lot of other racing situations, especially in Europe, especially if you are racing an international field. There can be a lot of shoving. It's part of the race. You're sort of defending your space in a way that's not going to end up in a disqualification. But absolutely, there's contact, there's always going to be someone stepping on your foot from the side or whatever. But it was definitely a surprise to be in the position to be disqualified for something like that. Because I did have lots of races where there were much more egregious things."

Paul McMullen on controlling fear: "Fear, you channel. I did something I started in high school, when I used to sometimes do three-four races in a row, and that was I would find a quiet place, lay on my back with my feet on my equipment bag—no music or anything—and I would kind of do what they do in meditative yoga where I would breathe in through my mouth and out through my nose. My mom taught me this because she was a respiratory therapist. Everyone experiences the butterflies in your stomach. Everyone experiences the thoughts of failure that replay in your head, they sort of get louder and louder the bigger the race.

"What I would consciously come to terms with was that I was fabricating the fear and the nervousness and by creating it, I could control it. I would take 15-20 minutes where I would almost fall asleep in sort of a meditation breathing style that would be full of positive thoughts of all of those scenarios where I was still able to win, and the affirmative confirmations from my teammates and my parents and my coach and my previous experiences of what had worked for me. And just let myself calm back down, and once my warm-up would get going, I would start at a lower threshold of fear and nervousness, and the exercise would kind of dissipate that building up of those nerves. And then if I needed another one, I would do it right after I would do my strides and go back to breathing that way, even as I'm putting my spikes on and whatever. Just remain very calm and very quiet. My teammates used to see this, and they could anticipate what was going to occur by my level of focus. I would stop talking and just become calm and focused right there in the moment, and have a little conversation with my coach and go out there. My teammates sometimes sensed when it was going to be a good one better than me. That's how I would do it. I could create it, I could control it, and I could bring those nerves down and get rid of them, so they wouldn't cloud my instincts that I would need when I was racing."

Sheila Reid on transitioning to college racing: "I think part of the appeal coming to the NCAA was being a really small fish in a big pond. I think if I'd stayed in Canada I would've risen to the top a lot quicker, but it definitely took more time and more work to be an NCAA champion. I guess I was surprised I was able to not only individually rise to the top but [be part of] the team that Villanova developed… I was fully expecting a challenge in the NCAA and I think I was really drawn to that because I think if you really want to grow as an athlete you really do have to challenge yourself. So I'm so glad that I did, because it prepared me for championship racing while on a much smaller scale. For the skill level that I was at, it was the biggest competition that I could get."

Sarah Brown on whether international racing is rougher: "I definitely would have said that two years ago, but I am at the point now where even in the U.S., there are some people who really don't mind throwing some elbows. You get the actual body touching, and the not-afraid-to-grab-you-and-move-you. I think it is definitely more prevalent on the international scene, but in the U.S., women have started to take on similar tactics."

Steve Scott on being alert in European races: "In Europe, everyone is of equal ability. Plus, it is a much more cynical form of running. There's a lot more bumping, pushing, boxing somebody in. In races like those, you definitely have to be a lot more aware of your surroundings. In U.S. races, whether it was the NCAAs, Div. 2 or Div. 1, you eventually are going to get out and find some space. But race over in Europe, and it's always going to come down to positioning, and who has the fastest kick in the last 150m or 200m. So that definitely opened my eyes as to being aware of your surroundings and thinking ahead. To say, okay, it's the second lap, I'm boxed in. If nobody opens up, I need to get outside. If you're running behind somebody, you've got to make sure you're running on their shoulder so that if someone comes by, you have a clear path to move with him. So, there's just always a lot more awareness, and you're not going to be looking ahead of you. You're constantly looking around, over your shoulder, at where everybody is—constantly being alert to the situation. You can't fall asleep in a race. You always have to be absolutely aware of everything that's going on around you."

Ron Warhurst on preparing for the chaos: "I have visions in my head about how to run a race, and you hope that the athletes have a similar vision. But once again, I'm up in the stands watching everything develop, and they're in the heat of battle. That's the difference. But the more times you go over it, the more times you talk about it—it's like anything else, the more experience you get in it, a situation that's chaos and you get confused in the chaos—the more times you're in the chaos, the more you feel comfortable. You know that's going to be there, and you focus what you're going to do. That's the biggest thing."

Thomas Wessinghage on how his tactics changed depending on his competition: "Normally I was the one who would try to kick. That's the way, let's say, I was brought up in the racing society. But then after about 10 years I encountered opponents who made it quite hard to pass them while kicking in a slow race. The likes of Steve Ovett and Sebastian Coe. And that is why I changed my tactics according to the race and the opponents within the race. In 1979 I won the World Cup in Montréal, a slow race and I was kicking on the home straight. There was no Steve Ovett around and three days later I raced him in London and I took it out to make the race fast. And so tactics changed according to the situation, the opponents and the way the race was run: slow race versus fast race."

Katie Mackey on watching your mushroom expenditures: "In running, consistency is key. If you can just stay healthy through the week, the month, the year, you're going to just naturally be stronger, and you're going to be able to train harder. I think having a breakthrough year is having a lot of training and consistency under your belt.

"The learning curve part of it, I do think that's really important because the 1500m is often tactical. Just learning the little things—when it's good to make moves, getting out in the first 100m. That's the thing that I really didn't do well my first couple years out is, I would be really aggressive. I would make really aggressive moves. I think trusting your instincts is good. I like to think of it as in Mario Karts, where you have the little mushrooms and you can press the gas pedal for a surge and you can have those little mushrooms disappear. But you only have a certain number of those. You can only tap into that system so many times before it comes back to bite you at the end when you really need that kick, when you're really trying to tap into that system again to pass people in the last 100m. So for example, that's something I had as a learning curve over the last couple of years where I trust my instincts but I've learned to make my moves more gradually which really does help in the last 100-150-200m of a race."

Peter Rono on keeping your strategy flexible: "The advice I would give prior to the championships is that you should have enough speed, you should have endurance, you should be able to change your strategy any time because when you go to the finals all twelve of you are capable of winning. You should go with your plan but you should be able to change your plan, should changes happen because there will be twelve strategies going into the finals. So I would say be prepared for those changes."

Todd Harbour: "I don't think I had the lead many races my freshman year. I ran until it was time to go beat people and I would just try to beat them."

"Patience is key in a 1500-meter race. The first few laps of the race position is not too important. In the last 600m, you must be very focused on the field and watch for people to begin a kick. It is good to ride on the shoulder of someone who is kicking instead of being the first to expend all of your energy."[5]
—Lopez Lomong,
here defeating Leo Manzano at the 2007 NCAA

Heather Kampf on being careful of too many moves: "Sometimes you just freak out and do all those little moves to try and fight for position. Going wide and throwing in spurts early on are costing you the opportunity to do those spurts a little bit later in the race. You've only got so much cash to spend while you're out there, and if you use it up too early, you're working on change in the last 100m. So yeah, I want to be more patient in terms of knowing that no matter where I am in the race on the first lap, it doesn't imply where I'm going to be at the end of the race."

Don Paige

Don Paige on deciding if you're a miler: "I trained as a miler, but the mile hurt a whole lot more than the half mile. In 1979 I won the NCAA in both the 800m and the 1500m. After that, I remember going to my coach, Mr. Elliott, and saying, 'Mr. Elliott, how do I determine in the Olympic year what I will specialize in?' He said, 'It's real easy. I'm going to ask you one question.' I said, 'You're going to ask me one question?'

"And he said, 'Oh, you're going to answer it just like that. You won't even have to think about it.' I said, 'Alright, I'm ready. What's the question?' He goes, 'Which one's easier?' I chuckled and said, 'The half mile.' Some people you ask that same question to, they would tell you the mile. Others they would tell you the half mile. That would happen with any athlete that runs a double. Rarely do they say they're both equal. For me, the mile was more painful."

Jenny Simpson on whether video playback is an advantage: "I think one of the ways that it has made an impact for me is when I was being coached by Julie [Henner], it helped us communicate as coach and athlete. There were things that I would experience in a race that from a bird's-eye view as a coach sitting in the stands were not very apparent. And vice versa. There are things that transpire in a race that I didn't recognize, and I was able to see it from her point of view. I had a really positive and quick learning curve by working that way with her. Having my experience in the race and being able to talk about it, and also being able to see what was happening in places that I couldn't see from my vantage point, and learning from that and being able to have a better idea of how to slightly alter either the way I thought about something or the way that I position myself the next time. I think that video can definitely be a very good tool.

"When you hear Ray Flynn talk about racing back in the day; they raced so often. They raced all the time. They would race all over the world and they would get the result sheets, and if you saw that somebody won by two or three seconds, you would automatically assume it was a runaway performance. Or if somebody won by 3/10 of a second, you assumed that it was a really close finish. The development of the race as the story plays out is a lot more than what you would see at the finish line. And so I think when I'm not at the Diamond League in New York City, I can still watch it and I still get to see exactly who looked good, who had a great finish, who led most of the race and I get the picture for myself. Even when I'm not there, I get to scout."

Amanda Eccleston on the video advantage: "When you watch a race, it looks very different than what you imagined in your head. When you think you made a move, when you think something happened in the race.... It is interesting how your mind can play tricks on you with that. I think, 'Oh, I moved at 300m,' and then I watched it, and it's completely different. A lot of times you play a race back in your head, you think it went a certain way, and maybe you think you did something right. But then you watch it on video, and maybe you see the other athletes make moves you didn't at first notice, and you realize you could have responded here better, or that you did a good job at this point. I think there's a huge learning experience being able to watch it back because you can also watch all the other athletes, especially the winner, and you can see what did the winner do to help them conserve energy in the first part, what moves did they make that put them in a winning position. I think that's huge, because you just can't pay attention to all that when you are busy running a race."

Cory McGee on the importance of learning from video: "Since I was young, the coach I had was from Morocco actually, and he's a strategic runner and he always had me watching races. He had me watching El Guerrouj and the way that he would always stick to his plan and do the same thing every time, and sometimes it worked, sometimes it didn't. I think that it helped me to go back and watch and learn from my mistakes and see what I could correct, and also just compare it to the way that you were training at that time and be able to see okay, this is where I didn't have what it took to win, but I'm confident in my training and know when I get to that same point how it's going to feel. I think it's definitely a huge thing that you can look back on that and key off of it."

Ron Warhurst on avoiding traps: "You want to be in position to come from 500m out or 300m out. And then save a little bit for 150m to go. The problem is that sometimes they don't position themselves properly. [Nick] Willis used to have problems staying on the curve too long and get trapped because he always thought, 'I'm going to run the shortest distance.' That's a great philosophy if you are in a race that's just going to run as fast as you can and they line up behind each other with rabbits like they do in European races. But when you're in a tactical situation, you can't be on the curve and lock yourself in because if it's tactical and you've come down to 300m to go and the leaders make a break and you are trapped back there. They opened up 20 yards on you. You might have a hell of a kick and run them down by ten but you still lose by five. Now if you would have positioned yourself knowing that it's coming down to that—you'll know after a half a mile if it's going to come down to the end—you've got to start getting yourself out and making yourself get to the front group so that when they make a move, you can cover it and give yourself a chance to run on the outside. You can run in the outside of lane one or the inside of lane two, but if it's a tactical race, it doesn't matter. So you're running a little longer distance. It puts you in a position to move when you need the speed, it doesn't make a difference if you run a little farther if you're going to win the race. You don't want to put yourself in a position where you know it's going to be tactical, and you still get trapped on the inside."

Jeff Atkinson on Matthew Centrowitz and the ease within the storm: "Centrowitz is just the master. He's a spectacularly gifted tactician. He is instinctual about when to slide up and find little crevices in the pack without expending any extra energy at all. He's great at that. It's just what you need to do well at that event. And so he has had some nice finishes based on his ease within the storm. If you can imagine a school of fish coming upriver and they're all kind of swimming together, they don't really freak out when they're side-by-side with everyone else. They move in unison as they react to everything around them, like a flock of birds. There are some people who are just relaxed in the event and some people who are not. If you can run relaxed in an environment like he has, it's really to your benefit."

Cory McGee on feeling good during the race: "In a good race the part that's most fun is probably halfway through when you look around and you know that you feel good and everybody else might not. I don't know if fun is the right word, but it kind of makes it worth it. Whenever you can almost take a step back and evaluate the situation whether you're running the 1500m or the mile. There are a couple moments of doubt within the race—you get to one where you can tell everyone is feeling it a little bit and you feel good and you're going to challenge for the win. I love that, that's a great feeling."

Amanda Eccleston on men racing differently than women, and overthinking: "That definitely can be true. I know sometimes when I look at my competitors and I look at what their strengths are, and I think, 'Oh they can kick, and they're strong, how do I beat them?' It seems like I'm thinking too much about what to do.

"One thing I do think about guys is actually they do race more competitively. If you're watching anything from a professional mile to a prelim in a conference meet, they're usually in an incredibly tight pack until 400m to go. And they're all confident of being able to kick. Really, sometimes it's cracked me up in these Big 10 meets. They will jog almost slower than the women for the prelim first three laps, and they'll just have a sprint race at the end. I think that women aren't always willing to take that risk quite as much. Also there's a wider range of women; they're not going to be in such a big pack. Maybe it's that more men are in a closer time range or that they're just more willing to be more competitive and take more risks. That could be the overthinking by women, thinking, 'Oh, I don't want to make this a big messy sit-and-kick. I want to make sure I'm out of it and ahead of everybody.' I do know, sometimes I do find myself overanalyzing a bit. I just try to rely more on my instincts, because it is easy to get caught up thinking about plans, and then when they don't go exactly the way you thought in a race, that can be a little scary, if you're not ready for that."

Sarah Brown on keying on other runners in a race: "I've done things like that before, like I know this person is going to the front so I should follow them. But I don't necessarily go specifically after someone. I guess mentally I know who some of the top runners are, so I know if they make a move, I need to make a move with them. But it's not directed toward one person. It's also on a subconscious level."

Gabe Grunewald on paying attention to the clock: "Usually I'm pretty aware of who's around me. If it's a race where place is more important than time, I have a pretty good idea of what to expect out of my competitors. I think sometimes I use them as benchmarks at times to see where they're at and what they're doing. But other times if you're going for a standard or season best, I've learned that you do need to pay attention to the clock. At this level, there are so many clocks on the track, it's hard to not look at it sometimes.

"It really depends on the race though, if it's a championship type situation or is it early in the year and I'm just looking to get race experience, I try to just forget about splits. When I'm racing a lot of the Americans who I race a lot, I'm definitely aware where they're at. It's a little bit different in international fields. I don't know nearly as much about those competitors, so on those ones you're always keying off of something, it's either the clock or your competitors, and sometimes you just pick one of them."

Kyle Merber on how believing you can do something is the first step: "One of the things that's really important is being able to gauge your fitness a little better. One of the big things that I would say I recently learned is you have to take steps in progressing and confidence and that makes a really big difference. I didn't realize when I was in high school how big of a deal believing you could do something could be. I just figured if you were in 4:15 mile shape you were in 4:15 mile shape and that's the end of it. But the thing that I kind of realize now is that everything I do isn't necessarily to get in better shape but to believe that I'm in better shape. And once you convince yourself that you are in shape to run a certain time, that's the first step in doing so. So maybe I'm in 3:52 mile shape right now, but I got into a race, and I only thought I was in 3:54 shape, so my mind only allowed my body to take me to 3:54. Sometimes you have to take these little incremental steps. Sometimes it's PRing little by little. Sometimes it's having a great workout or feeling great. Now what I've learned is the manipulation of the mind and how much more important it is to think that you can do something then it just being physical barriers."

Abdi Bile on what you need to be a good miler: "What I tell [the young people I coach] is the 1500m is a very tough race. Number one you have to have 10,000m endurance and you have to have 400m speed. And so it is a very tough combination. From 800m on, you just have to pay attention, you

Gabe Grunewald

have to prepare yourself for a good kick. You have to basically be ready to run an open 800m when you're running 1500m. Especially if the pace is slow. But if you go from the get-go, you have to have marathon endurance. It is a very tough race. It needs a lot of work. It's just a combination having the 400m speed and 10,000m endurance and maybe the power of a 100m runner or decathlete because it's a lot of power when you're all going all out. The mystique, the power, the endurance—it's very tough. So they shouldn't take it lightly."

Filbert Bayi: "Work hard. Have determination for what you are doing."

Todd Harbour on teaching milers how to race: "It's just a matter of making sure you're in position. Making sure you're ready to go and you're staying relaxed, staying out of boxes, not having to fight a lot. I think in the 1500m, you can't make too many moves. You got to be able to fit in there. I love watching an athlete be able to work himself out of the situation without too much effort. I think sometimes young runners spend too much effort trying to get to that perfect spot and then when it comes time to blast that last 300m they already used some of it. So teach them how to stay relaxed, don't panic even though you're not where you want to be.

"You want to prepare them for it. You don't want to overanalyze the situation, but you need to have at least a game plan of this might happen, or this might happen. That way, the athlete, they're prepared, they have a good sense of this is where I need to go."

Cory McGee on being in the mix: "I've been in quite a few races and I always try to be in the mix. I've gone through a few changes and had to get back to where I started. When I was younger, I was a frontrunner, and always led from the gun. I grew up in Mississippi where distance running isn't really that popular. In high school I just really liked to challenge myself, keying off of the times. I would travel a lot to races throughout the U.S. and I found that running from the gun when I faced girls who had more experience was pretty difficult and generally in the last 100m I would end up getting caught by one or two girls. That happened at the national championships freshman through senior year, I was leading with 50m to go and ended up getting second or third. I definitely had to learn patience. I think as a mile or 1500m runner that's one of the biggest struggles, because halfway through the race you feel great and that last 100m can just creep up on you.

"Anyway, the point is I definitely changed a lot in college and had to learn from Coach [Mike] Holloway and my other coaches just how to be a little more patient and how to hold on, and not kick with 600m to go but rather 200m. But at the same time, I want to be strong enough in the future where I can leave sooner in the race."

Cory McGee competing in Moscow
at the 2013 World Championships.

Francie Larrieu Smith on being ready to move quickly: "You have to have faith when you do run on the pole that it is going to open up. I think a lot of people are fearful of getting on the inside because they're fearful of getting boxed but the race will open up. It always does. So there are things that we always tell our kids to do well, that's if you get boxed in, just slow down and everyone else will go by. But if you're just patient enough it is going to open up. Someone is going to make a move. You will see an opening. But you just have to be totally aware of your surroundings and be ready to react immediately.

"I remember Brooks Johnson was talking about the importance of one's ability to automatically react and respond to deviations in your race plan and react to what was going on in the actual race itself. You just have to be ready to quickly move. Sometimes that has to do with your ability to just step it up for a couple of steps real quick, and then settle back in again. I used to practice my reaction time. Well, in weird ways like when I was driving and things like that. I know it's kind of crazy. I used to think about it, in terms of when the gun goes off, and taking that first step, and that sort of thing. We used to practice that and I think, too, there are drills that we do in practice with our kids. It's all about the neuromotor and the quickness. I would say that there are some people that are more gifted when it comes to that quickness, but I also believe that it is something you can work on. You may not be the best but you can certainly be better than what you are if you are diligent about working on it."

Paul McMullen on rough racing: "I think it's important to know that despite my size, never would I intentionally bump into someone or have contact. Never. That was always bad. It didn't help anybody. Now, hold my position, in terms of someone else initiating a bump? Sure. But I think that was kind of a misconception that a bigger guy can push his way around a 1500m race. The only thing I can say is that a guy my size just isn't affected as badly as a lighter weight guy. That's pretty much it."

Heather Kampf on making friends with the 1500m: "It took a while for me to make friends with the 1500m. I was in college and I would be out there and forget, am I on the second or the third lap? Where am I on the track? Because of the starting line being different than where the finish line is. That's something that I always loved about the mile, it was so easy to know exactly where you are in the race. There's that perfect symmetry that everyone talks about that's so fun for watching as well."

Jenny Simpson on getting tactical experience in high school: "I think that's one of the things that is kind of a trade-off from being a good or exceptional high school athlete, is that in high school, if you do show a lot of potential and you're really good and you train really hard, you have a lot of runaway races. At least when I was back in high school, it was even far less competitive. But if you were one of the top runners, you didn't need to learn how to run tactically in high school."

Coach Mike Scannell with Grant Fisher.

Mike Scannell on making the big move: "We never make a race plan where [Grant Fisher's] primary move—it will not be to the finish line. Does that make sense? We never go in a primary move without the ability for him to close at least that fast. Never, never, never we would never start the last quarter, push hard, and then relax on the backstretch. Maybe I shouldn't be saying that on tape. But it's my thought that when we go, we go for good. And I don't want any fading, until we hit the tape. Once you go, it's over. I want everyone else in the race to know they're second. Honestly, I am a very aggressive racer. When Grant Fisher goes, I want people to think it's over. And I want Grant Fisher to know that he's going to finish at this level. There will never be a case where he doesn't know how to finish what he starts."

Amanda Eccleston

Amanda Eccleston on the difference between racing NCAA Division 2 and Division 1: "In D2 I was one of the top mid-distance runners by my senior year and so I felt like I had a lot more control over the race. In most of my D2 finals, I did wait and sit and kick. I was able to relax a lot more. I sort of knew all the other runners. And I knew that I was capable of finishing harder and going harder at different points. Then when I got to D1, all of a sudden, you try and make moves, or you think it's going to play out a certain way, and everybody else is right there too. Everybody else is just as good, and as capable of making these tactical moves.

"So it was a bit scary, realizing that these girls can run just as fast if not faster, they know what they're doing because they're a lot more experienced at a higher level. So it was very different. You're with so many people who are so much closer in ability, whereas in D2, there is a lot more range. There might be 10 seconds between the girls at nationals, whereas in D1 there was three seconds between all of us in our PRs."

Ray Flynn on how racing prepares you for life: "The great thing about racing is it really mirrors life. You put your best effort out there and it doesn't always play out the way you want it to play out, but you lived to fight another day and you learn something from it, and you give it your best effort, and when you come up short, you have a lot of chances to come back out and have another shot at it."

Kevin Sullivan on NCAA vs Europe: "Collegiate running was more aggressive than what it was in high school, but there seemed to be more civility when it comes to American racing style versus European racing style."

Don Paige on not worrying about the splits: "I never listened to splits. I had no idea if it was fast or slow. Usually I'm just concentrating on what my competitors are doing in that race. Where I'm at, trying to stay out of trouble, not trying to get too far back. Some kickers have a tendency to go too far back, because obviously, we're dealing with some very high caliber athletes in the race, and it is nationals, and you expect that. I just focused on where I was in the race. Time never enters it. I mean, what am I going to do? If it's a fast time, I'm going to slow down and let them gain an extra 20m on me? I don't understand that theory, no. I'm not going to do that. If it's a slow time, am I going to take the lead and make it faster? Heck no! I'm definitely not going to do that."

Francie Larrieu Smith on coming to peace: "There were periods in my career I just went out and ran because I knew I was going to win unless I fell. And then there were periods where I sat and kicked, because I knew that was the best way for me to win a race. Then in the very end I would say, and this was actually a direct result of my experience in the 1984 Trials, I stopped worrying about my competition. I stopped listening to other people saying 'Francie is too old,' or 'Francie needs to get out of the sport.' I started loving what I was doing, and knowing that I wasn't going to win every race, but also knowing that anyone can win on any given day. Just training hard and doing my best. Not worrying so much about who was doing what. Knowing when I was going to the starting line, I was going to be racing some really good people, and just not worrying about it."

Ron Warhurst on sticking to your plan: "You don't want to put yourself out of an opportunity by being in the wrong position, so learning tactics is essential. Alan Webb would go right to the front and run away from people, and he found out in the college ranks that you can't do that. You have to be able to lay back. Run from the front, run from the side, run from the back. Know when to move and not just go from last to first in 20 yards. I think that's a big mistake a lot of people make. They're back and they panic and they try to make it all up within 50m. It's like a fartlek; they're going along and they panic, and they go all out. So I think that being aware of where you are in the race is very important when it comes to tactics for the mile, and knowing your competition helps, but once again, they have their tactics, you have yours. I don't like to let anybody else's tactics influence what my guys are doing. Because if they're doing what I think they're supposed to do, it doesn't make any difference what the other person's tactics are. You have to just respond to them. You know somebody's going to make a break, somebody's going to go; it doesn't matter who it is. You have to understand, that's the tactics of the situation. You have to have that mentality, but you have to have the ability to put yourself in that position. That's what racing is. Practice racing, and I like to do it in practice a lot.

"They say, 'God, I wasn't mentally prepared for that.' And I say, 'How do you get yourself mentally prepared for it? You do it in practice.' Some people say, 'Oh, we don't want to race in practice,' and I say, 'Oh yeah you do, because how else are you going to learn the emotional part of where you're going to be? You're out there training physically. You train to race, well, then you have to train yourself for tactics.' How do you learn that? You can do it in practice. You've got four or five guys. So racing means that you want to learn to position yourself. You've got five guys, you have one guy go in front, and two guys here and two guys here, and your turn is to stay in the back, and at a certain point, move yourself up into second place. You can't stay trapped and just let everybody go in practice. So the guy that led on that interval, he goes to the back, so it's his turn to follow. You learn to lead, you learn to be in the middle, you learn to be in the back.

"I think if you're in that position in practice a lot, there's a sense of claustrophobia in the group. The guy up in front is free. I like my guys to run just inside the lane line, that way you have time. If someone was to come up on your outside, you're not going to be trapped. And also, positioning is very important, running off the outside trail leg of the guy in front of you. Very important, because if you're running on the inside of his trail leg... Somebody comes up on your outside. You cannot pull out on the guy because this guy's trail leg is blocking you. You come up the inside, you have to slow down to go around the outside of that trail leg. If you're outside the trail leg, you have the space to go; you can respond to that. I talk about it all the time; this is what you have to be able to do. You have to be able to position yourself. If you're on the inside shoulder of the guy in front of you, his trail leg is back, and you run up close on his hip, and some guys come up on the right to pass, you cannot move out because that trail leg is coming out and blocking you. This guy goes by, the next guy goes by, and where are you? You're trapped. All of a sudden you went from second to fifth. And then you had to wait for this guy so you can get back and go outside his trail leg.... Now, if you're on the outside of his trail leg, and someone comes up on your shoulder, you've got a clear lane to run. But if you're on the inside, and someone comes up even to you, you're trapped. That's why I like guys running on the outside shoulder. That's very important for tactics, for being trapped and not trapped on the inside. It's very critical after the half mile, in collegiate races, in any race.

"So much of it is you have to keep your mind relaxed. You see some kids are in a panic, their eyes are bugging out of their head and they're pushing and shoving and they're losing it. [Matthew] Centrowitz has a good sense about himself. He's always in the right position. Kevin Sullivan had a great sense about himself. [Nick] Willis lets himself get too far back but he's learning to stay in it and move to the outside. Nate Brannen was tactical, unfortunately too tactical, in the Olympics. [Steepler] Tim Broe had a sense of tactics. The great ones do. You try to teach other boys by training them with [the ones who know tactics]. Watch what they do. You have to be able to think on your feet. You need to be superfit to race at the level these guys are racing. But I think tactics are tactics. High school kids can have good tactics. You need to know when to go and you explode on people. Or you just grind them. You come from 600m out. You don't just make a big sprint for 100m then slow down. You start grinding them. Or you wait till the last 100m. If you do that, you better be in the right position, you know. I think it's a matter of just practicing it and thinking about it."

Amanda Eccleston on seeing what you can do: "The actual racing is fun. The whole lead-up to it, especially the two-three hours before is the worst part. That's when you're just freaking out and wanting to get on the line. But usually when you're on the line, you're actually out there, it is the best part. Just to see what you're capable of. There are obviously races where you just feel awful and you're wanting to be done. When you have a bad day, you can sometimes just tell from the start, 'Wow, this just is not going to be good.' But for the most part it is exciting. It's exciting when you run and you feel strong, just to see how hard you can push yourself. And to see how you stack up against other people."

Kyle Merber

Kyle Merber on the fun part of racing: "I love the final 100m when you're just shoulder to shoulder with someone, and you can feel just how much they want it and how they're feeling and you're gauging off of them. Emotions are riding high but you know that you can stay calm. The last 100m of any race, especially in the mile.... I wouldn't even say the mile is a hard event. It's kind of just waiting and waiting and waiting to go, and it's how much do you have left. When you get to the point where it's, 'How much do I have left?,' that's the fun part."

Kevin Sullivan on hesitation: Remembering his third place finish in the NCAA 1500m as a freshman in 1994, Sullivan says, "Graham Hood and Erik Nedeau made real big moves with 300m to go and I was a little farther back and I wasn't feeling that great, I didn't make a strong decision at that point. At that point, at 300m to go, you've got to commit to the move, and I just kind of hesitated and was hoping that things would come back to me, which

294 | How to Race the Mile

didn't happen."

Sullivan ran 3:44.14, well behind Hood (3:42.10) and Nedeau (3:42.44)
He ran 3:36.78 later that season.

Gabe Grunewald on the last lap: "The last lap is always the most fun. For me, if I'm in the race and I'm feeling good, there's nothing like the last 200m, 150m of a race. It's the most exhilarating feeling just to be going at full speed in that race to the finish line, when you can start to see it."

Don Paige on knowing your competition: "You know, Mr. Elliott, that's what we called him back then. I call him 'Jumbo' now, but back then, he was Mr. Elliott. He taught us more about life than he did about track and field. Almost every Monday afternoon at 3 we would have a track meeting, and he would concentrate far more on real life issues than track and field. When he did talk about track, which was rare, he would stress competition. 'Life is a competition. Everything we do is a competition. Learn to compete.' I'd give him a quizzical look. 'Really?' He'd say. 'Think about it. You're in college. Not everyone in that classroom gets an A in college. So you're competing for grades. On the social scene, you're competing for a girlfriend, a gorgeous blonde girl, or whatever. In track and field, you're competing. You need to learn to compete. You need to be a master of competition.' I think he was a firm believer in you need to know your competition. I think he taught that through the business world. He related everything to the business world. He said, 'If I'm going in on a sales call, I want to know who my competitors are, what their products are, what their products cost, how long their products last, what the repair service on their products. I want to know everything about my competitors. Because I already know everything about my product. That way I can go in and I can sell that client the best product, which is mine.' And when you translate that to competition, the same thing happens. I would go into a race, and I would know the background of most of the athletes I was competing against. Were they a frontrunner, were they a kicker? You'd learn about their traits. Do you have to watch out? Does this guy drift in races? Because you have to be careful of people that don't hold their line and don't run proper, don't know etiquette. He wanted us to learn to compete, and I think that was a very valuable lesson, and I practice it every day."

Todd Harbour to high schoolers: "You have to be confident in whatever race strategy you have. You can't try to be something you're not. I mean, if you can't get out and run relaxed in the front, then you better not try to do it. You better try to get in a good position, and make sure that you're ready when the fight starts, you're ready to go. That you're relaxed, and you're ready to go, that you got yourself in a good spot. And that's not always possible. Things change, people move around you, they cut you off. You just have to stay relaxed. When the opportunity comes, you got to go. You have got to know when to go."

Sheila Reid on timing the kick: "So far as kicking later in races, I go back and forth on this. Oftentimes, I kick late, and a lot of the time that's because I don't want to take the lead until I know I can hold it. I think that's a really crucial point and it's something that I hear a lot from the coaches at Villanova. Such is the importance of making one move, because I find that in a race like a 1500m, you only have so many times you can switch gears before you run your legs out. So when I make my move I want to make sure it's the last one of the race. Otherwise I think you can kill that pop in your legs."

Ron Warhurst on training the kick: "I do a sprint drill. We do 150s. We do sprint 150s as much as we can. We do 150s especially in the spring when we're getting ready to run really fast. We come off the turn from 150m out and we do a fake race pace. And then we make the turn, put a cone there, and then we put another cone down the straightaway. So we come around the turn at race pace, which is 58-60 second pace for these guys. And then they have to concentrate on form. We practice relaxation. Shorten your arm stroke, shorten your stride. Shorten the stride to accelerate. They come round the turn, hit that mark, arms up, shorten their stride, and then they accelerate. Now they're maybe down to 56-second pace. Then they come down one more time with 50m to go, they have to shorten up and accelerate again by flipping the arms. They shorten their arm stroke. They don't overreach. I've seen Willis many times come down to 100m and then with 50m to go, go again. They practice it. Will Leer can do it. [Steeplechase bronze medalist Brian] Diemer could do it. I do 150s and we get going really fast in the early season because it's a mechanical thing. It's not an aerobic/anaerobic training device where you're doing speed work. We're doing mechanical work. We call it mechanical race pace. People go on about strength training and speed training. Well strength training is repeat miles, speed training is repeat 200s. We do six 150m strides. There's a rhyme and a reason to why we do them.

"We do another thing that we started two years ago. Willis came up with it and it sounded like a good idea. I learn as much from them as they learn from me. I still have 80% of the basics. The basics are there for me. And working with these guys you change it up. So we call it speed Sunday. They do their long run on Saturday. And on speed Sunday they'll go down there and they'll already have their 80-85 or 70-75 miles a week in depending on where we are in the season. What they'll do is we'll warm up with a 2-3 mile run, then they'll stretch and they'll do a couple of 100s almost on the fly. And then we'll run a 150m and a 150m and a 200m and then we'll sprint a

150m in 18 or 19 which is about a 25-second 200m pace. Then they jog 250m, then they'll do another 150m the same, and then they'll run a 200m in 24 or 25. And then they take a 400m jog, and then they'll go 150m fast with a 250m jog, 150m fast with a 250 jog and then a 300m in 37-39. We're talking 50-51 second pace. And they'll take a 400m to 500m jog and then we'll do another 150m. And we're still maintaining 18-19-second pace which is about 25-second pace [for 200]. And that could be adjusted to high school times. Then, we'll do the 150m again and we'll run a 400m. That's known as Speed Sunday.

"That's when we're working on speedwork. And the reason they can do that is because they've been doing the 150s, changing acceleration. Once we get up into the 300s and 400s, then it becomes speed-centered. But just doing the 150s, it isn't. Because it's not aerobic/anaerobic. You don't get lactic acid. But what you do is teach your muscles to contract and go hard, fast. In the beginning they might get a little sore, but what helps them not get sore is the fact that we do hill training. We run harder hills... It's pretty snappy, and it's an uphill, so you still get the strength in the legs from the bounding. We don't need to do a lot of weight work for our legs because we do hill training. We don't need to do bounding drills because we're running up hills all the time. And then from there we go back to the track and really crank."

Don Paige on competition and the strategy of not having a strategy: "The big difference I believe between the older generation and the later generation: rarely did I have a race plan. Reason being, I'm not a front runner. I'm not a pace runner. I'm a competitor. I compete. So if they want to go out in 65 seconds, I'll go out in 65 seconds. If the race is going to go out in 55 sec, I'll go out in 55. If that's what the race is doing at that moment, I'm there to compete. If [Steve] Scott, [Steve] Lacy and [Ray] Flynn, they all want to go through whatever time they want, I'm going to be there with them. That's competition.

"One of the things I get most frustrated with—some of these younger kids in the last 10-15 years or so. You'll read quotes or see interviews, and they'll talk about a race plan and they'll talk about planning their splits. 'I'm real thrilled, I hit my splits just the way I wanted them. I ran 3:50.5.' I'm like, great, you ran 3:50.5, but you finished seventh place, buddy. How can you be happy with that? You didn't compete. You ran a fast time. For a lot of kids today, it's all about running fast. When I was a younger athlete, the great John Walker and I were having dinner. He said, 'Don, you know, I can only tell you one thing. People remember who finished first. They rarely remember how fast you ran. Most people know I won the gold medal at the Olympics. Very few of them could tell you how fast I ran.' That always stuck with me. When you take that, and combine it with competing, if you get in a fast race, you'll run a fast time. But the goal is to win, the goal is not to run a fast time. If you play a football game, your goal is to score points, not that you played a good game or you blocked a couple passes. People have got to understand, it's about winning and losing. I don't understand this new tactic about running for pace.

"If [the leaders] want to go out that hard—I trained just as hard as they do, is my belief. My belief is they hurt just as much as I hurt. I'm willing to put up with whatever pain I need to put up with, to do what I have to do. In 1978 when I lost [the NCAA 1500m] I went off to find a quiet spot. I did cry; I did a self-evaluation. What the heck just happened? How did they beat me? I never bought into my teammate's theory that they were older, they were more experienced, that they were better. I said, 'What do I need to do to beat them the next time I run?' That's what I concentrated on. I said I obviously need to train harder. I need to get stronger. I need to put in more distance. I need to put in more speedwork. You know, you just start building. And that is what competition is all about. But in 1978, a race plan? My race plan was to win. I couldn't tell you what my time was, I couldn't tell you today what it is. And I couldn't tell you how much I lost by. But I could tell you I lost and finished fourth, and I wasn't happy."

Sam Penzenstadler on the difference between high school and college racing: "In high school, there might be three or four guys at your level when you're running 4:20-ish. It was never too competitive. But in the college race, no matter what level you're at, there are going to be a lot of people running at your level. In the prelims at nationals, that was a very strategic race. I remember there were elbows being thrown everywhere. You had to speed up, and slow down. I never really had to do that in high school. It's a lot different and harder. It takes a lot out of you in a race. You get used to that."

Be careful of sandbagging with too many excuses: Your opponents will get wise to you. That was the case for Glenn Cunningham, one of the world's greatest milers of the 1930s. Prior to the 1936 Olympics, he complained to a reporter that he had stiffness in his legs. Rival Gene Venzke, then the indoor record holder for the 1500m and mile, countered, "Glenn always runs a little faster when there is something wrong with him."[7]

Amanda Eccleston on the race she would like to do over: "My junior year at Hillsdale, at the D2 outdoor nationals, I ended up finishing fifth place there. And I remember coming off the final curve at about 100m to go—I think I was in fifth at 100m to go as well—a bunch of girls swung wide and for some reason I just kind of tucked in and just settled for fifth behind them. I remember crossing the line, and I was about a second behind the winner. That's when I realized, I could have won that and I probably should have if I had gone to the outside. I think that was the one race where I first realized, wow, I could be a national champion. And I just didn't commit to going all the way for it at that point. That one definitely really bugged me for a long time, but at the same time it was great, because going into my senior year, I decided, you know what, I'm capable of this and I think my goal is to win both indoor and outdoor mile and 15, and then it ended up happening. So even though it was frustrating at the time, it was a big lesson for me, just to show me what was possible."

Don Paige on the psychology of winning: "I never looked back and thought I did something wrong, or anything like that, during the race. I looked at it as was I not mentally tough enough? Did I not put up with enough pain? Was I not strong enough so I could have a better kick? That's how I evaluated it, because those are the only two options. A. you didn't put up with enough pain, or B. sometimes you have to put up with more pain because you're not fit enough. You know, I think it all comes back to your mental ability and how tough you are and how much training you put in. Rarely did I walk on that track thinking anybody on that track trained harder than I did, or that they were better than me. I almost never thought that. I didn't know I was going to win, but I didn't want them to beat me. I didn't like losing. There's an old saying, when you talk to people, if I were going to go out and recruit a new athlete, and I could ask them one question, I'd ask them, 'Do you like to win, or do you hate to lose?' And if the kid says, 'I love to win,' I would say, that's great, and I'd turn around and walk away. Because really, you want those kids who hate to lose. That is a much stronger feeling than loving to win."

Kyle Merber: the way that you run makes a difference: "A big thing about the level that I am currently racing at is there are a lot of people running the same times, but it's the way that you run a certain time that makes the difference. Or even the positioning yourself and moving not too early, not too late. That makes the difference between first and seventh. In a time trial a lot of people would run extremely similar times but [how they're racing] goes a really, really long way for people, and that's what separates the people who are winning every race versus the people who are finishing mid pack. It's just your ability to do that."

Andy Bayer on the best part of a race: "The finish. At least if I'm closing well, the finish is the fun part. I always feel like getting off the line, you're a little stressed trying to get into the right position. That's when most of the pushing and shoving happens. The 1500m, it's short enough, the third lap, that's when it starts hurting, at least if it's a fast race. Then when you get to the bell lap you know, 'I can finish now.' It's kind of fun to try and pass as many guys as possible or win. Definitely the last 50m unless you have a bad race, and that's probably the worst part of a race."

Sheila Reid on the learning curve to world class: "I still have a long way to go before I'm world class. I suppose that's the biggest thing. It's not enough to run an A standard. These women are just so much better right now, their speed is so much better. Some of them close in 57, which means their top-end 400m speed has to be so much faster than mine currently is. And it's not something that can't be worked on, but there's so much work to be done. And that's what I realize. And I realize it's not that I'm not putting in the work, it's a developmental thing. There's a learning curve, but there's a training aspect that takes time. You can't rush these things. There are no short cuts to getting that kind of speed, that raw speed, that some people like [Abeba] Aregawi and even Jenny [Simpson] have.

"In terms of learning, I guess the biggest difference is that in college, I think it was easier to run my best race because there were maybe a handful of girls who were all at the same level. Now everybody is really good. And everybody is there with a lap to go, and I think when it's that crowded, when there are that many people at the same level competing for the same thing, things can get messy, and it's easy to just kind of get blown out the back, quite frankly. The depth of the competition is huge so you almost have to be that much better than everyone else to be really competitive and to get through prelims and rounds feeling good. Just having clean races, I think that's the biggest thing. Learning to have your best race in those kinds of situations. [You need to be] learning to run around people all of the time."

Ron Warhurst on watching for the move, not the person: *Warhurst makes the valid point that often in the final stages of a race, it's important not to key on specific competitors. Doing that can cause the runner to focus too much on someone who might not be having a great day, and ignore the athlete who did come ready to race.*

"It happened to Kevin Sullivan at the World Championships in 2001. He geared himself in the semis off of two Kenyans who were real fast. And he stayed back with them even though the heat was extremely slow. And these Kenyans were 30 yards off the pace. He stayed back because these Kenyans, he thought they were going to go. With 300m to go, there were already six guys up front. Sully moves out and makes the big run. They took five [to the final] and he was the seventh-place guy. Sully didn't make the final. There's a typical example of racing your competition.

"You can do that with 500m to go, or 400m to go. Who's going to light it up? Some people like to go from 500m out, tactically some like to go at 400m, right at the bell, and some like to go at 300m. So you have to know which guys are going to go, but you have to understand, it doesn't matter who goes. Somebody's going from 500m out to get the pace going. [Hicham] El Guerrouj, he used to make a move at the 700-800m mark, he'd start picking the pace up and be in position from 800m out, to 500m to go. And then he would start grinding from 500m out. He would do it every time. He would go to the front, and he would try to control the pace. Instead of going to the front and slowing down, he would go to the front and he was on. So you kind of knew he was going to do that."

In general, though, when the racing starts, Warhurst is clear: "It doesn't matter who goes." Be ready and in position.

Peter Rono on the pressure: "The thing is once you win, it's not very easy for a champion. I know the pressure the great runners have. When you are the top guy, it can be very easy to get up there, but to remain up there is always the biggest challenge. So you give it your best."

Katie Mackey on the possibilities of racing: "I just love that when you stand on the line, anything can happen, anything is possible. I just really love that feeling. It's really fun for me to get out there and realize, all of us have trained as hard as we can, to get to this point, so let's get out there and bring the best out of each other. That is really fun to me."

Steve Scott on how sometimes not caring can help: "To give you an idea of how important it is to stay relaxed, I was in Ingelbrecht, racing in a 3000m. It was a small meet in this little town. The whole town comes out to watch it. It was the marquee race. It was a 3K and there wasn't anything else. When I raced 1500m or mile, I always cared how I did because of world rankings. There was the pride thing, but there were also bonuses from shoe companies.... So whenever you race 1500m or mile, if you lose, you're not going to be ranked #1. You can't afford to lose one race all season. But an odd distance race, like a 3K, it's like who cares. How I do is not going to affect my mile/1500m ranking. And that was basically my attitude going into this race. I didn't care at all. Like I talked about how I hated to lead, well this was possible for me if I was in the right frame of mind, but it was so difficult for me to get into that frame of mind. It had to be a situation where you didn't care, and that was this race. It was Thomas [Wessingage's] hometown; it was his crowd, so I was like, 'Okay, let's make a good showing. I'm going to go out and start running 60, and hold it for as long as I can. He'll come by me on the last lap, shoot me down, and so be it.' So that was my tactic. I didn't have any pressure. I didn't care. So the race started. Of course I go to the lead. Thomas is right behind me. I'm right at 60s, or 60-point, and we get to the last lap, and naturally, Thomas goes flying by me, but he's not leaving me. So I go chasing after him. And down the homestretch we're side by side. I passed him and I win the race in 7:36.69 which was a new American record. I didn't go into the race saying I had to win, I didn't go into the race saying I have to break this American record. I didn't even know what the record was. I just said I was going to go as hard as I can for as long as I can, and I don't care what happens. That shows how your mentality can also affect the success or failure of your tactics."

Shannon Rowbury:

"It's a distance where championship races tend to be tactical and almost everyone can be in the race until the last lap. If something goes wrong there isn't much room for error. To make the Olympic team is going to be very challenging and those who do so will have to be very fit, stay on their feet, get to the final and race well tactically."[6]

Ron Warhurst on teaching college racing to freshmen: "You say, look, you're a turd. You're not a superstar. Learn from this. This is how you do it. Watch the older guys. Watch them do it. This is how you're supposed to do it, this is how you're going to do it. And then they have to go trial-and-error, trial-and-error, trial-and-error, and hopefully by the time they're juniors they've got the savvy. And you don't have to worry about that. You say, this is where you're supposed to be, with 600m to go you've got to be in position to move. So much of this is experience."

Renato Canova: "Tactically, a winner must understand that, if the race is more tactical, his first goal is not to run less distance staying always in the first lane, but it is to be free to decide when and where to eventually attack. For that reason, I can't stand athletes saying, after the race, "they boxed me," because this is not a problem of other runners, but only of the athlete himself. A top athlete never puts himself in condition to be boxed!"

Marty Liquori on tactics being instinctual: "To be a successful tactician you must not only be in better physical condition than your competitors, you must also be stronger mentally. Your mind must be able to control your body, your mind must be able to recognize instantly the sudden opening and sweep you swiftly through it, without stopping to ask your legs and your lungs and the rest of your body how they're doing. You can't stop and think, 'If I go now I'm going to be really hurting the last two hundred yards.' You must simply go, utilizing your racing knowledge and secured by the thought that you can endure whatever hurt must follow."[9]

The Final Word

The intelligent competitor not only learns by doing, but learns by seeing and listening. Athletes can and should learn from their own experiences; however, the best competitors also learn from the experiences of others. Considering how short most competitive running careers are, it seems a pity to waste precious racing opportunities to a lack of understanding of the strategies needed.

As a coach, when I see any of my young runners disappointed after a race, I routinely ask what they learned from it. What do they need to do next time to handle that particular situation? Simply stated, there is no such thing as a bad race as long as the athlete has learned something from it and comes to the next race better prepared to compete.

Younger runners reading this book may not have found the perfect answer to their specific questions regarding racing. My hope is that now, at least, they know the right questions to ask themselves.

—Jeff Hollobaugh

INDEX OF NAMES DROPPED

A quick guide to many of the names prominently mentioned, as well as those interviewed and quoted.

PRs as of February 2015—times might have improved since then for active athletes.

AJ Acosta
USA, born 1988.
PRs: 800—1:49.64 ('12), 1500—3:36.41 ('12), Mile—3:53.76 ('10), 3000—7:50.92 ('15), 5000—13:46.87 ('10).
The 2006 US Junior champ, he made All-America eight times while at Oregon. Placed second in the 2010 NCAA 1500.

Saïd Aouita
Morocco, born 1959.
PRs: 800—1:43.86 ('88), 1000—2:15.16 ('88), 1500—3:29.46 ('85), Mile—3:46.76 ('87), 2000—4:50.81 ('87), 3000—7:29.45 ('89), Steeple—8:21.92 ('87), 2M—8:13.45 ('87), 5000—12:58.39 ('87), 10,000—27:26.11 ('86).
Won bronze in the 1983 World Champs 1500. The next year he struck gold in the Olympic 5000. Won the 1987 Worlds in the 5000m, and in 1988 earned Olympic bronze in the 800m. Set five world records. Was the first to break 7:30 in the 3000m and 13:00 in the 5000m. Lives in Florida and owns a sport clothing company.

Abeba Aregawi
Sweden, born 1990.
PRs: 800—1:59.20 ('13), 1500—3:56.54 ('12).
Placed 5th in the 2012 Olympics for Ethiopia, then switched citizenship to Sweden with a short-lived marriage to her coach. Won gold at the 2013 Worlds.

Jeff Atkinson
USA, born 1963.
PRs: 800—1:48.75 ('92), 1500—3:35.15 ('89), Mile—3:52.80y ('88).
As a high schooler in Manhattan Beach, California, ran 4:19. Was a walk-on at Stanford, where he finished 4th in the NCAA 1500m his senior year. Won the 1988 Olympic Trials and placed 10th in the Games that year. Currently coaches high schoolers at Palos Verdes (CA) and manufactures skateboards at Shaggo.com.

Andy Bayer
USA, born 1990.
PRs: 800—1:48.97 ('13), 1500—3:34.47 ('13), Mile 3:52.90 ('13), 3000—7:43.84 ('13), Steeple—8:25.71 ('14), 5000—13:32.74 ('11).
Ran 4:12.51 for 1600m as an Indiana high schooler. At Indiana University, won the NCAA 1500m as a junior. That same year, he won three Big 10 titles and placed fourth in the Olympic Trials. In 2014, he started training for the steeplechase, running 8:25.71 in his third career race.

Filbert Bayi
Tanzania, born 1953.
PRs: 800—1:45.32 ('74), 1500—3:32.16 ('74), Mile—3:51.0 ('75), Steeple—8:12.48 ('80), 5000—13:18.2 ('80).
Set 1500m world record at age 20 in winning Commonwealth Games. Broke Jim Ryun's mile world record at age 21. Denied the 1976 Olympics because of a boycott, and troubled by chronic malaria, he never reached his full potential as a miler. He concentrated on the steeplechase later in his career and won the silver medal in 1980. Currently operates an educational foundation and a number of schools in Tanzania.

Bryan Berryhill
USA, born 1977.
PRs: 800—1:46.03 ('01), 1500—3:35.48 ('01), Mile—3:54.87 ('01), 3000—8:01.14 ('01).
The Colorado State runner won the NCAA indoors and out in 2001. Now he coaches track and cross country at the University of Wyoming.

Abdi Bile
Somalia, born 1962.
PRs: 800—1:43.60 ('89), 1000—2:14.50 ('89), 1500—3:30.55 ('89), Mile—3:49.40 ('88), 3000—7:42.18 ('94).
Born into a nomadic family with 15 children, he began running when he realized it might get him to school in the United States. A star at George Mason, he won NCAA

titles in 1985 and 1987. Noted for his ferocious kick, he won the 1987 World Championships 1500m. Dogged by injuries, he missed the 1988 and 1992 Olympics, and the 1991 Worlds. Today he lives in the U.S. and has been national coach for several Middle Eastern nations.

Mike Boit
Kenya, born 1949.
PRs: 800—1:43.57 ('76),
1000—2:15.30 ('77),
1500—3:33.67 ('79),
Mile—3:49.45 ('81),
3000—7:45.61 ('82),
5000—13:35.70 ('82).
Primarily an 800m runner, Boit graduated from the legendary St. Patrick's High School in Iten in 1969, years before Colm O'Connell began coaching there. He won bronze in the 1972 Olympic 800m. He competed for Eastern New Mexico in 1973-1976, as did his brother Tom. Missed the 1976 and 1980 Olympics because of political boycotts. While he competed in the 800m at most championships, he was also a steady performer in the 1500/mile in the Coe-Ovett era, and placed second in two of Coe's mile world records. Won the 1500m at the African Championships in 1979. Now is a professor at Kenyatta University. Along with noted coach John Manners, is co-founder of the Kenyan Scholar-Athlete Project to encourage Kenyan youth to attend elite American universities.

Sarah Brown
USA, born 1986.
PRs: 800—2:02.25 ('10),
1500—4:05.27 ('13),
Mile—4:26.67 ('14),
3000—9:04.87 ('13),
5000—16:20.78 ('09).
As Sarah Bowman, was a major prep star from Virginia, clocking 4:36.95. At Tennessee she won 10 SEC crowns—the most in conference history—and captured the 2009 NCAA Indoor mile. She also ran on two American Record relays, and one world record. Placed 8th in the World Indoor 1500m in 2010. Finished 6th in the 2012 Olympic Trials.

Charlotte Browning
Great Britain, born 1987.
PRs: 800—2:02.52 ('10),
1500—4:09.86 ('10),
Mile—4:31.24 ('10),
3000—9:21.77 ('10).
5000—16:35.29 ('14).
She won NCAA titles indoors and out in 2010 for Florida.

Dick Buerkle
USA, born 1947.

PRs: 1500—3:39.8 ('78),
Mile—3:54.93 ('78),
5000—13:23.20 ('80),
10,000—28:25.00 ('74).
Only a 4:28 high school miler, the New York native developed into a top 5000m runner at Villanova. He won two U.S. titles at the distance and also the 1976 Olympic Trials. In the 1978 indoor season, he concentrated on the mile, setting the world indoor record. Since his athletic retirement, he has worked primarily as a Spanish teacher.

Tom Byers
USA, born 1955.
PRs: 800—1:47.2 ('83),
1000—2:16.1 ('81),
1500—3:35.75 ('82),
Mile—3:50.84 ('82),
3000—7:48.85 ('83).
Only a 4:20 high school miler, he placed second at USA nationals as a freshman, clocking 3:37.5 that year. Retired for a few years before coming back in the 1980s as a professional, and occasionally, a rabbit. Now a businessman in Ohio.

Fermín Cacho
Spain, born 1969.
PRs: 800—1:45.37 ('91),
1000—2:16.13 ('93),
1500—3:28.95 ('97),
Mile—3:49.56 ('96),
3000—7:36.61 ('96).
A skillful kicker, Cacho emerged from a village in northern Spain that had no track, and made it to the world stage in 1990, winning silver at the Euro Indoors. In 1991 he

placed 5th in the World Champs and the next year he surprised with Olympic gold. He captured World silvers in 1993 and 1997, and the Olympic silver in 1996. Long considered a big-meet kicker, he never produced a time that matched his accomplishments until late in his career. His 3:28.95 European record lasted for 16 years. Currently working in sports development in Spain with GO Fit.

Mary Cain
USA, born 1996.
PRs: 800—1:59.51 ('13),
1000—2:35.80 ('14),
1500—4:04.62 ('13),
Mile—4:24.11 ('14),
3000—8:58.48 ('14),
2M—9:38.68 ('13),
5000—15:45.46 ('13).
Teenage phenomenon turned pro while still in high school. Coached by Alberto Salazar.
She won the 2013 USA Indoor mile, and the 2014 World Junior 3000.

Peter Callahan
USA, born 1991.

PRs: 800—1:48.66 ('11),
1500—3:39.27 ('14),
Mile—3:58.76 ('12).
Won 2010 US Junior title. Anchored Princeton's indoor national championship DMR in 2013. He ran for New Mexico as a grad student, placing fourth in 2014 NCAA.

Renato Canova
Italy, born 1944.
Coach of many African distance stars, a list that includes world record holders and many world champions. Most notable miler he coaches is Silas Kiplagat. Currently working with the Chinese Federation.

Matt Centrowitz
USA, born 1955.
PRs: 1500—3:36.70 ('76),
Mile—3:54.94 ('82),
3000—7:48.20 ('78),
2M—8:26.82 ('79),
5000—13:12.91 ('82),
10,000—28:32.7 ('83).
As a prep was the top high school miler in the country. At Oregon, he broke Prefontaine's school 1500m record. Made the 1976 and 1980 Olympic teams in the 1500m. Won four straight USA titles at 5000m. Now coaches at American University.

Matthew Centrowitz
USA, born 1989.
PRs: 800—1:45.86 ('13),
1000—2:19.53 ('15),
1500—3:31.09 ('14),
Mile—3:50.53 ('14),
3000—7:46.19 ('12),
5000—13:20.06 ('14).
A skilled tactician, the son

of Matt Centrowitz (above) won the 2011 NCAA 1500m crown for Oregon. He captured the USA title that same year. He won bronze in the World Champs 1500m in 2011, silver in 2013, and in between placed fourth in the 2012 Olympics. Won his second USA 1500m championship in 2013.

Sebastian Coe
Great Britain, born 1956.
PRs: 400—46.87 ('79),
800—1:41.73 ('81),
1000—2:12.18 ('81),
1500—3:29.77 ('86),
Mile—3:47.33 ('81),
2000—4:58.84 ('82).
Won two Olympic gold medals at 1500m (1980 & 1984), and silvers at 800m those same years. Set a total of 11 world records during his career. Since retirement, has served in the British Parliament and as chairman of the London Organizing Committee for the 2012 Games.

Eamonn Coghlan
Ireland, born 1952.
PRs: 800—1:47.78 ('77),
1500—3:35.6 ('81),
Mile—3:49.78 ('83),
3000m—7:37.60 ('80),
5000—13:19.13 ('81),
10,000—28:19.3 ('86).
The "Chairman of the Boards" was renowned for his dominance of the indoor mile scene. Won four NCAA titles while at Villanova. In 1983 he became the first man to break 3:50 indoors. Placed fourth in the 1976 Olympic 1500m, and

fourth in the 1980 Olympic 5000m. Won the first World Championship at 5000m in 1983. He became the first man over age 40 to break the four-minute mile, which he had done a total of 83 times in his career. Since retirement he has served as an Irish senator.

Steve Cram
Great Britain, born 1960.
PRs: 800—1:42.88 ('85),
1000—2:12.88 ('85),
1500—3:29.67 ('85),
Mile—3:46.32 ('85),
2000—4:51.39 ('85),
3000—7:43.10 ('83),
2M—8:14.93 ('83),
5000—13:28.58 ('89).
The 1983 World Champion, he won Euro golds in 1982 and 1986, and silver in the 1984 Olympics. Set three world records, and was the first man to break the 3:30 barrier for 1500. Now a top athletics commentator for BBC TV.

Glenn Cunningham
USA, 1909-1988.
PRs: 800—1:49.7 ('36),
1500—3:48.4 ('36),
Mile—4:04.4 ('38).
Dominated American miling in the 1930s despite having his legs severely damaged by a fire in childhood. Set world records in the 800m and mile. He won silver in the 1936 Olympics. Served in the Navy and was athletic director at Cornell College.

Mark Deady
USA, born 1967.
PRs: 1500—3:35.83 ('88).

The Indiana athlete placed third in the 1988 NCAA meet and he also made the semis of the 1988 Olympics. Now a vice president at Mutual of America.

Amanda Eccleston
USA, born 1990.
PRs: 800—2:04.23 ('14),
1500—4:08.08 ('14),
Mile—4:30.43 ('14),
3000—9:21.23 ('13),
5000—16:13.07 ('13).
Ran 5:13.06 for 1600m in high school as Amanda Putt. Won NCAA D2 crowns at 800m and 1500m for Hillsdale. Competed for Michigan while doing graduate work, improving greatly to place fifth in the NCAA. In her first year as a pro, dropped her best to under 4:10 and made the finals at USA Nationals.

Hicham El Guerrouj
Morocco, born 1974.
PRs: 800—1:47.18 ('95),
1000—2:16.85 ('95),
1500—3:26.00 ('98),
Mile—3:43.13 ('99),
2000—4:44.79 ('99),
3000—7:23.09 ('99),
2M—8:06.61 ('03),
5000—12:50.24 ('03).

The dominant runner of his era captured golds in the 1500m and 5000m in the 2004 Olympics. Also won four straight golds in the 1500m at the World Champs.

Herb Elliott
Australia, born 1938.
PRs: 800—1:46.7 ('58),
1500—3:35.6 ('60),
Mile—3:54.5 ('58).
Fiercely competitive, he never lost a 1500/mile race as an adult. Won gold in both the 880y and mile at the 1958 Commonwealth Games. A few weeks later, he set world records at 1500m and the mile. In 1960, he won the Olympic gold with a world record performance. Retired from running at age 22. Later had great success in business .

James "Jumbo" Elliott
USA, 1915-1981.
Considered one of the greatest coaches of all time. As coach of Villanova University from 1949 to 1981, he coached five Olympic gold medalists out of 28 Olympians. His teams won eight NCAA team titles. Individually, his athletes captured 82 NCAA crowns and set 66 world records. Only a part-time coach, he sold construction equipment for a living.

Joe Falcon
USA, born 1966.
PRs: 1500—3:33.6 ('90),
Mile—3:49.31 ('90),
3000—7:46.42 ('89),

2M—8:24.43 ('91),
5000—13:20.49 ('90),
10,000—28:21.24 ('93).
Won the 1988 NCAA title
for Arkansas, in addition
to five other NCAA
crowns including cross
country and indoor track.
He won the Bislett Dream
Mile in 1990. Currently a
police officer and school
board member in
Arkansas.

German Fernandez
USA, born 1990.
PRs: 1500—3:34.60 ('12),
Mile—3:55.02 ('09),
3000—7:47.97 ('09),
5000—13:25.46 ('09).
A high school superstar
from California, as a
freshman at Oklahoma
State he won the NCAA
1500m. Won six Big 12
conference titles and in
2010 finished 8th in NCAA
Cross Country, helping
his school to the victory.

Grant Fisher
USA, born 1997.
PRs: 1500—3:42.89 ('15),
Mile—3:59.38 ('15),
2M—8:43.57 ('15).
Winner of the adidas
Dream Mile in 2014 and
2015.

Mac Fleet
USA, born 1990.
PRs: 800—1:46.32 ('13),
1500—3:38.35 ('13),
Mile—3:56.77 ('14).
US Junior champion in
2009, he had high school
mile best of 4:02.90.
NCAA champion in 2013
and 2014 for Oregon.
Seven time All-America.

Katie Flood
USA, born 1992.
PRs: 800—2:07.33 ('12),
1500—4:11.38 ('12),
Mile—4:28.48 ('12),
3000—8:55.31 ('12),
5000—15:45.60 ('14).
She won the 2012 NCAA
title for Washington. Six-
time All-America.

Ray Flynn
Ireland, born 1957.
PRs: 800—1:48.30 ('80),
1500—3:33.5 ('82),
Mile—3:49.77 ('82),
3000—7:41.60 ('84),
5000—13:19.52 ('84).
Starred at East
Tennessee State as an
All-American in both track
and cross country. In his
long career, ran 89 sub-
4:00 miles. Irish record-
holder in the mile; helped
Ireland to a world record
in the 4 x mile relay in
1985. Placed second in
the 1980 Euro Indoors,
and was a two-time
Olympian at 5000m.
Currently heads Flynn
Sports Management.

Gabe Grunewald
USA, born 1986.
PRs: 800—2:01.38 ('13),
1500—4:01.48 ('13),
Mile—4:27.94 ('12),
3000—8:42.64 ('13),
5000—15:33.64 ('14).
As Gabriele Anderson,
ran only 5:08.60 as a high
schooler, though she was
an 800m state champ.
Blossomed at Minnesota,
where she eventually
placed second in the
2010 NCAA 1500m.
Succesful despite battling
two different cancers. In
2014, she won the USA
Indoor 3000m.

Suzy Favor Hamilton
USA, born 1968.
PRs: 800—1:58.10 ('00),
1500—3:57.40 ('00),
Mile—4:22.93 ('98),
3000—8:46.16 ('00),
5000—15:06.48 ('00).
As a Wisconsin high
school star, ran 4:18.62
for 1500m. At the
University of Wisconsin,
she won nine NCAA titles.
A three-time Olympian,
she won four USA titles
outdoors and three
indoors.

Todd Harbour
USA, born 1959.
PRs: 800—1:47.22 ('80),
1500—3:33.99 ('82),
Mile—3:50.34 ('81),
2000—4:59.28 ('82),
5000—13:30.57 ('84).
As a Baylor star, he
finished second three
times in a row in the
NCAA 1500. Won silver in
the 1979 Pan-Am Games.
Now head track and cross
country coach at his alma
mater.

Len Hilton
USA, 1947-2000.
PRs: 1500—3:36.4 ('74),
Mile—3:55.9 ('73),
3000—7:48.0 ('72),

5000—13:40.20 ('72). The first Texan to break the four-minute mile, Hilton ran for Houston from 1967-71. Made the 1972 Olympic team in the 5000m, finishing third at the Trials. Won the USA mile championship in 1973 and 1975. Broke the four-minute barrier 32 times. He was noted for having a great kick. Later served as a corporate executive in the energy industry.

Steve Holman
USA, born 1970.
PRs: 800—1:44.98 ('95),
1000—2:16.68 ('99),
1500—3:31.52 ('97),
Mile—3:50.40 ('97),
3000—7:42.49 ('96),
5000—13:47.63 ('92).
Ran 4:09.26 for 1600m in high school. He won the 1992 NCAA 1500m. A semifinalist in the 1992 Olympics, the Georgetown alum finished ninth in the 1999 Worlds, after winning the USA title that year. Now works in retail investing.

Kelly Holmes
Great Britain, born 1970.
PRs: 800—1:56.21 ('95),
1000—2:32.55 ('97),
1500—3:57.90 ('04),
Mile 4:28.04 ('98),
3000—9:01.91 ('03).
A frequent medalist in international competition, she won the 800/1500m double at the 2004 Olympics. Has since worked in broadcasting and as president of Commonwealth Games England.

Shelby Houlihan
USA, born 1993.
PRs: 800—2:01.12 ('14),
1500—4:10.89 ('14),
Mile—4:30.77 ('15),
3000—9:03.71 ('15),
5000—16:11.63 ('14).
Arizona State athlete won the NCAA title in 2014 after she finished seventh the previous year.

Brian Hyde
USA, born 1972.
PRs: 800—1:49.86 ('97),
1000—2:18.46 ('95),
1500—3:35.84 ('95),
Mile—3:56.41 ('97),
3000—8:03.20 ('97)
William & Mary star placed 7th in 1995 NCAA and he ran 2nd in the USA Champs in a virtual dead heat with winner Paul McMullen. Now a physical therapist.

Gabe Jennings
USA, born 1979.
PRs: 800—1:46.83 ('01),
1500—3:35.21 ('00),
Mile—3:58.25 ('09),
3000—7:58.40 ('98),
5000—13:44.60 ('00),
Mar—2:19:32 ('05).
While at Stanford, he won NCAA titles in the 1500m and the indoor mile in 2000. Won the Olympic Trials that same year. Pursuing career in environmental law.

Ben Jipcho
Kenya, born 1943.
PRs: 800—1:47.1 ('75),
1500—3:33.16 ('74),
Mile—3:52.17 ('73),
3000—7:44.4 ('73),
Steeple—8:13.91,
2M—8:16.38 ('73),
5000—13:14.30 ('74).
Won the steeple silver in 1972, and golds in the steeple and 5000m at the 1974 Commonwealth Games. He is famous for rabbiting the 1968 Olympic 1500m final. Living in retirement in Kenya.

Heather Kampf
USA, born 1987.
PRs: 800—2:00.04 ('13),
1000—2:40.90 ('14),
1500—4:06.16 ('14),
Mile—4:30.07 ('15).
As Heather Dorniden, won 400m and 800m state titles as a Minnesota prep. At the University of Minnesota, competed in every track and cross country NCAA championship possible. Nine-time All-American. Won the NCAA Indoor 800m as a freshman. Has won two USA road mile championships. Competed in the World Indoor 1500m in 2014. Has steadily moved from the 800m into the 1500m, where she finished 6th at USA nationals in 2014.

Kip Keino
Kenya, born 1940.
PRs: 800—1:46.41 ('72),
1500—3:34.91 ('68),
Mile—3:53.1 ('67),
3000—7:39.6 ('65),
Steeple—8:23.64 ('72),
2M—8:25.2 ('65),
5000—13:24.2 ('65),
10,000—28:06.4 ('68).
After placing fifth in the 1964 Olympics 5000m, became one of the all-time greats. Won the 1968 gold in the 1500m over Jim Ryun after taking silver in the 5000m. In 1972, won

steeplechase gold and a 1500m silver. Also won three Commonwealth golds. His 3000m and 5000m bests were both world records. In later years, became chairman of the Kenyan Olympic Committee. His son Martin was a two-time NCAA champion.

Silas Kiplagat
Kenya, born 1989.
PRs: 800—1:44.8 ('12), 1500—3:27.64 ('14), Mile—3:47.88 ('14), 3000—7:39.94 ('10), 5000—13:55.0 ('13).
He placed seventh in the 2012 Olympics after winning silver in the previous year's World Champs.

Asbel Kiprop
Kenya, born 1989.
PRs: 800—1:43.15 ('11), 1500—3:27.72 ('13), Mile—3:48.50 ('09), 3000—7:42.32 ('07), 5000—14:12.9 ('13).
Finished fourth in both the 2007 and 2009 Worlds, but got the 2008 Olympic gold after Rashid Ramzi's disqualification. Troubled with injury, he finished last in the 2012 Olympic final, but the next summer placed second in the Continental Cup.

Bernard Lagat
USA, born 1974.
PRs: 800—1:46.00 ('03), 1000—2:16.18 ('08), 1500—3:26.34 ('01), Mile—3:47.28 ('01), 2000—4:54.74 ('14), 3000—7:29.00 ('10), 2M—8:09.49 ('13), 5000—12:53.60 ('11).

Won Olympic bronze (2000) and silver (2004) for Kenya before taking U.S. citizenship in 2005. Also earned silver in the 2001 Worlds. In 2007, representing the U.S., he won the 1500m and the 5000m at the World Champs. In 2009, won bronze in the 1500m at Worlds, and scored a 5000m silver in 2011.

Lawi Lalang
Kenya, born 1991.
PRs: 800—1:48.88 ('11), 1500—3:33.20 ('13), Mile—3:52.88 ('14), 3000—7:36.44 ('14), 5000—13:00.95 ('13), 10,000—28:14.63 ('13).
Recruited to Arizona despite having never raced before, because his brother Boaz had run 1:42.95 and 3:52.18. Captured the NCAA cross country title a year later, and the NCAA Indoor mile in 2013. In all, won eight NCAA titles.

Francie Larrieu Smith
USA, born 1952.
PRs: 1500—4:05.09 ('76), Mile—4:27.52 ('79), 5000—15:15.2 ('88), 10,000—31:28.92 ('91), Marathon—2:27:35 ('91).

Ran 4:16.8 for 1500m as a high school junior. Winner of 1972 Olympic Trials 1500m. A 16-time U.S. champion at various distances. Over long career competed in four Olympic Games at distances from 1500m to the marathon. She set 13 world indoor records and 35 American records. Flag bearer for the U.S. team at the 1992 Olympics. Currently coaching at Southwestern University in Texas.

Seneca Lassiter
USA, born 1977.
PRs: 800—1:45.51 ('99), 1500—3:33.72 ('99), Mile—3:54.21 ('01), 3000—8:05.87 ('99), 5000—13:39.82 ('02).
Won 1997 and 1998 NCAA titles for Arkansas, and ran second in 1999. Made World Champs teams in 1999 and 2001 but didn't get out of the heats. Finished sixth in World Indoor in 2001. Retired after being sanctioned by USATF for his pacemaking in the World Cup in 2002.

Will Leer
USA, born 1985.
PRs: 1:47.69 ('08), 1500—3:34.26 ('14), Mile—3:51.82 ('14), 3000—7:39.38 ('13), 2M—8:19.11 ('11), 5000—13:21.55 ('13).
Pomona grad was only a 4:16.41 runner in the high school 1600. He won four NCAA D3 titles. In 2013 won USA indoor titles at the mile and 3000.

Marty Liquori
USA, born 1949.
PRs: 1500—3:36.0 ('71),
Mile—3:52.2 ('75),
5000—13:15.06 ('77).
The third American to
break four-minutes while
in high school, he starred
at Villanova. Made the
Olympic team as a
college freshman in 1968.
In 1969 he defeated Jim
Ryun to win both the
NCAA and USA titles.
Was ranked No. 1 In the
world in 1969 and 1971.
Missed 1972 and 1976
Olympic years because of
injury. Won the 5000m at
the 1977 World Cup. Has
had a varied career since
then as a TV
commentator, store
owner, and is currently a
professional jazz
musician in Florida.

Liu Dong
China, born 1973.
PRs: 800—1:55.54 (93),
1500—3:56.31 ('97),
5000—16:03.41 ('97).
One of the pupils of
controversial coach Ma
Junren. Won the World
Junior gold in 1992 and
the next year captured
gold at the World
Champs. She now lives in
Spain and still competes
occasionally.

Jack Lovelock
New Zealand, 1910-1949.
PRs: 1500—3:47.8 ('36),
Mile—4:07.6 ('33).
Broke mile world record in
1933. Gold medal winner
in the 1936 Olympics,
setting a world record in
the race. A doctor during
WWII, he died tragically
young when he fell in

front of a train in
Brooklyn.

Katie (Follett) Mackey
USA, born 1987.
PRs—800—2:02.00 ('13),
1500—4:04.60 ('13),
Mile—4:27.78 ('14),
3000—8:59.41 ('13),
5000—15:04.74 ('14).
As a Colorado high
schooler, she ran 4:58.4
at 1600m as a
sophomore. Was All-
State ten times but never
won a state title. Starred
at Washington, winning
two Pac-10 titles in the
1500m and making NCAA
All-American eight times.
Has steadily improved
since then, placing 3rd in
the USA 1500m in 2014.

Taoufik Makhloufi
Algeria, born 1988
PRs: 800—1:43.53 ('14),
1500—3:30.40 ('14),
Mile—3:52.16 ('14).
In 2011, failed to make
the finals at the World
Champs. A year later he
dominated the Olympic
race to win gold.

Leo Manzano
USA, born 1984.
PRs: 800—1:44.56 ('10),

1000—2:19.73 ('09),
1500—3:30.98 ('14),
Mile—3:50.64 ('10),
3000—8:14.59 ('06).
Texas grad won two
NCAA miles indoors and
two NCAA 1500m crowns
outdoors. Known for his
final stretch kick, he
captured silver at the
2012 Olympics.

Cory McGee
USA, born 1992.
PRs: 800—2:04.13 ('15),
1500—4:06.67 ('13),
Mile—4:32.10 ('13),
3000—9:10.48 ('14),
5000—16:03.06 ('14).
Won 22 state track and
cross country titles as a
Mississippi high schooler.
She won the 2011 USA
Junior 1500m and the
Pan-Am Junior gold.
Finished third in the 2013
USA 1500m, and
represented the United
States at the 2013 World
Championships. NCAA
runner-up in 2014, after
three other top 10 finishes
for the University of
Florida.

John McDonnell
USA, born 1938.
Won All-America honors
six times as a runner
himself. Became the
winningest coach in
NCAA history at
Arkansas, where he
guided his teams to a
total of 42 NCAA team
championships. Now
retired, he runs a cattle
ranch.

Paul McMullen
USA, born 1972.
PRs: 800—1:45.71 ('01),
1500—3:33.89 ('01),

Mile—3:54.94 ('01), 3000—8:04.67 ('00), 5000—13:59.40 ('97). A football player and 4:19.9 runner in high school, he won the 1995 USA Champs and the 1996 Olympic Trials. Finished 10th in both the 1995 and 2001 World Championships. Known for his brash, confident style, he lost two toes in a lawnmower accident in 1997 but recovered well enough to record most of his PRs after that. Now working as a safety consultant in the home security industry.

Kyle Merber
USA, born 1990. PRs: 800—1:47.23 ('15), 1500—3:35.59 ('12), Mile—3:54.76y ('14); 3000—8:09.01 ('10), 5000—14:02.91 ('10). A 4:12.11 high school miler in New York, he broke 4:00 in his second year of college at Columbia. He made the NCAA final in 2010. Won the Ivy League 1500m in 2012, and set the American collegiate record with his 3:35.59.

Noureddine Morceli
Algeria, born 1970. PRs: 800—1:44.79 ('91), 1000—2:13.73 ('93), 1500—3:27.37 ('95), Mile—3:44.39 ('93), 2000—4:47.88 ('95), 3000—7:25.11 ('94), 5000—13:03.85 ('94). Coached by his brother, a one-time world class runner himself, Morceli competed for Riverside Community College in

California in 1989-90. He became the dominant miler in the world through most of the 1990s, winning the World Champs in 1991, 1993 and 1995, and following that with the 1996 Olympic gold. Broke the 1500m record in 1992 with his 3:28.86, and again in 1995 (3:27.37). His 1993 mile world record of 3:44.39 cut nearly two full seconds off Steve Cram's 1985 record. He also set world records at 2000m and 3000m.

Treniere (Clement) Moser
USA, born 1981. PRs: 800—1:59.15 ('07), 1000—2:37.86 ('15), 1500—4:02.85 ('13), Mile—4:27.49 ('15), 3000—9:03.54 ('13), 5000—15:11.00 ('13). Georgetown grad has won USA outdoor 1500m titles four times. She is coached by Alberto Salazar.

Dub Myers
USA, born 1964. 800—1:47.51 ('84), 1500—3:37.89 ('84), Mile—3:55.31 ('86). He won the 1986 NCAA title for Oregon after top-5 finishes the previous three years.

Noah Ngeny
Kenya, born 1978. 800—1:44.49 ('00), 1000—2:11.96 ('99), 1500—3:28.12 ('00), Mile—3:43.40 ('99), 2000—4:50.08 ('99), 3000—7:35.46 ('00).

Won silver at the Worlds in 1999, and followed up with gold at the 2000 Olympics. Never ran nearly as fast in the five years of his career that followed, partly due to a 2001 car accident. Currently coaching in Kenya.

Sonia O'Sullivan
Ireland, born 1969. PRs: 800—2:00.69 ('94), 1500—3:58.85 ('95), Mile 4:17.25 ('94), 3000—8:21.64 ('94), 5000—14:41.02 ('00), 10,000—30:47.59 ('02), Mar—2:29:01 ('05). Starred at Villanova, winning five NCAA titles. Won silver at 1500m in the 1993 Worlds, though most of her honors have come at longer distances. Has won World golds at 5000m and cross country, and has won three European golds. Currently an athletics commentator, and has written two books.

Steve Ovett
Great Britain, born 1955. PRs: 800—1:44.09 ('78), 1000—2:15.91 ('79), 1500—3:30.77 ('83), Mile—3:48.40 ('81), 2000—4:57.71 ('82), 3000—7:41.3 ('77), 2M—8:13.51 ('78), 5000—13:20.06 ('86). Known for his devastating kick, Ovett won the 1980 Olympic gold at 800m, and scored bronze at 1500m. He also won the 1978 European 1500m and two World Cups. Set five world records at 1500m and the mile. Has

since been an athletics commentator for CBC.

İlham Tanui Özbilen
Turkey, born 1990.
PRs: 800—1:44.00 ('13), 1000—2:15.08 ('14), 1500—3:31.30 ('13), Mile—3:49.29 ('09), 3000—7:50.61 ('12). Özbilen set the world junior record in the mile in 2009. He also won the 1500m at the World Athletics Final that year, and was part of the Kenyan team that broke the world record for the 4 x 1500m. In June 2011, he was persuaded by his Turkish manager to switch nationalities. He won the silver at 1500m in the 2012 World Indoors, and finished eighth in the London Olympics.

Don Paige
USA, born 1956.
PRs: 800—1:44.29 ('83), 1000—2:18.06 ('83), 1500—3:37.33 ('79), Mile—3:54.19 ('82). While at Villanova, he won both the NCAA 800m and 1500m in a 35-minute span in 1979. Placed second in USA 1500m that year. In 1980, won Olympic Trials 800m and later defeated world record holder Sebastian Coe, ranking No. 1 in the world. Has since worked as a track design consultant.

Sam Penzenstadler
USA, born 1992.
PRs: 800—1:48.86 ('14), 1500—3:39.77 ('14), Mile—3:58.21 ('14),

3000—8:10.97 ('14), 5000—14:10.41 ('14). Ran a 4:18.33 for 1600m as a Wisconsin high schooler. Improved greatly his junior year at Loyola when he broke 4:00 for the first time. The Missouri Valley Conference 800m champ surprised many by kicking to third in the NCAA 1500m in 2014.

Natalija Piliušina
Lithuania, born 1990.
PRs: 800—2:01.59 ('13), 1500—4:09.51 ('12), Mile—4:32.26 ('13). Finished seventh in the Euro 800m in 2012. The next year she won the NCAA 1500m. Won All-America honors seven times for Oklahoma State. Has struggled with injury since then.

Steve Prefontaine
USA, 1951 –1975.
PRs: 1500—3:38.1 ('73), Mile—3:54.6 ('73), 3000—7:42.6 ('74), 2M—8:18.29 ('74), 5000—13:21.87 ('74), 10,000—27:43.6 ('74). A legendary runner in the U.S., Prefontaine was known for his scrappy racing style and brash attitude. Won three NCAA cross country titles and four straight in the 3M/5000m. Placed fourth in the 1972 Olympic 5000m after driving the pace for the last mile. At one point, held every American record from 2000m to 10,000m. Died at the height of his career in an auto accident.

Jason Pyrah
USA, born 1969.
PRs: 800—1:46.62 ('00), 1500—3:35.21 ('96), Mile—3:55.14 ('96), Steeple—8:47.49 ('00). He placed fourth in the 1992 NCAA meet for BYU. Made Olympic teams in 1996 and 2000, placing 10th in the Olympic final in 2000. Now a sports medicine manager.

Sheila Reid
Canada, born 1989.
PRs: 800—2:04.60 ('13), 1500—4:02.96 ('13), Mile—4:27.02 ('13), 3000—8:44.02 ('13), 5000—15:23.64 ('12). From Newmarket, Ontario, she ran 4:34 in high school for 1500m. She won 12 Big East titles at Villanova University. In 2010 she won the NCAA cross country, and the next spring she became the first ever to capture the NCAA 1500m and 5000m in the same meet. She won a second NCAA XC crown in 2011. In 2012, she represented Canada

in the Olympic 5000m. Now trains with the Oregon Track Club.

Peter Rono
Kenya, born 1967.
PRs: 800—1:46.66 ('88), 1500—3:34.54 ('89), Mile—3:51.41 ('91), 2000—4:59.55 ('96), 3000—7:41.94 ('92).
Won silver at 1986 World Juniors, and in 1988 became the youngest Olympic 1500m champion ever. The next year he placed second in the NCAA for Mount St Mary's. Currently works for New Balance.

Shannon Rowbury
USA, born 1984.
PRs: 800—2:00.47 ('10), 1500—3:59.49 ('14), Mile—4:20.34 ('08), 3000—8:29.93 ('14), 2M—9:20.25 ('14), 5000—14:48.68 ('14).
She won 2007 NCAA indoor mile for Duke. Bronze medalist at 2009 World Champs. Olympic finalist in 2008 and 2012.

Jim Ryun
USA, born 1947.
PRs: 800—1:44.3+ ('66), 1500—3:33.1 ('67), Mile 3:51.1 ('67), 5000—13:38.2 ('72).
The first U.S. high schooler to break four minutes in the mile, he competed in the 1964 Olympics after his junior year in high school. Later he set world records as a freshman and sophomore at the University of Kansas. Won the 1500m silver at the 1968 Olympics. In 1972, he fell

in heats at the Olympics. He ran for two years as a professional after that. He represented Kansas as a Republican in the U.S. House of Representatives from 1996-2007.

Archie San Romani
USA, 1912-1994.
PRs: 1500—3:49.9 ('36). Mile—4:07.2 ('37), 2000—5:16.8 ('37).
Emporia State star won the NCAA mile in 1936 and 1936. Placed fourth in the 1936 Olympics. Set a 2000m world record in 1937. Shared a name with his son, who ran 3:57.6 for the mile in 1971.

Mike Scannell
USA, born 1963
Two-time Olympic Trials marathoner. He coached Omar Kaddurah, the 2011 Pan-Am Junior champion, and Grant Fisher, who won the high school Dream Mile in 4:02.02 as a junior.

Steve Scott
USA, born 1956.
PRs: 800—1:45.05 ('82), 1000—2:16.40 ('81), 1500—3:31.76 ('85), Mile—3:47.69 ('82), 2000—4:54.71 ('82), 3000—7:36.69 ('81), 5000—13:30.39 ('87).
A 1:52.0 800m runner in high school, Scott starred at UC Irvine, where he won the 1978 NCAA 1500m crown after being second the previous year. Was the top-ranked U.S. miler for 10 separate years, and captured the bronze at the 1983 World

Champs. He has run more sub-4:00 miles than any other man, with a total of 137. Currently coaching at Cal State San Marcos.

Jenny Simpson
USA, born 1986.
PRs: 800—2:00.45 ('13), 1500—3:57.22 ('14), Mile—4:25.91 ('09), 3000—8:42.03 ('09), Steeple—9:12.50 ('09), 5000—14:56.26 ('13).
An eight-time state champion as a Florida high schooler, she ran a 4:47.33 for 1600m as a junior. Developed into a steeplechase star at Colorado, setting three American records, winning three NCAA titles in the event, as well as two USA titles. Steeple 9th-placer in 2008 Olympics. Switched focus to 1500m after 2009. Won 2011 World Champs, and silver in 2013. Diamond League champion in 2014.

Mary (Decker) Slaney
USA, born 1958.
PRs: 800—1:56.90 ('85),

1000m—2:34.65 ('88), 1500m—3:57.12 ('83), Mile—4:16.71 ('85), 3000—8:25.83 ('85), 5000—15:06.53 ('85), 10,000—31:35.3 ('82). The dominant American runner of the 1970s and '80s—when healthy. She held every American record from 800m to the 10,000m. Won a historic 1500/3000m double at the 1983 World Championships. Made the finals of both events in the 1988 Olympics, after her controversial fall in the 1984 Games.

Peter Snell
New Zealand, born 1938. PRs: 800—1:44.3 ('62), 1000—2:16.6 ('64), 1500—3:37.6 ('64), Mile—3:54.03 ('64). Trained by the legendary Arthur Lydiard, he won the 800m gold in 1960 and the 800/1500m double in 1964. Set a total of five world records in his relatively short career. Now he is director of the Human Performance Center at the University of Texas Southwestern Medical Center at Dallas.

Jim Spivey
USA, born 1960. PRs: 800—1:46.5 ('82), 1000—2:16.54 ('84), 1500—3:31.01 ('88), Mile—3:49.80 ('86), 2000—4:52.44 ('87), 3000—7:37.04 ('93), 2M—8:24.14 ('86), 5000—13:15.86 ('94). A 4:06.2 miler in high school, he ran for Indiana where he won the 1982

NCAA. Captured bronze at the 1987 Worlds. Winner of the 1984 and 1992 Olympic Trials. Made three Olympic teams and five World Championships. Currently coaches and works for Asics.

Lennart Strand
Sweden, 1921- 2004 PRs: 800—1:51.8 ('49), 1500—3:43.0 ('47), Mile—4:04.8 ('45). Originally a competitive rower, he did not start running until age 23. Made his first breakthrough as a rabbit for Gunder Hägg and Arne Anderson. By 1946, he had become one of the leading milers in the world. He won five Swedish titles at 1500m during a time when the nation dominated world miling. He won gold at the 1946 European Champs, and captured the silver in the 1948 Olympics. In between he tied Hägg's world record for the 1500m.

Kevin Sullivan
Canada, born 1974. PRs: 800—1:47.06 ('95), 1500—3:31.71 ('00),

Mile—3:50.26 ('00), 3000—7:40.17 ('07), 5000—13:19.27 ('07). A sub-four minute miler while still in high school, he starred at the University of Michigan and ran in 22 World Championships (indoors, outdoors and XC) and three Olympic Games. Won 16 Big 10 and four NCAA titles including the 1995 indoor and outdoor crowns. Placed fifth in both the 1995 Worlds and the 1995 Olympics. Currently the cross country coach at the University of Michigan.

Morgan Uceny
USA, born 1985. PRs: 800—1:58.37 ('11), 1000—2:37.61 ('13), 1500—4:00.06 ('11), Mile—4:29.39 ('15). Four-time All-America at Cornell. Favorite at 2011 Worlds, but fell in final. Winner of the 2008 Olympic Trials. She made the 2012 Olympic final, but fell.

Gene Venzke
USA, 1908-1992. PRs: 1500—3:49.9 ('36), Mile—4:08.2 ('40). Penn star placed third in the 1934 NCAA. Placed ninth in the 1500m final at the 1936 Olympics. A three-time national champion, he set several world indoor records.

Tony Waldrop
USA, born 1951. PRs: 800—1:47.2 ('72), 1500—3:39.8 ('74), Mile—3:53.2 ('74). Won the NCAA indoor

1000y for North Carolina in 1973, and the indoor mile crown in 1974. He set a world indoor record of 3:55.0 in 1974. The next year, he won gold at the Pan-Am Games. Retired from track young to pursue a career in academics. Now the president of the University of South Alabama.

John Walker
New Zealand, born 1952
PRs: 800—1:44.92 ('74), 1500—3:32.4 ('75), Mile—3:49.08 ('82), 3000—7:37.49 ('82), 5000—13:19.28 ('86).
The first man to break the 3:50 barrier in the mile with his historic 3:49.4 in 1975. The following year he won the Olympic 1500m gold. He won medals three times in the Commonwealth Games. In his long career as a world-class miler, he became the first man to break the 4:00 barrier 100 times, ending his career with 135 such races. Diagnosed with Parkinson's Disease, he now runs an equestrian shop and is involved in local government in New Zealand.

Ron Warhurst
USA, born 1943.
As a runner, Warhurst competed for Western Michigan, though he did not make the top seven for the team's NCAA wins in 1964 and 1965. He served in the Marine Corps in the Vietnam War and earned two Purple Hearts and the Navy Commendation Medal. When he came home he took up coaching, and served as the cross country coach for the University of Michigan for over 35 years. He has coached 44 All-Americans, 7 Olympians, and approximately 20 sub-4:00 milers. At the 2008 Olympics, three of his runners made the 1500m finals. Currently he coaches at the ATI Running Institute in Ann Arbor.

Alan Webb
USA, born 1983.
PRs: 800—1:43.84 ('07), 1000—2:20.32 ('05), 1500—3:30.54 ('07), Mile—3:46.91 ('07), 3000—7:39.28 ('05), 2M—8:11.48 ('05), 5000—13:10.86 ('05), 10,000—27:34.72 ('06).
The fastest miler in U.S. high school history at 3:53.43, Webb set the American record for the distance in 2007. Made two World Championship finals but he never medaled. Retired from competitive running in 2014 to concentrate on the triathlon.

Thomas Wessinghage
Germany, born 1952.
PRs: 800—1:46.56 ('76), 1000—2:16.40 ('77), 1500—3:31.58 ('80), Mile—3:49.98 ('83), 2000—4:52.20 ('82), 3000—7:36.75 ('81), 2M—8:30.2 ('82), 5000—13:12.78 ('82).
Won the 1982 Euro gold at 5000m over world record holder David Moorcroft. Competed in two Olympics when young, but missed his chance to run in the Games when he was at his best because of boycott and injury. Now a prominent orthopedic doctor.

Andrew Wheating
USA, born 1987.
PRs: 800—1:44.56 ('10), 1000—2:17.44 ('12), 1500—3:30.90 ('10), Mile—3:51.74 ('10).
Only started running track his senior year of high school. At Oregon, won the 2009 NCAA 800m, and the next year won the 800/1500m double. Made the 2008 Olympic team at 800m, and in 2012 made it in the 1500m.

Graham Williamson
Great Britain, born 1960.
PRs: 800—1:45.6 ('83), 1000—2:16.82 ('84), 1500—3:34.01 ('83), Mile—3:50.64 ('82).
Ran 3:37.68 at age 18. Euro Junior champion in 1979, and a semi-finalist at the Worlds in 1983. Recurrent injury problems ended his career early. Now works for adidas.

Nick Willis
New Zealand, born 1983.
PRs: 800—1:45.54 ('04), 1000—2:16.58 ('12), 1500—3:29.91 ('14), Mile—3:49.83 ('14), 3000—7:36.91 ('14), 5000—13:20.33 ('14).
Michigan alum still coached by Ron Warhurst. Won the NCAA indoor mile in 2005. He has been a finalist at two

World Championships and two Olympics, capturing the silver in 2008.

Rick Wohlhuter
USA, born 1948.
PRs: 800—1:43.9 ('74), 1000m—2:13.9 ('74), 1500—3:36.4 ('75), Mile—3:53.3 ('75).
Just a 1:51.9 half-miler in high school, the former Notre Dame runner set a world record in the 880y (1:44.1) in 1973, a time superior to the 800m world record at the time. A year later, he broke the world record for 1000m. Won USA titles at 800m in 1973 and 1974. Won bronze in the 1976 Olympic 800m, and ran sixth in the 1500m. Has worked as a financial manager.

Sydney Wooderson
Great Britain, 1914-2006.
PRs: 800—1:48.4 ('38), Mile—4:04.2 ('45), 5000—14:08.6 ('46).
Called the "Mighty Atom" because of his 5-6 frame, he set world records at 800m and the mile. Never successful in the Olympics, but he won the mile gold in the 1934 Empire Games and European Championship gold at both 1500m (1938) and 5000m (1946).

Dave Wottle
USA, born 1950.
PRs: 800—1:44.3 ('72), 1500—3:36.2 ('73), Mile—3:53.3 ('73).
The Ohio native took up running as a child to gain strength. Ran 4:20.2 to win the Ohio state title in high school. While at Bowling Green, won the 1972 NCAA 1500m and the 1973 NCAA mile. Considered himself primarily a miler, but surprised everybody in equaling the world record in the 1972 Olympic Trials 800m. At the Games he produced nearly perfect even splits to kick to the gold by 0.03. After retiring from running, he served as an administrator for Rhodes College for 29 years.

Ruth Wysocki
USA, born 1957.
PRs: 800—1:58.65 ('84), 1500—4:00.18 ('84), Mile—4:21.78 ('84), 3000—8:49.93 ('85), 5000—16:26.83 ('97).
Winner of the 1984 Olympic Trials, making the Olympic finals in both the 800m and 1500m that same year. She placed seventh in the 1997 World Champs as a 40-year-old.

Natalya Yevdokimova
Russia, born 1978.
PRs: 800—1:58.75 ('03), 1500—3:57.73 ('05), Mile—4:24.40 ('03).
The European Junior Champion in 1997, her best as a senior was her fourth place finish in the 2004 Olympics.

Zamira Zaytseva
Uzbekistan, born 1953.
PRs: 800—1:56.21 ('83), 1500—3:56.14 ('82), Mile—4:22.5 ('81), 3000—8:35.74 ('85).

Competed for the Soviet Union. In a relatively short career marked by fast times in domestic meets, her best international performance was her silver in the 1983 World Champs 1500m. She had also won silver at the previous summer's European Champs. Retired after 1985.

NOTES

Quotes that came from direct interviews with the author are not cited, nor are quotes that came from press conferences. All other quotes come from the following sources and are utilized under the doctrine of fair use.

PREFACE
1. "Tactics and Strategy," *BMC News*, Spring 2002.
2. Associated Press, "Holman hopes home crowd helps him," *Gadsden Times* (Gadsden, AL), May 29, 1996.

CHAPTER 1: Tactics Back in the Day
1. Aaseng, Nathan. *Track's Magnificent Milers*. Minneapolis: Lerner, 1981.
2. "Lovelock Kept Sprint A Secret Until Games," *The Montreal Gazette*. August 7, 1936.
3. "Lovelock Kept Sprint A Secret Until Games," *The Montreal Gazette*. August 7, 1936.
4. Grantland Rice, "The Sportlight," *The Deseret News*, August 8, 1936.
5. Associated Press, "I Say, Cunningham," *Lawrence Journal-World* (Lawrence, KS), Jun1 15, 1939.
6. "British Writers Make Suggestions." *Ottawa Citizen* (Ottawa, ON), June 16, 1939.
7. Associated Press, "Wisconsin Flash Wins Mile Race," *The Telegraph-Herald* (Dubuque, IA), June 18, 1939.
8. Associated Press, "Mishap Mars Race as Fenske Wins Mile Classic." *The Palm Beach Post* (Palm Beach, FL), June 18, 1939.
9. Bob Mamini. "Sport-o-Scope: Maybe it was condition." *The Calgary Herald* (Calgary, AB). June 24, 1939.

CHAPTER 2: Successful Front-Running
1. Pugh, L.G.C.E. "The Influence of Wind Resistance in Running and Walking and the Mechanical Efficiency of Work Against Horizontal or Vertical Forces." *The Journal of Physiology*. 1971. 213, pp. 255-276.
2. Vicki Huber Rudawsky. "In distance racing, stay true to your style." Delawareonline.com web. June 26, 2013.
3. Earl Nurse & Lauren Said-Moorhouse, "Catch him if you can! Tanzania's forgotten record-breaking runner." *CNN African Voices*. May 20, 2014.
4. United Press Internatioal, "Jipcho Becomes Second Fastest Miler With 3:52 Race." *The New York Times*..July 3, 1973.
5. Dave Anderson, "Ben Jipcho Answers the Mile Record," *The New York Times*, May 22, 1975.
6. Associated Press, "Bayi Cracks World Mark," *The Observer-Dispatch* (Utica, NY), February 3, 1974.
7. Ron Reid, "A Record Goes Bust," *Sports Illustrated*, May 26, 1975.
8. Associated Press, "Bayi Makes Point With Record Mile," *The Milwaukee Sentinel* (Milwaukee, WI), May 19, 1975.
9. Neil Amdur, "New Mile Record Sparks Comparisons," *Sarasota Herald-Tribune* (Sarasota, FL), May 17, 1975.
10. *United Press International*, "Buerkle runs past favored Bayi," *Ellensburg Daily Record* (Ellensburg, WA), January 14, 1978.
11. Anita Verschoth, "Putting It All Up Front," *Sports Illustrated*, January 23, 1978.

12. Associated Press, "Distance runner Buerkle to retire," *The Southeast Missourian* (Cape Girardeau, MO), July 7, 1980.
13. Cathy Henkel, "No competition for Decker?" *Eugene Register-Guard* (Eugene, OR), May 30, 1983.
14. Bert Rosenthal (AP), "Decker, Smith double up in Helsinki," *The Spokesman Review* (Spokane, WA), Aug. 14, 1983.
15. Bert Rosenthal (AP), "Decker has tough luck, but still wins," *Daily News* (Bowling Green, KY), Jan. 25, 1985.

CHAPTER 3: The Pitfalls of Leading
1. Ralph Bernstein (AP), "Liquori Upsets Keino Strategy," *The Day* (New London, CT), May 18, 1970.
2. Ken Doney (AP), "Poor steals show in final day," *Daily News* (Bowling Green, KY), June 28, 1976.
3. Neil Cawood, "Wohlhuter turns the double play," *Eugene Register-Guard* (Eugene, OR), June 28, 1976.
4. Associated Press, "Upsets records mark last day of Trials," *The Bulletin* (Bend, OR), June 28, 1976.
5. Bert Rosenthal (AP), "When Bryan Hyde ran the Fastest Outdoor 1,500-Meter Time in the World," May 30, 1995.
6. "Golden double for Holmes," BBC Sport, Web, August 28, 2004.
7. Snell, Peter & Gilmore, Garth. *No Bugles, No Drums*. Auckland: Minerva, 1965. Page 128.

Chapter 4: The Mid-Race Move
1. Andrea Adelson (AP), "Quick pace pays off this time for Webb," *Eugene Register-Guard* (Eugene, OR), August 9, 2005.
2. Peter Gambaccini, "Alan Webb," *Runner's World* online, August 19, 2005.
3. Sebastian Coe, "How I went extra mile to be best middle-distance runner I could be," *The Telegraph* (London), Apr. 5, 2009.

Chapter 5: The Long Kick
1. Toni Reavis, "Don't train too hard, don't make it too easy," Toni Reavis – Wandering in a Running World, blog, 2014.
2. John Clarke, "Sporting Nation," Australian Broadcasting Corporation, documentary, 2012.
3. Associated Press, "Liquori, Ryun 'Dream Mile' Showdown Set," *Observer-Reporter*, May 15, 1971.
4. "James Dunaway (AP), "Ryun given 'paper advantage' over Liquori in dream mile," *The Free Lance-Star* (Fredericksburg, VA), May 12, 1971.
5. Associated Press, "Liquori Wins 'Dream Mile,'" *Sarasota Journal* (Sarasota, FL), May 14, 1971.
6. Ralph Bernstein (AP), "Liquori Wins Dream Mile," *The Owosso Argus-Press* (Owosso, MI), May 17, 1971.
7. Bert Rosenthal (AP), "Africans sweep distance events in final day of World Track," *Gainesville Sun* (Gainesville, FL), September 7, 1987.
8. Hank Lowenkron (AP), "Sullivan bests Hood in battle of NCAA milers," *The Daily Courier* (Prescott, AZ), March 13, 1995.
9. D. Orlando Ledbetter, "Jennings' pace leaves field behind," *Milwaukee Journal-Sentinel* (Milwaukee, WI), July 17, 2000.
10. Amy Shipley, "Matthew Centrowitz learns the strategy behind speed," *The Washington Post* (Washington, DC), April 12, 2012.
11. Dave Milner, "Catching up with Jim Spivey: legendary miler leaves mark on

Tennessee," *Tennessee Running* (tnrunning.com), November 15, 2006.

12. Ron Speer (AP), "Mills, Liquori Post NCAA Track Upsets," *Reading Eagle* (Reading, PA), June 22, 1969.

Chapter 6: The Short Kick

1. Bob Payne, "Oregon's Prefontaine 'Great'—Not Yet 'Greatest,' *The Spokesman-Review* (Spokane, WA), April 27, 1971.
2. Bruce Welch, "Amazing Last Quarter by Elliott in Mile Title," *The Age* (Melbourne, Australia), March 18, 1958.
3. Ranny Green, "Burly 'Must Get 6-Yard Lead' to Win," *Eugene Register-Guard* (Eugene, OR), October 19, 1964.
4. Dick Leutzinger, "Burly Happy to Be Back, Disappointed at Showing," *Eugene Register-Guard* (Eugene, OR), October 29, 1964.
5. Jim Ryun, "Middle Distance," *The Lakeland Ledger* (Lakeland, FL), July 15, 1976.
6. Steve Cram, "World Athletics 2013: Steve Cram on winning gold 30 years ago," bbc.com, Aug. 14, 2013.
7. Ovett, Steve with Rodda, John. *Ovett: An Autobiography*. London: Willow Books, 1984. Pages 165-166.
8. Gary Van Sickle, "Hacker fades out of 1,500, out of Olympics," *The Milwaukee Journal* (Milwaukee, WI), July 24, 1988.
8. Phil Hersh, "Coe Loses 1,500 And Appeal In What May Be Big-time Farewell," *Chicago Tribune* (Chicago, IL), September 10, 1989.
9. Guillermo Domínguez, "Fermín Cacho: "La plata de Atlanta tiene tanto valor o más que el oro de Barcelona," *Libertad Digital* (Madrid, Spain), July 2, 2014.
10. "Mehdi Baala échoue au pied du podium," *L'Express* (France), August 19, 2008.
11. Fairfax Media, "Willis reveals the secret to his success," Stuff.co.nz, August 21, 2008.
12. Texas Longhorns. "Leo Manzano shares life experiences, discusses Olympic performance." Online video clip. YouTube. April 5, 2013.
13. Franek Fartlek. "Leo Manzano im Interview by Fartlek (ISTAF 2013). Online video clip. YouTube. November 23, 2013.
14. Kenny Moore, "Bernard Lagat is Not Done Yet," *Runner's World* (online), January 14, 2010.
15. McConnell, Lynn. *Conquerors of Time*. York: SportsBooks Ltd, 2009. Page 35.
16. Interview with George Trevor, *New York Sun*, as cited in Lynn McConnell, *Conquerors of Time*, SportsBooks Ltd (York, UK), 2009, p. 35.
17. Kenny Moore, "Out of Nowhere," *Runner's World* (online), August 18, 2009.

Chapter 7: How to Beat a Kicker

1. Davis J. Walsh, "Hail Kansas' Cunningham! Greatest Miler in World," *The Miami News* (Miami, FL), March 18, 1937.
2. "Great Mile Starts Cunningham On New Career," *Reading Eagle* (Reading, PA), Mar. 18, 1937.
3. Dennis Neeld (AP), "Keino May Try For 3 Medals," *Reading Eagle* (Reading, PA), Feb. 18, 1968.
4. Associated Press, "Sacrifice pays off for runner," *The Gadsden Times* (Gadsden, AL), March 18, 1975.
5. Oliver E. Kuechle, "US Wins Relays; Keino Beats Ryun," *The Milwaukee Journal* (Milwaukee, WI), October 21, 1968.
6. "Rose Wilts After Yifter Does Double." *The Glasgow Herald* (Glasgow, Scotland), September 3, 1977.
7. Ovett, Steve with Rodda, John, *Ovett: An Autobiography*. London: Willow Books, 1984. Page 58.

8. Butcher, Pat. *The Perfect Distance - Ovett & Coe: The Record-Breaking Rivalry*, London: Phoenix 2004.
9. Butcher, Pat. *The Perfect Distance - Ovett & Coe: The Record-Breaking Rivalry*, London: Phoenix 2004.
10. Maloney, Andrew & McDonnell, John. *John McDonnell: The Most Successful Coach in NCAA History*. Fayetteville: University of Arkansas Press, 2013.
11. Bale, John & Sang, Joe. *Kenyan Running: Movement Culture, Geography and Global Change*. Oxford: Routledge, 2013.
12. Jerry Uhrhammer, "Ryun. Prefontaine talking little as mile confrontation nears," *Register-Guard* (Eugene, OR), June 3, 1971.

Chapter 8: Running the Rounds

1. James Emerson and Brian Hill, "Gender Differences in Competition: Running Performance in 1,500 Meter Tournaments," *Eastern Economic Journal* (2014) 40, 499–517.
2. Andrew Renfree, Graham J. Mytton, Sabrina Skorski, Alan St Clair Gibson, "Tactical Considerations in the Middle Distance Running Events at the 2012 Olympic Games," *International Journal of Sports Physiology and Performance* (Impact Factor: 2.68). 08/2013.
3. Coe, Sebastian with Miller, David. *Running Free*. New York: St. Martin's Press. Page 131.

Chapter 9: Racing Indoors

1. John Ortega, "Lagat Is Now More Confident by a Mile," *Los Angeles Times* (Los Angeles, CA), January 21, 2001.
2. Marv Schneider (AP), "Indoor track reaches climax," *Park City Daily News* (Park City, UT), February 23, 1984.
3. Associated Press, "Scott charges Coghlan with rough-house tactics," *The Tuscaloosa News* (Tuscaloosa, AL), February 16, 1981.
4. John Nicholson (AP), "Bekele, Lagat prepared for Wanamaker showdown," *The Victoria Advocate* (Victoria, TX), February 3, 2006.

Chapter 10: Racing Behind Rabbits

1. Associated Press, "Filbert Bayi Guns Down Track Rabbits," *Bangor Daily News* (Bangor, ME), February 24, 1977.
2. Ovett, Steve with Rodda, John, *Ovett: An Autobiography*. London: Willow Books, 1984. Page 101.
3. Simon Turnbull, "Athletics; Pacemaker who missed the point; Athletics World Cup: American 1500m man faces disciplinary action for quick-slow-slow show," *Independent on Sunday* (London, England), September 22, 2002.

Chapter 11: Tools in the Toolkit

1. Associated Press, " 'Fibber' Bayi 'Resets' AAU, Garden Scene," *Observer Reporter* (Washington, PA), February 25, 1977.
2. Snell, Peter & Gilmore, Garth. *No Bugles, No Drums*. Auckland: Minerva, 1965. Page 35.
3. Maloney, Andrew & McDonnell, John. *John McDonnell: The Most Successful Coach in NCAA History*. Fayetteville: University of Arkansas Press, 2013.
4. Mike Rosenbaum, "Jim Ryun's Distance-Running Tips," About.com, nd.
5. Liquori, Marty & Myslenski, Skip. *On the Run: In Search of the Perfect Race*. New York: William Morrow, 1979. Page 174.

Chapter 12: The Unexpected
1. Brenda Martinez (@bmartrun), Twitter, Sept. 2, 2014.
2. Guillermo Domínguez, "Fermín Cacho: "La plata de Atlanta tiene tanto valor o más que el oro de Barcelona," *Libertad Digital* (Madrid, Spain), July 2, 2014.
3. "Morceli Wins 1500m for God and Country," *Sydney Morning Herald* (Australia), August 3, 1996.
4. Associated Press, "Olympic 1500 Final," Aug. 3, 1996.
5. Jere Longman, "An Olympic Fall Lifts Moroccan," *The New York Times* (New York, NY), August 7, 1997.
6. Associated Press, "Hamilton, Plumer continue their strange rivalry in Prefontaine Classic," *The Dispatch* (Lexington, NC), June 22, 1991.
7. "Graham Williamson," www.scottishdistancerunninghistory.co.uk, nd.
8. Mike Rosenbaum, "Jim Ryun's Distance-Running Tips," About.com, nd.
9. Gary Cohen, "Shannon Rowbury," garycohenrunning.com, June 2012.
10. Shannon Fears, "Some athletes feel agony of defeat," *The Register-Guard* (Eugene, OR), June 28, 1987.

CHAPTER 13: General Advice
1. Guillermo Domínguez, "Fermín Cacho: "La plata de Atlanta tiene tanto valor o más que el oro de Barcelona," *Libertad Digital* (Madrid, Spain), July 2, 2014.
2. Amy Shipley, "Matthew Centrowitz learns the strategy behind speed," *The Washington Post* (Washington, DC), April 12, 2012.
3. Martin Lader (UPI), "Masback in 1,500-meter final," *Beaver County Times* (Beaver, PA), July 29, 1979.
4. Elliott, Herb with Trengrove, Alan. *The Herb Elliott Story*, New York: Thomas Nelson, 1961.
5. Maloney, Andrew & McDonnell, John. *John McDonnell: The Most Successful Coach in NCAA History*. Fayetteville: University of Arkansas Press, 2013. Page 113.
6. Ed Odeven, "Q&A with Olympic runner Lopez Lomong," Ed Odeven Reporting (blog), July 1, 2013.
7. Gayle Talbot. "True to Form: Berlin Olympics Yet To Produce One Surprise." *Reading Eagle* (Reading, PA), August 5, 1936.
8. "Shannon Rowbury," garycohenrunning.com, June 2012.
9. Liquori, Marty & Myslenski, Skip. *On the Run: In Search of the Perfect Race*. New York: William Morrow, 1979. Page 164.

PHOTO CREDITS

All photos used by expressed written permission.

Chapter 1: Tactics of Old
Walter George & William Cummings – public domain.
Glenn Cunningham – public domain.
Jack Lovelock – Alexander Turnbull Museum.
Wooderson headline –*The Pittsburgh Press* (Nov. 11, 1939)

Chapter 2: Successful Front Running
Steve Prefontaine – Jeff Johnson.
Dick Buerkle – Jeff Johnson.
German Fernandez – Phil Shockley / OSU University Marketing.
Lawi Lalang – University of Arizona-Athletics.
İlham Tanui Özbilen — Erik van Leeuwen - GNU Free Documentation License.
Jenny Simpson, et al – Randy Miyazaki, Track and Field PhotoMagazine.
Heather Kampf – Jeff Hollobaugh.

Chapter 3: The Pitfalls of Leading
Kip Keino – Jeff Johnson.
Brian Hyde – William & Mary Athletics Media Relations.
Kelly Holmes – Russell Garner – Creative Commons Attribution-Share Alike 2.0 Generic License.
Andy Bayer – Indiana University Athletics Media Relations.

Chapter 4: The Mid-Race Move
Gunder Hägg – Stockholms stadsarkiv. Creative Commons license.
Jeff Atkinson – StanfordPhoto.com.
Alan Webb — Erik van Leeuwen - GNU Free Documentation License.
Will Leer – Randy Miyazaki, Track and Field PhotoMagazine.

Chapter 5: The Long Kick
Herb Elliott – Olympics.org. Creative Commons license.
Marty Liquori - Koch, Eric / Anefo - Dutch National Archives, The Hague, Fotocollectie Algemeen Nederlands Persbureau. Creative Commons license.
Steve Scott – University of California at Irvine.
Ruth Wysocki – Jeff Johnson.
Abdi Bile – Allgedo News Media Network.
Kevin Sullivan – Michigan Photography.
Michael Stember, et al –StanfordPhoto.com
Lee Emanuel – UNM Athletics.
Morgan Uceny, et al – Randy Miyazaki, Track and Field PhotoMagazine.
Abeba Aregawi – Erik van Leeuwen - GNU Free Documentation License.
Jim Spivey – Jeff Johnson.
Marty Liquori/Jim Ryun – Jeff Johnson.

Chapter 6: The Short Kick
John Walker – Jeff Johnson.
Don Paige – Jeff Johnson.
Mark Deady – Indiana University Athletics Media Relations.
Sheila Reid – Phil Roeder - Creative Commons Attribution 2.0 Generic license.

Taoufik Makhloufi – Herwin Thole — Creative Commons Attribution 2.0 Generic license.
Richie Harris – Jeff Johnson.
Dave Wottle – Jeff Johnson.

Chapter 7: How to Beat a Kicker
Kip Keino – Stemeli10 - Creative Commons Attribution-Share Alike 4.0 International license.
Steve Ovett – Ken Hackman, U.S. Air Force
Trenier Moser & Mary Cain – Randy Miyazaki, Track and Field PhotoMagazine.
Steve Prefontaine – Jeff Johnson.

Chapter 8: Running the Rounds
Moscow 1500 semi – Randy Miyazaki, Track and Field PhotoMagazine.
Paul McMullen – Eastern Michigan University.
Jenny Simpson – Randy Miyazaki, Track and Field PhotoMagazine.
Amanda Eccleston – Michigan Photography.
2012 Trials Semi – Randy Miyazaki, Track and Field PhotoMagazine.

Chapter 9: Racing Indoors
Steve Prefontaine – Jeff Johnson.
Sarah Brown & Sally Kipyego (2) – Randy Miyazaki, Track and Field PhotoMagazine.
Steve Scott, et al – East Tennessee State University.

Chapter 10: Racing Behind Rabbits
Todd Harbour – Baylor Athletics.
Kevin Sullivan – Michigan Photography.
Silas Kiplagat – André Zehetbauer under Creative Commons Attribution-Share Alike 2.0 Generic license.
Jenny Simpson – Randy Miyazaki, Track and Field PhotoMagazine.
Leo Manzano – Randy Miyazaki, Track and Field PhotoMagazine.
Katie Mackey – PhotoRun – courtesy of Brooks.

Chapter 11: Tools in the Toolkit
Crowded pack – Randy Miyazaki, Track and Field PhotoMagazine.
2010 NCAA women – Michael Bruscas, University of Washington Athletic Communications.
Natalija Piliušina - Bruce Waterfield/Oklahoma State Athletics.
Steve Scott – Jeff Johnson.
Matthew Centrowitz/Leo Manzano – Randy Miyazaki, Track and Field PhotoMagazine.

Chapter 12: The Unexpected
Shelby Houlihan – Randy Miyazaki, Track and Field PhotoMagazine.
Sarah Brown – University of Tennessee Athletic Media Relations
Jim Ryun – Jeff Johnson.
Jenny Simpson – Randy Miyazaki, Track and Field PhotoMagazine.

Chapter 13: General Advice
Ron Warhurst – Michigan Photography.
Kevin Sullivan – Michigan Photography.
Heather Kampf – Eric Miller/Minnesota Gopher Athletics.

Lopez Lomong – NAU Athletics.
Gabe Grunewald – Eric Miller/Minnesota Gopher Athletics.
Cory McGee – Randy Miyazaki, Track and Field PhotoMagazine.
Grant Fisher – Jeff Hollobaugh.
Amanda Eccleston – Michigan Photography.
Kyle Merber – Jeff Hollobaugh.
Shannon Rowbury – Gary Rowbury - Creative Commons Attribution-Share Alike 3.0 Unported license.

Chapter 14: Index of Names Dropped
Dick Buerkle – Jeff Johnson.
Mary Cain – Randy Miyazaki, Track and Field PhotoMagazine.
Hicham El Guerrouj – Sebastien - Creative Commons Attribution-Share Alike 2.0 generic license.
Len Hilton – University of Houston Athletic Communications.
Lawi Lalang – University of Arizona-Athletics.
Jason Pyrah – BYU Athletic Communications.
Jenny Simpson – Colorado Sports Information Service.
Lennart Strand – public domain.

Photo of author – courtesy of Peter Draugalis.

Acknowledgements

A book of this scope would not be possible without the help of many people, from those that were gracious with their time in sharing their experiences, to those who helped with their support of the production and publication. I apologize to any whose names I have misplaced: Jeff Atkinson, Karl Bangert, Andy Bayer, Filbert Bayi, Cathy Beal, Abdi Bile, Eric Braschwitz, Sarah Brown, Dick Buerkle, Joe Burgireno, Peter Callahan, Renato Canova, Walt Chadwick, Dianne Dudley, Amanda Eccleston, Tony Ettwein, Mike Fanelli, Grant Fisher, Ray Flynn, John Geer, Gabe Grunewald, The Haas Family, Chip Hadler, Todd Harbour, Bob Hersh, Greg Hollobaugh, Riley Hollobaugh, Mirko Jalava, Charlie Janke, Jeff Johnson, Heather Kampf, Ann Kehn, Ryan Lamppa, Francie Larrieu Smith, Sieg Lindstrom, Gary Loubert, Katie Mackey, Cory McGee, Paul McMullen, Kyle Merber, MichianaTiming.com, Michael Newton, Sonia O'Sullivan, Sam Penzenstadler, Sheila Reid, Kirk Reynolds, Marcus Rogers, Peter Rono, Bill Rose, Saline Cross Country, Mike Scannell, Steve Scott, Jenny Simpson, Kent Stone, Kevin Sullivan, Jodi & Ryan Talbott, Mike Timpa, Ron Warhurst, Tony Waldrop, Thomas Wessinghage, Rick Wohlhuter, Dave Wood, Dave Wottle, Ruth Wysocki.

A special thanks for proofreading and editorial assistance to:

Andy Ames, Ray Antel, Joe Burgireno, Rachel DaDamio, Amanda Eccleston, Jessica Eddings, Tony Ettwein, Abby Hackett, Asa Kelly, David Mitchell, Don Passenger, Nick Stanko, Dave Testa.

Typos linger, even in the best books. Our apologies. Please help us get it right in future printings by alerting us to the mistake and the page number in a quick email. Also, this book is likely to see a second edition in a few years. If you have suggestions of races that might fit, or other information to include, please contact the author at jeff@mercury-chronicle.com.

About the Author

Jeff Hollobaugh has been an athletics journalist for three decades, and has a particular fascination with racing: the art of what happens between the firing of the gun and the finish. In the past, his writing has appeared in *Track & Field News* (he is a past managing editor), as well as ESPN.com and *Michigan Runner*. He has covered six Olympic Games and ten IAAF World Championships. He is the editor of Michtrack.org, a non-profit site that promotes high school track & cross country in Michigan. Much of his recent writing can be found at Mercury-Chronicle.com. In the interest of transparency, he reveals that his best mile was a 4:37 to win the Allen Park vs. Trenton dual meet of 1979. He used a long kick (chapter 5).

The author is available for book talks and signings. Please contact him at jeff@mercury-chronicle.com.

Also available on Amazon and directly from the author:

The 100 Greatest Track & Field Battles of the 20th Century (2012)

You've read the book, and hopefully enjoyed it. If you want to support this and other indie publishing ventures, the best thing you can do is please leave a review on Amazon.com and Goodreads.com.

Made in the USA
Middletown, DE
08 February 2017